James Tyndale Mitchel

The Statutes at Large of Pennsylvania from 1682 to 1801

Volume XIII

James Tyndale Mitchel

The Statutes at Large of Pennsylvania from 1682 to 1801
Volume XIII

ISBN/EAN: 9783741114588

Manufactured in Europe, USA, Canada, Australia, Japa

Cover: Foto ©Lupo / pixelio.de

Manufactured and distributed by brebook publishing software
(www.brebook.com)

James Tyndale Mitchel

The Statutes at Large of Pennsylvania from 1682 to 1801

THE

$\mathfrak{Statutes}$ at $\mathfrak{Large}$

OF

PENNSYLVANIA

FROM

1682 to 1801

COMPILED UNDER THE
AUTHORITY OF THE ACT OF MAY 19 1887 BY
JAMES T. MITCHELL AND HENRY FLANDERS
COMMISSIONERS

VOLUME XIII
1787-1790

HARRISBURG, PA.:
HARRISBURG PUBLISHING CO., STATE PRINTER.
1908.

THE STATUTES AT LARGE OF PENNSYLVANIA.

CHAPTER MCCCXXVI.

AN ACT FOR FURNISHING THE QUOTA OF TROOPS REQUIRED BY CON-
GRESS FOR THE PROTECTION OF [THE] WESTERN FRONTIERS AND
OTHER PURPOSES THEREIN MENTIONED.

(Section I, P. L.) Whereas the United States in congress assembled by their resolution of the third day of October in the
year of our Lord one thousand seven hundred and eighty-seven
reciting, that whereas the time for which the greater part of the
troops on the frontiers are engaged will expire in the course of
the ensuing year did resolve, that the interests of the United
States require that a corps of seven hundred troops should be
stationed on the frontiers to protect the settlers on the public
lands from the depredations of the Indians, to facilitate the
surveying and selling of the said lands, in order to reduce the
public debt and to prevent all unwarrantable intrusions thereon; and also that in order to save the great expense of transporting new levies to the distant frontiers of the United States,
and also to avail the public of the discipline and knowledge of
the country acquired by the troops on the frontiers, it is highly
expedient to retain as many of them as shall voluntarily re-
engage in the service; and did therefore further resolve that
seven hundred non-commissioned officers and privates be raised
for the term of three years, unless sooner discharged, and that
the same be furnished by the several states therein named in

certain specifièd proportions, whereof the quota or proportion of this state is required to be two hundred and sixty.

And whereas the legislature of this commonwealth in compliance with the said requisition of congress is desirous to facilitate the measures of the United States in the most speedy and effectual manner.

[Section I.] (Section II, P. L.) Be it enacted, and it is hereby enacted by the Representatives of the Freemen of the Commonwealth of Pennsylvania in General Assembly met, and by the authority of the same, That there be forthwith raised and levied by voluntary enlistment in this state two hundred and sixty able bodied men to be arranged as non-commissioned officers and privates in the service of the United States to continue for and during the term of three years unless sooner discharged.

[Section II.] (Section III, P. L.) And be it further enacted by the authority aforesaid, That the supreme executive council be and they are hereby authorized and empowered to appoint and commissionate the proportion of officers to be furnished by this state according to the seventh article of the confederation and perpetual union, and agreeably to the establishment mentioned in the resolutions of Congress herein in part recited.

[Section III.] (Section IV, P. L.) And be it further enacted by the authority aforesaid, That the said officers and men shall severally and respectively when embodied be and they are hereby declared to be liable and subject to such rules and regulations as Congress or a committee of the states have formed or hereafter shall form for the government of the troops or army of the United States and that the pay, rations and subsistence of the said officers and soldiers shall be agreeable to the act of congress of the twelfth day of April in the year of our Lord one thousand seven hundred and eighty-five, provided that all such pay, rations, subsistence and other expenses of supporting said troops be furnished and provided by the United States.

[Section IV.] (Section V, P. L.) And be it further enacted by the authority aforesaid, That the president and the supreme executive council be and they are hereby authorized and em-

powered to draw on the treasurer of this state in favor of the
commanding officer of the said troops for the sum of five hundred and twenty dollars for the purpose of giving two dollars
advance to each non-commissioned officer and private that shall
be enlisted, which sum shall be charged to the United States
and repaid to this commonwealth out of the first month's pay
to be drawn for said troops, and also that the said president
and supreme executive council draw in manner aforesaid for
the further sum of two hundred and sixty dollars to be distributed by the said commanding officer for the expenses of the re-
cruiting service in such manner as to him may appear reasonable and just.

Passed November 10, 1787.   Recorded L. B. 3, p. 333.

CHAPTER MCCCXXVII.

AN ACT TO PROVIDE FOR THE WAGES OF MEMBERS OF THE STATE
CONVENTION, AND TO DEFRAY THE EXPENSES OF HOLDING THE
SAME.

(Section I, P. L.) Whereas it [is] necessary to determine the
allowance to be made to the members of the state convention
which is to be held for the purpose of considering the proposed
federal constitution and also to provide for the same, together
with the incidental expenses of the said convention.

[Section I.] (Section II, P. L.) Be it therefore enacted, and it
is hereby enacted by the Representatives of the Freemen of the
Commonwealth of Pennsylvania in General Assembly met, and
by the authority of the same, That the same allowances be made
of wages and mileage to attending members of the state convention as is now made to the members of the general assembly,
and that the same together with the incidental expenses of the
convention be paid by warrant on the state treasurer and drawn
by the president or chairman of the convention, and countersigned by the comptroller-general.

Passed November 10, 1787.   Recorded L. B. No. 8, p. 333.

CHAPTER MCCCXXVIII.

AN ACT TO ALTER AND AMEND AN ACT ENTITLED "AN ACT FOR ERECTING AND OPENING A LOAN OFFICE FOR THE SUM OF FIFTY THOUSAND POUNDS."[1]

(Section I, P. L.) Whereas the bills of credit emitted and made current by an act of assembly passed the sixteenth day of March in the year of our Lord one thousand seven hundred and eighty-five, have suffered a considerable depreciation, and the restoration of their credit may be affected by taking out of circulation such and so many of them as shall be received by the trustees of the loan office in discharge of the mortgages to them made for sums borrowed of them, over and besides the sum of twenty-thousand pounds which by the said act is directed to be annually canceled and burned.

[Section I.] (Section II, P. L.) Be it therefore enacted, and it is hereby enacted by the Representatives of the Freemen of the Commonwealth of Pennsylvania in General Assembly met, and by the authority of the same, That it shall and may be lawful for any mortgagor of any messuages, lands or rents, mortgaged to the trustees of the loan office in pursuance of an act of assembly passed the fourth day of April in the year of our Lord one thousand seven hundred and eighty-five, entitled, "An act for erecting and opening a loan office for the sum of fifty thousand pounds." or his heirs, executors, administrators or assigns to pay the whole, or any part or parts of the moneys borrowed and due by and upon such mortgages, and for the said trustees to receive the same in part or in full of the same, at any time or times before the time specified in the said mortgage deeds, anything in the last recited act to the contrary notwithstanding.

[Section II.] (Section III, P. L.) And be it further enacted by the authority aforesaid, That all the bills of credit emitted by the said first above mentioned act which shall be paid to and

---

[1]Chapter 1159.

received by the said trustees in part or in full discharge of any
of the said mortgages, in pursuance of the said act for that
purpose made or of this act shall be paid into the treasury of
this state on or before the last day of every month in which
the same shall be paid to the said trustees and shall not be re-
loaned or re-issued on any account whatsoever but the same
bills shall be canceled by the treasurer and reserved to be
burned and shall be burned in the same manner as the said
annual sum of twenty-thousand pounds is directed to be canceled and burned by the fifty-ninth section of the act first herein above recited, anything in the said act for erecting and opening the said loan office to the contrary notwithstanding.

Passed November 27, 1787.   Recorded L. B. No. 3, p. 385.

CHAPTER MCCCXXIX.

A SUPPLEMENT TO THE ACT ENTITLED "AN ACT TO ALTER AND
AMEND AN ACT ENTITLED 'AN ACT TO REMEDY THE DEFECTS OF
THE SEVERAL ACTS OF ASSEMBLY HERETOFORE MADE FOR REGU-
LATING THE ELECTIONS OF JUSTICES OF PEACE THROUGHOUT
THIS STATE AND TO ESTABLISH A PERMANENT MODE FOR HOLDING
SUCH ELECTIONS AND TO AUTHORIZE THE JUSTICES OF THE PEACE
OF THE CITY OF PHILADELPHIA TO HOLD THE COURTS OF RECORD
OF THE SAID CITY AND TO MAKE FURTHER PROVISIONS FOR THE
DUE ELECTION AND RETURN OF JUSTICES OF PEACE ELECT."[1]

(Section I, P. L.) Whereas it appears to this house that for
the purposes of holding orphans' courts and the accelerating
other public businesses falling under the jurisdiction of the
county courts it will be useful and convenient to the citizens of
this state that a number of justices necessary to compose a
court should reside so near together that a court may be easily
assembled in cases wherein their immediate intervention is
necessary:

[Section I.] (Section II, P. L.) Be it enacted by the Freemen of
the Commonwealth of Pennsylvania in General Assembly met
and it is hereby enacted by authority of the same, That every

Passed February 27, 1788.   Recorded L. B. No. 3, p. 336.
[Passed March 4th, 1786, Chapter 1205.

district in which a county town is situate within this state now erected or hereafter to be erected shall be entitled to three justices of the peace of the proper county upon the election of the freeholders of the respective districts in which such towns are situate as soon as the president or vice-president in council shall think proper to grant the same and the freeholders of the several districts aforesaid shall as in other cases elect and return a double number of justices of the peace elect accordingly any law heretofore made enacted to the contrary notwithstanding.

CHAPTER MCCCXXX.

AN ACT AUTHORIZING THE SUPREME EXECUTIVE COUNCIL TO DRAW AN ORDER ON THE TREASURER OF THIS STATE FOR THE SUM OF SEVENTY-NINE POUNDS TEN SHILLINGS IN FAVOR OF ALEXANDER McDOWELL.

Whereas by a petition presented to this house by Alexander McDowell it is therein set forth that he was appointed a surveyor of one of the districts in the late purchase, that after he had [carried] out his division line and before he had executed one warrant he received orders from the supreme executive council to desist, by means of which he has been subjected to considerable expenses and as the running of the aforesaid line is rendered useless he has prayed for relief in the premises, and it is just and reasonable that the expenses aforesaid be paid. Therefore:

[Section I.] (Section II, P. L.) Be it enacted and it is hereby enacted by the Representatives of the Freemen of the Commonwealth of Pennsylvania in General Assembly met and by the authority of the same, That the supreme executive council be and they are hereby authorized to draw an order on the treasurer of this state for the sum of seventy-nine pounds ten shillings being the balance due to him.

Passed February 27, 1788. Recorded L. B. No. 3, p. 336.

CHAPTER MCCCXXXI.

AN ACT FOR VESTING THE PUBLIC STORE HOUSE AND TWO LOTS OF GROUND IN THE BOROUGH AND COUNTY OF LANCASTER IN THE TRUSTEES OF FRANKLIN COLLEGE FOR THE USE OF THE SAID INSTITUTION.

(Section I, P. L.) Whereas from a full conviction of the utility of establishing seminaries of learning in this commonwealth an act of assembly was passed the tenth day of March one thousand seven hundred and eighty-seven to incorporate a college and charity school in the borough and county of Lancaster under the title of Franklin College:

And whereas it hath since been represented to this house by the petition of the trustees of the said college that their funds, notwithstanding the former bounty of the legislature, are inadequate to the good purposes intended, wherefore they have prayed this house to convey to the said college two certain lots or pieces of ground on Queen Street in the said borough with the public store house thereon being:

And whereas it appears reasonable and proper that the said petition should be granted:

[Section I.] (Section II, P. L.) Be it therefore enacted and it is hereby enacted by the Representatives of the Freemen of the Commonwealth of Pennsylvania in General Assembly met and by the authority of the same, That the said two lots of ground as they are situated on the west side of Queen street in the said borough with their appurtenances and all the estate, right, title, interest, property claim and demand of the state of Pennsylvania in and to the same shall be and they are hereby granted and vested in the trustees of Franklin college in the borough and county of Lancaster and their successors forever to and for the use of the said institution.

Passed February 27, 1788. Recorded L. B. No. 3, p. 337.

CHAPTER MCCCXXXII.

AN ACT TO INCORPORATE THE SOCIETY FOR PROPAGATING THE GOSPEL AMONG THE HEATHEN FORMED BY MEMBERS OF THE EPISCOPAL CHURCH OF THE UNITED BRETHREN OR UNITAS FRATRUM.

(Section I, P. L.) Whereas it has been represented to this house by the Reverend John Ettwein, one of the bishops of the church called Unitas Fratrum or the United Brethren, and the Reverend John Meder, pastor in ordinary of the said church in the city of Philadelphia, that since the year of our Lord one thousand seven hundred and forty when the said church began to make settlements in America the principal aim of their members coming over from Europe was to carry the glorious truths of the Gospel to the Indians here, that they have without intermission continued their labors among the Indians and notwithstanding the increase of expenses and other difficulties are resolved to pursue and support this commendable work and for this purpose have formed a society for propagating the Gospel among the heathen and entered into certain rules of association (a copy whereof they have subjoined to their petition) and prayed to incorporate the said society:

And whereas the propagation of the Gospel among the Indians of America is of great importance to the citizens of this and other the United States and may by the blessing of God be conducive to the peace and security of the inhabitants and settlers of our frontiers, and by living examples of the missionaries and the converts the savages may be induced to turn their minds to the Christian religion, industry and social life with the citizens of the United States:

And whereas this house is disposed to exercise the powers vested in the legislature of the commonwealth for the encouragement of all pious and charitable purposes:

[Section I.] (Section II, P. L.) Be it therefore enacted and it is hereby enacted by the Representatives of the Freemen of the

Commonwealth of Pennsylvania in General Assembly met and
by the authority of the same, That the Reverend John Ettwein,
bishop, Frederick William Von Marshall, gentleman, the Reverend Andrew Hubner and Paul Munster, Hans Christian Von
Schweinitz, gentleman, the Reverend David Zeisberger, junior,
John August Klingsohr, Jeremiah Dencke, Charles Gotthold
Reichel, Daniel Koehler, Christian Benzein and Godfrey Prae-
zel, the present directors, the Reverend Bernhard Adam Grube,
Frederick Peter senior and Jacob Van Vleck, the present assistant directors of the said society, the Reverend John Herbst,
John Medar, Francis Boahler, James Birkby, Lewis Boehler,
and Abraham Reinecke and others, the ministers in the different brethrens congregations and their successors and all other
members of said society who have and hereafter shall subscribe the rules of the said society be and they are hereby made,
declared and constituted to be a corporation and body politic
and corporate in law and in fact, to have continuance forever
by the name, style, and title of "The society of the United
Brethren for propagating the Gospel among the heathen."

[Section II.] (Section III, P. L.) And be it further enacted
by the authority aforesaid, That the said corporation and their
successors by the name, style and title aforesaid, shall forever
hereafter be persons able and capable in law to purchase, have,
receive, take, hold and enjoy in fee simple or of less estate
or estates, any lands, tenements, rents, annuities, liberties,
franchises and other hereditaments, by the gift, grant, bargain,
sale, alienation, enfeoffment, release, confirmation or devise
of any person or persons bodies politic and corporate, capable
and able to make the same and further that the said corporation and their successors may take and receive any sum or
sums of money and portion of goods and chattels that have
been or hereafter shall be given or bequeathed to them or the
said society by any person or persons, bodies politic or corporate, able and capable to make a bequest or gift thereof. Provided, That no misnomer of the said corporation and their successors shall defeat or annul any gift, grant, devise or bequest
to the said corporation if the intent of the donor shall sufficiently appear upon the face of the gift, testament or other

writing whereby any estate or interest was intended to pass
to the said corporation; nor shall any non-user of the rights,
liberties, privileges and authorities, or any of them, hereby
granted to the said corporation, create or cause a forfeiture
thereof.

[Section III.] (Section IV, P. L.) And be it further enacted by
the authority aforesaid, That all donations and contributions,
rents interests and profits arising from the real and personal
estate of the aforesaid corporation shall by the said directors
and their successors from time to time be applied and laid out
for the maintenance and support of [their] missionaries and
their assistants, for building and supporting places of public
worship and schools, providing books for the better educating,
instructing and civilizing the children of the converts and
others among the nations who shall be desirous to commit their
youths to the care and instructions of the said missionaries and
for such other pious and charitable uses as are conformable to
the true design and intent of the said society.

[Section IV.] (Section V, P. L.) And be it further enacted
by the authority aforesaid, That the said corporation and their
successors, shall not by deed or otherwise, grant, alien, convey
or otherwise dispose of any part or parcel of the real estate in
the said corporation vested or to be vested or charge or encumber the same to any person or persons whatsoever except by
and with the consent of a majority of the regular contributing
members of the said society convened for that purpose.

[Section V.] (Section VI, P. L.) And be it further enacted
by the authority aforesaid, That the said directors and assistant directors and their successors or a majority of them shall
and may from time to time convene the members of the said
society to make rules, by-laws and ordinances and to transact
everything requisite for the good government and support of
the affairs of the said society agreeable to their stated rules.
Provided always, That the said rules, by-laws and ordinances
or any of them be not repugnant to the laws and statutes in
force within this commonwealth.

[Section VI.] (Section VII, P. L.) And be it further enacted
by the authority aforesaid, That the said society and their suc-

cessors shall have full power and authority to make, have and use one common seal with such device and inscription as they shall think proper and the same to break, alter and renew at their pleasure.

[Section VII.] (Section VIII, P. L.) And be it further enacted by the authority aforesaid, That the said corporation and their successors by the name, style and title aforesaid shall be able and capable in law to sue and be sued, plead and be impleaded in any court or courts, before any judge or judges, justice or justices in all and all manner of suits, complaints, causes, matters and demands of whatsoever kind, nature or form they may be and all and every other matter and thing therein to do in as full and effectual a manner as any other person or persons, bodies politic or corporate in this commonwealth in the like cases may or can do.

[Section VIII.] (Section IX, P. L.) Provided also and it is further enacted by the authority aforesaid, that the clear yearly value or income of the messuages, houses, lands, tenements, rents, annuities or other hereditaments and real estate of the said corporation shall not exceed the sum of two thousand pounds lawful money of the state of Pennsylvania, to be taken and esteemed exclusive of the moneys arising from the contributions of the actual members and donations of the honorary members or other friends to the said institution.

Passed February 27, 1788. Recorded L. B. No. 3, p. 358.

CHAPTER MCCCXXXIII.

AN ACT TO INCORPORATE THE FIRST PRESBYTERIAN CONGREGATION OF THE BIG SPRING IN NEWTOWN TOWNSHIP IN CUMBERLAND COUNTY.

(Section I, P. L.) Whereas the members of the first Presbyterian Church of Big Spring in the county of Cumberland now under the pastoral care of the Reverend Samuel Wilson have in a petition to this house prayed that their said church may be incorporated and by law enabled as a body politic and corporate to receive and hold such charitable donations and bequests as have been or may from time to time be made to their society and vested with such powers and privileges as are enjoyed by the religious societies who are incorporated in the state of Pennsylvania:

And whereas it is just and right and agreeably to the true spirit of the constitution that the prayer of their said petition be granted.

[Section I.] (Section II, P. L.) Be it therefore enacted and it is hereby enacted by the Representatives of the Freemen of the Commonwealth of Pennsylvania in General Assembly met and by the authority of the same, That David Sterret, Robert Patterson, Charles Leiper, Randle Blair, John McKeehan, Samuel Finley and John Carson and their successors duly elected and appointed in such manner and form as hereinafter is directed be and they are hereby made and constituted a corporation and body politic in law and in fact to have continuance forever by the name, style and title of "The trustees of the First Presbyterian Church in Newtown Township in the County of Cumberland," that the said corporation and their successors by the name style and title aforesaid shall forever hereafter be capable and able in law as well to take, have, receive, hold and enjoy all and all manner of lands, tenements, rents, annuities, liberties, franchises and other hereditaments which at any time heretofore have been granted, bargained, sold, enfeoffed, released, devised or otherwise conveyed to the said Presbyterian church, the congregation worshipping there or to any other person or persons to their use or in trust for them, and the said lands, tenements, rents, annuities, liberties, franchises and other hereditaments are hereby vested and established in the said corporation and their successors forever according to the original use and intent for which such devises, gifts and grants were respectively made. And the said corporation and their successors are hereby declared to be seized and possessed of such estate and estates therein as in and by the respective grants, bargains, sales, enfeoffments, releases, devises or other conveyances thereof is or are declared, limited, or ex-

pressed, and also that the said corporation and their successors aforesaid at all times hereafter shall be able and capable
to purchase, have, receive, take, hold and enjoy in fee simple
or of any less estate [or estates] any lands tenements, rents, annuities, liberties, franchises and other hereditaments by the
gift, grant, bargain, sale, alienation, enfeoffment, release, confirmation or devise of any person or persons, bodies politic and
corporate capable and able to make the same: And further that
the said corporation as aforesaid may take and receive any
sum or sums of money and any manner or portion of goods
and chattels that have been or shall be given or bequeathed
to them by any person or persons, bodies politic and corporate
capable to make a bequest thereof and the said corporation
are declared to be capable and able and they are hereby authorized and empowered to grant, bargain, sell, convey, assure,
demise and to farm-let, place out at interest or otherwise dispose of the same in such manner as to them or a majority of
them, as hereinafter is directed shall deem most beneficial and
serviceable to the society. Provided always, That the said
trustees and their successors shall not by any deed, fine or
recovery or by any other way or means grant, bargain, sell,
alien, or otherwise dispose of any manors, messuages, lands,
tenements or hereditaments, the real estate of the said church .
in them or their successors vested or hereafter to be vested,
nor charge nor encumber the same to any person or persons
whatever except the same be done by consent of a majority of
the regular members of the said church qualified to vote as
hereinafter is directed.

[Section II.] (Section III, P. L.) And be it further enacted
by the authority aforesaid, That the said trustees and their
successors or the majority of two-thirds of them met from time
to time either on their own adjournments or on public notice
from the desk or pulpit of said church the preceding Lord's
day, commonly called Sunday, immediately after divine service
before the congregation is dismissed or after regular notice in
writing left at the house of each trustee and the particular
business having been mentioned as least one meeting of the
trustees before, be authorized and empowered to make rules,

2—XIII

by-laws and ordinances and to do everything needful for the
good government and support of the secular affairs of the said
church. Provided, That the said rules, by-laws and ordinances
or any of them be not repugnant to the laws of this commonwealth and that all their proceedings be fairly and regularly
entered in a church book to be kept for that purpose. Provided also, That the said trustees and their successors do and
shall yearly and every year upon the day of election of new
trustees render a full and satisfactory account plainly stated
to the congregation or a committee of the congregation appointed to receive the same of all and every part of their proceedings while in trust.

[Section III.] (Section IV, P. L.) And be it further enacted
by the authority aforesaid, That the said corporation shall
always consist of seven members called and known by the
name, style and title of "The trustees of the First Presbyterian
Church in Newtown Township in the County of Cumberland,"
and shall at all times hereafter be chosen by ballot by a majority of the members met together as shall have been enrolled in
the aforesaid book as stated worshippers with the said church
for no less than the space of one year and shall have paid one
year's pew rent or other annual sum of money not less than
one dollar for the support of the pastor or other officers of the
church or other necessary expenses of the said church and shall
not at the time of voting be more than one year in arrear for
the same.

Provided always, That the making sale and disposition of any
part or parcel of the real estate of the said corporation as well
as the election of trustees and all matters that require the
consent and concurrence of the major part of the congregation shall be determined by the plurality of the [votes of the]
members so met, that the said trustees and their successors
met as aforesaid be authorized and empowered to elect from
among themselves a president and to elect from among themselves or other members of the said congregation a treasurer
and secretary and the whole or any of them to remove, change,
alter or continue at pleasure as shall seem most for the benefit
of the said church and corporation.

[Section IV.] (Section V, P. L.) And be it further enacted
by the authority aforesaid, That the said corporation and their
successors shall have full power and authority to make, have
and use one common seal, with such device and inscription as
they shall think proper and the same to break, alter and renew
at pleasure.

[Section V.] (Section VI, P. L.) And be it further enacted by
the authority aforesaid, That the said corporation and their
successors by the name, style and title aforesaid shall be capable and able in law to sue and be sued, plead and be impleaded in any court or courts, before any judge or judges,
justice or justices in all manner of suits, complaints, pleas,
causes, matters and demands of whatever nature, kind or form
they may be and all and every matter and thing therein to do
in as full and effectual a manner as any other person or persons, bodies politic and corporate within this commonwealth
may or can do.

[Section VI.] (Section VII, P. L.) And be it further enacted
by the authority aforesaid, That the pastor or minister of
the said church for the time being shall be entitled to vote
equally with any other member of the said congregation and
that all and every person or persons qualified to vote and elect
as aforesaid shall and may be capable and able to be voted
and elected a trustee.

[Section VII.] (Section VIII, P. L.) And be it further enacted
by the authority aforesaid, That the said David Sterret, Robert
Patterson, Charles Leiper, Randle Blair, John McKeehan, Samuel Finley and John Carson the first and present trustees hereby incorporated shall be and continue trustees until removed
in the manner following, that is to say, two sevenths in number
of the said trustees being the two first herein named shall
cease and discontinue and their appointment determine on
the first Tuesday in November, which shall be in the year of
our Lord one thousand seven hundred and eighty-nine and
two-sevenths being the second two herein mentioned shall
cease and discontinue and their appointments determine on the
first Tuesday in November which shall be in the year of our
Lord one thousand seven hundred and ninety and on the first

Tuesday in November in the year then next following three sevenths being the last three in number of the said trustees shall in like manner cease and discontinue and their appointment determine, on which in each of the aforesaid mentioned years, repectively new elections shall be held of other trustees in stead and in place of those whose appointments shall have ceased and terminated, which manner of discontinuance, determination and new appointments or election shall be continued on the said first Tuesday in November in every year hereafter forever, so that no person shall be or continue a trustee longer than three years together without being re-elected, which may be done whenever and as often as the members of the said congregation qualified to vote as afore described shall think fit.

Provided always, That whenever any vacancy shall happen by death, refusal to serve or other removal of one or more of the said trustees an election shall be held as soon as conveniently can be done and some fit person or persons chosen and appointed as before directed to supply such vacancy and that the remaining trustees have power to call a meeting of the electors of the congregation for such purposes.

[Section VIII.] (Section IX, P. L.) Provided always and be it further enacted by the authority aforesaid, that the clear yearly value, interest and income of the lands, tenements, rents, annuities and other hereditaments and real estate of the said corporation shall not exceed the sum of five hundred pounds gold or silver money at the current value thereof in the commonwealth of Pennsylvania exclusive of pew rents and other free contributions belonging to the aforesaid congregation, which said money shall be received by the said trustees and disposed of by them for the purpose and in the manner hereinbefore directed and described.

Passed February 27, 1788. Recorded L. B. No. 3, p. 354.

CHAPTER MCCCXXXIV.

A SUPPLEMENT TO AN ACT ENTITLED "AN ACT FOR RAISING BY WAY OF LOTTERY THE SUM OF FORTY-TWO THOUSAND DOLLARS FOR IMPROVING THE PULIC ROADS LEADING FROM THE CITY OF PHILADELPHIA TO THE WESTERN PARTS OF THIS STATE AND TOWARDS THE IMPROVING THE NAVIGATION OF THE RIVER SCHUYLKILL."

(Section I, P. L.) Whereas the net produce of the lottery directed to be drawn by an act of general assembly of this commonwealth passed on the fifteenth day of March in the year of our Lord one thousand seven hundred and eighty-four doth not amount to a sum sufficient to answer very extensively the good purposes intended thereby, so that it is conceived by this house that the conduct of the business in the hands of commissioners would create an unnecessary expense and it is considered that the moneys will be more economically expended if the supreme executive council shall be invested with a power to direct the mode of applying the said moneys by contract or otherwise as they shall deem proper:

And whereas the moneys so to be raised by the lottery before mentioned were directed by the said recited act to be appropriated agreeably to the laws then existing or which might thereafter be enacted for that purpose and it is thought most conducive to the end [proposed] that the application should be made to such parts of the roads and river as can be effectually benefited by the sum now raised, leaving the further improvement thereof to future exertions.

[Section I.] (Section II, P. L.) Be it therefore enacted, and it is hereby enacted by the Representatives of the Freemen of the Commonwealth of Pennsylvania in General Assembly met and by the authority of the same, That the supreme executive council of this state be and they are hereby vested with full powers and authorities to direct the application of the produce of the lottery aforesaid in manner following, that is to say, one full and equal moiety or half part thereof heretofore appropriated to the repairing the western roads shall be expended

and laid out on the road leading from the middle bridge on
Schuylkill to Lancaster, beginning at the western side of the
said river and extending so far as can with the sum hereby
alloted therefor be effectually repaired and rendered perman-
ently passable, but if the said sum shall not be sufficient in the
opinion of the said council according to the best information
they can obtain to extend to the repairs of a certain part of the
said road called Jones' lane, which has heretofore been in the
winter season for the most part impassable, then and in such
case the said council shall and they are hereby directed to cause
that part of the said road to be in the first instance effectually
repaired and amended and if it shall be thought proper, altered
so as to be rendered shorter and to run over better ground, and
apply the residue of the said moiety so far as the same will
go in manner hereinbefore directed, And the said supreme executive council are hereby farther authorized and empowered
to direct the other moiety or half part of the said moneys to be
applied by contract or otherwise to the improving the navigation of the river Schuylkill in such way and manner as to them
shall seem expedient, having regard to the principles on which
the application of the other moiety is directed to be made so
that what shall be laid out shall effectually improve the part to
which it is applied, lest by extending the object too far the
design may be defeated. And the said supreme executive
council are hereby authorized and empowered to draw orders
on the state treasurer to whom the managers of the said lottery
are hereby directed to pay over the sum produced by the same
for such sums not exceeding the amount of the sum so produced as the said supreme executive council shall from time to
time deem necessary.

Passed March 3, 1788. Recorded L. B. No. 3, p. 339.

The Statutes at Large of Pennsylvania.

CHAPTER MCCCXXXV.

AN ACT FOR ERECTING A CERTAIN DISTRICT OF COUNTRY IN WHICH THE COURT HOUSE IN CHESTER COUNTY STANDS INTO A COUNTY TOWN.

(Section I, P. L.) Whereas a number of the inhabitants of Chester county have petitioned this house that a certain district of country in the which the court house of the said county stands may be erected into a county town and that the inhabitants of the said town may be entitled to a like number of justices of the peace with other county towns and it appearing that the public convenience will thereby be promoted:

[Section I.] (Section II, P. L.) Be it therefore enacted and it is hereby enacted by the Representatives of the Freemen of the Commonwealth of Pennsylvania in General Assembly met and by the authority of the same, That a certain district of country within the county aforesaid, bounded as follows, viz, beginning at the line which divides the townships of East Bradford and Goshen at the corner of the lands of Charles Ryan and John Darlington, thence along the lines of the said Charles Ryan and the lands late of Thomas Williamson, of Gideon Williamson and of Thomas Darlington, Junior, to lands of George Matlack, thence along the lines of the lands of George Matlack, William Sharpless, Jonathan Matlock and John Patton to a line of the land of Doctor Joseph Moore, thence to the line of the land of Isaiah Matlack, thence along the lines of the said Isaiah Matlack's land and of the lands of Doctor Joseph Moore and Thomas Hoops to the road called the Goshen street, thence along the said street to the land of Benaniel Ogden, being the line which divides the township of East Bradford from the township of Goshen, and from thence to the place of beginning, be and hereby is erected into and constituted the county town of and for the said county of Chester, by the name and title of "West Chester," and is hereby invested with and entitled to all the rights, privileges, immunities and advantages of a county town within this commonwealth.

Passed March 3, 1788. Recorded L. B. No. 3, p. 388.

CHAPTER MCCCXXXVI.

AN ACT TO ENABLE THE COMMISSIONERS OF THE COUNTY OF
CHESTER TO SELL AND CONVEY A CERTAIN LOT OF LAND IN THE
TOWNSHIP OF EAST CALN AND COUNTY AFORESAID FOR THE USE
OF THE SAID COUNTY.

(Section I, P. L.) Whereas in and by an act of assembly
passed the twentieth day of March, one thousand seven hundred and eighty certain commissioners therein named were
empowered to purchase and take assurance of a lot of land in
some convenient part of the county of Chester and thereon to
erect a court-house and prison, in consequence of which powers
and for said uses the said commissioners purchased a lot of
land in the township of East Caln.

And whereas in and by one other act passed the twenty-
second day of March one thousand seven hundred and eighty-
four other commissioners were appointed for the purposes mentioned in the above recited act with a proviso, confining said
commissioners to certain limits upon which the buildings were
to be erected.

And whereas the commissioners appointed by the act last
recited have executed their trust by erecting a court-house and
prison in the township of Goshen by which the lot of land in
East Caln is rendered of no use:

And whereas the commissioners of said county have by petition prayed that a law may be passed enabling them to sell
and convey the said lot.

[Section I.] (Section II, P. L.) Be it therefore enacted and
it is hereby enacted by the Representatives of the Freemen of
the Commonwealth of Pennsylvania in General Assembly met
and by the authority of the same, That the commissioners in
and for the county of Chester or any two of them be and they
are hereby empowered and directed to expose to sale by public
vendue to the highest bidder a certain lot of land lying and
being in the township of East Caln, purchased from Rosanna

Sheward for the use of said county by William Clingan, Thomas Bull, John Kinkead, Roger Kirk, John Sellers, John Wilson, and Joseph Davis, commissioners under the act first recited, bounded as follows, viz, beginning at a marked hickory sapling, standing on the north side of the Conestogo road, thence by said road north seventy degrees and an half east, ten perches to a post, thence by lands of said Rosanna Sheward north eighteen degrees west sixteen perches to a post, thence by said Rosanna Sheward's land south seventy-one degrees and a half west ten perches to a post thence south eighteen degrees and a half east sixteen perches to the place of beginning, containing one acre be the same more or less.

[Section II.] (Section III, P. L.) And be it further enacted by the authority aforesaid, That the commissioners of the county aforesaid, be and they hereby are authorized and empowered to give assurances in the law to the purchaser or purchasers, his, her or their heirs and assigns forever and the moneys arising therefrom shall be appropriated to the use of the county in the same manner that county rates and levies are appropriated.

Passed March 3, 1788. Recorded L. B. No. 3, p. 339.

CHAPTER MCCCXXXVII.

AN ACT TO ENABLE THE OWNERS AND POSSESSORS OF A CERTAIN TRACT OF MARSH AND MEADOW LAND THEREIN DESCRIBED SITUATE IN THE COUNTIES OF PHILADELPHIA AND CHESTER TO KEEP THE BANKS DAMS, SLUICES AND FLOOD GATES IN REPAIR AND TO RAISE A FUND TO DEFRAY THE EXPENSE THEREOF.

(Section I, P. L.) Whereas there is a certain parcel of marsh and meadow land situate in the township of Kingsessing in the county of Philadelphia, commonly known by the name of Boone's Island and Carcus-Hook marsh, and also other parcels of drained marsh situate in the township of Tinicum in the county of Chester the whole of which several parcels is con-

tained within the bounds following to wit, beginning at the
fast land of Christopher Elliott to the southward of said Elliott's house and adjoining to a piece of marsh which he has
embanked at his own expense, thence by Darby creek to Green
creek, thence by said Green creek and Plumb creek to the river
Delaware thence up the same to Bow creek and up Bow creek
to Boone's creek and thence up the said Boone's creek to the
fast land near the house of the widow Cocks, thence by the
fast land to the dam now in use over Kingsessing creek to
Boone's, Knowles's Blankeney's and the State Islands, thence
crossing by the said dam to the fast land on the north side of
the said creek, thence by the several courses of the said fast
land to the place of beginning, which said tract or parcel of
marsh and meadow land hath been and now is embanked but
inasmuch as the banks, dams, sluices and flood-gates made for
the stopping out the tide waters from the same and for prevent-
the overflowings thereof cannot be equitably and sufficiently
maintained without a law.

[Section I.] (Section II. P. L.) Be it therefore enacted and
it is hereby enacted by the Representatives of the Freemen of
the Commonwealth of Pennsylvania in General Assembly met
and by the authority of the same, That the said tracts and
parcels of meadow lands are hereby divided into the two certain divisions following, that is to say, from a certain creek
called Bow creek including the eastern dam and sluice over
said Bow creek and thence to the fast land on Carcus-hook
and Boone's island shall be henceforth called and named the
Northern division and from the said Bow creek including the
western dam and sluice over the said Bow creek and thence to
Plumb creek shall be henceforth called and named the southern
division and that the said owners occupiers and possessors of
meadow land in the northern division shall be called and named
the Tinicum company and the owners, occupiers and possessors
meadow land in the southern division shall be called and named
named the Kingsessing company.

[Section II.] (Section III, P. L.) And be it enacted by the
authority aforesaid, That it shall and may be lawful for the
said companies respectively or as many of them as shall think

fit to meet together on the third Monday in March yearly and
every year at the town of Darby or such other convenient place
as shall hereafter be appointed by the managers of each respective division or any two of them to be chosen by virtue of this
act of which place and time of meeting the treasurer of each
division respectively shall notify the owners and occupiers
thereof by three advertisements at least in each township or
division ten days before the day appointed for such meeting
and then and there by a majority of those met shall choose by
ticket in writing three fit persons owners or possessors of land
in each respective division before described to be managers and
one fit person to be treasurer of the said divisions respectively
for the year then next ensuing.

[Section III.] (Section IV, P. L.) And be it enacted by the
authority aforesaid, That if any of the owners or possessors
elected managers as aforesaid on due notice given in writing
of his election by some of the company present at the said election shall refuse or afterwards neglect to do the duty required
of him or them by this act, he or they so refusing or neglecting
his duty shall forfeit and pay to the treasurer for the time
being of his or their division the sum of three pounds to be
added to the common stock of the company of said division
unless he or they shall have served two years successively in
the said office next before his or their said appointment, which
fine shall be recovered in the manner hereinafter directed for
the recovery of other money payable to the treasurer of the said
divisions respectively and the other managers or a majority of
them shall proceed in the execution of their office without him
or them or if they think fit may choose others of the said owners or possessors to be manager or managers in the place of him
or them so refusing or neglecting, and if the person so elected
treasurer shall refuse or neglect to take upon him the duties
or to give the securities required by this act or shall misbehave
himself, or by death or otherwise be rendered incapable to execute the said office, in any of these cases the managers for
the time being shall choose another fit person to be the treasurer for that year.

[Section IV.] (Section V, P. L.) And be it enacted by the authority aforesaid, That every treasurer hereafter to be chosen shall before he takes upon him the execution of his office enter into an obligation with at least one sufficient surety in double the value of the money that doth or may probably come into his hands during the continuance of his office as near as can be estimated by the managers, conditioned that he will once in every year or oftener if required, render his accounts to the said managers or a majority of them and well and truly account, adjust and settle with them when required for and concerning all moneys that are or shall come to his hands by virtue of this act, or that belong to the owners of the land in the said divisions respectively, and shall well and truly pay the balance that shall appear on such settlement to be in his hands to such persons and to such services as any two of the managers for the time being shall order and appoint and not otherwise, and that he will do and execute all other matters and things as treasurer to the said owners respectively according to the true intent and meaning of this act and that he will at the expiration of his office well and truly pay or cause to be paid and delivered all the money then remaining in his hands together with the books of accounts concerning the same and all other papers and writings in his keeping belonging to the owners of the said divisions respectively unto his successor in the said office.

[Section V.] (Section VI, P. L.) And be it enacted by the authority aforesaid, that the banks, dams, sluices and floodgates which belong to the said districts respectively shall hereafter be maintained and supported by the managers respectively in common for which purpose it shall and may be lawful for the said managers of each respective division or any two of them as often as they shall see occasion to meet together and lay such assessments and taxes on every acre of land in their said respective districts as they shall judge to be necessary for the benefit and security of the same. Provided always, That previous to such reparation and maintenance in common, those banks which are now deficient shall be made and put in equal good order with the best at the expense and cost of the respec-

tive owners to which they now belong, by the managers of
the respective districts, and the owners or occupiers of land on
which the banks are, shall sow the said banks with grass seed
from time to time when necessary and shall mow and keep
them clean at such times as the managers shall order and
direct.

[Section VI.] (Section VII, P. L.) And be it enacted by the
authority aforesaid, That the managers for the time being of
each respective division or any two of them shall have the
power of disposing of all moneys paid to the treasurer by virtue
of this act and of hiring and appointing at the expense of the
said divisions respectively any person or persons from time to
time to inspect the condition of all the banks, dams, sluices and
flood-gates belonging to the said divisions and to offer and pay
such rewards as they think necessary out of the common stock
for the destruction of such vermin as usually damage the banks
and dams as well as for all other general services of the said
divisions respectively.

[Section VII.] (Section VIII, P. L.) And be it enacted by
the authority aforesaid, That the managers of the said districts or a majority of either of them respectively are hereby
authorized, empowered and required to raise and repair a certain dam commonly called Boone's dam in such manner as
shall to them appear most effectual and shall have full power
and authority to assess and levy on all the lands in the said
districts such sums of money as may be necessary for the said
purpose and collect the same by the methods hereinafter
directed.

[Section VIII.] (Section IX, P. L.) And be it enacted by the
authority aforesaid, That the managers of the said districts
or a majority of them may, if it shall appear to them necessary, make a dam and sufficient sluice therein across Bow creek
near its junction with the Delaware in such place and manner
as shall in their opinion be most suitable and raise money to
defray the expense thereof by a tax on the said districts and
when the said dam and sluice is fully perfected they shall be
thereafter maintained and supported by the managers of the
said northern division.

[Section IX.] (Section X, P. L.) And be it enacted by the
authority aforesaid, That the major part of the managers for
the time being of each district respectively shall at least three
times in each year hereafter at such times as they think necessary by written or printed advertisements published in three
or more places in each district at least ten days before the
time therein to be appointed, require the owners or [occupiers]
of all meadow lands in the said districts respectively to cut all
ransted, elders, poke, thistles, burdock and other weeds which
may be injurious to the said meadows and should the owners
or occupiers of the said lands or any of them neglect to cut
or mow the same at such times as they shall be so required it
shall and may be lawful for the said managers and they are
hereby enjoined and required to hire and employ a sufficient
number of men to cut or mow the same and fine the said owner
or occupier for their neglect in any sum not exceeding the cost
of the said cutting or mowing and recover the money so expended and the fine so imposed in like manner as other sums
of money are by this act directed to be recovered, which fines
shall be applied to the benefit of the said districts respectively.

[Section X.] (Section XI, P. L.) And be it enacted by the
authority aforesaid, That all creeks or ditches which now are
or hereafter shall be made in the said districts of the width
of nine feet and of the depth of three feet shall be deemed and
considered in law as lawful fences and enclosures, and if any
owner or occupier shall find on his or her land so enclosed as
aforesaid any swine or hogs it shall and may be lawful for the
said owner or occupier to seize and take off such swine or hogs
whether yoked and ringed or not and being legally attested before the next justice that such swine or hogs were taken in
his or her meadow lands so enclosed, the said justice shall forthwith order and direct the treasurer of the said district respectively to advertise the same and within five days sell at public
auction all such swine and after deducting all reasonable cost
divide the remainder equally between the managers for the use
of the district wherein such swine were taken and the person
so taking them up.

(Section XII, P. L.) And whereas the cutting or making drains or ditches in suitable places and securing those now made or which may hereafter be made will greatly conduce to the better improvement of the said meadows:

[Section XI.] Be it therefore enacted by the authority aforesaid, That the major part of the managers of the said districts respectively shall at such times and so often as they see occasion direct and order that new drains or ditches be made where necessary or those which are already made scoured and apportion the cost of making and scouring the same amongst those benefited thereby or order such compensation to those who may be injured as shall appear to them just and reasonable and compel payment in the manner hereinafter directed.

[Section XII.] (Section XIII, P. L.) And be it further enacted by the authority aforesaid, That if any owner or occupier shall think him her or themselves aggrieved by any act, order, account, proceeding or neglect of any of the said managers of either division, such owner or occupier shall if he or they think proper choose two fit and disinterested persons, and the said managers or any two of them shall choose two other fit and disinterested persons, who, if occasion be, son so chosen or any three of them shall finally settle the same and all matters and things in dispute that shall be referred to them by the parties.

[Section XIII.] (Section XIV, P. L.) And be it enacted by the authority aforesaid, That the orders of any two of the managers on the treasurer of the respective divisions for the time being shall be complied with by the said treasurer and shall be good vouchers to indemnify him for the payment and delivery of the money and effects committed to his care by virtue of this act and that all bonds, mortgages, deeds, and conveyances in trust for the use of the said owners, shall be taken in the name of the treasurer of the Tinicum or Kingsessing companies respectively and be payable to him and his successors and shall be mentioned to be for the use of the owners thereof, and with or without assignment shall be good and available in law to his successor or successors in the said trust, for the use of the owners as aforesaid and shall be recoverable in any court of

record in this commonwealth where the same may be cognizable as fully and effectually to all intents and purposes as if
the same were private property and duly assigned in all the
forms of law and the receipts and discharges of such succeeding treasurer or treasurers for any such sum or sums of money
paid to him or them shall be effectual in law.

[Section XIV.] (Section XV, P. L.) And be it enacted by
the authority aforesaid, That if the banks, dams, sluices, floodgates and other conveniences made or to be made for the security and preservation of the said meadows shall be out of repair
in either of the divisions aforesaid and the managers of such
division wherein the said banks, dams, sluices, floodgates and
other conveniences so out of repair as aforesaid may be shall
neglect or refuse upon notice given thereof by the managers
of the other division or any of them to make, amend and repair
the same, that then and in every such case it shall and may
be lawful for the managers of the division from whom such
notice shall be given to enter into the said division so out of
repair, and to make, amend and repair the same and to recover
and levy the costs, charges and expenses thereof in the same
manner as if they were the managers of and for the division
so out of repair, any thing herein contained to the contrary
thereof notwithstanding.

[Section XV.] (Section XVI, P. L.) And be it further enacted by the authority aforesaid, That if any person or persons shall wickedly and maliciously cut through, break down
or damage any of the banks, dams, sluices or floodgates to the
aforesaid divisions or either of them belonging, or shall let in
any creek or water to annoy, injure or overflow any of their
neighbor's lands and shall thereof be convicted before the justices of the court of quarter sessions of either of the said counties of Philadelphia or Chester in which the same may happen,
in all such cases the person or persons so offending shall be
fined treble the value of the damages, to be assessed by two
or more indifferent persons to be appointed by the said courts
respectively to value the same, one third part of which fine
shall be paid to the persons injured and the remaining two
thirds thereof shall be added to the common stock of the re-

spective division for the general use and benefit thereof.

[Section XVI.] (Section XVII, P. L.) And be it enacted by the authority aforesaid, That if any of the said owners, occupiers or possessors of meadow lands within the aforesaid districts, shall neglect or refuse to pay the several sums of money that shall from time to time be rated, assessed or imposed by the major part of the managers of either of the said divisions for paying and discharging their respective proportions for maintaining the banks, dams, and sluices to the said districts or either of them belonging, or for making or scouring drains or ditches when thereunto required as aforesaid, for the space of thirty days after demand made by the treasurer of the respective division, it shall and may be lawful to and for the said several treasurers, by the direction of the major part of the managers for the time being respectively, in his own name to sue for and recover the several sums of money so charged and assessed in the same manner as debts not exceeding ten pounds are by law recoverable, and give this act and the said assessment or the said account in evidence. Provided always, That such delinquent owner, occupier or possessor shall not be entitled to stay of execution for any longer time than ten days, or it shall and may be lawful to and for the several treasurers, by the directions of the managers as aforesaid in his own name to apply to some justice of the peace of the county for his warrant of distress for levying the said sums of money so neglected or refused to be paid, directed to the constable of the township where the meadows are, which said warrant the said justice of the peace is hereby empowered and directed to grant accordingly, to be by the said constable levied on the tract or piece of marsh meadow belonging as aforesaid to such owner or owners so neglecting and deliver the same over unto the managers respectively for the time being, who, or a major part of them, are hereby empowered and authorized to let the same on rent, or any part thereof that may be sufficient, belonging to such delinquent owner or owners so neglecting as aforesaid from time to time for so long time as until the rent or rents arising therefrom shall as nearly as may be computed, pay all

3—XIII

such sum or sums of money so assessed, charged or imposed, together with all costs and reasonable expenses arising thereon
for his, her or their neglect or refusal to pay the same as aforesaid and no longer. Provided always, That in letting out the
said meadow land the said managers do publicly notify the
leasing thereof and let the same to the highest bidder at public
sale.

[Section XVII.] (Section XVIII, P. L.) And be it further
enacted by the authority aforesaid, That it shall and may be
lawful for the said managers respectively to meet together as
often as they shall see occasion, to direct the necessary repairs, and the said managers or a majority of them for the time
being respectively are hereby empowered, authorized and required to enter upon and inspect, at least four times in each
year the condition of all the said banks, dams, sluices, floodgates and other conveniences necessary for stopping out the
tides and draining the water from the said meadows, and it
shall and may be lawful to and for the said managers respectively or any of them together with such workmen, horses,
carts, barrows and other tools as they shall think necessary, to
enter into and upon any of the lands of the said divisions where
a breach or defect now is or shall hereafter happen to be and
then and there to dig and carry earth or purchase suitable
materials to make, amend and repair the said banks, dams,
sluices and floodgates and all other conveniences necessary for
stopping out the tide or for draining the waters off the meadows
in such manner and by such ways and means as they the
said managers or a majority of them respectively shall think
fit and reasonable, any law, usage, or custom of this commonwealth to the contrary in anywise notwithstanding.

[Section XVIII.] (Section XIX, P. L.) And be it further
enacted by the authority aforesaid, That the managers of the
said districts respectively shall each of them have and receive ten shillings per day for each day that they shall be
employed in the several duties required of them and the treasurers shall have such compensation for their services as a major
part of the managers of each respective division shall think
adequate.

[Section XIX.] (Section XX, P. L.) And be it enacted by
the authority aforesaid, That should the managers of a certain
district of meadows called Long-Hook company neglect to keep
and maintain the banks, dams, sluices and floodgates to the
said company belonging in good order and repair and the
owners or occupiers of meadow lands in the aforesaid southern
division be injured thereby, or should the managers of the said
southern division neglect to do their duty according to the true
intent and meaning of this act, in either case it shall and may
be lawful for the managers of the said company and division or
a majority of either of them to enter into the company or
division so neglecting in the same manner and with the same
powers and authorities as is given to the managers of the
aforesaid divisions in the fifteenth section of this act.

(Section XXI, P. L.) And whereas a dam hath been made
across Mingo or Kingsessing creek, nearer the mouth of the
said creek than the aforesaid dam called Boone's dam, with a
sluice or sluices therein, and should the managers thereof neglect to keep the said sluice or sluices in good order and repair
and properly laid to discharge the waters of the said creek, the
meadow lands in the aforesaid northern division may be greatly
damaged to the injury of the owners and occupiers of land in
the said division:

For remedy whereof:

[Section XX.] Be it enacted by the authority aforesaid, That
should those who may have the care and management of the
said lower dam and sluice or sluices refuse or neglect to keep
the same in good order and repair and properly laid in order
sufficiently to discharge the waters from the said creek,
that then and in such case if the managers of the said northern
division and those who may have the care and management
of the said dam and sluice or sluices disagree respecting the
order and repair of the same they may refer all matters in
dispute to three or more indifferent persons whose judgment
shall be conclusive, but should those who may have the care
and management of the said dam neglect or refuse to refer
the matters in difference as aforesaid, the managers of the
said northern division or a majority of them may apply to some

justice of the peace of the county in which the said lands are,
who is hereby authorized and required to appoint three or
more indifferent persons to settle all such matters in dispute,
whose orders and directions respecting the same shall be binding on all parties, but should those who may have the care and
management of the said dam in either case neglect to perform
their duty when determined as aforesaid it shall and may be
lawful for a major part of the managers of the said northern
division to alter, amend and repair the same agreeable to the
decision of the said referees or of those appointed by the said
justice and recover the moneys so expended and cost to be
taxed by the said justice in the same manner as is directed in
the seventeenth section of this act.

[Section XXI.] (Section XXII, P. L.) And be it enacted by
the authority aforesaid, that an act of assembly of the province of Pennsylvania entitled, "An act to enable the owners
and possessors of a certain tract of marsh and meadow land
'therein described situate in the counties of Philadelphia and
Chester to keep the banks, dams, sluices and floodgates in repair and to raise a fund to defray the expense thereof,"[1] and
another act of assembly of the said province entitled "A supplement to an act entitled "An act to enable the owners and
possessors of a certain tract of marsh and meadow land therein
described situate in the counties of Philadelphia and Chester
to keep the banks, dams, sluices and floodgates in repair and
to raise a fund to defray the expense thereof "[2] and another act
of Assembly of the said province entitled "An act for the new
regulation of the allotments of banks, dams, sluices and floodgates belonging to the Tinicum company owners and possessors of drained meadow land in the township of Ridley in
the county of Chester,"[3] and also another act of assembly of
the said province entitled "An act for amending each and
every of the acts of assembly of this province heretofore made

Passed March 10, 1788. Recorded L. B. No. 8, p. 841.

[1]Passed February 17, 1762, Chapter 474.

[2]Passed March 4, 1763, Chapter 491.

[3]Passed February 78, 1769, Chapter 591.

[4]Passed February 15, 1765, Chapter 528.

for embanking and draining several parcels of marsh land
situate. In the counties of Philadelphia and Chester and
for repairing and maintaining the banks, dams, and sluices
thereunto belonging,"[1] so far as they relate to the aforesaid
districts or divisions shall be and are hereby repealed and made
null and void.

CHAPTER MCCCXXXVIII.

AN ACT TO INCORPORATE AND ENDOW AN ACADEMY OR PUBLIC
SCHOOL IN THE BOROUGH OF READING IN THE COUNTY OF BERKS.

(Section 1, P. L.) Whereas the education of youth has ever
been found to be of the most essential consequences as well to
the good government of states and the peace and welfare of
society, as to the profit and ornament of individuals, insomuch
that from the experience of all ages it appears that seminaries
of learning when properly conducted have been public bless-
ings to mankind so that much of the happiness and prosperity
of every community depends on the proper instruction of youth
who must succeed the aged in the important business of life,
and as an academy or public school in the borough of Reading
and county of Berks for the education of youth is likely to contribute to the welfare of the community and this house cheer-
fully concurring in so laudable a work:

Therefore:

[Section 1.] (Section II. P. L.) Be it enacted and it is hereby
enacted by the Representatives of the Freemen of the Commonwealth of Pennsylvania in General Assembly met and by the
authority of the same, That there shall be and hereby is erected
and established In the borough of Reading in the county of
Berks an academy or public school for the education of youth
in useful arts, sciences and literature by the name, style and
title of "Reading Academy."

[1]Passed February 15, 1765, Chapter 523.

[Section II.] (Section III, P. L.) And be it further enacted
by the authority aforesaid, That the first trustees of the said
academy shall consist of the following persons, viz: the Hon-
orable Thomas Mifflin, Esquire, the Reverend William Ingold,
the Reverend Frederick Wildbohn, the Reverend William Boos,
Daniel Broadhead, Daniel Heister, Junior, James Biddle,
Joseph Heister, Collinson Read, Daniel Clymer, Doctor James
Diemer, Cadwalader Morris, George Ege, Joseph Sands, Christopher Lower, Charles Shoemaker, Nicholas Lutz, John Bishop,
Thomas Dundass, Paul Grosscup, John Eckert, John Otto,
Daniel Levam, Esquires, Jacob Winey, John Hartman, Henry
Hahn, Senior, Peter Nagle, John Strohecker and Daniel Udre,
to meet the fourteenth day of May one thousand seven hundred
and eighty-eight in the borough of Reading at the house of
John Hartman, which said trustees and their successors to be
elected as hereinafter mentioned shall forever hereafter be and
they are hereby erected, established and declared to be one body
politic and corporate in deed and in law to all intents and purposes with perpetual succession by the name and title of "The
Trustees of the Academy in the Borough of Reading and county
of Berks," by which name and title they and their successors
shall be competent and capable in law and in equity to take
and hold to them and their successors for the use of the said
academy any estate in any messuages, lands, tenements, hereditaments, goods, chattels, moneys or other effects, by the
gift, grant, bargain, sale, conveyance, assurance, will, devise
or bequest of any person or persons whatsoever capable of
making the same, and the same messuages, lands, tenements,
hereditaments and estates, real and personal to grant, bargain,
sell, convey, assure, devise and to farm, let out on interest or
otherwise dispose of for the use of the said academy, either to
build rebuild or enlarge or otherwise alter the school house for
the accommodation of the scholars at the aforesaid academy
or to erect or make any new building in such manner as to them
or at least seven of them shall seem most beneficial to the institution and to recover the rents, issues, profits, income and interest of the same and to apply the same to the benefit, use and
support of the said academy and by the same name and title

as aforesaid to sue, commence, prosecute and plead and be impleaded in any court or courts, before any judge or judges, justice or justices in all and every manner of suits, complaints,
pleas, causes, matters and demands of whatsoever nature, kind
or [form] they may be and all and very matter and thing
therein to do in as full and effectual a manner as any other
person or persons, bodies politic or corporate within this commonwealth may or can do, and to hold, enjoy and exercise all
such powers, authorities and jurisdictions touching and concerning the premises which shall be incidentally necessary
thereto in every case, matter or thing relative to the management or in anywise necessary for the good government of the
aforesaid academy.

[Section III.] (Section IV, P. L.) And be it further enacted
by the authority aforesaid, That the said trustees and their
successors, shall have full power and authority to use one
common seal with such device and inscription thereon as they
shall think proper, under and by which all deeds, certificates
and acts of the said corporation shall pass and be authenticated
and the said seal to break alter and renew at their pleasure.

[Section IV.] (Section V, P. L.) And be it further enacted
by the authority aforesaid, That any seven of the said trustees
shall be a quorum to transact all the business of the said academy, particularly of making and enacting ordinances and by-
laws for the government of the said academy, of electing trustees in the room of those who shall be removed by death or
resignation, of electing and appointing masters and tutors of
said academy, of agreeing with them for their salaries and removing them for misconduct and breaches of the laws of the
institution, of appointing a secretary, stewards, managers and
other necessary officers for taking care of the estate and managing the concerns of the corporation and shall determine all
matters and things, although the same be not herein particularly mentioned, which shall occasionally arise and be event-
ually necessary to be determined and transacted by the said
trustees. Provided always, That no ordinance or by-laws shall
be of force which shall be repugnant to the laws of this com-

monwealth and that all their laws and proceedings be fairly
and regularly entered in a book to be kept for that purpose.

[Section V.] (Section VI, P. L.) And be it further enacted
by the authority aforesaid, That no misnomer of the said corporation shall defeat or annul any gift, grant, devise, or bequest
to the said corporation provided the intent of the parties shall
sufficiently appear upon the face of the gift, grant, will or other
writing whereby any estate or interest was intended to pass to
the said corporation, nor shall any disuser or nonuser of the
rights, liberties, privileges, jurisdictions and authorities hereby
granted to the said corporation create or in anywise cause a
forfeiture thereof.

[Section VI.] (Section VII, P. L.) And be it further enacted
by the authority aforesaid, That no sale or alienation of the
real estate of the said corporation which shall have been made
by the said trustees or their successors bona fide for a valuable
consideration, in case the possession thereof pass immediately
to the purchaser or purchasers thereof and continue in him, her
or them, his, her or their heirs or assigns shall be invalidated
for want of proving that seven of the trustees of the said corporation consented to such sale or alienation, unless the same
be controverted within the space of seven years, from and after
the sale and delivery of such real estate to the purchaser or
purchasers thereof.

[Section VII.] (Section VIII, P. L.) And be it further enacted by the authority aforesaid, That five thousand acres of
land together with six per centum allowance for roads be laid
off and surveyed within the unappropriated lands of this commonwealth be and they are hereby granted to the said trustees
of Reading Academy in the county of Berks to have and to
hold the same to them, their successors and assigns forever.
And on the application of the said trustees or of any person
duly authorized by them, the secretary of the land office of this
state, he shall and hereby is required to grant and issue such
and so many warrants to be directed to the surveyor general,
requiring him to survey or cause to be surveyed for the trustees of the said academy such and so many tracts of land with
such number of acres in each warrant as shall be applied for

at each application in such places not otherwise appropriated by acts of assembly of this commonwealth as shall in the whole amount to the said quantity of five thousand acres with the usual allowance and the surveyor-general shall receive and enter all such warrants in his office and issue copies thereof directed to his deputies in the different counties and districts within the state and the said deputies shall duly execute the same and make returns thereof and thereupon such proceedings shall be had and patents or grants of confirmation for the same shall be issued and granted to the said trustees of the said academy in like manner and form and having like force and effect as the like proceedings and patents have been and are conducted and granted in case of private persons making application for and taking up lands under the laws of this commonwealth, provided that no warrant issue for less than five hundred acres and that the same be included in one survey.

[Section VIII.] (Section IX, P. L.) And be it further enacted by the authority aforesaid, That all and every the tract and tracts of land hereby directed to be surveyed for the use of the said academy shall be so done at the charge of this state and the president or vice-president in council are hereby authorized and empowered to draw orders on the treasurer of this state to pay and defray all the charges arising thereupon.

Passed March 10, 1788.   Recorded L. B. No. 3, p. 848.

CHAPTER MCCCXXXIX.

AN ADDITIONAL SUPPLEMENT TO THE ACTS FOR THE REGULATION OF THE MILITIA OF THE COMMONWEALTH OF PENNSYLVANIA.

(Section I, P. L.) Whereas the present laws for the regulation of the militia of this commonwealth prove very burthensome and expensive to those who spend their time in attending on muster days as well as to those who from conscientious scruples or otherwise neglect or refuse to give such attendance and

and have attached themselves to the battalions from which
they have been respectively formed and others influenced by
their example may be desirous of forming like companies from
other battalions.

[Section V.] (Section VI, P. L.) Therefore be it enacted by
the authority aforesaid, That it shall and may be lawful for the
volunteers composing the aforesaid companies of light infantry
to elect by ballot one captain, one first and one second lieutenant, and that the non-commissioned officers of such companies shall be appointed in like manner as is usual in the
other militia and the said companies respectively may consist of
sixty-eight men, exclusive of officers provided such number have
joined or hereafter shall join such companies, and shall be attached to and act with the battalion from which they are or
shall be formed and be subject to like rules and regulations as
the other militia of this state.

[Section VI.] (Section VII, P. L.) And be it further enacted
by the authority aforesaid, That whenever forty volunteers
from any battalion within this commonwealth shall [signify]
to the commanding officer thereof their intention of forming
a company of light infantry and shall be willing to equip and
clothe themselves in uniform for that purpose, it shall be lawful for them to elect their officers and thereafter they may consist of like number and shall be governed and regulated in like
manner as the companies mentioned in the section last preceding.

Passed March 22, 1788. Recorded L. B. No. 8, p...... The Act in
the text was repealed by the Act of Assembly passed April 11, 1793,
Chapter 1696.

CHAPTER MCCCXL.

AN ACT FOR DESTROYING THE BILLS OF CREDIT OF THIS COMMON-
WEALTH EMITTED IN PURSUANCE OF AN ACT OF GENERAL AS-
SEMBLY PASSED THE FIRST DAY OF JUNE ONE THOUSAND SEVEN
HUNDRED AND EIGHTY ENTITLED "AN ACT FOR FUNDING AND RE-
DEEMING THE BILLS OF CREDIT OF THE UNITED STATES OF
AMERICA AND FOR PROVIDING MEANS TO BRING THE PRESENT
WAR TO A HAPPY CONCLUSION."[1]

(Section I, P. L.) Whereas in pursuance of the above recited
act bills of credit of this state to the amount of one million four
hundred and ninety-five thousand dollars were emitted on the
credit of this state, to be redeemed thereby on or before the
thirty-first day of December in the year one thousand seven
hundred and eighty-six with interest at five per centum per
annum, and the redemption thereof guaranteed by the United
States in case of the insolvency of this state through the desola-
tion of war:

And whereas four tenths of the said bills of credit so emitted
were subjected to the orders of the United States and to be
credited to this state in the accounts with the United States
and the remaining six tenths were placed in the continental loan
office to be delivered over to the treasurer of this state from
time to time in proportion as the payments were made of the
quota required of this state in the requisition of Congress for
sinking the old continental bills of credit.

And whereas by a negotiation between the United States
and this commonwealth in the year one thousand seven hundred and eighty-one, the residue of the said four-tenths not
then issued by the United States was exchanged for a like sum
in bills of credit of this state of another emission which was
paid to the United States by the treasurer of this state whereby the said residue became redeemed.

And whereas this state hath paid to the United States her

---

[1] Chapter 912. Passed June 1st, 1780.

full quota of the requisition of Congress for sinking the old
continental bills of credit and is thereby entitled to receive the
whole of the six-tenths aforesaid:

And whereas by an act of general assembly passed the seventeenth day of March one thousand seven hundred and eighty-
six,[1] funds were assigned for the redemption of all such of
the bills of credit aforesaid as had been issued by the United
States or by this State which had not been otherwise redeemed:

And whereas it is proper and necessary that the said bills
when redeemed should be sunk and destroyed:

Therefore:

[Section I.] (Section II, P. L.) Be it enacted and it is hereby
enacted by the Representatives of the Freemen of the Commonwealth of Pennsylvania, in General Assembly met and by the
authority of the same, that all the bills of credit emitted in
pursuance of the said first recited act which now are or hereafter may be in the treasury of this state, be examined, counted,
burnt and destroyed from time to time in such manner as the
general assembly shall see fit to direct.

Passed March 22, 1788.   Recorded L. B. No. 3, p. 351.

CHAPTER MCCCXLI.

A SUPPLEMENT TO THE ACT ENTITLED "AN ACT FOR REGULATING
THE MEASUREMENT OF CORN AND SALT IMPORTED INTO THE PORT
OF PHILADELPHIA."[2]

(Section I, P. L.) Whereas large quantities of coal are imported or brought into the port and city of Philadelphia for sale
in the measurement whereof frequent disputes arise:

[Section I.] (Section II, P. L.) Be it therefore enacted and it
is hereby enacted by the Representatives of the Freemen of the
Commonwealth of Pennsylvania in General Assembly met and

---

[1] Chapter 1212.
[2] Passed September 22, 1785, Chapter 1199.

by the authority of the same, That the measurer of corn and salt
imported or brought into the port and city of Philadelphia for
sale shall be the measurer of all coal imported or
brought into the said port and city of Philadelphia for sale
and that the said measurer shall at his own cost provide a
sufficient number of two bushel tub measures and have the
same compared with and regulated by the public standard
measure kept in the city of Philadelphia and shall have the
same powers and be subject to the same rules, regulations and
penalties as are by the said act directed for the measurement
of corn and salt imported into the city and port of Philadelphia.

[Section II. (Section III. P. L.) And be it further enacted by
the authority aforesaid, That the allowance for measurement
of coal imported into the city and port of Philadelphia shall
be at the rate of one shilling for every hundred bushels, to
be paid by the buyers, and one shilling for every hundred
bushels to be paid by the sellers who shall cause the same to
be filled into the measures, and no more.

And whereas considerable quantities of lime are from time to
time imported and brought into the city of Philadelphia, the
district of Southwark and township of the Northern Liberties
and disputes concerning the admeasurement thereof frequently
occur:

[Section III.] (Section IV, P. L.) Be it therefore enacted and
it is hereby enacted by the authority aforesaid, That in case
any dispute shall hereafter arise respecting the admeasurement of lime imported or brought for sale into the said city of
Philadelphia or parts adjacent thereto within one mile from
the court house in the said City the same shall be determined
by the measurer hereinbefore appointed for corn, salt and
coals, who is hereby authorized and empowered to measure
according to the usual and proper mode of measuring that
article, all lime concerning the admeasurement whereof disputes may happen at the instance of either of the parties between whom such dispute or difference may arise and the said
measurer shall be paid by the party who shall be found by the
said measurer in the wrong in such dispute or difference the

sum of one penny for every bushel so measured and the determination of the said measurer in the premises shall be final
between the parties.

Passed March 28, 1788. Recorded L. B. No. 3, p. 361

CHAPTER MCCCXLII.

AN ACT FOR OPENING AND ESTABLISHING CERTAIN ROADS IN THE COUNTIES OF NORTHAMPTON AND LUZERNE.

(Section I, P. L.) Whereas the opening of roads through the
unsettled parts of this state will greatly promote its settlement and population and increase its domestic and
foreign commerce, its manufactures and agriculture, and divers
persons citizens of this state have already subscribed considerable sums of money and divers other persons are disposed
to subscribe further sums for the purpose of opening roads from
Pocona Point in the county of Northampton to a place known
by the name of Mount Ararat and thence to the New York line
at the intended carrying place between the rivers Susquehanna
and Delaware, as also from the said Mount Ararat to the most
proper place at or near the mouth of the river Tioga.

And whereas the said roads will conduce to the immediate
settlement of an extensive tract of country, will promote both
the export and Indian trade of this state and by communication with other roads already begun will render Pennsylvania
the most eligible route for the emigrants from the northern
and eastern parts of the United States:

And whereas it is just and proper that such important efforts
of private citizens of this commonwealth and which tend to increase the general wealth and power of the state should be
patronized and assisted by the legislature thereof:

[Section I.] (Section II, P. L.) Be it therefore enacted and it
is hereby enacted by the Representatives of the Freemen of the
Commonwealth of Pennsylvania in General Assembly met and

by the authority of the same, That the roads aforesaid shall
be laid out and opened as nearly as conveniently may be in
the following directions, that is to say, one of the said roads
shall begin at or near to Pocona Point in the county of Northampton and shall run from thence as shall appear most proper
in the opinion of the commissioners to be appointed as herein
after mentioned, to or near to a place in the said county, known
by the name of Mount Ararat, another of the said roads shall
be run from and at the termination of the road aforesaid at
or near Mount Ararat to such a point in the line dividing the
state of New York from this state, and lying between the rivers
Susquehanna and Delaware, as shall be deemed most proper by
the said commissioners and the last of the said three roads
shall run from (or as near as may be from) the said Mount
Ararat to the most proper place in the opinion of the said
commissioners at or near the mouth of the river Tioga and
each of the said roads shall be laid out sixty-feet wide.

[Section II.] (Section III, P. L.) And be it further enacted
by the authority aforesaid, That the supreme executive council
be and they are hereby authorized and empowered to appoint
five commissioners for the purposes aforesaid and the
said commissioners or any two of them are hereby
authorized and directed to lay out and open or cause
to be laid out and opened the said roads and highways throughout their several main courses aforesaid, in
such manner and in such directions (having regard to the face
and nature of the country) as they shall deem proper, and they
shall proceed to perform the said services at such time and in
such manner as to them may appear most convenient and practicable, and the said commissioners shall report their proceedings in the premises together with an exact account of their
expenditures to the president or vice-president in council, who
are hereby authorized and empowered to establish the said
roads as reported and the said roads or highways when they
shall be so established shall be to all intents and purposes
public state highways and the courses and distances shall be

4—XIII

entered in the council books, which entry shall be deemed a record thereof.

[Section III.] (Section IV, P. L.) And be it further enacted by the authority aforesaid, That the sum of one thousand pounds of money not already appropriated shall be and the same is hereby appropriated to the purposes of this act and the president or vice-president in council are hereby authorized to draw on the treasurer of this state for the same in favor of the said commissioners for the purpose aforesaid.

[Section IV.] (Section V, P. L.) And be it further enacted by the authority aforesaid, That each of the said commissioners shall if required by the president or vice-president in council give security before the issuing of any such draft or order on the treasury to and for the faithful discharge of his trust.

Passed March 28, 1788.   Recorded L. B. No. 3, p. 363.

CHAPTER MCCCXLIII.

AN ACT FOR THE PURPOSE OF GRANTING THE SUM OF ONE HUNDRED POUNDS FOR THE RELIEF OF JAMES McMANAS.

(Section I, P. L.) Whereas it hath been represented to this house by the petition of James McManas and by other testimony it doth appear, that while employed in the service of this state as a laborer in running the northern boundary line thereof said James McManas did receive such wounds and bruises by the falling of a tree in a storm on said James McManas that he is thereby rendered totally incapable of ever supporting himself by labor, and it being consistent with the principles of humanity and justice that some provision be made for his present support.

[Section I.] (Section II, P. L.) Therefore be it enacted and it is hereby enacted by the Representatives of the Freemen of the Commonwealth of Pennsylvania in General Assembly met and by the authority of the same, That the president or

vice-president in council are hereby authorized and empowered
to draw an order on the state treasurer in favor of James Mc-
Manas for the sum of one hundred pounds to be placed in the
hands of the managers of the house of employment of this city
for his immediate support.

Passed March 28, 1788.   Recorded L. B. No. 3, p. 362.

CHAPTER MCCCXLIV.

AN ACT TO EXONERATE JOSEPH FRY, DOOR KEEPER OF THE HOUSE
OF REPRESENTATIVES OF THE FREEMEN OF COMMONWEALTH OF
PENNSYLVANIA IN GENERAL ASSEMBLY, FROM ANY CHARGE FOR
RENT OR OTHER DEMANDS FOR OR ON ACCOUNT OF HIS OCCUPY-
ING OF PART OF THE WESTERN WING OF THE STATE HOUSE AND
CONSUMING THE HERBAGE OF THE STATE HOUSE YARD.

(Section I, P. L.) Whereas it has been represented to this
house by Joseph Fry, door-keeper thereof, that an account has
been exhibited against him by the comptroller-general for a
sum by way of rent for his occupying of the part of the western
wing of the state house in which he and his family dwell, and
for the herbage of the state house yard heretofore consumed
by cattle for his use:

And whereas it appears to this house that such charges have
not been customary against former door-keepers and that the
privileges for which the said Joseph Fry is considered by the
comptroller-general as liable to make compensation are but
a reasonable allowance for extra services and the care of the
state house which the said Joseph Fry is obliged constantly
to exercise as well during the sitting as in the recess of the
house:

[Section I.] (Section II, P. L.) Be it enacted and it is hereby
enacted by the Representatives of the Freemen of the Commonwealth of Pennsylvania in General Assembly met and by
the authority of the same, That all charges, claims and demands whatsoever which are or may be made against the said

Joseph Fry, his executors or administrators for or on account of
the premises are hereby extinguished and released to the said
Joseph Fry, his executors and administrators and the door-
keeper to the general assembly for the time being is hereby
permitted without rent or charge on account of the same to
occupy as heretofore the said apartments.

Passed March 29, 1788.   Recorded L. B. No. 3, p. 362.

CHAPTER MCCCXLV.

AN ACT TO EXPLAIN AND AMEND AN ACT ENTITLED "AN ACT FOR
THE GRADUAL ABOLITION OF SLAVERY."[1]

(Section I, P. L.) For preventing many evils and abuses arising from ill disposed persons availing themselves of certain
defects in the act for the gradual abolition of slavery passed
on the first day of March in the year of our Lord one thousand
seven hundred and eighty[1]:

[Section I.] (Section II, P. L.) Be it enacted, [and it is hereby
enacted] by the Representatives of the Freemen of the Commonwealth of Pennsylvania in General Assembly met and by
the authority of the same, That the exception contained in the
tenth section of the aforesaid act relative to domestic slaves
attending upon persons passing through or sojourning in this
state and not becoming resident therein shall not be deemed
or taken to extend to the slaves of such persons as are inhabitants of or resident in this state or who shall come here
with an intention to settle and reside, but that all and every
slave and slaves who shall be brought into this state by persons inhabiting or residing therein or intending to inhabit or
reside therein shall be immediately considered, deemed and
taken to be free to all intents and purposes.

[Section II.] (Section III, P. L.) And be it further enacted
by the authority aforesaid, That no negro or mulatto slave or
servant for term of years (except as in the last exception of the

tenth section of the said act is excepted) shall be removed out
of this state with the design and intention that the place of
abode or residence of such slave or servant shall be thereby
altered or changed or with the design and intention that such
slave or servant if a female and pregnant shall be detained and
kept out of this state till her delivery of the child of which she
is or shall be pregnant or with the design and intention that
such slave or servant shall be brought again into this state,
after the expiration of six months from the time of such slave
or servant having been first brought into this state without his
or her consent, if of full age, testified upon a private examination before two justices of the peace of the city or county in
which he or she shall reside, or being under the age of twenty-
one years, without his or her consent testified in manner aforesaid, and also without the consent of his or her parents if any
such there be, to be testified in like manner aforesaid, whereof
the said justices or one of them shall make a record and deliver to the said slave or servant a copy thereof, containing the
name, age, condition and then place of abode of such slave or
servant, the reason of such removal and the place to which he
or she is about to go. And if any person or persons whatever
shall sell or dispose of any such slave or servant to any person
out of this state or shall send or carry or cause to be sent or carried any such slave or servant out of this state for any of the
purposes aforesaid, whereby such slave or servant would lose
those benefits and privileges which by the laws of this state
are secured to him or her and shall not have obtained all such
consent as by this act is required testified in the manner before mentioned, every such person and persons, his and their
aiders and abettors shall severally forfeit and pay for every
such offence the sum of seventy-five pounds to be recovered in
any court of record by action of debt, bill, plaint, or information
at the suit of any person who will sue for the same, one moiety
thereof when recovered for the use of the plaintiff, the other
moiety for the use of the poor of the city, township or place
from which such slave or servant shall be taken and removed

[Section III.] (Section IV, P. L.) And be it further enacted

by the authority aforesaid, That all persons who now are or
hereafter shall be possessed of any child or children born after
the first day of March, one thousand seven hundred and eighty,
who would by the said act be liable to serve till the age of
twenty-eight years, shall on or before the first day of April one
thousand seven hundred and eighty-nine, or within six months
next after the birth of any such child, deliver or cause to be
delivered in writing to the clerk of the peace of the county,
or the clerk of the court of record of the city of Philadelphia
in which they shall respectively inhabit the name, surname
and occupation or profession of such possessor and of the county, township, district or ward in which they reside and also
the age (to the best of his or her knowledge) name and sex of
every such child or children, under the pain and penalty of
forfeiting and losing all right and title to every such child and
children, and of him, her or them immediately becoming free,
which said return or account in writing shall be verified by
the oath or affirmation of the party which the said clerks are
hereby respectively authorized and required to administer, and
the said clerks shall make and preserve records thereof, copies
and extracts of which shall be good evidence in all courts of
justice when certified under their hands and seals of office.
For which oath or affirmation and entry or extract the said
clerks shall be respectively entitled to one shilling and sixpence
and no more, to be paid by him or her who shall so as aforesaid make such entry or demand the extract aforesaid:

And whereas it has been represented to this house that
vessels have been fitted out and equipped in this port for the
iniquitous purpose of receiving and transporting the natives
of Africa to places where they are held in bondage and it is
just and proper to discourage as far as is practicable such
proceedings in future:

[Section IV.] (Section V, P. L.) Be it therefore enacted and
it is hereby enacted by the authority aforesaid, That if any
person or persons shall build, fit, equip, man or otherwise prepare any ship or vessel within any port of this state, or shall
cause any ship or other vessel to sail from any port of this state

for the purpose of carrying on a trade or traffic in slaves, to, from or between Europe, Asia, Africa or America, or any places or countries whatever, or of transporting slaves to or from one port or place to another in any part or parts of the world, such ship or vessel, her tackle, furniture, apparel and other appurtenances shall be forfeited to the commonwealth and shall be liable to be seized and prosecuted by any officer of the customs or other person by information *in rem* in the supreme court or the county court of common pleas for the county wherein such seizure shall be made, whereupon such proceedings shall be had both unto and after judgment as in and by the impost laws of this commonwealth in cases of seizures is directed: And moreover all and every person and persons so building, fitting out, manning, equipping or otherwise preparing or sending away any ship or vessel knowning or intending that the same shall be employed in such trade or business contrary to the true intent and meaning of this act, or anywise aiding or abetting therein shall severally forfeit and pay the sum of one thousand pounds, one moiety thereof to the use of the commonwealth and the other moiety thereof to the use of him or her who will sue for the same by action of debt, bill, plaint or information.

And whereas the practice of separating which is too often exercised by the masters and mistresses of negro and mulatto slaves or servants for term of years, in separating husbands and wives and parents and children, requires to be checked so far as the same may be done without prejudice to such masters or mistresses.

[Section V.] (Section VI, P. L.) Be it enacted by the authority aforesaid, That if any owner or possessor of any negro or mulatto slave or slaves or servant or servants for term of years shall from and after the first day of June next separate or remove or cause to be separated or removed a husband from his wife, a wife from her husband, a child from his or her parent or a parent from child, of any or either of the descriptions aforesaid, to a greater distance than ten miles with the design and intention of changing the habitation or place of abode of such husband, or wife, parent or child, unless such child shall be above the age of four years or unless the consent of such slave or servant for life or years shall have been obtained and testified in the manner hereinbefore described, such person or persons shall severally forfeit and pay the sum of fifty pounds with costs of suit for every such offense to be recovered by action of debt, bill, plaint or information, in the supreme court or in any court of common pleas, at [the] suit of any person who will sue for the same, one moiety thereof when recovered, for the use of the plaintiff the other moiety for the use of the poor of the city, township or place from which such husband or wife, parent or child shall have been taken and removed.

[Section VI.] (Section VII, P. L.) And be it further enacted by the authority aforesaid, That if any person or persons shall from and after the passing of this act by force or violence take and carry or cause to be taken and carried, or shall by fraud, seduce or cause to be seduced, any negro or mulatto from any part or parts of this state to any other place or places whatsoever with a design and intention of selling and disposing or of causing to be sold, or of keeping and detaining, or of causing so to be, as a slave or servant for term of years, any such person and persons, their aiders and abettors, shall on conviction thereof in any court of quarter sessions for any city or county within this commonwealth forfeit and pay the sum of one hundred pounds to the overseers of the poor of the city or township from which such negro or mulatto shall have been taken or seduced as aforesaid and shall also be confined at hard labor for any time not less than six months nor more than twelve months and until the costs of prosecution shall be paid.

[Section VII.] (Section VIII, P. L.) And be it further enacted by the authority aforesaid, That the justices of the courts of common pleas for the counties of this state respectively be and they are hereby required and enjoined to cause [this] act to be publicly read at least twice in each term for the two terms next following the passing of this act.

Passed March 29, 1788. Recorded L. B. No. 3, p. 370. See the Act of Assembly passed December 8, 1789, Chapter 1476.

CHAPTER MCCCXLVI.

AN ACT TO LAY A DUTY ON FOREIGN BARLEY AND MALT IMPORTED INTO THIS STATE.

(Section I, P. L.) Whereas it appears to this house that considerable quantities of foreign malt not the produce or manufacture of this or any other of the United States have been imported into this state, whereby the price hath been so reduced as greatly to discourage the raising of barley, although the soil and climate of this and the neighboring states are well adapted to the production thereof, and whereas it is expedient to give all due encouragement and preference to the agriculture and manufactures of this state:

[Section I.] (Section II, P. L.) Be it therefore enacted and it is hereby enacted by the Representatives of the Freemen of the Commonwealth of Pennsylvania in General Assembly met and by the authority of the same, That from and after the first day of October next there shall be levied, collected and paid to the use of this commonwealth for every bushel of barley or malt imported into this state not of the growth and manufacture of this or some one of the United States, the sum of two shilings and sixpence and the same duty shall be collected, secured and paid in like manner as the impost of two and a half per centum is or shall be collected, secured and paid in and by an act entitled "An act to encourage and protect the manufactures of this state by laying additional duties on the importation of certain manufactures which interfere with them"[A] and shall be subject to like regulations, seizure and forfeiture, and entitled to like drawbacks upon re-exportation, and the collector of the port of Philadelphia shall be subject to like account and responsibility for the same.

Provided always, that any barley really and bona fide imported by or for any person or persons inhabitants of this state, for seed, shall not be subject to the duty hereby imposed.

Passed March 29, 1788. Recorded L. B. No. 3, p. 274.

CHAPTER MCCCXLVII.

AN ACT TO ENCOURAGE AND PROTECT THE MANUFACTURES OF THIS STATE.

(Section I, P. L.) Whereas it is necessary for the encouragement of the arts and manufactures of this state that measures should be taken to prevent ill designing persons from exporting the tools, utensils and machines employed in the manufactures now established or likely so to be and from seducing artificers and manufacturers to leave this country.

[Section I.] (Section II, P. L.) Be it therefore enacted and it is hereby enacted by the Representatives of the Freemen of the Commonwealth of Pennsylvania in General Assembly met and by the authority of the same, That if any person or persons shall on any pretense whatever export, load or put on board or cause or procure to be exported, loaden or put on board or shall pack or cause or procure to be packed in order to be laden or put on board of any ship or vessel bound to any place beyond the sea or not within the United States of America or shall lade or cause or procure to be laden on board of any boat or other vessel or shall bring, or cause to be brought to any quay, wharf or other place in order to be so laden or put on board any such ship or vessel or shall wilfully and maliciously destroy or render useless any machine, engine, tool, press, utensil or implement whatever used in or proper for the woolen, cotton, linen silk, iron or steel manufactures that now are or hereafter may be established in this state, or any part or parts of such machine, engine, tool, press, utensil or implement, or shall buy, purchase, collect or procure any such machine, engine, tool, press, utensil or implement or any part thereof for any of the purposes aforesaid, he or they so offending shall for every such offense not only forfeit and lose all such machines, engines, tools, presses, utensils and implement or parts or parcels thereof, together with the packages and all other goods packed therewith, if any there be, but upon complaint made thereof upon

the oath or affimation of one or more credible witness or witnesses it shall and may be lawful for any justice of the peace
to issue his warrant to bring the person or persons so complained of before him or any other justice, and if such per-
sor. or persons shall not thereupon give such an account of the
use or purpose to which such machines, engines, tools, presses,
utensils and implements or parts or parcels thereof are intended to be appropriated as shall be satisfactory to such justice it shall and may be lawful for such justice to bind the person or persons so charged to appear at the next court of oyer
and terminer or quarter sessions of the peace to be held for
the city or county in which the offense shall be committed with
reasonable sureties for his or their appearance, or to commit
such person or persons in default of giving such security until
the next court of oyer and terminer or quarter sessions of
the peace for the said city and county and in case such
person or persons shall be convicted at such court of oyer and
terminer or quarter sessions of the peace of any of the offenses
aforesaid. he or they shall forfeit and pay for every such offense
a fine of three hundred and fifty pounds and shall also suffer imprisonment in the common gaol of the city or county in which
such offense shall have been committed for the space of twelve
months without bail or mainprize and until such fine shall be
paid together with the costs of prosecution.

[Section II.] (Section III, P. L.) And be it further enacted by
the authority aforesaid, That it shall and may be lawful for
any person or persons whatsoever to seize and secure all such
machines, engines, tools, presses, utensils and implements or
parts or parcels thereof as shall be found or discovered to be
laden and put on board or intended to be laden and put on
board of any ship, vessel or boat and intended to be exported
contrary to the true intent and meaning of this act together
with the packages and all other goods packed therewith if any
such there be and after condemnation thereof in due course of
law the same shall be publicly sold to the best bidder by the
sheriff of the city or county in which the same shall be condemned and one moiety of the produce arising by the sale thereof after deducting the charges of the condemnation and sale
shall be to the use of the commonwealth and the other moiety
to the person who shall seize and prosecute the same as aforesaid.

[Section III.] (Section IV, P. L.) And be it further enacted by the authority aforesaid, That if any captain or master of any ship, boat or vessel, shall knowingly and designedly permit any such machine, engine, tool, press, utensil or implement or any part or parcel thereof to be put on board of his ship, boat or vessel, with design to export the same contrary to the meaning and intent of this act, such captain or master shall for every such offense forfeit and pay a fine of three hundred and fifty pounds and shall also suffer imprisonment in the common gaol of the city or county in which the said offense shall be committed for the space of twelve months, and until the said fine together with the costs of prosecution shall be paid.

[Section IV.] (Section V, P. L.) And be it further enacted by the authority aforesaid, That if any person or persons shall have in his or their custody, power or possession any such machine, engine, tool, press, utensil or implement or any part or parcel thereof with intention to export the same contrary to the intention of this act or to destroy the same or render it useless, upon complaint thereof made by the oath or affirmation of one or more credible witness or witnesses it shall and may be lawful for any justice of the peace to issue his warrant to seize such machine, engine, tool, press, utensil and implement or the parts or parcels thereof and to bring the person or persons so complained of before him or any other justice of the peace and if such person or persons shall not give a satisfactory account of the case or purposes to which such machines, engine, tool, press, utensil and implement or the parts or parcels thereof were intended to be applied, it shall and may be lawful for such justice to cause such machine, engine, tool, press, utensil or implement or the parts or parcels thereof to be detained and to bind the person or persons so charged to appear at the next court of oyer and terminer or quarter sessions of the peace for the county in which the offense shall have been committed, with reasonable sureties for his or their appearance and in default of such security to commit such person or persons to the common gaol of the city or county and in case any such person or persons shall be convicted at such court

of oyer and terminer or quarter sessions of the peace of having
in his or their custody, power or possession, any such machine,
engine, tool, press, utensil or implement or any part or parcel
thereof with such intent as aforesaid, the person or persons
convicted thereof shall for every such offense forfeit and [lose]
all such machines, engines, tools, presses, utensils and implements, and the parts and parcels thereof to the use of the commonwealth and of the prosecutor in manner aforesaid and shall
also forfeit and pay a fine of three hundred and fifty pounds
and shall suffer imprisonment in the common gaol of the city
or county wherein he or they shall be convicted for the space
of twelve months without bail or mainprize and until such
fine shall be paid together with the costs of prosecution.

[Section V.] (Section VI, P. L.) And be it further enacted
by the authority aforesaid, That if any person or persons shall
contract with, entice, persuade or endeavor to seduce or encourage any artificer or workman concerned, skilled or
employed in, or who shall have worked at or been employed in
or who is skilled in the woolens, cotton, linen, silk, iron or steel
manufactures which now are or hereafter may be established
in this state, to go out of this state to parts beyond the sea or to
any place not within the United States of America and
shall be duly convicted thereof, every such person shall for
every such offense forfeit and pay a fine of one hundred pounds
and be committed to the common gaol aforesaid, there to
remain without bail or mainprize for the space of four months
and until such fine shall be paid together with the costs of
prosecution.

[Section VI.] (Section VII, P. L.) And be it further enacted by the authority aforesaid, That if any suit or action
shall be commenced against any person or persons for what
he or they shall do in pursuance of this act such suit or action
shall be commenced within six months next after the fact
committed and the person or person so sued may plead the
general issue and give this act and the special matter in evidence and if the plaintiff or prosecutor shall become non-suit
or suffer a discontinuance or if a verdict shall be given against

him or judgment entered against him on demurrer, the defendant shall recover double costs.

[Section VII.] (Section VIII, P. L.) And be it further enacted by the authority aforesaid, That nothing in this act contained shall be construed to prevent or prohibit the exportation of wool and cotton cards or of such other tools or implements as are or may be usually manufactured for sale and exportation within this state or any [of] the United States of America.

[Section VIII.] (Section IX, P. L.) And be it further enacted by the authority aforesaid, That this act shall be and continue in force for and during the term of two years from and after the publication thereof and from thence to the end of the then next session of the general assembly and no longer.

Passed March 29, 1788. Recorded L. D. No. 3, p. 368.

CHAPTER MCCCXLVIII.

AN ACT FOR FACILITATING THE REDEMPTION OF THE BILLS OF CREDIT EMITTED IN THE YEAR ONE THOUSAND SEVEN HUNDRED AND EIGHTY-ONE AND FOR REDEEMING PART OF THE FUNDED DEBT OF THIS STATE, FOR EXTENDING THE TIME FOR PATENTING LANDS WHICH WERE LOCATED BEFORE THE DECLARATION OF INDEPENDENCY AND FOR GIVING A RIGHT OF PRE-EMPTION TO ACTUAL SETTLERS FOR PROCURING WARRANTS FOR LANDS BY THEM OCCUPIED.

(Section I, P. L.) Whereas in and by an act of the general assembly of this commonwealth passed the twenty-eighth day of March in the year of our Lord one thousand seven hundred and eighty-seven, entitled, "An act for facilitating the redemption of the bills of credit emitted in the year one thousand seven hundred and eighty-one and for redeeming part of the funded debt of this state by the speedy collection of the arrearages due for unpatented lands which were located before the declaration of independency."[1] wherein it is enacted that

---

[1] Chapter 1283.

If any person entitled to lands within this state and yet remaining unpatented, shall refuse or neglect to pay or secure the purchase money or arrearages thereof with interest every such person so refusing or neglecting shall be barred and precluded from all the benefit intended by this act, with respect to further time of payment and [the] mode of such payment and shall be forthwith prosecuted and proceeded against by the sale of his said lands according to law as if this act had not been made

And whereas the before recited act by its own limitation expires the tenth day of April next, within which time so limited the citizens cannot obtain a confirmation of their grants, it is therefore deemed expedient further to extend the same.

[Section I.] (Section II, P. L.) Be it therefore enacted and it is hereby enacted by the Representatives of the Freemen of the Commonwealth of Pennsylvania in General Assembly met and by the authority of the same, That the time limited in the act above recited for paying or securing to the state the payments for lands held or claimed by any citizen of this commonwealth by location or any other office right obtained before the tenth day of December one thousand seven hundred and seventy-six, and yet remaining unpatented be and hereby is extended to every matter and thing contained in the act aforesaid to the tenth day of April in the year of our Lord one thousand seven hundred and eighty-nine.

[Section II.] (Section III, P. L.) And be it further enacted by the authority aforesaid, That every person entitled to demand a patent for land in this state on paying one fourth part of the amount of the purchase money now due with the interest thereon in lawful money of this state or in the bills of credit emitted by virtue of an act passed the seventh day of April one thousand seven hundred and eighty-one together with the whole of the office fees in current lawful money shall at his option pay the residue of such purchase money and interest in lawful money or bills of credit aforesaid or in funded certificates of this state, on which certificates the interest shall be computed and allowed till the time of such payment.

Provided nevertheless, That such payment or payments be

made and completed before the tenth day of April in the year of our Lord one thousand seven hundred and eighty-nine.

[And] whereas by an act passed the thirtieth day of December in the year of our Lord one thousand seven hundred and eighty six entitled, "An act for giving during a limited time a right of pre-emption to the actual settlers within this state"[1] and as said act by its own limitation will expire the tenth day of April next and as it is deemed just and reasonable that the actual settlers within this state who have not procured warrants for the lands by them occupied should be allowed longer time for completing the same.

[Section III.] (Section IV, P. L.) Be it enacted by the authority aforesaid, That the act above recited be and hereby is extended in every matter and thing to the tenth day of April in the year of our Lord one thousand seven hundred and eighty-nine, anything in the said act to the contrary notwithstanding.

Passed March 29, 1788. Recorded L. B. No. 3, p. 366. See the Acts of Assembly passed March 21, 1789, Chapter 1422; March 29, Chapter 1502; April 13, 1791, Chapter 1576.

CHAPTER MCCCXLIX.

AN ACT TO SUSPEND AN ACT ENTITLED "AN ACT FOR ASCERTAINING AND CONFIRMING TO CERTAIN PERSONS CALLED CONNECTICUT CLAIMANTS THE LANDS BY THEM CLAIMED WITHIN THE COUNTY OF LUZERNE AND FOR OTHER PURPOSES THEREIN MENTIONED.

(Section I. P. L.) Whereas by an act entitled "An act for ascertaining and confirming to certain persons called Connecticut claimants the lands by them claimed within the county of Luzerne and for other purposes therein mentioned"[2] it is among other things enacted that certain commissioners therein named or thereafter to be appointed should within a limited time meet together within the said county for the purpose of receiving and examining the claims of the said claimants and ascertaining and confirming the same:

[1]Chapter 1259.
[2]Passed March 28, 1787. Chapter 1265.

And whereas when these commissioners had met in pursuance of the said law they were interrupted in their proceedings by the combinations, threatenings and outrageous violence of certain lawless people in the said county of Luzerne and obliged to fly for the preservation of their lives

And whereas doubts have also arisen concerning the construction, true intent and meaning of said law for which and other causes it hath become very difficult to determine the same and to adjust the compensation to be made to those persons who will be divested of their property by the operation of the said law if the same shall be carried into effect:

And whereas the time in which these commissioners were to receive claims has expired but their other powers still remain, which if immediately executed without further provisions and regulations being previously made will tend to embarrassment and confusion:

[Section I.] (Section II, P. L.) Be it therefore enacted, and it is hereby enacted by the Representatives of the Freemen of the Commonwealth of Pennsylvania in General Assembly met and by the authority of the same, That so much of the said law as empowers the said commissioners to ascertain and confirm the claims of the said people called Connecticut claimants and all and every part of the said act which gives any power and authority to the said commissioners be and the same is hereby suspended until the legislature of this commonwealth shall by a law for that purpose to be enacted make further provisions and regulations in the premises and shall direct and require the said commissioners to proceed in the exercise of their said powers.

Passed March 29, 1788.   Recorded L. B. No. 3, p. 368.

CHAPTER MCCCL.

AN ACT FOR THE RELIEF OF JAMES PARKER AN INSOLVENT DEBTOR
CONFINED IN THE GAOL OF THE CITY AND COUNTY OF PHILADEL-
PHIA.

(Section I, P. L.) Whereas James Parker a prisoner confined
for debt in the gaol of the city and county of Philadelphia
hath by his petition to this general assembly represented that
by reason of his legal residence being without the limits of this
state he is not entitled to the benefit of the general laws of this
commonwealth for relief of insolvent debtors:

And whereas this house by a committee of their body have
searched into the circumstances of the case and are willing
to enable the petitioner to support himself and family by his
industry:

[Section I.] (Section II, P. L.) Be it therefore enacted and
it is hereby enacted by the Representatives of the Freemen of
the Commonwealth of Pennsylvania in General Assembly met
and by the authority of the same, That the county court of
common pleas in and for the county of Philadelphia be and
they are hereby authorized and required upon the petition of
the said James Parker to grant unto him relief in like manner and upon the same terms as by the laws of this commonwealth now in force is provided for insolvent debtors who
are confined in execution for debt to any one person to the
value of forty shillings and upwards, and the discharge thereupon to be made by the said court of the prisoner aforesaid
shall be as valid and their proceedings as effectual to all intents as any discharge or proceeding in the case of any insolvent debtor under the existing laws of this commonwealth
for the relief of insolvent debtors who severally are indebted
or owe to any one creditor to the value of forty shillings and
upwards, would or may be although the said James Parker may
not have resided within this state for the space of two years
next before his imprisonment or confinement aforesaid.

[Section II.] (Section III, P. L.) And be it further enacted by the authority aforesaid, That if any creditor or creditors of the said James Parker doth or shall not reside within this state at the time of such proceedings before the said court that the service of notice of the application to the said court or of any rule or order of the same court in the premises on the known agent or attorney within this state of such creditor or creditors shall be equally good and effectual as if the same notice or notices was or were served on the person or persons of such creditor or creditors, but if such creditor or creditors shall have no such agent or attorney within this state, the said court on satisfactory proof that due diligence hath been used to find out such agent or attorney and that none can be found shall and may notwithstanding proceed to discharge the said James Parker in like manner as if such notice had been actually given.

Passed March 29, 1788. Recorded L. B. No. 3, p. 369.

CHAPTER MCCCLI.

AN ACT FOR VESTING IN THOMAS GORDON, HIS HEIRS AND ASSIGNS CERTAIN ESTATES FORFEITED TO THIS COMMONWEALTH BY VIRTUE OF HIS ATTAINDER OF HIGH TREASON.

(Section I, P. L.) Whereas Thomas Gordon of the township of Oxford and county of Philadelphia was commanded by proclamation of the supreme executive council bearing date the twenty-second day of June which was in the year of our Lord one thousand seven hundred and seventy-nine to surrender himself to some one of the justices of the supreme court or of the justices of the peace of one of the counties within this state on or before Thursday the fifth day of August then next following and also abide his legal trial on pain that he the said Thomas Gordon not rendering himself and abiding his legal trial as aforesaid should from and after the said fifth day of August one thousand seven hundred and seventy-nine stand and be attainted of high treason and suffer such pains and penalties and undergo all such forfeitures as persons attainted of high treason ought to do:

And whereas the aforesaid Thomas Gordon did not render himself and abide his legal trial as by said proclamation he was commanded to do, he thereby became attainted of high treason and his estate a forfeiture to the commonwealth:

And whereas it appears from satisfactory evidence produced to this house that the said Thomas Gordon was a minor and absent from this continent at the time of his attainder, having been placed on board a British vessel in the port of Philadelphia in the year one thousand seven hundred and seventy-eight by his mother who was also his guardian) much against his own inclination, by reason whereof it became impossible for him to obey the aforesaid proclamation:

And whereas consistent with justice and equity the said Thomas Gordon ought not to suffer by means of the imprudence of a guardian to whose authority the laws of the state had subjected him:

Therefore:

[Section I.] (Section II, P. L.) Be it enacted, and it is hereby enacted by the Representatives of the Freemen of the Commonwealth of Pennsylvania in General Assembly met and by the authority of the same, That all and every the lands, tenements, or other estates real and personal whatsoever and wheresoever which were or would have vested in the aforesaid Thomas Gordon provided he had never became attainted of high treason and which by means of such attainder as aforesaid have been or may or can be forfeited to and vested in this commonwealth, shall be and they are hereby restored to and vested in the aforesaid Thomas Gordon, his heirs and assigns forever in as full and effectual a manner to all intents and purposes as if the said attainder of high treason had never happened and the claim of this state to said estates acquired under and by virtue of such attainder is hereby fully released and forever relinquished.

Passed March 29, 1788. Recorded L. B. No. 3, p. 365. See the Act of Assembly passed September 27, 1791, Chapter 1584.

CHAPTER MCCCLII.

AN ACT FOR ALLOWING A FURTHER TIME TO DISTRIBUTE THE DONA-
TION LANDS PROMISED TO THE TROOPS OF THIS COMMONWEALTH.

(Section I, P. L.) Whereas agreeably to an act of general
assembly, passed the twenty-fourth day of March one thousand
seven hundred and eighty-five entitled, "An act for directing
the mode of distributing the donation lands promised to the
troops by this commonwealth" (1) the term therein limited for
the claimants to come in and obtain their respective quantities
of lands hath expired and it is just and reasonable that a
further time be allowed them:

[Section I.] (Section II, P. L.) Be it enacted and it is hereby enacted by the Representatives of the Freemen of the Commonwealth of Pennsylvania in General Assembly met and by
the authority of the same, That it shall and may be lawful for
all and every person or persons who would have been entitled
to lands under the said recited act had they respectively applied
for the same within the time therein limited or their heirs or
devisees to make their applications for and obtain patents of
confirmation of their respective proportions of the said lands
in like manner as in and by the said recited act is directed
within one year after the passing of this act, but not afterwards, anything in the said recited act to the contrary in anywise notwithstanding, of which public notice shall immediately
be given by the supreme executive council in one or more of the
newspapers of Philadelphia, Carlisle and Pittsburg and the
surveying, drawing, numbering, draughting and patenting and
all other matters and things touching or concerning the said
lands and the claimants thereof, which in and by the said recited act are directed, shall forthwith commence in manner
and form and subject to the same terms prescribed by the recited act aforesaid.

¹Passed March 24, 1785, Chapter 1189.
Passed September 13, 1768.   Recorded L. B. No. 3, 377.

CHAPTER MCCCLIII.

AN ACT TO INCORPORATE THE MEMBERS OF THE RELIGIOUS SOCIETY OF ROMAN CATHOLICS BELONGING TO THE CONGREGATION OF SAINT MARY'S CHURCH IN THE CITY OF PHILADELPHIA.

(Section I, P. L.) Whereas the members of the religious society of Roman Catholics inhabiting the city and vicinity of Philadelphia and belonging to the congregation worshipping at the church of Saint Mary in Fourth street between Spruce and Walnut streets in the said city have requested this house to pass a law to incorporate them and to enable them to manage the temporalities of their church as other religious societies within this state have been enabled to do, and it is reasonable to grant their request:

[Section I.] (Section II, P. L.) Be it therefore enacted and it is hereby enacted by the Representatives of the Freemen of the Commonwealth of Pennsylvania in General Assembly met and by the authority of the same, That the members of the religious society of Roman Catholics inhabiting the city and vicinity of Philadelphia and belonging to the congregation worshipping at the church of Saint Mary aforesaid are and from and immediately after the passing this act shall be and they are hereby erected into and declared to be one body politic and corporate in deed and in law by the name, style and title of "The Trustees of the Roman Catholic Society worshipping at the church of Saint Mary in the City of Philadelphia," and that they the said trustees by the name aforesaid and their successors to be elected as hereinafter mentioned shall have perpetual succession and shall be able and capable in law to purchase, take, have, hold, receive and enjoy to them and their successors in fee simple or for any lesser estate any lands, tenements, rents, hereditaments or real estate, whose yearly value in the whole shall not exceed the sum of five hundred pounds, by grant, gift, bargain and sale, will, devise or otherwise, and also to purchase, take, hold, possess and enjoy any moneys, goods and chattels or personal estate whatsoever by gift, grant, will, legacy or bequest and the same lands, tenements, rents, hereditaments and real and personal estate (excepting always the said church called Saint Mary's, and the lot of ground grave yard and appurtenances thereto belonging or therewith now used and occupied containing in breadth on Fourth and Fifth Streets, sixty-three feet and in depth three hundred and ninety-six feet) to give, grant, demise or otherwise dispose of as to them shall seem meet, for the use of the said religious society, and also that the said trustees by the name aforesaid shall be able and capable in law to sue and be sued, implead and be impleaded, answer and be answered unto, defend and be defended, in any suits or actions and in all or any courts or jurisdictions whatsoever, and that it shall and may be lawful for the said trustees by the name aforesaid to devise, make, have and use one common seal to authenticate all and every the acts deeds and instruments touching their business and the same at pleasure to break, alter and renew, and generally that the said trustees by the name aforesaid, shall have, hold and enjoy, all and singular the rights, privileges, liberties and franchises incident and belonging to a private or religious corporation or body politic as fully and effectually as any other private or religious corporation or body politic within this state has right to have, hold and enjoy the same.

[Section II.] (Section III, P. L.) And be it further enacted by the authority aforesaid, That the first trustees of the said corporation shall be and consist of the following persons, viz: the Reverend Robert Molyneaux, the Reverend Francis Beeston, the Reverend Lawrence Graesal, the present pastors of the said church, and George Meade, Thomas Fitzsimons, James Byrne, Paul Esling, John Cottringer, Joseph Eck, Mark Wilcox and John Carrol, members of the congregation worshipping in the said church, and the future trustees of the said corporation shall be and consist of the pastors of the said church for the time being, duly appointed, not exceeding three

in number, and of eight lay members of the congregation worshipping in the said church, to be appointed and elected in
the manner hereinafter mentioned.

[Section III.] (Section IV, P. L.) And be it further enacted
by the authority aforesaid, That all and every the members
of the said congregation (holding a pew or part of a pew in
the said church and paying for the same not less than fifteen
shillings by the year and not being in arrear for the said con-
tribution more than six months), shall meet on the Tuesday of
Easter week in the year one thousand seven hundred and
eighty-nine and so in every year forever thereafter at such place
in the said city as shall be appointed by the said trustees,
whereof notice shall be given in the said church at the close of
divine worship on the morning of the preceding Sunday and
then and there shall choose by ballot the said eight lay trustees in manner aforesaid by a majority of those members so
qualified who shall so meet between the hours of eleven before
noon and one in the afternoon of every such day and the trustees so chosen shall continue to be trustees of the said corporation until the next election and if the pastors of the said
church duly appointed shall on any day of such election exceed
the number of three they shall among themselves agree which
three of them the said pastors shall be trustees for the ensuing
year and shall openly declare in the presence of all the electors
so met at the time of concluding the said election the names
of all the said pastors and members who shall be so appointed
and chosen trustees of the said corporation and their names
shall be entered in the books of the said corporation for that
purpose to be kept and the said pastors so appointed and members so chosen trustees as aforesaid shall be and continue trustees of the said corporation until the close of the next election.

[Section IV.] (Section V, P. L.) And be it further enacted by
the authority aforesaid, That it shall and may be lawful to and
for the said trustees and their successors from time to time as
occasion shall require to meet together for the purpose of transacting the business of the society under their care, of the time
and place of which meetings due notice shall be given to all the

said trustees at least one day before, at which meetings the eldest pastor present shall be president and if seven of the said trustees shall attend they shall form a quorum or board and shall have power by a majority of voices present to make, ordain and establish such rules, orders and regulations for the management of the temporal business, the government of their shools, [and] disposing of the estate of the said corporation as to them shall seem proper. Provided that such rules, orders and regulations be reasonable in themselves and not repugnant to the constitution and laws of this state.

Passed September 13, 1788. Recorded L. B. No. 3, p. 378.

CHAPTER MCCCLIV.

AN ACT TO ALTER AND AMEND SO MUCH OF THE SEVERAL IMPOST LAWS OF THIS STATE AS CONFINES THE ALLOWING OF DRAW- BACKS ON GOODS EXPORTED TO THE ORIGINAL IMPORTERS THERE- OF AND OBLIGES THE EXPORTER TO PRODUCE CERTIFICATES OF THE LANDING OF SUCH GOODS.

(Section I, P. L.) Whereas the drawing back the duties and imposts laid by the several laws of this commonwealth on the importation of goods, wares and merchandise when the same shall be bona fide exported for sale and consumption in other states or foreign countries tends to the increase of the commerce of this state and the said drawbacks are by the said laws confined to the original importers of such goods:

[Section I.] (Section II, P. L.) Be it therefore enacted and it is hereby enacted by the Representatives of the Freemen of the Commonwealth of Pennsylvania in General Assembly met and by the authority of the same, That from and after the passing of this act all the duties and imposts which have been or shall be paid or secured to be paid upon the importation of any goods, wares, or merchandise into this state shall be drawn back, allowed or remitted to any person exporting the same in the manner and form prescribed and directed in the acts for allowing drawbacks on goods, wares and merchandise· exported except as is herein excepted:

And whereas certificates of the landing of goods, wares and merchandise exported in the manner prescribed by the acts aforesaid cannot in many places be procured or is attended with great expense and difficulties.

[Section II.] (Section III, P. L.) Be it enacted by the authority aforesaid, That from and after the passing of this act, the bonds which shall be given on the exportation of goods, wares and merchandise to any port or place not within the United States shall be canceled on the oath or affirmation of the master of such vessel wherein any goods, wares and merchandise may be exported as aforesaid, specifying the delivery thereof at the port of discharge, agreeably to the conditions of the said bonds or on the oath or affirmation of the consignee of such goods, wares and merchandise, anything in the said acts to the contrary notwithstanding.

[Section III.] (Section IV, P. L.) And be it further enacted by the authority aforesaid, That so much of the said laws as is hereby altered and supplied be and is hereby repealed.

Passed September 20, 1788. Recorded L. B. No. 3, p. 381.

CHAPTER MCCCLV.

AN ACT TO INCORPORATE THE PRESBYTERIAN CHURCH OF MIDDLE OCTARARA IN BART TOWNSHIP IN THE COUNTY OF LANCASTER.

(Section I, P. L.) Whereas the minister, elders and other members of the Presbyterian Church of Octarara in Bart township in the county of Lancaster by their petition have prayed that their said church may be incorporated and by law enabled as a body corporate and politic to receive and hold such charitable donations and bequests as may from time to time be made to their society and vested with such powers and privileges as are enjoyed by the other religious societies who are incorporated in this state:

And whereas it is just and right and also agreeable to the true spirit of the constitution that the prayer of their said petition be granted:

[Section I.] (Section II, P. L.) Be it therefore enacted and it is hereby enacted by the Representatives of the Freemen of the Commonwealth of Pennsylvania in General Assembly met and by the authority of the same, That Robert Baily, John Paxton, John Johnston, Andrew Work, John Anderson, Thomas Whiteside, Samuel McClelland, Alexander Morrison [and] the Reverend Nathanial W. Semple, the present pastor of said church, and their successors duly elected and appointed in such manner and form as hereinafter is directed be and they are hereby made and constituted a corporation and body politic in law and in fact to have continuance forever by the name, style and title of "The Trustees of the Presbyterian Church of Middle Octarara in Bart Township in the county of Lancaster."

[Section II.] (Section III, P. L.) And be it further enacted by the authority aforesaid, That the said corporation and their successors by the name, style and title aforesaid shall forever hereafter be able and capable in law as well to take, receive and hold all and all manner of lands, tenements, rents, annuities, franchises and other hereditaments which at any time or times heretofore have been granted, bargained, sold, enfeoffed, released, devised or otherwise conveyed to the said church and congregation or to the religious congregation worshipping therein now under the pastoral charge and care of the Reverened Nathanial W. Semple or to any other person or persons to their use or in trust for them and the same lands, tenements, rents, annuities, liberties, franchises and other hereditaments are hereby vested and established in the said corporation and their successors forever according to their original use and intention. And the said corporation and their successors are hereby declared to be seized and possessed of such estate and estates therein as in and by the respective grants, bargains, sales, enfeoffments, releases, devises or other conveyances thereof is or are declared, limited or expressed, as also that

the said corporation and their successors aforesaid at all times
hereafter shall be capable and able to purchase, have, receive,
take, hold and enjoy in fee simple or of any other less estate
or estates any lands, tenements, rents, annuities, liberties,
franchises and other hereditaments by the gift, grant, bargain,
sale, alienation, enfeoffment, release, confirmation or devise
of any person or persons, bodies politic or corporate capable
and able to make the same, and further that the said corporation may take and receive any sum or sums of money, any
manner or portion of goods and chattels that shall be given or
bequeathed to them by any person or persons, bodies politic
or corporate capable to make a gift or bequest thereof, such
money, goods and chattels to be laid out by them in a purchase
or purchases of lands, tenements, messuages, houses, rents,
annuities, or hereditaments to them and their successors forever, or the moneys lent on interest or otherwise disposed of
according to the intention of the donors.

[Section III.] (Section IV, P. L.) And be it further enacted
by the authority aforesaid, That the rents, profits and interest
of the said real and personal estate of the said church and corporation shall by the said trustees and their successors from
time to time be applied for the maintenance and support of the
pastor or pastors of the said church, for salaries to their clerk
and sexton, in the maintenance and support of a school and in
repairing and maintaining their lot and house of public worship, burial ground, parsonage house or houses, school-house or
houses and other tenements which now do or hereafter shall
belong to the said church and corporation.

[Section IV.] (Section V, P. L.) And be it further enacted by
the authority aforesaid, That if hereafter the building for
public worship or any other tenement belonging to the said
church and corporation shall be burnt, endamaged or otherwise rendered unfit for use or if hereafter the said house of
public worship shall appear to be too small to accommodate the
congregation, whereby it shall become necessary to rebuild or
repair the same, that then and in such case it may be lawful
for the said corporation and their successors to make sale or

otherwise dispose of any part or parcel of the said real or personal estate other than the site of the house of public worship, burial ground or burial grounds, parsonage house or houses, school house or houses, for the purposes aforesaid, and not otherwise.

[Section V.] (Section VI, P. L.) Provided always, and be it further enacted by the authority aforesaid, That in the disposal and application of the public moneys of the said corporation or in the making sale or disposition of any part or parcel of the real or personal estate of the said corporation for any of the purposes aforesaid, the consent and concurrence of the major part of the regular members of the said church, qualified as hereinafter is directed, shall be had and obtained and the votes hereinafter directed to be taken shall be by ballot, and also that the said trustees in like manner qualified shall be admitted to vote therein as members of the said church.   Provided, nevertheless, That no deed or other conveyance made by the said trustees or their successors bona fide and for valuable consideration for any part of the real estate of the said corporation, in case the possession thereof immediately pass to the purchaser and continue in him, his heirs and assigns, shall be invalidated or called in question for want of the consent and concurrence aforesaid or for want of conformity to this act unless the same be done within seven years from and after the sale and delivery of the possession of such real estate to the purchaser and purchasers thereof.

[Section VI.] (Section VII, P. L.) And be it further enacted by the authority aforesaid, That the said trustees and their successors shall not by deed, fine or recovery or by any other ways or means, grant, alien or otherwise dispose of any manors, messuages, lands, tenements or hereditaments in them or their successors vested or hereafter to be vested nor charge nor encumber the same to any person or persons whatsoever except as hereinbefore is excepted.

[Section VII.] (Section IX, P. L.) And be it further enacted by the authority aforesaid, That the said trustees and their successors or the majority of any five of them met from time to time after public notice given the preceding Lord's day commonly called Sunday from the desk or pulpit of the said church immediately after divine service before the congregation are dismissed, or after regular notice in writing left at the house of each trustee and the particular business having been mentioned at least one meeting before, be authorized and empowered and [they] are hereby authorized and empowered to make rules, by-laws and ordinances and to do everything needful for the good government and support of the secular affairs of the said church. Provided always, That the said by-laws, rules and ordinances or any of them be not repugnant to the laws of this commonwealth and that all their proceedings be fairly and regularly entered into a church book to be kept for that purpose and also that the said trustees and their successors by plurality of votes of any five or more of them met as aforesaid, after such notice as aforesaid, be authorized and empowered and they are hereby authorized and empowered to elect and appoint from among themselves a president and also to elect and appoint from among themselves or others a treasurer and secretary or any of them at their pleasure to remove, change or alter or continue as to them, or a majority of any five or more of them so met as aforesaid from time to time shall seem to be most for the benefit of the said church and corporation.

[Section VIII.] (Section X, P. L.) And be it further enacted by the authority aforesaid, That the said corporation and their successors shall have full power and authority to make, have and use one common seal with such device and inscription as they shall think proper and the same to break, alter or renew at their pleasure.

[Section IX.] (Section XI, P. L.) And be it further enacted by the authority aforesaid, That the said corporation and their successors by the name of "The Trustees of the Presbyterian Church of Middle Octarara in Bart Township in the County of Lancaster" shall be able and capable in law to sue or to be sued, plead and be impleaded in any court or courts, before any judge or judges, justice or justices, in all and all manner of suits, complaints, pleas, causes, matters and demands, of whatsoever kind, nature or form they may be, and all and every matter and thing therein to do in as full and effectual a manner as any other person or persons, bodies politic or corporate within this commonwealth may or can do.

[Section X.] (Section XII, P. L.) And be it further enacted by the authority aforesaid, That the said corporation shall always consist of nine members called and known by the name of "The Trustees of the Presbyterian Church of Middle Octarara In Bart Township in the county of Lancaster" and the said members shall at all times hereafter be chosen by way of ballot by a majority of such members met together of the said church or congregation as shall have been enrolled in the aforesaid book as stated worshippers with the said church for not less than the space of one year and shall have paid one year's pew rent, or other annual sum of money not less than seven shillings and six-pence for the support of the said pastor or pastors or other officers of the said church, their lot and house of public worship and other lots and tenements belonging to the said church and corporation and towards the other necessary expenses of the said church and shall not at the time of voting be more than one year behind or in arrears for the same. Provided nevertheless, That the pastor or pastors of the said church for the time being shall be entitled to vote equally with any member of the said church or corporation. And provided also, That all and every person or persons qualified as aforesaid to vote and elect, shall and may be capable and able to elect a trustee aforesaid, except in case of the said church having two pastors, one of them only to be eligible at the same time.

[Section XI.] (Section XIII, P. L.) And be it further enacted by the authority aforesaid, That the said Robert Baily, John Paxton, John Johnston, Andrew Work, John Anderson, Thomas Whiteside, Samuel McClelland, Alexander Morrison and Nathaniel W. Semple, the first and present trustees hereby incorporated, shall be and continue trustees aforesaid until they shall be removed in manner following, that is to say, one third part in number of the trustees aforesaid, being the third part herein first named and appointed, shall cease and discontinue and their appointment determine on Monday next after the first Lord's day, commonly called Sunday, in May which will be in the year one thousand seven hundred and eightyeight, upon which day a new election shall be had and held of so many others in their stead and place by a majority of the persons met and qualified agreeable to the purport, true intent and meaning of this act, to vote and elect as aforesaid, and on the Monday next after the first Lord's day, commonly called Sunday, in May in the year following, the second third part in number of the trustees herein named shall in like manner cease and discontinue and their appointment determine and a new election to be had and held of so many in their place and stead in like manner and on the Monday next after the first Lord's day commonly called Sunday in May in the year then next following the last third part in number of the said trustees shall in like manner cease and discontinue and the appointment determine and a new election be had and held in like manner as hereinbefore is directed and that in the same manner and by the like mode of rotation one third part in number of the said trustees shall cease, discontinue and their appointment determine and a new election of the said third part be had and held in manner aforesaid on the Monday next after the first Lord's day commonly [called] Sunday, in the month of May in every year forever, so that no person or persons shall be or continue a trustee or trustees of the said church for any longer time than three years together, unless he be reelected. Provided always, That the persons belonging to the said church who are in and by this act authorized and empowered to elect shall and may be at liberty to reelect any one or more of the trustees whose time shall have expired on the day of the said annual election whenever and so often as they shall think fit. Provided also, That whenever any vacancy shall happen by the death, refusal to serve or removal of any one or more of the trustees aforesaid pursuant to the directions of this act an election shall be had of some fit person or persons in his or their place and stead so dying, refusing or removing as soon as conveniently can be done, and that the person or persons so elected shall be, remain and continue as a trustee or trustees aforesaid, for so long without a new election as the person or persons in whose place and stead he or they shall have been so elected as aforesaid would or might have remained and continued and no longer. And that in all cases of a vacancy happening by the means in this act last mentioned the remaining trustees shall be empowered to call a meeting of the electors for supplying the said vacancy, such meeting to be notified and published in like manner as hereinbefore is directed and appointed for notifying and publishing the meeting of the trustees.

[Section XII.] (Section XIV, P. L.) Provided always, and it is hereby enacted by the authority aforesaid, That the clear yearly value or income of the messuages, houses, lands, tenements, rents, annuities or other hereditaments and real estate of the said corporation shall not exceed the sum of five hundred pounds lawful money of the state of Pennsylvania, to be taken and esteemed exclusive of the moneys arising from the letting of the pews and the contributions belonging to the said church, which said money shall be received by the said trustees and disposed of by them in the manner hereinbefore described, pursuant to the vote or votes of the members of the said church duly qualified to vote and elect as aforesaid.

Passed September 20, 1788. Recorded L. B. No. 3, p. 381.

CHAPTER MCCCLVI.

AN ACT FOR THE RELIEF OF THE SUFFERING INHABITANTS OF THE TOWNSHIPS OF WAYNE AND DERRY IN THE COUNTY OF CUMBERLAND.

(Section I, P. L.) Whereas by the repeated depredations and incursions of the savages during the late war the inhabitants

6—XIII

of the townships of Wayne and Derry in Cumberland county were driven from their habitations and otherwise much distressed and impoverished so as to be rendered unable to pay their respective proportions of the public taxes:

[Section I.] (Section II, P. L.) Be it therefore enacted and it is hereby enacted by the Representatives of the Freemen of the Commonwealth of Pennsylvania in General Assembly met and by the authority of the same. That the commissioners of and for the said county of Cumberland or any two of them be and they are hereby authorized and required to exonerate and discharge each and every of the inhabitants of the said townships of Wayne and Derry in the county aforesaid of and from all taxes and assessments and of and from all and every sum and sums of money taxed or assessed, or which might or could had this act not been made, have been taxed or assessed on them and on each and every of them for the years of our Lord one thousand seven hundred and eighty-one and one thousand seven hundred and eighty-two.

Passed September 20, 1788. Recorded L. B. No. 3, p. 408.

CHAPTER MCCCLVII.

AN ACT TO COMPENSATE THE SERVICE OF LIEUTENANT-COLONEL FRANCIS MENTGES IN INSPECTING THE MILITIA OF THE STATE AND THE PUBLIC ARMS AND STORES.

(Section I, P. L.) Whereas it appears to the general assembly that Lieutenant-Colonel Francis Mentges hath rendered some services in inspecting the militia of the state and the public arms under the direction of the supreme executive council, which services are yet uncompensated:

[Section I.] (Section II, P. L.) Be it therefore enacted and it is hereby enacted by the Representatives of the Freemen of the Commonwealth of Pennsylvania in General Assembly met and by the authority of the same, That the supreme executive council be authorized and they are hereby authorized and directed to draw their warrant on the state treasury in favor of Lieutenant-Colonel Francis Mentges for the sum [of] one hundred pounds as a full compensation for the services rendered as aforesaid.

Passed September 20, 1788.   Recorded L. B. No. 3, p. 409.

CHAPTER MCCCLVIII.

AN ACT TO SUSPEND FOR SIX MONTHS THE POWERS OF THE COMMISSIONERS OF THE SEVERAL COUNTIES OF THIS STATE TO MAKE SALE OF UNSEATED LANDS FOR NON-PAYMENT OF TAXES.

(Section I, P. L.) Whereas the strict execution of the law directing the sale of unseated lands for non-payment of taxes has, by reason of the small proportion they generally yield on the sale of their supposed or real value, become extremely oppressive, and it is necessary and just as well for the more easy recovery of the taxes imposed on located uncultivated lands the property of persons residing at a distance therefrom, as for the protection of the owners of such property against divers inconveniences and losses to which they have been and may be subjected, that alterations and amendments in the laws for imposing taxes should be made and enacted by a future assembly:

[Section I.] (Section II, P. L.) Be it enacted and is it hereby enacted by the Representatives of the Freemen of the Commonwealth of Pennsylvania in General Assembly met and by the authority of the same, That the commissioners of the several counties within this state be and they are hereby restricted and prohibited from making sale of any unseated lands whatsoever in their respective counties by reason of the non-payment of taxes for and during the term of six months from and after the passing of this act, any law to the contrary notwithstanding.

Passed September 22, 1788.   Recorded L. B. No. 3, p. 410.

CHAPTER MCCCLIX.

AN ACT FOR ERECTING CERTAIN PARTS OF THE COUNTIES OF WEST-
MORELAND AND WASHINGTON INTO A SEPARATE COUNTY.

(Section I. P. L.) Whereas the inhabitants of those parts of
the counties of Westmoreland and Washington, which lie most
convenient to the town of Pittsburgh have by petition set forth
that they have been long subject to many inconveniences from
their being situated at so great a distance from the seat of
judicature in their respective counties, and that they conceive
their interest and happiness would be greatly promoted by
being erected into a separate county comprehending the town
of Pittsburgh and as it appears just that they should be relieved
in the premises and gratified in their reasonable request:

[Section I.] (Section II, P. L.) Be it enacted and it is hereby
enacted by the Representatives of the Freemen of the Commonwealth of Pennsylvania in General Assembly met and by
the authority of the same, That all these parts of Westmoreland [and Washington] counties lying within the limits and
bounds hereinafter described shall be and hereby are erected
into a separate county, that is to say, beginning at the mouth
of Flaherty's run, on the south side of the Ohio river, from
thence by a straight line, to the plantation on which Joseph
Scott, Esquire, now lives, on Montour's run, to include the
same, from thence by a straight line, to the mouth of Miller's
run on Chartier's creek, thence by a straight line to the mouth
of Perry's mill run on the east side of Monongahela river,
thence up the said river, to the mouth of Becket's run, thence
by a straight line to the mouth of Sewickly Creek on Youghiogany river, thence down the said river to the mouth of Crawford's run, thence by a straight line to the mouth of Brush
creek on Turtle creek, thence up Turtle creek to the main fork
thereof, thence by a northerly line until it strikes Puckety's
creek, thence down the said creek to the Allegheny river,.

thence up the Allegheny river to the northern boundary of the state, thence along the same to the western line of the state, thence along the same to the river Ohio and thence up the same to the place of beginning, to be henceforth known and called by the name of Allegheny county.

[Section II.] (Section III, P. L.) And be it further enacted by the authority aforesaid, That the inhabitants of the said county of Allegheny shall, under the limitation hereafter mentioned, at all times hereafter enjoy all and singular the jurisdictions, powers, rights, liberties and privileges whatsoever, which the inhabitants of any other county of this state do, may or ought to enjoy by the constitution and laws of this state.

(Section IV, P. L.) And whereas the line by this act established, dividing the said county of Allegheny from the counties of Westmoreland and Washington, will intersect several of the election districts of the counties of Westmoreland and Washington as heretofore established, so as to separate the same and leave the different parts thereof in each of the said counties of Allegheny, Westmoreland and Washington:

And whereas there will not be sufficient time before the next general election to run and clearly ascertain the said division line and to establish new and proper election districts within the counties aforesaid:

For remedy whereof:

[Section III.] Be it further enacted by the authority aforesaid, That until the said line, dividing the said county of Allegheny from the said counties of Westmoreland and Washington shall be duly run and ascertained, and until new and proper election districts within the said counties of Westmoreland and Washington shall be established, the general election of Westmoreland and Washington counties, including such parts of them and each of them as by this act are cut off and erected into a separate county called Allegheny and all other elections by the freemen thereof and all things whatsoever touching and concerning the same, shall be and continue and be carried on and held at such places and in like manner as if this act had not been made, and until the time aforesaid it shall and may be lawful for the freemen of such parts of the said county of Allegheny as heretofore lay within the county of Westmoreland and the freemen of such parts of the said county of Allegheny as heretofore lay within the said county of Washington respectively to vote at such times and places and in such manner and for such officer or officers as they might or could have done had this act not been made, and that from and after the division line dividing the said county of Allegheny from the counties of Westmoreland and Washington shall be duly run and ascertained, the general elections and all other elections by the freemen of the said county of Allegheny shall be held at such time and times as the laws and the constitution of this commonwealth shall direct, at the town of Pittsburg, where it shall and may be lawful for the freemen of the said county of Allegheny who are or shall be duly qualified by law, to elect at the times and under the regulations stipulated and directed by the constitution and laws of this state, a councillor, a representative to serve in the general assembly, censors, sheriffs, coroners, and commissioners, which said officers, when duly elected and qualified, shall have and enjoy all and singular such powers, authorities and privileges with respect to their said county as such officers, elected in and for any other county, may, can or ought to do and the said election shall be conducted in the same manner and form and agreeable to the same rules and regulations as now are or hereafter may be in force in the other counties of this state.

(Section V, P. L.) And in order that a due representation of the freemen of this commonwealth may be preserved and kept up:

[Section IV.] Be it further enacted by the authority aforesaid, That from and after the time when the division line dividing the said county of Allegheny from the said counties of Westmoreland and Washington shall be duly run and ascertained as aforesaid the freemen of the said county of Westmoreland shall, at their general elections instead of three representatives to serve in the general assembly of this commonwealth, choose and return two only and no more, anything to the contrary in any law notwithstanding.

[Section V.] (Section VI, P. L.) And be it further enacted
by the authority aforesaid, That the justices of the supreme
court and the justices of oyer and terminer and general gaol
delivery of this state shall have like powers, jurisdictions and
authorities in the said county as in other counties of this state
and are hereby authorized and empowered to deliver the gaols
of the said county of capital and other offenders in like manner
as they are authorized to do in the other counties of this state.

[Section VI.] (Section VII, P. L.) And be it further enacted
by the authority aforesaid, That the justices of the courts of
quarter sessions and common pleas now commissioned within
the limits of the said counties and those that may hereafter ·
be commissioned or any three of them, shall and may hold
courts of general quarter sessions of the peace and gaol delivery
and courts of common pleas and shall have all and singular
such powers, rights, privileges, jurisdictions and authorities
to all intents and purposes as other justices of the courts of
general quarter sessions and justices of the common pleas in
other counties of this state may, can or ought to have in their
respective counties, which courts shall sit and be held for the
said county (until the trustees hereinafter appointed shall have
erected a court house, agreeably to the directions of this act) ·
in the town of Pittsburgh four [times] in each and every year,
on the Tuesday next preceding the county courts of Fayette
county, and [sic] [and the court of quarter sessions] shall sit
three days in each session, if occasion be, and no longer, and
also, that orphans' courts in and for the said county of Allegheny shall be held in such manner and shall have such powers,
authorities and jurisdictions as are by the laws and constitution of this commonwealth provided as to the orphans' courts
of any county or counties within this commonwealth.

[Section VII.] (Section VIII, P. L.) And be it further enacted
by the authority aforesaid, That it shall and may be lawful
for George Wallace, Devereaux Smith, William Elliot, Jacob
Bausman and John Wilkins, or any three of them, to make
choice of any of the lots set apart for public buildings in the
reserved tract opposite the town of Pittsburgh and thereon

to erect a court house and prison sufficient to accommodate the
public business of the county within the space of five years
from and after the passing of this law, and, if needful, to hire
or otherwise procure a temporary building to serve as a court
house and prison until the public buildings can be erected as
aforesaid.

[Section VIII.] (Section IX, P. L.) And be it further enacted
by the authority aforesaid, That it shall and may be lawful
for the said trustees to call upon the commissioners of the said
county for any sum of money not exceeding five hundred pounds
for the purpose of erecting a court house and prison for the use
of the said county, and the said commissioners are hereby authorized and empowered to levy and collect the said sum of five
hundred pounds within said county for the uses aforesaid in
the same manner that county rates and levies are usually
raised in this state. Provided nevertheless, That not more
than one fifth part of the said sum shall be levied and collected
in one year.

[Section IX.] (Section X, P. L.) And be it further enacted
by the authority aforesaid, That no action or suit already commenced in the courts of Westmoreland and Washington or
either of them before the enacting of this law against any
person living within the bounds of the said county shall be
stayed or discontinued by this act or by anything in the same
contained, but the same actions already commenced as aforesaid may be prosecuted to final issue and judgment thereupon
rendered in like manner as if this act had not been made, and
it shall and may be lawful for the justices of the said counties
respectively to issue processes to their respective sheriffs for
carrying on and obtaining the full and legal effects of such
suits in the same manner as if the parties resided within the
counties of Westmoreland and Washington.

[Section X.] (Section XI, P. L.) And be it further enacted
by the authority aforesaid, That the sheriffs, coroners and
public officers of the counties of Westmoreland and Washington shall continue to exercise the duties of their respective
offices within the county of Allegheny until similar officers

are appointed agreeably to law within the said county of Allegheny, and that all arrearages of excise and public taxes shall be paid into the hands of the present collectors to be by them accounted for in manner and form as if this act had never been passed.

[Section XI.] (Section XII, P. L.) And be it further enacted by the authority aforesaid, That the sheriffs, treasurers, collectors of excise and all such officers as have heretofore usually given bail for the faithful discharge of their respective offices who may hereafter be appointed or elected in the said county of Allegheny, before they or any of them shall enter upon the execution of their respective offices, shall give sufficient security in the like sums, in the like manner and form and for the like uses, trusts, and purposes as such officers are obliged by law for the time being to do in the counties of Westmoreland and Washington.

[Section XII.] (Section XIII, P. L.) And be it further enacted by the authority aforesaid, That it shall and may be lawful to and for Eli Coulter, Peter Kidd and Benjamin Lodge, or a majority of them, and they are hereby required and firmly enjoined within six months next after the publication of this act to run, mark out and distinguish the boundary lines between the said counties of Westmoreland, Washington and Allegheny, and the aforesaid Eli Coulter, Peter Kidd, and Benjamin Lodge or any two of them who are actually employed in running and marking the line between the counties aforesaid, shall have and receive for their services at the rate of twenty shillings per diem each and no more, and the charges so accrued shall be defrayed by the said county of Allegheny and to that end levied and raised by the inhabitants thereof in such manner as other public money for the use of the said county by law ought to be raised and levied.

Passed September 24, 1788. Recorded L. B. No. 3, p. 412. See the Act of Assembly passed April 13, 1791, Chapter 1577.

CHAPTER MCCCLX.

A SUPPLEMENT TO AN ACT ENTITLED "AN ACT TO DIVIDE WASHING-
TON COUNTY INTO ELECTION DISTRICTS."[1]

(Section I, P. L.) Whereas the freemen of the fifth district of
Washington county have by their petition set forth that they
labor under great inconvenience in attending upon their elec
tions, the place of meeting (which is at Joshua Meek's not
being central:

For remedy whereof:

[Section I.] (Section II, P. L.) Be it enacted and it is hereby
enacted by the Representatives of the Freemen of the Commonwealth of Pennsylvania in General Assembly met and
by the authority of the same, That from and after the passing
of this act the boundary line of the fifth district shall begin
at the mouth of Flaherty's run, thence along the county line
to the plantation of Joseph Scott, Esquire, on Montour's run,
thence to Armstrong's mill on Miller's run, thence with the
boundary line described in the act to which this is a supplement.   And the freemen of the [said] fifth district shall hold
their elections at the house of Elizabeth McCanless.

[Section II.] (Section III, P. L.) And be it further enacted
by the authority aforesaid, That so much of the said act en
titled "An act to divide Washington county into election districts," (2) as far as the same respects the boundary line which
divides the fifth and third districts and ordains the place of
election for the fifth district to be at the house of Joshua
Meeks is hereby repealed and declared null and void.

[1] Passed September 20, 1787. Chapter 1310.
[2] Ante.
Passed September 26, 1788.   Recorded L. B. No. 3, p. 415.

CHAPTER MCCCLXI.

— —

AN ACT TO ERECT THE TOWNSHIPS OF PENNS AND BEAVER IN THE COUNTY OF NORTHUMBERLAND INTO A SEPARATE DISTRICT AND ALTER THE PLACE OF HOLDING ELECTIONS IN THE THIRD DISTRICT IN THE SAID COUNTY OF NORTHUMBERLAND.

(Section I, P. L.) Whereas the freemen of Penns and Beaver townships in the county of Northumberland have by their petition set forth that they labor under very great inconvenience on account of the distance many of them live from the place of holding the annual elections and by means of the troublesome streams of water which they have been obliged to pass over in their way to the said election:

For remedy whereof:

[Section I.] (Section II, P. L.) Be it enacted and it is hereby enacted by the Representatives of the Freemen of the Commonwealth of Pennsylvania in General Assembly met and by the authority of the same, That the townships of Penns and Beaver in the county of Northumberland aforesaid shall from and after the passing of this act be struck off and separated from the first district in the said county and established and erected into a separate district called the sixth district in the county aforesaid and that the freemen of the said sixth district now erected as aforesaid shall hold their elections at the house of Albright Swineford in Penns township aforesaid, anything contained in a former law obliging the inhabitants of the said townships to attend their elections at the county town notwithstanding:

And whereas the inhabitants of the third district in the said county of Northumberland have by their petitions set forth that by the division of their districts by a law passed the nineteenth day of September one thousand seven hundred and eighty-six, without altering the usual place of election in the old district the said place is rendered very inconvenient to the petitioners:

For remedy whereof:

[Section II.] (Section III, P. L.) Be it enacted by the authority aforesaid, That the freemen of the third district of Northumberland shall from and after the passing of this act hold their elections at the dwelling house of Andrew Billmeyer in Buffeloe township, anything in a former law directing the said elections to be held at Foutz's or Green's mill to the contrary thereof notwithstanding.

Passed September 26, 1788. Recorded L. B. No. 3, p. 418.

CHAPTER MCCCLXII.

AN ACT TO ALTER CERTAIN ELECTION DISTRICTS WITHIN THE COUNTIES OF DAUPHIN AND FRANKLIN AND TO ESTABLISH NEW ONES THEREIN.

(Section I, P. L.) Whereas the freemen of part of Derry and Lower Paxtang township in the county of Dauphin and the freemen of the townships of Lurgan and Southampton in the county of Franklin have by their petitions set forth that they labor under very great inconveniences in attending their elections occasioned by the too great distance from the places appointed by law for holding their said elections:

For remedy whereof:

[Section I.] (Section II, P. L.) Be it enacted and it is hereby enacted by the Representatives of the Freemen of the Commonwealth of Pennsylvania in General Assembly met and by the authority of the same, That from and after the passing of this act; that part of Derry township, now included in the second election district of the county of Dauphin and that part of Lower Paxtang township included within the third district of the said county be struck off into a sixth district by the lines hereafter described, viz., beginning

at a stone mill situate in Lower Paxtang township near the
bank of the Susquehanna river distant about three miles from
Middletown, thence in a straight line to Jacob Brandt's, thence
in a straight line to Christopher Earnest's on Swatara creek,
thence down the same to a ford commonly called the Island
ford, thence across the said creek and along the boundary line
between the companies of Captain James Cluni and Captain
Robert McKee to a road that divides the townships of Londonderry and Derry, thence along the said road to Conawaga creek,
thence along the said creek to the Susquehanna river, thence
up the Susquehanna river including the islands to the stone
mill aforesaid, and the freemen of the said sixth district now
erected shall hold their elections at the house now occupied by
Conrad Nolfly in the town of Middletown, in Lower Paxtang
township aforesaid.

[Section II.] (Section III, P. L.) And be it further enacted
by the authority aforesaid, That the freemen of the townships
of Lurgan and Southampton in the county of Franklin shall
be the fifth district in the said county and the freemen of the
aforesaid townships shall meet and hold their elections at
the house now occupied by Joseph Finley in the township of
Southampton.

[Section III.] (Section IV, P. L.) And be it further enacted
by the authority aforesaid, That so much of the act entitled
"An act to regulate the general elections of this commonwealth and to prevent frauds therein,"[1] so far as the same
respects the boundaries of the second and third election districts interfering with the district now laid off be and it is
hereby repealed and declared null and void.

[Section IV.] (Section V, P. L.) And be it further enacted
by the authority aforesaid, That so much of an act entitled
"An act to divide the county of Franklin into election districts
and to alter the place for holding the general elections in the
sixth district of the county of Bedford and for making the
townships of Greenwood and Rye in the county of Cumberland

---

[1] Passed September 13, 1785, Chapter 1175.

a sixth district for the purpose of holding their general elections,"² as is hereby altered be and the same is hereby repealed.

Passed September 27, 1788.   Recorded L. B. No. 8. p. 419.

CHAPTER MCCCLXIII.

AN ACT TO EXONERATE THE FRONTIER INHABITANTS OF WASHING-TON COUNTY FROM THE PAYMENT OF TAXES.

(Section I, P. L.) Whereas the frontier inhabitants of Washington county have by their petition set forth that they are greatly distressed and impoverished by the frequent incursions and depredations of the Indians so as to be rendered unable to comply with the demands of government in paying their taxes, and therefore have prayed this house to give them relief by exoneration:

And whereas it is deemed just and reasonable to give the citizens of Washington county that relief which they have prayed for:

[Section I.] (Section II. P. L.) Be it therefore enacted and it is hereby enacted by the Representatives of the Freemen of the Commonwealth of Pennsylvania in General Assembly met and by the authority of the same, That it shall and may be lawful for the commissioners of the county aforesaid or any two of them to hear, judge of and determine upon all applications that shall be made by the frontier inhabitants of said county in pursuance of this act, and in all cases [where] said commissioners have due information either from their own knowledge or by the oath or affirmation of one or more credible witnesses (which oath or affirmation the said commissioners are hereby empowered to administer) that the person so applying has been actually driven from his or her habitation, or been otherwise distressed by the depredations of the Indians, then and in such case the commissioners shall extend to such

² Passed September 10, 1787, Chapter 1301.

applicants the benefits of this act and grant them exoneration
either from the whole or such part of their tax as the commissioners shall think they are entitled to by this act, and that
this act shall continue for and during the term of two years.

[Section II.] (Section III, P. L.) And be it further enacted
by the authority aforesaid, That the said commissioners shall
annually transmit to the general assembly of this state a
list of the names of the persons so exonerated and stating the
amount of the sum so remitted.

Passed October 3, 1788.   Recorded L. B. No. 3, p. 403.

CHAPTER MCCCLXIV.

A SUPPLEMENT TO AN ACT ENTITLED "AN ACT TO ALTER AND
AMEND AN ACT ENTITLED 'AN ACT FOR GRANTING AND DISPOSING
OF THE UNAPPROPRIATED LANDS WITHIN THIS STATE.' "[1]

(Section I, P. L.) Whereas in and by an act of general
assembly of this commonwealth entitled, "An act to alter and
amend an act of assembly, entitled, 'an act for granting and
disposing of the unappropriated lands within this state,' "[2] it
is enacted and declared that the price of the unappropriated
lands within this state which have been purchased or should
be purchased by certain commissioners for that purpose appointed should be fixed at thirty pounds for every one hundred
acres of the same land and so in proportion for greater or
less quantities thereof, and it was by the same act directed that
payments of the same price should be made before the issuing
of the warrant for surveying each tract thereof respectively,
either in gold or silver money or in the bills of this state which
be dated on the twentieth day of April, Anno Domini one
thousand seven hundred and eighty-one or in certain certificates
which are particularly described in another act of general
assembly of this commonwealth entitled, "An act for opening

(1) Passed December 21, 1784, Chapter 1122.
(2) Ante

the land office and for granting and disposing of the unappropriated lands within this state,"[1] that was published on the first day of April, Anno Domini one thousand seven hundred and eighty-four. And whereas the land office of this state for the sale and distribution of the unappropriated lands aforesaid within the purchase aforementioned was in and by the act last recited directed to be on the first day of May which was in the year of our Lord one thousand seven hundred and eighty-five and the same was accordingly opened on that day:

And whereas on or about the said first day of May and afterwards considerable quantities of the same lands were applied for and warrants of survey issued to divers persons, but for and during many months last past, very few applications have been made for the purchase of said lands and it is reasonable to suppose that the best and most valuable of the lands within the purchase so as aforesaid made of the Indian nations (not specially appropriated nor reserved) have been surveyed and set apart by virtue of warrants issued upon the applications aforesaid, and it is judged proper that the price of the residue of the lands within the said purchase (not specially appropriated nor reserved, should be reduced and accommodated so as to induce persons to become purchasers thereof:

[Section I.] (Section II, P. L.) Be it therefore enacted and it is hereby enacted by the Representatives of the Freemen of the Commonwealth of Pennsylvania in General Assembly met and by the authority of the same, That from and after the first day of March next the price of the unappropriated lands of this state within the seventeen districts in the counties of Northumberland and Luzerne, being a part of the purchase last made of the Indian nations as aforesaid shall be twenty pounds for every hundred acres of the same and no more and so in proportion for greater or less quantities thereof, and that the same price shall be payable before the issuing of each warrant of survey respectively for any quantity thereof, in gold or silver money at the rates after which the same are commonly current in this state or in the bills of credit of this

[1] Passed April 1, 1784, Chapter 1094.

commonwealth which are dated on the sixteenth day of March
in the year of our Lord one thousand seven hundred and eighty-
five or in certificates of this state which have been or shall be
issued according to law and the bearers whereof are entitled
to receive of the treasurer of this commonwealth an annual
interest thereon after the rate of six per centum half yearly
and no other satisfaction for the said price.   Provided always,
That this act shall not extend to any lands which have been
or which shall be surveyed by virtue of any warrant heretofore issued for the surveying of lands within the late purchase
made by this commonwealth as aforesaid.

Passed October 3, 1788.   Recorded L. B. No. 3, p. 434.

CHAPTER MCCCLXV.

AN ACT TO ESTABLISH A BOARD OF WARDENS FOR THE PORT OF PHILADELPHIA AND FOR OTHER PURPOSES THEREIN MENTIONED.

(Section I, P. L.) Whereas the act entitled, "An act appointing wardens for the port of Philadelphia"[1] is by its own
limitation nearly expired:

Therefore:

[Section I.] (Section II, P. L.) Be it enacted and it is hereby
enacted by the Representatives of the Freemen of the Commonwealth of Pennsylvania in General Assembly met and by
the authority of the same, That immediately after the passing
of this act a board of wardens for the port of Philadelphia consisting of seven discreet and skilful persons to be named and
appointed [by the supreme executive council] of this commonwealth shall be established, and that it shall and may be lawful for them and they are hereby enjoined and required as soon
as conveniently may be after they shall have been named and
appointed as aforesaid to meet together at some convenient

[1]Passed February 26, 1773, Chapter 641.

7—XIII

place in the city of Philadelphia, having first taken oath or
affirmation hereinafter directed, and for them being so met to
choose one of their own number to be the master warden who
shall be styled the master warden and shall continue in the
said office of master warden during the space of one year and
the clerk of the said board, who, it is hereby declared, shall be
the same person who shall be the tonnage officer for the time
being shall keep fair minutes and entries of all the orders,
regulations and transactions of the said master warden and
board of wardens in a book to be kept for that purpose and
shall have and receive a salary of one hundred
pounds per annum, which with the perquisites in
this section mentioned, shall be in full for all services as clerk of the wardens and the said minutes
and entries shall be made public and submitted to the inspection of any person or persons who shall desire to see and peruse
them, he or they so desiring the inspection paying to the clerk
the sum of one shilling each time the books shall be examined,
and the said clerk shall give true copies of any such entries or
minutes made in the said book to such person or persons as
shall demand the same, he or they paying to the said clerk
three farthings for each line the said copy shall contain, every
line to consist of not less than twelve words; and the said clerk
shall be entitled to demand and receive for his own use the
sum of two shillings and sixpence for every vessel above fifty
tons and the sum of one shilling for every vessel under fifty
tons which shall be entered in his office, every time she shall
be entered; and the said wardens are hereby empowered to
have and use one common seal in their affairs and the same at
pleasure to change and alter.

[Section II.] (Section III, P. L.) And be it further enacted
by the authority aforesaid, That the said wardens shall meet
together on the first Monday in every month at ten o'clock in
the forenoon at a public office or place called the wardens'
office to be by them procured and kept, for the purpose of discharging the duties hereby enjoined them and shall at every
monthly meeting, remain and continue till one of the clock, in

order to dispatch such business as shall come before them in pursuance of this act and at all other times (Sundays only excepted) the master warden who shall be chosen annually in manner aforesaid shall attend at the said office from ten of the clock in the forenoon till one of the clock in the afternoon of every day during the year for which he shall be appointed for the dispatch of such business as shall come before him in pursuance of this act and shall have full power and authority to do and perform all and every act, matter and thing herein enjoined and required of him and shall be paid fifteen shillings for each day that he shall so attend or be employed and in case of the refusal, death, absence, or inability of any such master warden to do and perform the duties by this act enjoined and required of him, the said wardens shall, as soon as conveniently may be and as often as occasion may require meet at the said office and choose another fit person of their own number to be master warden of the said board for and during the remainder of the said year and the master warden so to be chosen shall during that time be vested with all the powers and authorities and do and perform all the duties which are by this act given to or enjoined on any master warden of the said board.

[Section III.] (Section IV, P. L.) And be it further enacted by the authority aforesaid, That there shall be no other meeting of the said wardens or any of them in pursuance of this act than the meetings aforesaid unless the master warden for the time being shall think it necessary to call a general meeting of all the wardens, which he is hereby authorized to do as often as he may think proper by issuing his order to the clerk directing him to cause them to be summoned to meet on three hour's notice to hear and determine all such matters and things which shall or may come before them as wardens of the port of Philadelphia, but at all other times the master warden alone for the time being shall [be and he is] hereby vested with full power and authority to do and discharge all the duties required of the wardens by this act except the making of contracts or disposing of moneys, which shall only be done by the board of

wardens at their monthly meetings aforesaid or by a majority
of them when specially convened in the manner hereinbefore
directed [and for that purpose] during all the time in which
his attendance at the office is by this act required he shall be
attended by the clerk of the said board of wardens and no other
warden or wardens than the master warden for the time being
shall be entitled to any further or other pay than for their
actual attendance at the said monthly meetings or when they
shall be specially summoned and shall attend in the manner
hereinbefore directed and in such cases they shall be entitled
to seven shillings and six pence per diem and no more and the
said clerk shall moreover attend as collector of tonnage at the
said office during all the usual hours of business observed at
the custom house.

[Section IV.] (Section V, P. L.) And be it further enacted
by the authority aforesaid, That the said master warden for the
time being or so many of the wardens as shall attend at the
said monthly meetings or on being specially convened in manner aforesaid shall have full power and authority to examine
all persons offering themselves to serve as pilots to and from
the port of Philadelphia as to their knowledge and skill in
pilotage and to grant three kinds of certificates, the first to
such pilots as shall be qualified to pilot ships or vessels of any
draught of water, the second to pilots for ships or vessels not
exceeding in draught of water twelve feet, the third to pilots
for vessels not exceeding in draught of water nine feet.

[Section V.] (Section VI, P. L.) And be it further enacted
by the authority aforesaid, That the said persons upon the
receipt of the said certificates shall pay [the sum of] five shillings and no more, and shall give bond with one sufficient
surety to the president of the supreme executive council for the
time being in any sum not exceeding one hundred pounds nor
less than fifty pounds conditioned that they will truly and faithfully perform all and every the duties and services required
of them by this act and shall deliver up such certificates to
the said wardens to be cancelled upon their being declared void
and such person or persons incapable of acting as pilots,
agreeably to the directions of this act.

[Section VI.] (Section VII, P. L.) And be it further enacted by the authority aforesaid, That the certificates heretofore granted to any pilot or pilots by any former board of wardens and not vacated shall for the space of one month from and after the passing of this act and no longer be of the same force and effect as if the said certificates were granted in pursuance of the directions of this act, and that all securities taken in consequence of any certificates shall be and continue to all intents and purposes of the same force and effect as any security or securities taken or to be taken in pursuance of this act may or can be.

[Section VII.] (Section VIII, P. L.) And be it further enacted by the authority aforesaid, That no person shall be entitled to receive a certificate as a first rate pilot unless he shall have served a regular apprenticeship of at least four years to the business of a pilot nor a certificate as a second rate pilot unless he shall have served aforesaid three years nor a certificate as a third rate pilot unless he shall have served as aforesaid two years. Provided nevertheless, That no person who has heretofore obtained a certificate as a second or third rate pilot from any board of wardens shall be disqualified from obtaining a renewal thereof on account of his not having served such apprenticeship.

[Section VIII.] (Section IX, P. L.) And be it further enacted by the authority aforesaid, That every pilot who shall conduct any ship or vessel from the port of Philadelphia to the capes of Delaware or from the said capes to the said port shall have and receive [for] his trouble the sum of five shillings for every half foot of water which such vessel shall draw under and up to [twelve] feet and for every half foot of water which such vessel shall draw more than twelve feet the sum of ten shillings and so in proportion for any less distance, to be settled and adjusted by the master warden of the board for the time being or [by] any board of wardens and shall also receive over and above the said sums for every vessel which shall not be the property of a citizen or citizens of the United States or of some or one of them twenty shillings. Provided, That the said pilot shall not have or receive any reward for any supernumerary inches under six. And the said master warden for the time being or any board of wardens shall and be and they are hereby authorized and required to settle and adjust the reward which shall be due from any master, owner or merchant of a ship or other vessel to the pilot thereof for any extraordinary time he shall be detained in the river or bay by the said master, owner or merchant in the service of the said ship or other vessel. Provided, The same shall not exceed fifteen shillings per diem, which said reward when so adjusted if not paid on demand shall be sued for and recovered in the same manner before any justice of the peace as the pilotage of the vessel is hereinafter directed to be recovered.

[Section IX.] (Section X, P. L.) And be it further enacted by the authority aforesaid, That every pilot who shall pilot any ship or vessel into the port of Philadelphia shall within forty-eight hours next after her arrival make report thereof at the wardens office, specifying the names of the master and vessel and the depth of water she draws and if any pilot shall neglect or refuse so to do he shall forfeit and pay for every such offense the sum of five pounds, to be recovered as other fines are in and by this act directed to be recovered.

[Section X.] (Section XI, P. L.) And be it further enacted by the authority aforesaid, That from and after the publication of this act no person or persons whatsoever shall be capable of suing, commencing or prosecuting any action, suit or complaint at law against any person or persons whatsoever for any sum or sums of money that shall be claimed for pilotage of any ship or vessel in the said river or bay of Delaware unless he or they shall have obtained a certificate as aforesaid of his or their being duly qualified to act as a pilot or pilots and unless such pilotage shall be performed during the force of such certificate. And that if any ship or vessel shall be brought or navigated up to the port of Philadelphia (except as hereinafter excepted) or carried from thence by any person or persons not having such certificate if such qualified pilot may be had or procured that then and in every such case the master,

owner or merchant of such vessel on due proof thereof shall
forfeit and pay to the collector of tonnage to be by him paid
over to the wardens or master warden of the board for the time
being for the use of the pilot who shall have first offered himself [a sum of money equal to one fourth part of the pilotage
of the said vessel, settled and ascertained by virtue of this act]
provided such offer shall have been made before such ship or
vessel shall have arrived as high up the river as Reedy Island,
and that the said collector shall not under the penalty of fifty
pounds to be paid to the wardens for the uses in this act mentioned give a receipt to such person or persons so navigating
such vessel, for the tonnage thereof agreeable to the directions
of this act until such fourth pilotage shall be paid [sic], except
the making of contracts or disposing of moneys which shall
only be done by the board of wardens, at their monthly meetings aforesaid or by a majority of them when specially convened in the manner hereinbefore directed.

And in order to prevent vessels from departing from this
port without pilots and thereby evading the payment of pilotage.

[Section XI.] (Section XII, P. L.) Be it enacted by the authority aforesaid, That from and after the passage of this act
no ship or vessel of the burden of fty tons and not more than
one hundred tons shall be entitled to or permitted to clear at
the naval office till the master or owner thereof shall produce
to the naval officer a certificate from the tonnage officer of their
having lodged in his hands a sum equal to one fourth of what
the pilotage of such ship or vessel from this port would amount
to agreeably to the directions of this act, which said sum shall
be paid to the pilot who shall carry such ship or vessel to sea
on proof thereof being made and on failure of such proof the
said sum shall be forfeited to the commonwealth and be accounted for and paid by the tonnage officer in such manner
as in and by this act is directed as to other moneys received
by the tonnage officer.

[Section XII.] (Section XIII, P. L.) And be it further enacted by the authority aforesaid, That it shall and may be law-

ful, upon complaint made to any justice of the peace and he
is hereby empowered and required to issue forth his precept
in writing under his hand and seal in the nature of a summons,
capias, or attachment as the case may require directed to any
constable commanding him to bring or cause to come before
him any person or persons against whom such complaint shall
be made respecting any demand, matter, cause, controversy
or dispute, that shall or may arise between pilots, masters of
vessels, merchants or others respecting pilotage and thereupon
proceed to hear the proofs and allegations of the said parties
or such of them as shall appear and to determine and pass judgment thereon and also to award process under his hand and
seal against the body or the goods of the person or persons
against [whom] such judgment shall be given for the sum due
with costs of suit as are generally recovered before a justice
of the peace on debts under ten pounds, and the said justice
shall keep fair entries and records of all his proceedings from
the commencement of the first process to the final end of such
suit.   Provided nevertheless, That in all cases in this act mentioned, where power is given to the master warden for the time
being or to any board of wardens to settle or adjust any matter
or thing, the same shall be deemed and taken for conclusive
evidence before such justice.

[Section XIII.] (Section XIV, P. L.) And be it further enacted by the authority aforesaid, That the said wardens or so
many of them as shall attend at any stated monthly meeting
shall be and they are hereby authorized and empowered from
time to time to make such orders and rules as shall be useful
and necessary for governing and better regulating the pilots
aforesaid, and to impose and lay any penalty for the breach of
such orders and rules not exceeding ten pounds to be recovered
by the said wardens for the uses in this act mentioned and shall
cause the said orders and rules to be recorded in their office
and to be printed and published for the information of all
whom it may concern, which said orders and rules shall be
inviolably observed, and executed by all persons concerned,
according to the tenor, true intent and meaning thereof.   Pro-

vided, They be not repugnant to the laws of this commonwealth and shall be approved by the president or vice president and supreme executive council of this commonwealth.

[Section XIV.] (Section XV, P. L.) And be it further enacted by the authority aforesaid, That before the said wardens shall take upon themselves the office of wardens each and every of them shall take an oath or affirmation before some justice of the peace for the city and county of Philadelphia that he will well and faithfully, to [the] best of his skill, understanding and judgment, perform, do, execute and discharge the office and duty of a warden of the port of Philadelphia according to the directions of this act.

[Section XV.] (Section XVI, P. L.) And be it further enacted by the authority aforesaid, That if it shall so happen that any first rate pilot having his boat attending him shall be carried out to sea by any ship or vessel contrary to his inclination, the master or owner of such ship or vessel shall pay to such pilot, his executors or administrators the sum of six pounds per month for every month he shall be necessarily absent until his return to the said capes, or in case he shall die while so absent then to the time of his death and if no boat shall attend such pilot, the said master or owner shall pay him the sum of four pounds per month as aforesaid, and if any second rate pilot shall be carried off as aforesaid, having his boat attending him as aforesaid, he shall be paid the sum of five pounds per month, if without his boat, three pounds ten shillings per month, and if any third rate pilot shall be carried off as aforesaid, having his boat attending him, he shall be paid three pounds per month, if without his boat, forty-five shillings per month, by the said master or owner of such ship or vessel, which shall so convey or carry off such pilots respectively, for every month until his death or return to the said capes aforesaid. And if any master of any ship or vessel shall carry off to sea any pilot contrary to his inclination when his boat or any other boat is ready and offers to take him from such ship or vessel and the same may be done without endangering the vessel aforesaid, every such master shall for every such offence forfeit and pay to the said pilot so carried off the sum of three hundred pounds to be recovered by action of debt, plaint, or information and the owner or owners of every such ship or vessel shall also forfeit and pay to every such pilot the sum of fifty pounds to be sued for and recovered in manner aforesaid which sums shall be recovered and paid over and above the wages aforesaid.

And whereas disputes have arisen between the owners of vessels in ward bound and pilots, by reason of their detention in the river in the winter season:

For remedy whereof:

[Section XVI.] (Section XVII, P. L.) Be it enacted by the authority aforesaid, That when any ship or vessel inward bound shall be safely moored at Reedy island and be there detained by ice, it shall and may be lawful for the master of any such ship or vessel, after being so detained for six days to discharge his pilot and in such case, the said pilot shall be entitled to receive and recover full pilotage as if he had conducted such ship or vessel to the port of Philadelphia.

[Section XVII.] (Section XVIII, P. L.) And be it further enacted by the authority aforesaid, That if any pilot duly qualified in virtue of this act shall neglect or refuse on due notice given to him to aid and assist any ship or vessel which shall be in distress within six leagues to the southward of Cape Henlopen or the same distance to the northward of Cape May or in the river or bay of Delaware aforesaid or in case any ship or vessel shall be lost or damaged by the manifest neglect of the pilot having charge of her, every such pilot so refusing to aid or assist or neglecting his duty shall on due proof made thereof before any board of wardens, at any of their said monthly meetings or when they shall be specially convened in manner aforesaid be rendered incapable of exercising the office or duty of a pilot, and the certificate before given shall be utterly void and all contracts and agreements made or to be made by and between any pilot and the master of a ship or vessel in distress for his aid and assistance shall be also void and such pilots shall be entitled to ask, demand and recover

no more than a reasonable reward for his said aid, assistance
and service any such contract notwithstanding.   Provided always nevertheless, That if any pilot on endeavor-
ing to assist or relieve any ship or vessel in distress shall suffer
loss or damage in his boat, her sails, tackle, rigging or appurtenances, the master or owner of such ship or vessel shall be
liable to pay to such pilot the value of such loss or damage over
and besides the said reasonable compensation for his services.

[Section XVIII.] (Section XIX, P. L.) And be it further enacted by the authority aforesaid, That if any person or persons
shall conceive him or themselves aggrieved by any judgment
given by any justice in pursuance of this act, it shall and may
be lawful for such person or persons to appeal to the next
county court of common pleas to be held for the county where
the said judgment shall be given, which said appeal shall be
allowed by the said justice upon sufficient security being given
for the prosecuting the same to effect and that the proceedings
on such appeal shall be prosecuted on the same terms, in the
same manner and under the same penalties as are directed
by the laws of this commonwealth in cases of appeals from the
judgment of any justice of the peace.

[Section XIX.] (Section XX, P. L.) And be it further enacted by the authority aforesaid, That if any person or persons whosoever shall take up any anchor and stock or any
anchor without a stock or any cable within the bay or river
Delaware, every such person or persons shall as soon as conveniently may be bring or cause to be brought every such
anchor or anchor and stock or cable to the port of Philadelphia and deliver the same to the master warden for the time
being, under the penalty of one hundred pounds to be paid
to the wardens for the uses herein mentioned or to the person
who shall rightfully own such anchor or anchor and stock or
cable and upon the delivery of such anchor or anchor and stock
or cable to the master warden for the time being he shall, without delay advertise the said anchor or anchor and stock or cable
so delivered three times in some of the public newspapers
published in the city of Philadelphia unless the owner there-

of or his factor shall appear and claim the same and shall permit and suffer the said anchor or anchor and stock or cable to be viewed by any person or persons who shall make application to him for that purpose and if any person or persons shall claim and make satisfactory proof of his or their right and property in any such anchor or anchor and stock or cable within the space of three months next after the date of the first advertisement before the master warden for the time being or any board of wardens or of his or their right and property in such anchor or anchor and stock or cable the said cable or cables or anchor and anchor and stock the property whereof shall be so proved shall be restored to such claimants upon he or they paying such salvage for the same as the said board of wardens shall deem reasonable, together with the costs and expenses accruing thereon, but if no person or persons shall within the time aforesaid claim and make proof of his or their property in such cable anchor or anchor and stock then and in such case the said master warden for the time being shall at the end of two months from the date of the first advertisement, expose the said cable or cables, anchor or anchor and stock to sale at public vendue at some public place in the city of Philadelphia, having first given due and timely notice thereof and after deducting the charges and expenses accruing thereon pay the money proceeding from such sale to the person or persons who took up the said cable or anchor or anchor and stock so sold.

And whereas, a light-house has been erected on Cape Henlopen and sundry buoys, beacons and piers have been and are to be fixed in the bay and river Deleware for the more convenient and safe navigation to and from the said port of Philadelphia

[Section XX.] (Section XXI, P. L.) Be it further enacted by the authority aforesaid, That if any person or persons shall after the publication of this act remove and destroy or be aiding and assisting in the removal or destruction of any of the said buoys, beacons or piers or shall burn or otherwise destroy or be aiding and assisting in burning or destroying the said light house and shall be convicted thereof in any court of quarter sessions for any city or county in this state where he, she or they shall be apprehended or to which he, she or they shall be brought if apprehended in any place out of this state shall forfeit and pay the sum of one thousand pounds, for the use of this commonwealth and shall also be confined at hard labor for any time not exceeding seven years:

And whereas it is expedient and necessary that the said light-house, buoys, beacons, and piers should be duly supported, repaired and maintained and further provision made for the wages, salary, rent and other expenses hereinbefore mentioned:

[Section XXI.] (Section XXII, P. L.) Be it therefore enacted by the authority aforesaid, That from and after the publication hereof there shall be laid, raised, collected and paid from every ship or vessel, (except as hereinafter [is] excepted) coming into or going out of any port of this state the following duties of tonnage, that is to say, from every such ship or vessel the property whereof in whole or in part shall be owned by or belonging to any person or persons not being a citizen or citizens of the United States or of some or one of them or of the territories thereunto belonging, one shilling and two pence per ton, upon all and from every such ship or vessel the property whereof shall be wholly in and be owned by or belonging to any person or persons who shall be a citizen or citizens of the United States or of some or one of them or of the territories thereunto belonging, of seven pence per ton, all of which said duties of tonnage shall be accounted, taken and paid according to the measure of every such ship or vessel, to be made and taken by the collector of the said duty of tonnage in the port or place where they shall arrive, enter and clear and the master or owner of every such ship or vessel shall within forty-eight hours after the arrival thereof at the port or place of their discharge or unloading in this state, cause or procure such ship or vessel to be entered in the office of the collector of tonnage, appointed or to be appointed for collecting the said duties of tonnage and at the time of such entry and before he or they shall unload or break bulk shall either pay to the said

collector the sum of money due and payable for the tonnage
of all such ships or vessels or shall give good and sufficient
security by bond to the said collector to be approved of by
him, to pay the said duty of tonnage to the said collector or
his successors for the uses aforesaid within the space of six
weeks under the penalty of twenty pounds to be paid to the
said collectors for the uses in this act mentioned.

[Section XXII.] (Section XXIII, P. L.) And be it further
enacted by the authority aforesaid, That the master or owners
of all ships or other vessels (except as is hereinafter excepted)
now building or hereafter to be built within this state shall
within forty-eight hours after demand made enter the same
ships or other vessels in the said collectors office and pay or
secure to be paid the like duties of tonnage according to the
rates aforesaid in manner aforesaid under the penalty of twenty
pounds to be paid to the collector of tonnage for the uses herein
mentioned. Provided always nevertheless, That in order that
the commerce of this commonwealth shall be increased and extended by promoting and facilitating a commercial intercourse
with the neighboring states whereby the number and quantity
of exportable articles may be increased all shallops and other
small vessels trading within the river and bay of Delaware
and all ships and other vessels not exceeding the burden or
measurements of fifty tons passing to or from any port within
this state and to or from any other port or ports within the
United States of America shall be freed and exempted from
the payment of any duty of tonnage whatsoever, and that all
other ships and vessels passing in like manner between any
port in this state and other port or ports in the said United
States shall not be subject to the payment of the said duty or
duties more than once in every twelve months during the continuance of any such ship or vessel in such trade without going
to any port not within the said United States. And provided
further, That any and every ship or vessel employed in the
coasting trade between this state and port or ports within the
United States and bringing into the port or ports of this state
no other goods, wares, or merchandise than those of the

growth, produce and manufacture of the said United States or
of some or one of them and such as may be lawfully imported
free from duty or impost by the laws of this state shall be
subject to the payment of seven shillings and six pence and
no more for every entrance and clearance at the naval office,
any law, usage or custom to the contrary notwithstanding.
And provided likewise, That no ship or vessel shall be exempted from the payment of tonnage duty except such ship
or vessel shall be the property of a citizen or citizens of this
state or of the United States or some or one of them.

And in order to prevent the owners of vessels subject to the
tonnage duty from evading the payment thereof:

[Section XXIII.] (Section XXIV, P. L.) Be it enacted by
the authority aforesaid, That from and after the passing of this
act the master or owner of every vessel which shall be of the
burden of fifty tons or upwards shall within forty-eight hours
next after the arrival of such vessel in this port, report the
said vessel to the tonnage officer who shall give a certificate
of such entry to the person making the same and if the master
or owner of such ship or vessel shall neglect or refuse to make
such report and entry he shall forfeit and pay the sum of
twenty pounds for the use of the commonwealth for every such
neglect or refusal, to be sued for and recovered in the same
manner as other fines are directed to be by this act.

[Section XXIV.] (Section XXV, P. L.) And be it further
enacted by the authority aforesaid, That it shall and may be
lawful for the tonnage officer as often as he shall think necessary to require from the master of any vessel of the burden of
fifty tons or upwards who shall claim an exemption from the
payment of tonnage duty by reason of such vessel being employed in the coasting trade, an oath or affirmation, which oath
or affirmation he is hereby authorized to administer, that the
said vessel has been employed in the manner directed by this
act and if the master or owner of such vessel shall refuse to
make oath or affirmation that such vessel has been so employed
during each and every voyage since the last payment of the
tonnage duty, every such ship or vessel shall be subject to

the tonnage in the same manner as other vessels are made subject to the payment of the same.

[Section XXV.] (Section XXVI, P. L.) And be it further enacted by the authority aforesaid, That for preventing disputes concerning the contents of vessels hereby made liable to the said duty of tonnage, the said tonnage shall be measured and computed in manner following, that is to say, every single decked ship or vessel shall be measured by the length of the keel and the breadth of the beam taken within board by the midship beam from plank to plank and the depth of the hold from the ceiling plank next the kelson to the under part of the deck plank, then multiply the length by the breadth and the product thereof by the depth and divide the whole by ninety-five, the quotient shall give the contents of the tonnage of such single decked vessel; and in order to find the length of keel, measure the gun deck, from the fore part of the stern post to the fore of the stem, from which deduct three-fifths of the beam for the rake forward and four inches out of the length of each foot of the stern post as high as the gun deck for the rake abaft, the remainder shall be the length of the keel. And every two decked ship shall be measured in the manner hereinafter directed, that is to say, the breadth to be taken within board by the midship beam, from plank to plank, multiplied by the length of the keel, to be measured as hereinbefore directed, and the product thereof multiplied by one half of the breadth, on the midship beam as aforesaid, the whole divided by ninety-five, the quotient shall be and is hereby declared to be the contents of the tonnage of every such two [decked] ship or vessel, according to which method and rules, all ships and vessels shall be measured and the several duties of tonnage thereby computed and collected accordingly, any law, usage, custom to the contrary notwithstanding.

And whereas from the freedom of commerce and the admission of foreign vessels many ships or vessels may arrive in the river Delaware, the commanders or masters whereof may not be duly informed of the duties enjoined on them by the act entitled "An act to prevent infectious diseases being

brought into the province,,[1] and the penalties to which they
may be subjected by not conforming to the regulations prescribed in and by the said act:

[Section XXVI.] (Section XXVII, P. L.) Be it therefore enacted by the authority aforesaid, That the master warden for
the time being shall cause an abstract of the said act to be
made, containing the substance of all such regulations and
duties therein made and enjoined as relate to the commanders,
masters or persons having charge of ships or vessels bound
to the port of Philadelphia, and have a competent number of
copies of such abstracts printed and distributed to and among
the licensed pilots so as to enable each and every of the said
pilots to furnish and deliver one of the said copies to the
commander or master of each and every inward bound vessel
he shall take charge of.

[Section XXVII.] (Section XXVIII, P. L.) And be it further
enacted by the authority aforesaid, That it shall be the duty
of each and every of the said pilots, and the same is hereby
enjoined, to deliver one of the said abstracts or copies to the
commander or master of every inward bound ship or vessel he
may take charge of as pilot or shall otherwise fully inform such
commander or master of the nature and purport of the said
regulations and of the duties thereby enjoined, and such pilot
shall not presume to conduct such ship or vessel nearer the city
of Philadelphia than is consistent with the said regulations
on pain of being suspended from exercising the duties and receiving the emoluments of a pilot for twelve months and of
forfeiting fifty pounds for every such offence to the said wardens for the uses herein mentioned.

[Section XXVIII.] (Section XXIX, P. L.) And be it further
enacted by the authority aforesaid, That the ballast of any ship
or vessel judged or deemed to be infectious under the act entitled, "An act to prevent infectious diseases being brought
into this province,"[2] shall not be brought up to the city of
Philadelphia, the district of Southwark or Northern Liberties,
but the same shall be thrown out or discharged at such con-

---

[1]Passed January 22, 1774, Chapter 691.
[2]See Ante.

venient and proper place as the health officer may direct and appoint, under the penalty of one hundred pounds to be recovered by the wardens and appropriated as hereinafter is directed.

[Section XXIX.] (Section XXX, P. L.) And be it further enacted by the authority aforesaid, That when and so often as any warrant of survey on vessels and goods [damaged,] or supposed to be damaged by stress of weather, accident at sea, bad stowage or other cause, shall be applied for to the court of admiralty or other competent jurisdiction the same shall be directed to the wardens of the port of Philadelphia for the time being, directing or requiring them or any two of them in the usual form to execute the same, and such warrant shall be so framed as to comprehend all the surveys which may be requisite to be made respecting any one vessel and the various parts or portions of her cargo, under which warrants the said surveyors may nevertheless make and return such and so many separate and distinct reports to the judge of the admiralty as the nature and circumstances of the case may require. And in case the said surveyors shall think the aid and assistance of a ship carpenter or other tradesman necessary to the forming of a proper judgment and report on any such survey they are hereby authorized to call to their aid any such tradesman as they shall choose and who shall be willing to join them in the said business, which tradesman so chosen and called, shall be taken and deemed to be a surveyor for that occasion, as fully and amply to all intents and purposes as if he had been named in the warrant and as a compensation to the said surveyors for performing the said duties they shall be allowed and paid by the parties respectively demanding or requiring any such survey as follows, to wit, to each of the two wardens who shall perform the service and also to the carpenter or other tradesmen so called to their assistance, ten shillings for every survey and return on a ship or other vessel and ten shillings each for every separate shipment or invoice of goods they shall so survey and report upon.

[Section XXX.] (Section XXXI, P. L.) And be it further en-

acted by the authority aforesaid, That if the collector of tonnage, or his deputy or deputies lawfully appointed, shall be
sued or prosecuted, for anything done in pursuance of this act,
he or they so sued or prosecuted may plead the general issue
and give this act and special matter in evidence for their justi-
fication and if upon trial thereof a verdict shall be given against
the plaintiff or he shall become non-suit or suffer a discontinuance, the defendant or defendants in such action shall recover
treble damages with full costs of suit. Provided also, That
the said collector or any other person, shall not be sued for
anything done in pursuance of this act unless such suit shall
be commenced within six months next after the pretended or
supposed injury shall be done or committed.

[Section XXXI.] (Section XXXII, P. L.) And be it further
enacted by the authority aforesaid, That the collector of tonnage appointed or to be appointed shall keep fair and true accounts in writing of all his transactions relating to the premises
and the duty of his office, which he shall from time to time submit to the view and inspection of the master warden for the
time being and to any board of wardens and shall also lay the
same before the comptroller-general for the purposes herein
after mentioned and the said collector shall deduct and retain
out of all moneys which he shall receive in pursuance of this
act for his trouble in executing the duties hereby enjoined him
six pounds for every hundred pounds and so in proportion for
any greater or lesser sum, for measuring, receiving and paying
as aforesaid, and the said state treasurer shall have and receive
for his trouble in receiving and paying the conveys coming into
his hands by virtue of this act the sum of ten shillings for every
hundred pounds and so in proportion for any greater or less
sum and no more.

[Section XXXII.] (Section XXXII. P. L.) [sic] Provided
always and be it further enacted by the authority aforesaid
That the said collector, before he enters upon the execution of
his office shall take an oath or affirmation before some justice
of the peace of the county of Philadelphia who is hereby empowered to administer the same and shall also become bound to

the president or vice-president of the supreme executive council of this Commonwealth in the sum of five hundred pounds with one or more sufficient sureties conditioned for the true and faithful execution of his said office.

[Section XXXIII.] (Section XXXIII. P. L.) And be it further enacted by the authority aforesaid, That the said wardens or such of them as shall attend at any or every of their monthly meetings aforesaid, shall nominate and appoint a careful and reputable person to be the keeper of the said light-house, who shall carefully and diligently attend his duty in kindling and keeping burning the lights from sun setting to the rising thereof and in placing the said lights so as they may be best seen by persons on board vessels coming into or going out of the said bay of Delaware and shall be allowed by the said wardens a reasonable compensation therefor. And in case such keeper shall neglect his duty in any part of the premises he shall forfeit and pay any sum of money according to the degree of his offense not exceeding the sum of two hundred and fifty pounds, one half thereof to him who shall sue or prosecute for the same by bill, plaint or information and the other half for the uses in and by this act declared. Provided always, That the said keeper before he enters upon the duties of his said office or takes charge of the said light house shall give one or more good and sufficient [sureties] to the president of the supreme executive council for the true and faithful performance and discharge of his duty in any sum not exceeding two hundred and fifty pounds.

[Section XXXIV.] (Section XXXV. P. L.) And be it further enacted by the authority aforesaid, That the said wardens shall repair and maintain in good order the said buoys, piers, beacons, and lighthouse and keep up the lights in the said house at all proper times or cause the same to be done and for [those] purposes shall draw orders on the State treasurer who shall discharge the same out of the moneys paid into his hands in pursuance of this act.

[Section XXXV.] (Section XXXVI. P. L.) And be it further enacted by the authority aforesaid, That all forfeitures,

penalties, sum and sums of money in this act mentioned and
not otherwise directed and appropriated shall be payable, sued
for, recovered and applied in manner and form following, that
is to say, all the said forfeitures, penalties, sum and sums of
money in and by this act made payable to the wardens or to the
master warden for the time being shall be sued for and recovered
by the said wardens and all such forfeitures, penalties, sum and
sums of money as are by this act made payable to the collector
of tonnage shall be sued for and recovered by the said collector
of tonnage and that all the said forfeitures, penalties, sum and
sums of money so as aforesaid payable to the said wardens or
to the master warden for the time being or to the collector of
tonnage which are under ten pounds shall be sued for and recovered with costs of suit before any justice of the peace of any
city or county within this State in like manner as other debts
under ten pounds are by the laws of this Commonwealth recoverable before any justice of the peace and subject to the like
appeal, security, trial and costs and that all such forfeitures,
penalties, sum and sums of money as amount to ten pounds or
upwards shall be sued for and recovered, with costs of suit by
action of debt, case, bill, plaint or information in any court of
record within this State or otherwise and that all the fines, forfeitures, penalties, sum and sums of money by this act made
payable to the said collector of tonnage or to the wardens or to
the master warden thereof for the time being shall (where it is
not herein otherwise directed) be by them respectively paid
to the State treasurer once in every three months, for the special use and purpose of paying off the salvage, rent, salaries,
wages and other incidental expenses arising from the due execution of this act and all other expenses, costs and charges
which have accrued by the execution of the several acts appointing or in anywise respecting, wardens for the port of
Philadelphia and also for the use and purpose of keeping and
maintaining the said light house, piers, beacons and buoys and
such other piers, beacons and buoys as any board of wardens
shall think it necessary to erect, sink or fix, in good order
and repair and to this end all the said fines, forfeitures.

penalties, sum and sums of money so as aforesaid to be
paid to the said treasurer in pursuance of this act shall
at all times remain in the hands of the said treasurer, specially
appropriated for the purpose and subject to the drafts of the
said master warden of the board of wardens for all or any of
the purposes aforesaid and for no other use or purpose whatsoever and to the end and intent that fair and just accounts shall
be kept and settlements made by the said wardens and collectors of tonnage of all their transactions in pursuance of this act,
they and every of them are hereby enjoined and required to
exhibit just and true accounts of all their proceedings in pursuance of this act once in every three months to the comptroller-
general who is hereby authorized and required to settle and
adjust the same in like manner as other accounts are settled
by him agreeable to the laws of this commonwealth subject to
the like appeal, security and trial and costs as are in other
cases of appeal from any settlement made before him and in
like manner to proceed and recover such balance or balances as
on such settlement or settlements shall be found due from them
or any of them.

[Section XXXVI.] (Section XXXVI, P. L.) And be it further enacted by the authority aforesaid, That all and singular
the sums of money which shall be paid to the collector of the
tonnage by virtue of this act for one fourth part of the pilotage
of all ships and vessels brought or navigated up to the port of
Philadelphia or carried from thence without a pilot and all
fines to be recovered from pilots for any breach of this act shall
be kept as a fund by the said collector for the use of distressed
and decayed pilots, their widows and children, to be distributed
by a society of pilots, to be formed for that purpose, and that
as soon as a society shall be formed by the said pilots consisting
of two-thirds of the whole number of first rate certificate pilots
at least and having a board of managers, treasurer and clerk,
the said collector shall pay to them or their orders, all the said
moneys to be by them kept, managed and distributed as aforesaid and so shall, once in every half year, pay over to the said
managers for the use aforesaid all the moneys by him to be re-

ceived from time to time or such one fourth part pilotage's and
the fines which may be recovered from pilots by virtue of this
act.

And to the end and intent that the navigation of the river
Delaware may not be injured by the extension of wharves to
an improper distance into the channel thereof within the port
of Philadelphia or by obstructions or encroachments of any
other kind.

[Section XXXVII.] (Section XXXVII, P. L.) Be it further
enacted by the authority aforesaid, That when and so often as
any person shall be desirous to extend any wharf or other building into the tide-way of the river Delaware from any part of
the city or liberties of Philadelphia, such person shall make application to the said board of wardens at any of their monthly
meetings aforesaid, stating in writing the nature, extent and
plan of such intended wharf or building and if it shall appear
to the board of wardens or a majority of them that such plan
and design may be lawfully executed and that the same will
not improperly encroach upon or injure the said channel and
harbor the board of wardens at any of their stated monthly
meetings, or when specially convened in manner aforesaid,
shall give their assent and license for erecting and extending
such wharf or building and cause the same to be recorded in
their office but if the said board of wardens shall deem it improper to give such assent and license and the party applying
shall think himself aggrieved by their resolutions he may make
such application to the supreme executive council who, after
hearing the reasons which induced the wardens to refuse their
assent, shall finally determine and award thereon as they may
think right and proper and if any person or persons after the
publication of this act shall extend any wharf or building within the city or liberties of Philadelphia into the river Delaware
beyond low water mark without license first had and obtained
from the wardens as aforesaid, or in case of their refusal from
the supreme executive council, he or they shall, on conviction
thereof, in the manner in and by this act directed forfeit and
pay to the said board of wardens the sum of one thousand

pounds to be by them recovered and applied in such manner as other fines, forfeitures or sums of money by this act made payable to them are directed to be recovered and applied.

And whereas it sometimes happens that vessels are injuriously impeded in the landing or discharging of their cargoes by being refused admittance to a wharf, although divers wharves or parts thereof may be unoccupied by any other vessel or occupied by such only as might, without material injury, be removed to some other situation.

And whereas it is just and proper that the owner or possessor of a wharf, though extended into the river beyond low water mark, should enjoy a reasonable right of preoccupancy thereof:

[Section XXXVIII.] (Section XXXVIII, P. L.) Be it enacted by the authority aforesaid, That no ship or vessel subject to the duties of tonnage shall be permitted to moor at or otherwise to occupy any wharf within the city or liberties of Philadelphia without leave first had and obtained from the owner or possessor thereof, Provided always, That if such leave be duly applied for by the owner, agent, master or other person having charge of such ship or vessel and refused by the owner or possessor of any wharf within the limits aforesaid, being vacant in the whole or in such part as may reasonably accommodate the ship or vessel [so applied for and such vacancies shall remain unoccupied by some ship or vessel] in which the owner or possessor of the wharf hath an immediate interest, for twenty-four hours after such application and refusal, it shall then and in such cases be lawful for the ship or vessel first applied for to be moored at and occupy such wharf for so long time as shall be requisite for the dispatch of her business, subject nevertheless to the control and direction of the master warden for the time being as hereinafter is mentioned.

[Section XXXIX.] (Section XXXIX, P. L.) And be it further enacted by the authority aforesaid, That when any ship or vessel subject to the duties of tonnage shall be moored at and occupy such wharf or end or side thereof within the said city or liberties affording proper convenience for such vessel to discharge and receive goods either with or without the leave and consent of the owner or possessor of such wharf and without any agreement being made for the rate or price of such wharf-age, it shall and may be lawful for the owner or possessor of such wharf to demand and receive for such wharfage any sum not exceeding the rate of five shillings per day for so long time as such vessel shall so occupy such wharf or part thereof, and for an outside berth the second vessel from a wharf shall pay not exceeding the rate of two shillings per day and the third vessel from a wharf shall pay not exceeding the rate of one shilling per day.

And whereas vessels being out of repair or for some other reason remaining unemployed or nearly so frequently occupy for an unreasonable length of time the wharves and situations best adapted for the dispatch of business to the great hindrance and obstruction of others:

[Section XL.] (Section XL, P. L.) Be it enacted by the authority aforesaid, That the master warden of the said board of wardens for the time being or any board of wardens be and they are hereby severally authorized and required on application to him or them made for the removal or any such ship or vessel to be removed to such other place or situation as the owner, master or other person having charge thereof shall choose and the said master warden or board of wardens shall approve and in case such owner or other person shall refuse or neglect to choose such other place or situation as shall be so approved or to make such removal of the vessel and the said master warden or the board of wardens shall direct within twenty-four hours after due notice given for that purpose such owner, master or other person having charge of such ship or vessel shall forfeit and pay to the said wardens the sum of five pounds per day for every day such ship or vessel shall afterwards remain unremoved as aforesaid, unless prevented by stress of weather or other reasonable cause of which the said master warden for the time being or board of wardens shall be the judge or judges, which forfeitures shall be recovered with costs of suit, by action of debt or by attachment of the said ship or vessel and her appurtenances at the suit of the said wardens as seamen's wages are recoverable and applied as is herein directed.

And in order to prevent the city of Philadelphia from being unnecessarily exposed to danger from fire:

[Section XLI.] (Section XLI, P. L.) Be it further enacted by the authority aforesaid, That if any person or persons whatsoever shall from and after the passing of this act burn or bream or caused to be burned or breamed any ship or other vessel or any part thereof at or near any wharf or wharves of this city or between South and Vine streets of the said city, he or they shall for every such offense forfeit and pay to the said wardens the sum of fifty pounds to be by them recovered and applied in such manner and to such uses as other fines, forfeitures and sums of money by this act made payable to them are directed to be recovered and applied.

And whereas inconveniences and mischiefs frequently happen for want of order and regularity in the placing, anchoring and mooring of vessels in the stream as well as at the wharves and docks:

[Section XLII.] (Section XLII, P. L.) Be it enacted by the authority aforesaid, That it shall and may be lawful for the said master warden or any board of wardens and he or they is and are hereby authorized and required to form and establish such rules and orders as they on due deliberation and advisement shall from time to time think requisite and proper for guarding against such inconveniences and mischiefs, which rules and orders shall be recorded in the office of the said wardens, and shall be printed and published for the information of all whom it may concern. And if any owner, master or other person having the charge or command of any ship or vessel within the harbor of Philadelphia shall wilfully or negligently disobey or refuse or neglect to comply with such rules and orders, after due notice thereof or neglect or refuse to comply with any reasonable order or directions of the said master wardens, for the time being or any of the wardens as aforesaid, respecting the placing, mooring or removing such ship or vessel within the said harbor, such owner, master or other person shall forfeit and pay to the wardens for the uses in this act mentioned the sum of five pounds for every such

time the same or a similar offense shall be repeated, for which
offense for the first time and ten pounds for each and every
forfeitures [and] fines such vessel and her appurtenances shall
be liable, as well as the person and effects of the offender or
offenders and the owners and all others concerned in any such
vessels shall be moreover debarred from recovering any compensation for any damages she may sustain in the mean-
[time], by any other vessel running foul of or injuring the same
or the tackle or apparel thereof, which said forfeiture shall
be and they are hereby made recoverable as hereinbefore is
directed for the recovery of other forfeitures, penalties and
sums of money.

[Section XLIII.] (Section XLIII, P. L.) And be it further
enacted by the authority aforesaid, That if any person or persons shall think himself or themselves aggrieved by any order
or sentence made by the master warden of the wardens for the
time being as aforesaid, it shall and may be lawful for such
person or persons to appeal therefrom to the board of wardens
on giving bond to the master warden of the wardens, with
sufficient surety, to abide and perform the final determination
of the board thereon, of the sufficiency of which security the
master warden of the wardens for the time being shall judge
and determine, which bond shall be executed and tendered
within twenty-four hours after notice of such order or sentence
and the party appellant shall prosecute such appeal to effect
before the board at their next meeting, or otherwise the appeal
shall be dismissed unless a satisfactory cause for a further continuance be shown to the board and if either of the parties
shall require it and the master warden for the time being shall
think it proper, a special meeting of the board shall be called
for the hearing of such appeal as early as may be and if upon
such hearing of such appeal, either at a stated or special meeting, the original order or sentence shall be affirmed, the board
shall award such reasonable costs to be paid by the appellant
as they shall adjudge to be adequate to the expenses occasioned by the appeal, including the established pay of the war-

dens and their clerks for so long time as they shall have attended on the said business.

And whereas injuries frequently happen by vessels accidentally or negligently running foul of each other and it is expedient that a summary and expeditious mode should be established for ascertaining such damages and awarding payment thereof by the party or parties who ought of right to pay the same:

Therefore:

[Section XLIV.] (Section XLIV, P. L.) Be it enacted by the authority aforesaid, That the party injured by such accident or negligence and claiming redress shall and may apply to the master warden for the time being, stating his claim of redress and pointing out the person or persons from whom the same is demanded, which master warden is authorized and required to appoint a time and place for the hearing and determination of such claim, of which notice shall be given in writing by the party claiming to the adverse party at least twenty-four hours before the time so appointed and the said master warden after due information by examination of witnesses, inspection, surveys or such other proper means as the case may require, shall adjudge and award such recompense for the damages sustained, as he shall think just and reasonable, to be paid by one party to the other for the same, together with such reasonable expenses as may have been incurred in obtaining such information and [the] award, certified under the hands of the said master warden shall be final and conclusive to the parties unless appealed from as aforesaid and shall be taken and deemed to be sufficient evidence of a debt incurred to maintain and support an action before any justice of the peace or in any court of record where the same may be cognizable, agreeably to the directions of this act and the party injured may prosecute thereon accordingly by summons or capias as the case may require or by attachment of the vessel which occasioned such damages at his option.

And whereas keeping up and maintaining, victualling and providing for the sloop commonly called the state sloop belonging to this commonwealth is found to be attended with a very heavy expense far exceeding the benefits arising therefrom:

Therefore:

[Section XLV.] (Section XLV, P. L.) Be it further enacted by the authority aforesaid, That the master warden of the wardens for the time being shall with all convenient dispatch from and after the passing of this act sell or cause to be sold the said sloop with her tackle, apparel and furniture for the best price that can be got for the same at public vendue at the coffee house or at some other public place in the city of Philadelphia after having given public notice of such intended sale and of the time and place thereof at least five days in one or more of the public newspapers printed in the city and to pay the moneys arising from such sale (after having first paid off and discharged all the wages due to the officers and crew belonging to the said sloop for their services on board of her, and such other costs and expenses as she may have incurred) to the state treasurer for the uses and purposes in this act mentioned as to fines, forfeitures, penalties and sums of money and subject to the like drafts and for no other use or purpose whatsoever.

[Section XLVI.] (Section XLVI, P. L.) And be it further enacted by the authority aforesaid, That the act of general assembly entitled, "An act appointing wardens for the port of Philadelphia and for other purposes therein mentioned,"[1] and one other act entitled "A supplement to an act entitled 'An act appointing wardens for the port of Philadelphia,' "[2] and to an act entitled, "An act to prevent infectious diseases being brought into this province"[3] and one other act entitled "An act for the further regulation of the port of Philadelphia and enlarging the power of the wardens thereof"[4] and one other act entitled, "A supplement to an act entitled 'An act for the further regulation of the port of Philadelphia and for enlarging the powers of the wardens thereof' "[5] and every

[1]See Ante.
[2]Passed March 18, 1775, Chapter 708.
[3]See Ante.
[4]Passed April 1, 1784, Chapter 1095.
[5]Passed Septemebr 23, 1784, Chapter 1116.

clause, matter or thing in them or any of them contained shall be and they are hereby repealed.

Passed October 4, 1788. Recorded L. D. No. 3, p. 385. See the Acts of Assembly passed March 27, 1789, Chapter 1417; September 29, 1789, Chapter 1461; April 13, Chapter 1572; April 11, 1793, Chapter 1696.

CHAPTER MCCCLVI.

AN ACT TO APPOINT COMMISSIONERS TO SETTLE THE ACCOUNTS OF CERTAIN COMMISSIONERS WHO BY A CERTAIN ACT OF ASSEMBLY PASSED THE NINTH DAY OF MARCH ONE THOUSAND SEVEN HUNDRED AND SEVENTY-ONE WERE APPOINTED TO SETTLE THE ACCOUNTS OF CERTAIN OTHER COMMISSIONERS WHO BY A CERTAIN ACT OF ASSEMBLY PASSED THE TWENTIETH DAY OF SEPTEMBER ONE THOUSAND SEVEN HUNDRED AND SIXTY-FIVE WERE APPOINTED TO SETTLE THE ACCOUNTS OF THE MANAGERS OF A LOTTERY WHICH HAD BEEN SET UP AND DRAWN FOR THE PURPOSE OF ERECTING A BRIDGE OVER SKIPPACK CREEK IN THE THEN COUNTY OF PHILADELPHIA (NOW MONTGOMERY) AND TO RECEIVE VOLUNTARY DONATIONS AND SUBSCRIPTIONS FOR PERFECTING SAID BRIDGE.

(Section I, P. L.) Whereas in and by the above recited act passed the twentieth day of September one thousand seven hundred and sixty-five, William Dewees, Michael Hillegas and Benjamin Davis were appointed commissioners for the purpose of erecting a bridge over said Skippack creek and in order to enable them to perform that duty they were empowered to settle with, sue for and recover from the managers of said lottery all such sums of money as they or either of them had received on account of said lottery or otherwise, for the purpose of erecting said bridge:

And whereas in and by the above recited act passed the ninth day of March one thousand seven hundred and seventy-one, Benjamin Jacobs, Jacob Umstat and John Kestar were appointed commissioners for building a bridge over said Skippack creek and for calling upon the first mentioned commissioners and compelling them to account for such sum or sums of money as they or any or either of them had received for the purpose of erecting said bridge:

And whereas a number of the inhabitants of said county of
Montgomery have petitioned this house setting forth that although a sum of money had been raised by lottery and subscriptions obtained for the purpose of erecting said bridge, yet
the good intentions of the contributors have not been carried
into effect and that travellers are subject to great dan-
gers, difficulties and delays consequent on the sudden risings
of the waters of said creek and that two of the last mentioned
commissioners are now deceased therefore praying this house
to appoint commissioners and grant them power to recover the
money which hath been received by any person or persons on
account of said bridge and to apply the same for the purpose
aforesaid:

And whereas it is just and reasonable to comply with the
prayer of said petitioners:

Therefore:

[Section I.] (Section II, P. L.) Be it enacted and it is hereby
enacted by the Representatives of the Freemen of the Commonwealth of Pennsylvania in General Assembly met and by the
authority of the same, That Anthony Cruthers, Thomas Davis
and William Armstrong are hereby nominated and appointed
commissioners for the purpose of erecting said bridge over
Skippack creek and in order to enable them to perform that
duty the said commissioners appointed by the last recited act,
their heirs, executors or administrators and all other persons
who have moneys in their hands on account of said bridge are
hereby required within three months after the passing of this
act upon the request of the commissioners appointed by this act
or a majority of them to render fair and just accounts of all
the moneys by them, any or either of them received for the purpose of erecting said bridge, as well as all debts due to them or
either of them on that account and upon settlement to pay unto
the said commissioners appointed by this act all such sum and
sums of money as they have respectively received, together with
all books of accounts, papers and vouchers respecting the same

1 Chapter 634.
2 Chapter 530.

and in default of payment as aforesaid it shall and may be lawful to and for the said commissioners hereby appointed or a majority of them to sue for and recover all such sums of money by action on the case or otherwise as may be proper, if above the sum of ten pounds in any court of common pleas within this commonwealth, if ten pounds or under before any justice of the peace, and upon trial to give this act and other legal proof in evidence, and if it shall appear to the court and jury or to the justice of the peace aforesaid on any trial by virtue of this act before them respectively had that the sum demanded or any part thereof is justly due, then the said court or justice as the case may be respectively shall give judgment against the defendant for so much as shall appear to be due, with costs of suit, and shall award execution for the same as is usually done in like actions before them respectively triable and determinable by the laws of this commonwealth but if no part of the sum demanded shall appear to be due as aforesaid, then the said court or justice respectively shall give judgment for the costs against the plaintiff, which costs shall be paid out of the moneys recovered or collected by virtue of this act.

[Section II.] (Section III, P. L.) And be it further enacted by the authority aforesaid, That the said commissioners appointed by this act, shall, under the penalty of fifty pounds lay a clear statement of their procedure in the recovery of the money due on account of said lottery or otherwise respecting said bridge before the grand jury of the said county at every court of quarter sessions until the whole is recovered at which time the grand jury shall make such allowance to the said commissioners for their time and trouble out of the money so recovered as aforesaid as shall appear just and reasonable.

[Section III.] (Section IV, P. L.) And be it further enacted by the authority aforesaid, That if the money to be collected by virtue of this act shall appear sufficient for the purpose of erecting said bridge, that then the said commissioners are hereby authorized and required to erect the same, and when completed to lay a clear statement of their accounts and transactions respecting the premises before the then next succeeding grand jury of the county for their inspection and approbation.

[Section IV.] (Section V, P. L.) And be it further enacted
by the authority aforesaid, That in case the money to be collected by virtue of this act should not be sufficient after deducting
the allowance made to said commissioners as aforesaid for the
purpose of erecting said bridge, that then and in such case, the
said commissioners are hereby required to pay the same into
the hands of the county treasurer for the time being to be by
him kept safe until an additional sum sufficient for that purpose can be otherwise procured, at which time the commissioners for the purpose of erecting said bridge are hereby authorized and empowered to draw an order or orders on said
county treasurer to the full amount of the sum paid into his
hands as aforesaid, which order or orders the said treasurer is
hereby enjoined and required to pay and discharge.

Passed October 3, 1788.   Recorded L. B. No. 3, p. 407.

CHAPTER MCCCLXVII.

AN ACT TO AUTHORIZE THE SUPREME EXECUTIVE COUNCIL TO DRAW
ON THE STATE TREASURER [FOR] A SUM OF MONEY FOR DEFRAY-
ING THE EXPENSE OF PURCHASING OF THE INDIANS LANDS ON
LAKE ERIE.

(Section I, P. L.) Whereas a purchase hath been made by
this commonwealth from the United States of a certain tract
of country lying on Lake Erie, bounded by part of the said lake,
part of the northern line of this state and by a meridian line
run from the said [northern] boundary of this state to Lake
Erie the said meridian being a part of the western boundary of
New York, and it is necessary to provide funds for defraying
the expenses of purchasing the claims of the Indian natives
to the said tract or parcel of land:

[Section I.] (Section II, P. L.) Be it enacted and it is hereby
9—XIII

enacted by the Representatives of the Freemen of the Commonwealth of Pennsylvania in General Assembly met and by the authority of the same, That the supreme executive council of this state be and they are hereby authorized and directed to draw an order or orders on the state treasurer for any sum or sums of money not exceeding twelve hundred pounds, which said sum or sums shall be paid by the state treasurer out of the duties and imposts [arising] on goods, wares and merchandise imported into this state under the acts of the twentieth day of September in the year of our Lord one thousand seven hundred and eighty-five and the fifteenth day of March in the year of our Lord one thousand seven hundred and eighty-seven. And the supreme executive council are hereby empowered and directed to apply the said sum or sums of money or such part thereof as shall be found necessary for and towards defraying the expenses of purchasing of the Indians the tract or parcel of land hereinbefore mentioned.

Passed October 3, 1788. Recorded L. B. No. 3, p. 406. See the Act of Assembly passed September 28, 1789, Chapter 1447.

CHAPTER MCCCLXVIII.

AN ACT TO INCORPORATE THE EPISCOPAL CONGREGATION OF SAINT JAMES AT PERKIOMEN IN THE TOWNSHIP OF NEW PROVIDENCE AND COUNTY OF MONTGOMERY.

(Section I, P. L.) Whereas the Episcopal congregation of Saint James Church at Perkiomen in the township of New Providence and county of Montgomery have petitioned this house that said congregation may be incorporated and by law enabled as a body corporate and politic to receive and to hold such charitable donations and bequests as have been or hereafter may be made to said congregation and vested with such powers and privileges as are invested in and enjoyed by other

religious societies which have already been incorporated by the
legislature of this state:

And whereas in compliance with the prayers of the petitioners and agreeable to the spirit of the constitution this house
is disposed to exercise the powers therein vested: •

Therefore:

[Section I.] (Section II, P. L.) Be it enacted and it is hereby
enacted by the Representatives of the Freemen of the Commonwealth of Pennsylvania in General Assembly met and by the
authority of the same, That the Reverend Slaitor Clay, the
present minister, James Shannon and Nathan Pawling, wardens, Henry Pawling, Senior, Edward Lane, John Bean, Henry
Newberry, Joseph Pawling, Robert Shannon, Benjamin Rittenhouse, Henry Pawling, Junior, John Pawling, Junior, vestrymen, and their successors, duly elected and appointed be
and they are hereby made and constituted a corporation and
body politic in law and in fact to have continuance forever by
the name, style and title of "The Minister, Wardens and Vestrymen of the Episcopal congregation of Saint James's Church
at Perkiomen in the Township of New Providence and County
of Montgomery:"

And whereas the aforesaid congregation are already possessed of real estates consisting of a certain messuage or tract
of land and parsonage house contiguous to said church, containing fifty acres, the donation and bequest of William Lane,
deceased and it is hoped similar donations may be made
to said church.

[Section II.] (Section III, P. L.) Therefore be it enacted by
the authority aforesaid, That the above named trustees and
their successors or a majority of them consisting of not less
than two-thirds of the whole number, shall have power to receive in trust for the benefit of said congregation all such charitable donations and bequests as already have been or hereafter may be made and also in case it shall be deemed for the
benefit or advantage of said congregation by a majority of [the]
trustees or their successors as aforesaid, they shall have power
to bargain, sell and convey all such real estate and donations

of land other than the site on which the church stands as
already is or hereafter may be made to said congregation and
in lieu thereof to purchase other real estate that may by said
trustees be deemed more beneficial to the secular interest of
said congregation, Provided nevertheless, That the clear yearly
income, rents and value of all such real estate and charitable
donations belonging to said congregation does not exceed the
sum of five hundred pounds specie.

[Section III.] (Section IV, P. L.) And be it further enacted
by the authority aforesaid, That the said corporation and their
successors by the name, style and title aforesaid shall forever
hereafter have, use and exercise all and singular the like powers, authorities, rights, privileges, immunities and shall be
subject to such regulations, provisions and directions and to
such limitations and restrictions as were given and granted to
the Episcopal Congregation of Saint Paul's Church in the city
of Philadelphia in and by an act of the general assembly entitled, "An act for incorporating Saint Paul's Church in the city
of Philadelphia"¹ passed the twenty-third day of September
in the year of our Lord one thousand seven hundred and eighty-
three.

¹ Passed September 23, 1783, Chapter 1041.
Passed October 3, 1788.   Recorded L. B. No. 3, p. 411.

- - - - - - - - - - -

CHAPTER MCCCLXIX.

___

AN ACT FOR VESTING A LOT OF GROUND HEREIN DESCRIBED WITH
THE BUILDINGS AND IMPROVEMENTS THEREON ERECTED AND
MADE IN THE TRUSTEES OF DICKINSON COLLEGE IN THE BOROUGH
OF CARLISLE IN THE COUNTY OF CUMBERLAND.

(Section I, P. L.) Whereas Thomas Penn and Richard Penn,
Esquires, late proprietaries of Pennsylvania, did by their patent bearing date at Philadelphia the third day of March in
the year of our Lord one thousand seven hundred and seventy-

three and recorded in the Rolls Office in Book A. A. volume
twelve page one hundred and twenty-seven &c., give, grant,
release and confirm unto John Montgomery, Robert Miller,
John Armstrong, James Wilson, George Stevenson, Robert Magaw, Stephen Duncan, William Lyon and William Irwin, a
lot of ground in the town (now borough) of Carlisle in the county of Cumberland, marked in general plan of the said town
number two hundred and nineteen and situated on the north
side of Pomfret street between Hanover street and Bedford
street and containing in breadth east and west sixty feet and
in length north and south two hundred and forty feet, bounded
southward with Pomfret street, eastward with lot number two
hundred and twenty-seven, northward with a twentyfeet alley
and westward with lot number two hundred and eleven to have
and to hold the lot of ground, hereditaments and premises, by the said patent granted with the appurtenances unto
the said John Montgomery, Robert Miller, John Armstrong,
James Wilson, George Stevenson, Robert Magaw, Stephen Duncan, William Lyon, and William Irwin in trust, nevertheless
that they and the survivors and survivor of them should and
would from time to time, and at all times forever thereafter
permit and suffer the same to be applied to the use and purpose
of keeping and maintaining a grammar school, to be kept and
taught in one or more proper houses or buildings on the same
lot of ground to be erected as by the said patent recorded as
aforesaid, reference being thereunto had, will more fully and
at large appear:

And whereas the trustees in the said patent named erected
a house on the said lot of ground for the purpose in the said
patent specified, in which house a grammar school was kept
and taught for several years:

And whereas on the ninth day of September in the year of
our Lord one thousand seven hundred and eighty-three [1] an act
was passed by the legislature of this commonwealth for the
establishment of a college at the borough of Carlisle, in the
county of Cumberland in the state of Pennsylvania (which col-

---

[1] Chapter 1029.

lege was by the said act called Dickinson College) under the
management, direction and government of a number of trustees, which said trustees and their successors elected in the
manner in the said act directed were by the said act elected,
established and declared to be one body politic and corporate
with perpetual succession in deed and in law, to all intents
and purposes whatsoever by the name, style and title of "The
Trustees of Dickinson College in the Borough of Carlisle in the
County of Cumberland:"

And whereas a number of the surviving trustees in the said
patent named and also a number of the inhabitants of the said
borough of Carlisle have presented a petition to this house
setting forth the substance of the said patent and stating also
that the trustees of Dickinson College have at a considerable
expense erected buildings on the said lot for the said college,
in which it hath been kept since the establishment thereof to
the present time and further setting forth that the petitioners
conceive that the good intentions of the said late proprietaries
are fully answered by the establishment of the said college in
Carlisle, as there is annexed to it a very respectable grammar
school, which is under the direction of the principal and under
the immediate care of a professor of languages and assistant
tutors:

Therefore the petitioners pray that this house would pass a
law to vest the said lot of land and premises with the appurtenances in the trustees of Dickinson College in the borough
of Carlisle in the county of Cumberland and their successors
for the use of the said college forever:

And whereas this house is satisfied of the truth of the facts
set forth as aforesaid and that it is the desire of the inhabitants
of Carlisle for whose use and benefit the said lot of ground was
granted as aforesaid that the same should be vested in the trustees of Dickinson College aforesaid for the use of the said college:

[Section I.] (Section II, P. L.) Be it therefore enacted and it
is hereby enacted by the Representatives of the Freemen of the
Commonwealth of Pennsylvania in General Assembly met and

by the authority of the same, That the said lot of ground so as aforesaid bounded and described and also all and singular the houses, buildings, edifices and improvements thereon made and erected and premises with the appurtenances to the same belonging or in anywise appertaining and the reversion and reversions, remainder and remainders thereof and all the estate, right, title, interest, claim and demand whatsoever of the said John Montgomery, Robert Miller, John Armstrong, James Wilson, Robert Magaw, Stephen Duncan, William Lyon and William Irwin the surviving trustees in the said patent named of, in, to and out of the premises with the appurtenances, shall from and after the passing of this act be vested in the trustees of Dickinson College in the borough of Carlisle, in the county of Cumberland and their successors forever for the use of the said college.

Passed October 3, 1788.   Recorded L. B. No. 3, p. 404.

CHAPTER MCCCLXX.

AN ACT IN AID OF AN ACT OF THE DELAWARE STATE FOR THE SETTLEMENT OF THE ACCOUNTS OF THE WILMINGTON LOTTERY.

(Section I, P. L.) Whereas by an act of the general assembly of Delaware entitled, "An act for the settlement of the accounts of the Wilmington lottery," passed at Dover on the third day of February one thousand seven hundred and eighty-seven it is enacted [that] James Gibbons, Joseph Smallcross, Thomas May, Vincent Bonsall and Isaac Hendrickson, gentlemen, all of the borough of Wilmington in the said state, or any three or more of them, be authorized, directed and empowered to settle and adjust all matters that now are or may afterwards arise in dispute respecting the said lottery and to call the managers of the said lottery before them and all other persons concerned or employed by and under them in the sale or disposal of tickets in the same for the purpose of a full and final settlement of the accounts of the same and appropriation of the profits and proceeds thereof according to the true intent and meaning of the original scheme and design of the same as set forth and expressed in the preamble of the said act:

And whereas the said James Gibbons, Joseph Shallcross, Thomas May, Vincent Bonsall and Isaac Hendrickson, or any three or more of them have full power and authority by the said act to call for the attendance of the said managers and every of them, their heirs, executors or administrators on giving them and each of them as the case may require fifteen days notice in writing of the time or times of such meeting and to bring their accounts and vouchers ready prepared for such settlement and in case the said managers or their legal representatives or any of them or any other person or persons who were employed in the sale or disposition of tickets in the said lottery under the said managers or any of them shall refuse to attend after such notice duly given as aforesaid, the said James Gibbons, Joseph Shallcross, Thomas May, Vincent Bonsall and Isaac Hendrickson or any three or more of them shall proceed to the settlement and adjustment of the said accounts to the best of their judgment ex parte and according to such evidence as may be offered to them by the other managers and parties attending and the said James Gibbons, Joseph Shallcross, Thomas May, Vincent Bonsall and Isaac Hendrickson or any three or more of them have full power and authority to issue their summons under their hands and seals to compel the appearance and attendance of such person or persons as can give any necessary evidence touching the adjustment and settlement of the said accounts, who shall be examined upon oath or affirmation to be administered by any justice of the peace of the county, &c., which said evidences so as aforesaid [summoned] are ordered and obliged by the said act to give their attendance under such pains and penalties as the court of common pleas in such case of neglect and refusal might and of right could order and inflict and such attending witnesses to be allowed the like per diem pay as witnesses in other cases in the common law courts to be paid by such delinquent manager three or more of them, the said commissioners to make due return and report under their hands and seals to the court of common pleas of the county of New Castle or to the supreme court or party as shall be adjudged by the said commissioners, or any of the said Delaware state, which may sit next ensuing the date of said report, of all suc hmatters and things as relate to the premises upon which report being so made and returned, such judgment, execution or process shall accordingly and without delay be awarded as is and has heretofore been the practice of the said court in cases of reports of auditors under rules of reference:

And whereas it hath been represented to this general assembly that although five-sixths of the net profits or proceeds of the said lottery were to be applied towards pious uses within this state, namely, the building a church to be called Saint John's Church in the Northern Liberties of the city of Philadelphia, and a proportionable number of tickets were sold to citizens of this state, yet a settlement of the accounts of the said lottery cannot be obtained, because the act of the assembly of Delaware state (as in part above recited) cannot enable the commissioners therein named to compel the appearance of persons [residing] out of the said state for the purpose of giving evidence or of settling and adjusting the said accounts:

For remedy whereof and in aid of the said act of assembly of the Delaware state:

[Section I.] (Section II, P. L.) Be it enacted by the General Assembly of the Commonwealth of Pennsylvania and by the authority of the same, That the said James Gibbons, Joseph Shallcross, Thomas May, Vincent Bonsal and Isaac Hendrickson, or any three or more of them, for the purpose of the final adjustment and settlement of the accounts of the said lottery, shall have power to meet within the city of Philadelphia and to exercise within the same and among all the citizens of this state all the [powers] and authority herein before recited and no other and to make due return and report under their hands and seals to the courts of common pleas of the counties of Philadelphia and Chester or either of them as the case may require, or to the supreme court of this state of all such matters

and things as relate to the premises upon which report being
so as aforesaid made and returned to the said courts or any of
them within their proper jurisdiction such judgment, execution
and process, shall accordingly and without delay be awarded,
as is [and] has heretofore been the practice of the said courts,
or any of them, in cases of reports of auditors under rules of
reference, Provided always nevertheless, That if any person or
persons shall deem him, her or themselves aggrieved by the determination of the said [commissioners] he, she or they shall
and may appeal to the court or courts aforesaid in this state
and a trial shall thereupon be had by a jury of the county according to the laws of this state, Provided also, That the said
managers shall previous to their issuing any summons or process, which they are hereby authorized to issue, apply to some
justice of the common pleas of this state who shall examine
into the cause and necessity of issuing the same and if the said
justice shall approve thereof and not otherwise, he shall and
may sign and allow the same and the said summons or process
shall not be valid without such signature and allowance.

Passed October 2, 1788.   Recorded L. B. No. 3, p. 415.

CHAPTER MCCCLXXI.

.AN ACT TO RECOMPENSE JOHN HAGUE FOR INTRODUCING INTO THIS
STATE A USEFUL MACHINE FOR CARDING COTTON.

(Section I, P. L.) Whereas John Hague in introducing into
this state a carding machine by means of which the establishment of a proposed extensive cotton manufactory may be
greatly facilitated has thereby rendered a public service worthy
of being recompensed by the legislature:

[Section I.] (Section II, P. L.) Be it enacted and it is hereby
enacted by the Representatives of the Freemen of the Commonwealth of Pennsylvania in General Assembly met and by
the authority of the same, That the supreme executive council

be authorized and directed and they are hereby authorized and
directed to draw their warrant in favor of John Hague on the
treasurer of this state for the sum of one hundred pounds as a
premium for the service rendered as aforesaid, the same to be
paid out of any of the moneys of the state not specially appropriated.

Passed October 3, 1788.   Recorded L. B. No. 3, p. 418.

CHAPTER MCCCLXXII.

AN ACT FOR THE PAYMENT OF AN ADDITIONAL SUM OF MONEY TO
GUNNING BEDFORD AND OTHERS FOR THEIR SERVICES IN ERECT-
ING A TRIUMPHAL ARCH IN THE CITY OF PHILADELPHIA.

(Section I, P. L.) Whereas the general assembly by their resolution passed on the second day of December one thousand
seven hundred and eighty-three did direct that a triumphal
arch should be erected at the upper end of Market street between Sixth and Seventh streets in the city of Philadelphia
to make public demonstration of joy on the definite treaty of
peace between the United States and Great Britain:

And whereas the sum mentioned and directed to be paid by
the tenor of the said resolution was inadequate to the design
and original plan, the completion of which amounted to more
than had been originally intended (but necessarily) as the expense accruing therefor:

And whereas it is but reasonable and just that due and full
compensation ought and of justice should be done to the person
or persons employed in constructing and erecting the said triumphal arch and that they should receive full and ample satisfaction therefor:

[Section I.] (Section II, P. L.) Be it enacted and it is hereby
enacted by the Representatives of the Freemen of the Commonwealth of Pennsylvania in General Assembly [met] and
by the authority of the same, That the executive council of this

commonwealth be authorized and they are hereby authorized to draw an order upon the treasurer of this state for the payment of the sum of one hundred and eighty-five pounds, money of Pennsylvania, being the full remaining balance of their account, which said order is to be drawn in favor of Gunning Bedford and others concerned in erecting the said triumphal arch.

Passed October 3, 1788.   Recorded L. B. No. 3, p. 420.

CHAPTER MCCCLXXIII.

AN ACT DIRECTING THE TIME, PLACES AND MANNER OF HOLDING ELECTIONS FOR REPRESENTATIVES OF THIS STATE IN THE CONGRESS OF THE UNITED STATES AND FOR APPOINTING ELECTORS ON THE PART OF THIS STATE FOR CHOOSING A PRESIDENT AND VICE-PRESIDENT OF THE UNITED STATES.

(Section 1, P. L.) Whereas the constitution of the United States declares and directs that "The house of representatives in the congress of United States shall be composed of members chosen every second year by the people of the several states; that the electors in each state shall have the requisite qualifications of electors of the most numerous branch of the state legislature"; that until the enumeration therein pointed out of the citizens of the United States shall be made, the number of representatives for this state shall be eight, [and] that "the times, places, and manner of holding elections for senators and representatives shall be prescribed in each state by the legislature thereof":

And whereas it is further declared and directed in and by the said constitution, that for the purposes of choosing a president and vice-president of the United States, "each state shall appoint in such manner as the legislature thereof may direct a number of electors equal to the whole number of senators and representatives to which the state may be entitled in the congress":

And whereas the convention which framed the said constitution resolved that as soon as [the conventions of] nine

states should have ratified the said constitution the United
States in Congress assembled should fix a day on which electors should be appointed by the state which should have ratified
the same and a day on which the electors should assemble to
vote for the president, and the time and place for commencing
proceedings under the said constitution. And that after such
publication the electors should be appointed and the senators
and representatives elected:

And whereas the United States in congress assembled by
their act of the thirteenth day of September in the present
year (reciting that the said constitution had been ratified in
the manner therein [declared] to be sufficient for the establishment of the same) did resolve that the first Wednesday in
January next be the day for appointing electors in the several
states ratifying the said constitution before the said day and
that the first Wednesday in February next be the day for the
electors to assemble in their respective states and vote for a
president:

And whereas a convention duly appointed by the people of
this state did by their act of the twelfth day of December in
the year of our Lord one thousand seven hundred and eighty-
seven in the name of the said people assent to and ratify the
said constitution:

In order therefore to carry the said constitution into effect.

[Section I.] (Section II, P. L.) Be it enacted and it is hereby
enacted by the Representatives of the Freemen of the Commonwealth of Pennsylvania in General Assembly met and by
the authority of the same, That the election of representatives
agreeably to the said constitution and the directions of this
act to serve in the congress of the said United States shall be
held by the citizens thereof qualified to vote for members of
assembly on the last Wednesday in November next, and of
electors agreeably to the said constitution on the first Wednesday of January next, of which elections due notice shall
be given by the sheriffs of the respective counties agreeably to
the election laws of this state at the places in the city of Philadelphia and in the several counties of this state prescribed by

the election laws aforesaid, in like manner as in and by the
said election laws is directed for the election of members of
the general assembly of this state. And all and every officer
and person whose duty it is or may be to attend, conduct and
regulate according to the election laws of this state the general
election to be held on the second Tuesday in October next, are
hereby authorized, enjoined and required to attend, conduct
and regulate the elections herein directed to be held for the
purposes aforesaid, in like manner as in and by the said election law is directed and the several powers and authorities to
them given by the laws of this state relating to the election of
members of assembly of this state are and shall be continued
and vested in the said officers and persons respectively for the
purposes of holding and conducting the said elections to be
held in pursuance of the directions of this act, as fully and
effectually to all intents and purposes as if the powers and
authorities aforesaid were herein particularly enumerated and
expressed, and in case of the death, absence or inability of
any of the said officers or persons before the holding the elections in and by this act directed to be held, others shall be
chosen or appointed in their stead according to the directions
of the said election laws and all and every person and persons
who shall or may be guilty of any neglect or abuse of the said
election laws or of any part thereof at any election to be held
in pursuance of this act shall be prosecuted and punished in
the same manner as if he or they, was or were guilty of the
like neglects, abuses or breaches of the said election laws in
the election of representatives to serve in the general assembly
of this state.

[Section II.] (Section III, P. L.) And be it further enacted
by the authority aforesaid, That every person coming to elect
representatives shall deliver in writing on one ticket or piece
of paper the names of eight persons to be voted for as representatives and that every person coming to vote for electors
agreeably to the said constitution and the directions of this
act shall deliver in writing on ticket or piece of paper the names
of ten persons to be voted for as electors agreeably to the said

constitution and for the purposes therein mentioned. The said
persons so voted for as representatives and electors to be
selected from the citizens and inhabitants of the state
at large who [are] duly qualified according to the said constitution to serve in the said respective stations, which said
tickets or ballots shall be received and dealt with in like
manner with those delivered in at the general elections for
members of assembly and councillors of this state.

[Section III.] (Section IV, P. L.) And be it further enacted
by the authority aforesaid, That after the polls in the several
districts shall be closed and the votes of the electors cast up
in manner and form directed by the laws of this state on that
subject, the names of the several persons voted for at the
several wards and districts in the city of Philadelphia and the
several counties of this state shall be written on parchment
or paper and the number of the votes for each candidate in
the wards and districts fairly enumerated and set down, which
numbers shall be written in words at length and not in figures
only, and the tickets and other papers relating to the elections
shall be sealed up and deposited in manner and form as directed
by the election laws of this state, and on such names and
numbers being so set down and written, the judges of the
several elections in the city of Philadelphia and in each and
every district in all and every county of this state, when assembled at the place for that purpose directed shall respectively within the space of three days after the said election,
sign and seal the papers or instrument on which the same are
so written and shall make out, sign, seal and execute duplicate
returns thereof, one whereof shall be delivered to the prothonotary of the county to be kept safely and one other copy thereof shall be delivered to the sheriff of the proper county to be
delivered or safely transmitted by him within ten days after
each respective election to the secretary of the supreme executive council of this state for the inspection and examination
of the said supreme executive council, and in the city of
Philadelphia and in such counties wherein the said election shall be holden at one place, the said elections shall

be carried on and conducted and the return thereof made in like manner as is herein directed. And the said supreme executive council, after having received the returns, papers and instruments aforesaid, from the said city and each and every of the counties aforesaid, shall enumerate and ascertain the numbers of votes for each and every candidate so as aforesaid chosen as representatives or electors respectively, and shall thereupon declare by proclamation issued by the said Council duly signed by the president and without delay dispersed through the state, the names of the eight persons highest in votes of the electors throughout the state and in consequence duly elected and chosen as representatives of and for the state in the congress of the United States and the names of the ten persons highest in votes and therefore elected as electors agreeably to the constitution aforesaid. And the said supreme executive council shall as soon as conveniently may be after such examination and declaration, transmit the same, together with the documents on which it is founded to the secretary of the United States in Congress assembled to be by him delivered to the house of representatives in the congress of the United States when they shall be assembled at the time and place by the present congress of the United States directed and fixed on.

[Section IV.] (Section V, P. L.) And be it further enacted by the authority aforesaid, That the electors so as aforesaid to be chosen shall assemble on the first Wednesday in February next at the borough of Reading and shall perform the duties enjoined on them by the said constitution agreeably to the directions thereof. And the same allowance of mileage and daily wages when travelling to, remaining at and returning from the place aforesaid shall be paid them and each and every of them as is by law allowed and paid to members of assembly of this commonwealth, the same to be paid by the treasurer of this state or the treasurer of the counties in which such electors respectively reside on warrants signed by the president of the meeting of such electors, if any they shall choose or by the majority of such electors exclusive of the per-

son in whose favor such warrants may or shall be respectively
drawn.

Passed October 4, 1788.   Recorded L. B. No. 3, p. 421.

CHAPTER MCCCLXXIV.

A SUPPLEMENT TO THE ACT ENTITLED "AN ACT TO ENFORCE THE
DUE COLLECTION AND PAYMENT OF TAXES WITHIN THIS COMMON-
WEALTH."[1]

(Section I, P. L.) Whereas the mode of compelling the payment of taxes directed to be raised by the act entitled "An
act for furnishing the quota of this state towards paying the
annual interest of the debts of the United States and for funding and paying the interest of the public debts of this state,"[2]
is found to be tedious and liable to abuse:

For remedy whereof:

[Section I.] (Section II, P. L.) Be it enacted and it is hereby
enacted by the Representatives of the Freemen of the Commonwealth of Pennsylvania in General Assembly met and by
the authority of the same, That if any person or persons who
is or are or have been rated or assessed by virtue of the said
recited act and in pursuance of the directions thereof shall refuse or neglect to pay and satisfy the sum or sums of money
which he, she or they is, are or have been so as aforesaid rated
and assessed, for the space of forty days after the same shall
be demanded of him by the collector of the proper township,
ward or district, or if any person or persons who shall be so
as aforesaid rated and assessed in pursuance of the said recited
act in any sum or sums of money, shall refuse or neglect to
pay the sum or sums of money for which he, she or they shall
be so as aforesaid rated or assessed, within the time in and
by the said act limited for the payment thereof to the collector

[1] Passed March 24, 1786, Chapter 1218.
[2] Passed March 16, 1785, Chapter 1137.

10—XIII

such as have been or shall be allowed them as aforesaid) the treasurer of the proper county is hereby authorized and required to issue his warrant under his hand and seal to the sheriff of the proper county directed commanding him to take the body and seize and secure all the estates, real and personal, of such delinquent or which shall come into the hands or possession of his heirs, executors or administrators and to make return thereof to the said treasurer at such time as he shall have apopinted by his said warrant.

[Section IV.] (Section V, P. L.) And be it further enacted by the authority aforesaid, That if the money so as aforesaid detained by such delinquent collector or for which he shall be as aforesaid accountable shall not be paid, together with all reasonable costs, within twenty days next after such seizure as aforesaid, the said treasurer shall by another warrant under his hand and seal to the said sheriff directed authorize and require him to sell and dispose, at public vendue (after having given twenty days public notice thereof) all such estate real and personal of such delinquent collector as he shall have as aforesaid seized and secured or so much thereof as shall be sufficient to satisfy and discharge such deficiency or deficiencies, together with all reasonable costs and charges, and the said sheriff shall pay to the said county treasurer so much of the money (if so much there shall be) arising from such sales as will be sufficient to pay and discharge such deficiencies and shall return the overplus, if any there be after all costs and charges are deducted, to the owner or owners, and where any lands tenements or hereditaments shall be sold by such sheriff in pursuance of this act, he shall convey the same by a deed, duly sealed and executed which shall convey all such right and estate as the delinquent had therein.

[Section V.] (Section VI, P. L.) And be it further enacted by the authority aforesaid, That if any justice or justices shall neglect or refuse within twenty days after demand made by the treasurer of any county within this state to render an account of all moneys received for taxes by the said justice or justices and also to pay the said moneys to such county treasurer or treasurers, a warrant or warrants shall be issued against such justice or justices in like manner as is herein-before directed for proceedings against delinquent collectors and such proceedings shall thereon be had to final judgment, execution and sale as are in and by this act directed respecting delinquent collectors. Provided always nevertheless, That nothing in this act contained shall be construed to prevent or impede the continuance or due prosecution to final judgment, execution and effect of any proceedings which have already been commenced under the said recited act, but the same shall be continued and prosecuted in like manner as if this act had not been made.

[Section VI.] (Section VII, P. L.) And be it further enacted by the authority aforesaid, That in case of neglect or refusal by any county treasurer to pay into the hands of the state treas-urer within twenty days after the settlement made with the comptroller-general and due notice thereof given to the state treasurer, any sum or sums of money belonging to this com-monwealth, received as taxes under the laws of the state, that then in such case the like proceedings shall be had by warrants from the state treasurer as are herein directed for the speedy recovery of public moneys in the hands of delinquent collectors, the balances due from such county treasurers to be ascertained on the settlements directed by the laws of this state to be made with the comptroller general who is hereby directed to make return to the state treasurer of the amount of such balances and settlements to the end that proceedings may be had as herein directed against any county treasurer or treasurers ap-pearing thereby to be in arrears to the state.

[Section VII.] (Section VIII, P. L.) And be it further en-acted by the authority aforesaid, That so much of the laws of this commonwealth as respect the collecting and paying of taxes as are hereby altered or suplied be and they are hereby repealed.

Passed October 4, 1788. Recorded L. B. No. 3, p. 425. See the Note to the Act of Assembly passed March 24, 1786, Chapter 1216 and the Act of Assembly passed March 28, 1789, Chapter 1424.

CHAPTER MCCCLXXV.

AN ACT FOR THE BETTER ASCERTAINING AND MAKING GOOD LOSSES
OF PUBLIC MONEYS BY ROBBERIES.

(Section 1, P. L.) Whereas sundry petitions have been preferred to this house by the collectors of taxes of different counties of this state setting forth that they have been robbed of divers sums of public moneys and praying to be exonerated from the payment thereof:

And whereas it would be unjust and severe to compel individuals from whom such sum or sums have been taken by force and violence and without their privity, connivance or consent to make good the loss or losses sustained thereby:

And whereas [inquiries] into the facts and circumstances alleged by such petitioners can be more properly and conveniently had in the respective counties wherein the said alleged robberies are set forth to have happened:

[Section 1.] (Section 11, P. L.) Be it therefore enacted and it is hereby enacted by the Representatives of the Freemen of the Commonwealth of Pennsylvania in General Assembly met and by the authority of the same, That in all cases wherein any collector or collectors of public money, their executors and administrators have before the passing of this act by their petitions to the general assembly prayed to be exonerated from the payment of such sum or sums of the public moneys aforesaid as any such collector or collectors has or have, before the passing of this act, made oath or affirmation before any judge of the supreme court or justice of the peace within this commonwealth of their having been robbed, the commissioners of the said respective counties shall cause suits to be instituted against such collector or collectors, their executors or administrators in the supreme court or in any county court of common pleas within this commonwealth in which the said robbery or robberies is or are alleged to have been committed, for all

such sum or sums of money which they, the said collector or
collectors, shall be found in arrear or which shall be demanded
from him or them, their executors or administrators, for or
on account of public taxes received or collected by him or
them: and in such suits the said collector or collectors, their
executors or administrators shall plead the general issue with
any other plea or pleas by leave of the court, and trial shall
be had by a jury of the country and the said collector or collectors, their executors or administrators, shall and may give
the special matter in evidence, and if it shall appear by legal
evidence to the said court or courts and juries that the said
collector or collectors were, before the passing of this act,
robbed of the sum or sums of public money of which he or they,
their executors or administrators have claimed in manner
aforesaid to be exonerated, and that no fraud or connivance at
or in the said robbery or robberies can be reasonably charged
on such collector or collectors and that prudential means for securing the moneys have not been neglected, then and in such
case the said jury or juries shall find for the defendant and
judgment shall be entered accordingly.

[Section II.] (Section III, P. L.) And be it further enacted
by the authority aforesaid, That where it shall be found in
manner aforesaid that any loss or losses were before the passing of this act sustained by said collector or collectors in manner aforesaid and the fact and the sum or sums shall be legally
ascertained and established as aforesaid, the commissioners of
the proper county shall give credit to and exonerate the said
collector or collectors, their executors or administrators from
the payment of such sum or sums of money so proved to have
been lost in manner aforesaid and shall forthwith assess, levy,
quota and cause to be collected from the proper county at large
all such sum or sums of public moneys lost as aforesaid together with legal costs sustained on such trial or trials in due
proportion from the several townships in like manner and
under the same powers and regulations as are or shall be given
[and] established by the laws of the state for raising taxes for

funding the debts and redeeming the bills of credit of this
state.

[Section III.] (Section IV, P. L.) And be it further enacted
by the authority aforesaid, That in all cases wherein such
oath or affirmation of any such robbery or robberies having
been committed has been made in manner aforesaid by any
such collector or collectors, and in which such collector or
collectors, his or their executors or administrators have in
manner aforesaid claimed to be exonerated from the payment
of any such money as aforesaid for the causes aforesaid, and
have, notwithstanding, paid the same or any part or parts
into the treasury of the proper county, it shall and may
be lawful for any collector or collectors, his or their executors or administrators, to commence and prosecute in any
of the courts aforesaid against the treasurer of the proper
county, his or their action or actions for the recovery thereof,
in which said action or actions, such proceedings and trials
as are hereinbefore mentioned shall be had and on due proof
being made of such robbery or robberies having been committed in manner aforesaid, before the passing of this act, such
collector or collectors, his or their executors or administrators
shall have and recover such sum or sums as shall have been
paid by him or them and of which it shall be proved in manner
aforesaid that such collector or collectors were before the
passing of this act robbed in manner aforesaid, and in every
such case the commissioners of the proper county shall forthwith assess, levy, quota and cause to be collected from the
proper county at large all such sum or sums as shall have
been recovered by such collector or collectors, his or their executors or administrators in manner aforesaid together with
the costs of suit, in due proportions from the several townships
in like manner and under the same powers and regulations as
are or shall be given and established by the laws of this commonwealth, for raising taxes for funding the debts and redeeming the bills of credit thereof.

Passed October 4, 1788. Recorded L. B. No. 3, p. 428. See the
Act of Assembly passed February 27, 1798, Chapter 1968.

CHAPTER MCCCLXXVI.

A SUPPLEMENT TO AN ACT OF GENERAL ASSEMBLY ENTITLED "AN ACT FOR ERECTING THE SOUTHERN SUBURBS OF THE CITY OF PHILADELPHIA INTO THE DISTRICT OF SOUTHWARK, FOR MAKING THE STREETS AND ROADS ALREADY LAID OUT THEREIN PUBLIC ROADS AND HIGHWAYS AND FOR REGULATING SUCH OTHER STREETS AND ROADS AS THE INHABITANTS THEREOF MAY HERE- AFTER LAY OUT AND FOR OTHER USES AND PURPOSES THEREIN MENTIONED.[1]

(Section I, P. L.) Whereas the district of Southwark is become populous and in many places closely built and requires some regulations. And in the act to which this is a supplement no provision is made for the erecting of public pumps to supply the inhabitants with water and secure them against the ravages of fire nor for regulating the descent of water courses or common sewers, all which are essentially necessary in cities and close built towns and whereas the pitching and paving the streets, lanes and alleys of the said district will greatly tend to the improvement thereof and the lighting and watching the same by night will be a great convenience and security against fires and robberies as soon as the said district shall be enabled to support the expense thereof:

[Section I.] (Section II, P. L.) Be it therefore enacted and it is hereby enacted by the Representatives of the Freemen of the Commonwealth of Pennsylvania in General Assembly met and by the authority of the same, That the supervisors of the streets, highways and landings, elected or to be elected in pursuance of the act for that purpose made and provided or a majority of them, by and with the consent of one or more of the justices of the peace for the said district or for such district for election of justices of the peace whereof the district of Southwark shall constitute [a] part, and a majority of the regulators of the said district shall from time to time as occasion may require dig such and so many wells and therein fix

---

[1] Passed March 26, 1762, Chapter 481.

pumps in such convenient places within the streets, lanes and alleys of the said district as to them shall appear necessary so as to supply the inhabitants with water in the most equal manner and the said pumps shall be kept in good order at the charge of the said district forever.

And whereas the pumps already fixed in the streets, lanes and alleys of the said district are frequently so much neglected as to be out of repair and totally unfit for use:

[Section II.] (Section III, P. L.) Be it therefore enacted by the authority aforesaid, That it shall and may be lawful for the said supervisors or a majority of them to confer with any person or persons who shall have fixed any pump or pumps in any of the streets, lanes, or alleys in the said district, and if any of them who have so fixed any pump or pumps shall agree to keep them in good order and repair to the satisfaction of a majority of the supervisors, he, she or they shall be entitled to demand and receive yearly for each pump so kept in repair the sum of thirty shillings from the said supervisors out of the public money in their hands and if any person or persons whatsoever, shall demand, exact or receive any sum or sums of money or any other recompense from any person or persons for any water drawn out of any pump or pumps so erected or to be erected within the streets, lanes, or alleys of the said district or shall in anywise molest or hinder any person or persons from drawing water therefrom, he, she or they being legally convicted thereof on the testimony of one or more credible witnesses before any justice of the peace for the said district or for such district for election of justices of the peace, whereof the district of Southwark shall constitute a part, shall forfeit and pay for the first offense the sum of five shillings, and for every subsequent offense ten shillings; the said money accruing by such fines and forfeitures to be applied for the purpose of carrying this act into execution. And if any pump or pumps erected, or to be erected by any private persons within the streets, lanes and alleys of the said district shall be out of repair for the space of two months successively, the same being proved by two reputable freeholders, to the satisfaction of

any justice of the peace for the said district or for such district for election of justices of the peace whereof the district of Southwark shall constitute a part the said justice shall issue an order, under his hand and seal directing the supervisors aforesaid to have such pump or pumps put in[to] good order and repair and so kept at the public charge forever.

[Section III.] (Section IV, P. L.) And be it further enacted by the authority aforesaid, That if any person or persons from and after the passing of this act shall wilfully or maliciously break or carry away the handle, pin or spear of any of the pumps within the said district or otherwise damage or injure any of the said pumps and shall thereof be legally convicted before any justice of the peace for the city and county of Philadelphia, he, she or they shall forfeit and pay to the said supervisors to be applied for the purpose of carrying this act into execution the sum of five pounds for every such offense on the first conviction and for every other such offense committed after the first conviction the sum of ten pounds, and it shall be lawful for the said justice to commit such offender to the common gaol of the said county until the said fines and the costs of prosecution be paid.

[Section IV.] (Section V, P. L.) And be it further enacted by the authority aforesaid, That the said supervisors or a majority of them for the time being and the said regulators or a majority of them, by and with the consent and approbation of one or more of the justices of the peace of the said district shall have full power and authority and they are hereby enjoined and required as soon as conveniently may be to regulate and direct the courses and degrees of descent and the distances from the sides of the streets, lanes and alleys of all and every the gutters, natural water courses and common sewers within the said district and to fix and ascertain the same so that the freeholders shall hereafter know with certainty how to erect their buildings and enclose their grounds in conformity thereto, and if it shall be necessary to carry any common sewer through the ground of any private person or body politic, the damages (if any) which shall or may accrue

to the owner or owners of such ground shall be ascertained
by two indifferent persons mutually to be chosen by the said
supervisors and the said owner or owners which persons not
agreeing shall have power to choose a third person and the
sum of money to be fixed by them or any two of them shall
be paid to the owner or owners by the said supervisors in satisfaction of the said damages out of the public moneys in their
hands and thereupon it shall be lawful for the said supervisors
with all necessary workmen, tools, implements, carts, carriages,
and horses to enter upon the said private grounds whenever
and as often as it shall be necessary, to make, amend, cleanse
and scour such water courses, and common sewers, doing nevertheless as little damage as possible to the adjoining grounds
and always putting up and leaving all enclosures and improvements thereon in as good a state as they were at the time of
their entry thereupon.

[Section VI.] (Section VII, P. L.) And be it further enacted
by the authority aforesaid, That the said supervisors shall, as
soon as conveniently may be after the gutters and water courses
in the streets, lanes, and alleys within the said district are
regulated, cause the same to be pitched or paved with brick or
stone, as the case may require and plant posts to defend the
same from being injured by carriages and also have a footway
paved four feet wide with brick or flat stone and keep an exact
account of the costs and charges arising therefrom and demand
and receive of and from each and every owner of the lots or
grounds opposite to which such gutters or water-courses shall
be so paved and posted the full amount of so much of the
expense thereof as shall be proportionate to the number of
feet front of ground held by such owner or owners respectively.
Provided always nevertheless, That all and every owner and
owners shall have the privilege of paving and pitching their
own fronts as aforesaid, so that they have it completed within
three months after notice given for that purpose by the supervisors or any two of them in writing under their hands. And
in case any owner or owners shall neglect or refuse to pay
such amount for one month after such footway and water

course shall be paved and posted opposite to his, her or their ground, it shall and may be lawful for the said supervisors to recover the same in the same manner and form as debts under forty shillings are by law recoverable.

And in case the grounds belong to minors or absent persons then the same shall be recovered against any person or persons having the care of such grounds belonging to said minor or absent owner and the receipts of the said supervisors for such money shall be good vouchers to all executors, administrators, guardians, trustees, or attorneys in fact against their principals.

[Section VI.] (Section VII, P. L.) And be it further enacted by the authority aforesaid, That if any person or persons shall wilfully or maliciously obstruct or stop up any public watercourse or common sewer already made or to be made and established within the said district and shall be thereof legally convicted in any court of record having jurisdiction within the county of Philadelphia, he, she or they shall forfeit and pay for such offense any sum to be fixed and assessed by such court not less than ten nor exceeding fifty pounds and for a repetition of the offense after the first conviction any sum not less than twenty nor exceeding one hundred pounds, which sums shall go to the [said] supervisors for the purpose of carrying this act into execution.

And in order to defray the costs, charges and expenses of carrying this act into execution:

[Section VII.] (Section VIII, P. L.) Be it further enacted by the authority aforesaid, That it shall and may be lawful for the said supervisors and the assessors of the said district together with one or more of the justices of the peace to meet at some convenient place and lay and assess a tax on the inhabitants and landed estate within the said district in the same manner and at the same time with the road tax in the act to which this is a supplement. Provided nevertheless, That the tax to be laid by virtue of this act shall not exceed two shillings and sixpence on every hundred pounds, agreeably to the county rates, without any exceptions in favor of mechanics, manufacturers or others.

And whereas inconveniences may arise from the elections for regulators and supervisors being held on the third Saturday in April and from a total change of them at any future election which may be prevented by an alteration in the time of election and continuing some of them for a longer time than one year:

[Section VIII.] (Section IX, P. L.) Be it therefore further enacted by the authority aforesaid, That from and after the passing of this act the election for choosing regulators and supervisors shall be held on the first Saturday in January annually and agreeably to the directions and restrictions contained in the act to which this is a supplement and that at the election to be held as aforesaid, the proper number of persons to fill both these offices shall be balloted for and he or they composing one equal third part of the number of officers for both these offices respectively, who shall have the greatest number of votes shall be the officers for three years thence next following and he or them composing another equal third part of the number of officers of both those offices respectively who shall have the next greatest number of votes shall be the officers for two years thence next following and he or they composing another equal third part of the number of officers for both these offices respectively who shall have the next or third greatest number of votes shall be the officers for one year thence next following; and that at the election which shall happen as aforesaid next after the said election now next coming, another number of persons sufficient to supply the places of those whose times shall expire by the directions aforesaid shall be chosen and continue in office for the term of three years, and so toties quoties in every year to supply the vacancies which shall arise. Provided always, That no person shall be excluded from the choice of the people on account of his having filled either of the said offices the preceding term of three years. And provided also, that [if] at the now next election two or more persons shall have an equal number of votes for the same office the term

for which each of them shall serve shall be determined by lots
to be drawn by the inspectors and judges of the election immediately after casting up the votes.

[Section IX.] (Section X, P. L.) And be it further enacted
by the authority aforesaid, That before the said supervisors
shall take upon themselves the duties by this act enjoined and
required, they and each of them shall take an oath or affirmation before one of the justices of the said district, or of such
district for election of justices of the peace whereof the district
of Southwark shall constitute a part, of the following tenor,
to wit: that they will well and truly, to the best of their skill,
knowledge and ability, discharge and fulfill the duties and services enjoined them by this act, that they will use their endeavors to collect the moneys arising as well by the taxes to
be imposed by virtue of this act as by the fines therein mentioned, and will apply the same to the uses and purposes therein
directed and to no other uses or purposes whatsoever.

[Section X.] (Section XI, P. L.) And be it further enacted by
the authority aforesaid, That the said supervisors and regulators shall be allowed out of the moneys arising by virtue of this
act the sum of six shillings each for each and every day they
shall be employed in attending to the services enjoined by this
act in full satisfaction for all their time, trouble and expenses.

[Section XI.] (Section XII, P. L.) And be it further enacted
by the authority aforesaid, That so soon as the services by this
act enjoined are so performed that the tax hereby authorized to
be levied and collected shall be no longer necessary for those
purposes, it shall and may be lawful for the said supervisors to
continue the said tax and to apply the moneys arising thereby
to the pitching and paving the streets, lanes and alleys, the
lighting and watching the said district or such parts thereof as
shall most immediately require to be lighted and watched by
night.

[Section XII.] (Section XIII, P. L.) And be it further enacted by the authority aforesaid, That the justices of the district of Southwark or of such district for the election of justices
of the peace whereof the district of Southwark shall be a part

or any one of them taking to their or his assistance two reputable freeholders of the said district, shall on or before the first Saturday in March in every year from and after the passing of this act, settle the accounts of the supervisors and allow them every reasonable charge, a fair statement of which accounts, shall be published in hand bills, in three or more of the most public places in the district aforesaid (and published in one or more of the newspapers which are most in circulation in the said district) and if any of the said supervisors shall refuse or neglect to settle their accounts as aforesaid, they and each of them refusing or neglecting shall forfeit and pay the sum of twenty pounds over and above the balance which may be found in his or their hands, to be recovered as debts under ten pounds are by law recoverable, to be applied for the purpose of carrying this act into execution.

[Section XIII.] (Section XIV, P. L.) And be it further enacted by the authority aforesaid, That every clause, matter and thing contained in the said act to which this is a supplement which is contradictory or repugnant to or in anywise altered by this act, be and the same is hereby repealed, annulled and made void and of no force and effect whatever.

Passed October 4, 1785. Recorded L. B. No. 3, p. 430.

CHAPTER MCCCLXXVII.

A SUPPLEMENT TO AN ACT ENTITLED "AN ACT FOR REGULATING THE FISHERY IN THE RIVER CONNESTOGA IN THE COUNTY OF LANCASTER."[1]

(Section I, P. L.) Whereas since the passing of an act for regulating the fishery in the river Connestoga in the county of Lancaster passed the twenty-second day of January one thousand seven hundred and seventy-four it has been found that many means and contrivances not guarded against in the said

[1] Passed January 22, 1774, Chapter 694.

law have been used, whereby the fish have been obstructed from
going up the said river and also whereby the spawn, fry or
brood of fish have been destroyed or spoiled:

Wherefore, for remedying such mischiefs and for the more
easy and effectual recovery of fines and forfeitures in this act
mentioned.

[Section I.] (Section II, P. L.) Be it enacted and it is hereby
enacted by the Representatives of the Freemen of the Commonwealth of Pennsylvania In General Assembly met and by
the authority of the same, That if any person or persons whatsoever from and after the passing of this act shall use or practice any of the means specified in the said act to which this is
a supplement to obstruct the said fish from going up the said
river or destroy or spoil any spawn, fry or brood of fish, of any
kind whatsoever or shall, by using any sweep net, draw net,
draught net, cast net, stalker, sturchel or shove net or nets of
any other name or description, or who shall use any seine or
seines (except for taking of shad in due season) in the said river
below the mouth of Muddy creek, for the taking of fish, every
person so offending being thereof legally convicted by the oath
or affirmation of one or more witnesses or by his or her own confession before any justices of the county of Lancaster, shall
forfeit and pay the sum of five pounds lawful money of this
commonwealth for every such offence or suffer two months
imprisonment without bail or mainprize, one moiety of which
forfeiture shall be paid to the informer or prosecutor and the
other moiety to the overseers of the poor of the township or
borough where such offender shall reside.   Provided always
nevertheless, That nothing in this act contained, shall be construed or understood to deprive or hinder any person or persons from drawing a seine or net for the taking of shad fish
from the fifteenth day of April to the twenty-fifth day of May
in every year in any part of the river of Connestoga. And provided also, That if either the prosecutor or person charged with
an offense against this act or the act to which this is a supplement shall be aggrieved by the judgment of the said jus-

11—XIII

tice, then and in such case either party may appeal to the next general quarter sessions of the peace who are to hear and determine the said appeal.

[Section II.] (Section III, P. L.) And be it further enacted by the authority aforesaid, That so much of the aforesaid act as relates to the forfeiture and imprisonment mentioned in the second section of the aforesaid act to which this is a supplement be and is hereby repealed and made null and void, anything to the contrary thereof in the said section contained [notwithstanding].

[Section III.] (Section IV, P. L.) And be it further enacted by the authority aforesaid, That the person or persons who shall hereafter prosecute in the name of the commonwealth any person offending against this act or the act to which this is a supplement, shall and may be a legal witness to prove such offence either before the justice or on an appeal, notwithstanding he, she or they are to receive one half of the forfeiture as aforesaid.

Passed October 4, 1788.Recorded L. B. No. 3, p. 435.

CHAPTER MCCCLXXVIII.

AN ACT TO GRANT THE SUM OF ONE HUNDRED AND EIGHTY-SEVEN POUNDS TEN SHILLINGS TO CAPTAIN WILLIAM ROSS IN CONSIDERATION OF HIS SERVICES TO THIS COMMONWEALTH.

(Section I, P. L.) Whereas Captain William Ross of the county of Luzerne hath manifested on every requisite occasion a zealous attachment to the government of Pennsylvania and hath been frequently called upon to support the laws of the state in the said county and been employed in suppressing insurrections and checking the violent and lawless proceedings of certain insurgents and rioters who have on many occasions disturbed the peace of the said county and in an attempt to take certain [persons] in the said county who, in violation of

the laws of this state, had captivated Colonel Timothy Picker-
ing, Esquire, the said captain William Ross received several
dangerous wounds which have disabled him from supporting
himself, he thereby having lost the use of his right hand and
being subjected to other bodily infirmities. And it being the
duty of this house to reward the faithful services of those who
expose their lives in defence of the laws and to relieve the distresses brought on individuals by such their laudable exertions:

[Section I.] (Section II, P. L.) Be it enacted and it is hereby
enacted by the Representatives of the Freemen of the Commonwealth of Pennsylvania in General Assembly met and by
the authority of the same, That the president or vice-president
in council be and they are hereby authorized and empowered
to draw an order on the state treasurer for the sum of one
hundred and eighty-seven pounds ten shillings in favor of the
said Captain William Ross as a full compensation and reward
for his services and all charges and expenses incurred by him
or chargeable to this state for or on account of the said
premises.

Passed October 4, 1788. Recorded L. B. No. 3, p. 416.

CHAPTER MCCCLXXIX.

AN ACT FOR REWARDNO THE PERSON OR PERSONS CONCERNED IN
APPREHENDING GEORGE SINCLAIRE ATTAINTED BY OUTLAWRY.

(Section I, P. L.) Whereas it hath been represented to this
house by the petition of David Linton that in the month of
March last he apprehended in the town of Manheim in the
county of Lancaster and safely lodged in the gaol of the said
county a certain George Sinclaire, who had been duly attainted
by outlawry in the supreme court of this state from several
robberies, burglaries and felonies by him committed within the
same:

And whereas it is just and proper that due encouragement be given to such as shall exert themselves in apprehending such malefactors:

[Section I.] (Section II, P. L.) Be it enacted and is it hereby enacted by the Representatives of the Freemen of the Commonwealth of Pennsylvania in General Assembly met and by the authority of the same, That the supreme executive council be and they are hereby authorized and empowered to draw an order on the treasurer of this state for the sum of fifty pounds in favor of the person or persons who was or were concerned in apprehending the said George Sinclaire, as aforesaid. And in case it shall appear to the executive council that other person or persons than the said David Linton were assisting in the taking the said malefactor so as justly to be entitled to a part or parts of the said sum herein granted, then the executive council are hereby authorized, empowered and directed to distribute the said sum to and among the said David Linton and his associates in such shares and proportions as to the executive council shall seem proper.

Passed October 4, 1788. Recorded L. B. No. 3, p. 437.

CHAPTER MCCCLXXX.

AN ACT TO INCORPORATE THE MEMBERS OF THE RELIGIOUS SOCIETY OF GERMAN ROMAN CATHOLICS OF THE CHURCH CALLED THE HOLY TRINITY IN THE CITY OF PHILADELPHIA.

(Section 1, P. L.) Whereas the members of the German religious society of Roman Catholics belonging to the church called the Holy Trinity and residing within the city of Philadelphia and the vicinity thereof have represented that they have at a considerable expense, purchased a lot of ground at the northwest corner of Spruce and Sixth streets in the said city, and nearly completed a house or church for the public worship of Almighty God, called the Holy Trinity, and have prayed to be incorporated and by law enabled to receive such donations

and bequests as have or hereafter may be made to their said
society as well as to manage the temporalities of their said
church as other religious societies within this commonwealth
may or can do, and it being just and reasonable as well as
conformable to the spirit of the constitution that the prayer
of their petition be granted:

Therefore:

[Section I.] (Section II, P. L.) Be it enacted and it is hereby
enacted by the Representatives of the Freemen of the Commonwealth of Pennsylvania in General Assembly met and by
the authority of the same. That the German subscribers and
others being or who shall hereafter become members of the
said religious society of German Roman Catholics now or hereafter worshipping at the said church called the Holy Trinity,
are and from and immediately after the passing of this act
shall be and they are hereby erected into and declared to be
one body politic and corporate in deed and in law, by the name,
style and title of "The Trustees of the German Religious society
of Roman Catholics of the Holy Trinity Church in the city of
Philadelphia," and that they the said trustees and their successors to be elected as hereinafter mentioned by the name
aforesaid shall have perpetual succession and shall be able and
capable in law to purchase, take, have, hold, receive and enjoy
to them and their successors in fee simple or for any lesser
estate, any lands, tenements, rents, hereditaments or real
estate, whose yearly value in the whole shall not exceed the
sum of five hundred pounds, by grant, gift, bargain and sale,
will, devise or otherwise and also to purchase, take, hold, possess and enjoy any moneys, goods, chattels or personal [estate]
whatsoever, by gift, grant, will legacy or bequest and the same
lands, tenements, rents, hereditaments and real and person
estate excepting always the said church called the Holy Trinity
and the lot of ground and appurtenances thereto belonging or
therewith now used or occupied, to give, grant, demise or otherwise dispose of as to them shall seem meet for the use of the
said religious society and also that the said trustees by the
name aforesaid shall be able and capable in law to sue and be

sued, implead and be impleaded, answer and be answered unto,
defend and be defended, in any suits or actions, and in all or
any of the courts or jurisdictions whatsoever. And that it
shall and may be lawful for the said trustees by the name aforesaid, to devise, make, have and use one common seal, to authenticate all and every the acts, deeds and instruments touching
their business and the same at pleasure to break, alter and
renew and generally that the said trustees by the name aforesaid shall have, hold and enjoy all and singular the rights,
privileges, liberties and franchises incident and belonging to
a private and religious corporation and body politic as fully
and effectually as any other private or religious corporation or
body politic within this state has right to have, hold and enjoy
the same.

[Section II.] (Section III, P. L.) And be it further enacted
by the authority aforesaid, That the first trustees of the said
corporation shall be and consist of the following persons, viz.,
the eldest pastor of the said church for the time being, George
Ernest Lechler, Senior, James Oellers, Christopher Shorty,
Senior, Henry Horne, Adam Premir, Anthony Hooky, Jacob
Threin and Charles Bauman, all members of said corporation
and subscribers towards the building of said [church].

And the future trustees of the said corporation shall be and
consist of the eldest pastor of the said church for the time
being, duly appointed, and of eight lay members of the congregation, worshipping in and contributors to the said church
to be appointed and elected in the manner hereinafter mentioned.

[Section III.] (Section IV, P. L.) And be it further enacted
by the authority aforesaid, That all and every the members of
the said church having subscribed to the building of the same
or who shall hereafter contribute any sum of money not less
than ten shillings annually, towards the support of the said
church, shall meet on Monday immediately after Whit-Sunday
which will be in the year of our Lord one thousand seven hundred and ninety and so on in every year forever thereafter at
such place in the said city as shall be appointed by the said
trustees, whereof notice shall be given in the said church at

the beginning of Divine Worship on Whit-Sunday in the morning and then and there shall choose by ballot the said eight
lay trustees in manner aforesaid by a majority of those members qualified to vote as aforesaid who shall so meet between
the hours of one and three of the clock in the afternoon of
every such day and the [trustees so chosen shall be and con-
tinue] trustees of the said corporation until the next election
and on the Sunday next after every such election the trustees
so elected shall be published in the said church and their names
entered in the books of the said corporation for that purpose
to be kept and the said eldest pastor for the time being so
appointed and members so chosen trustees as aforesaid shall
be and continue trustees of the said corporation until the
close of the next election at which time and place they shall be
prepared with and render a just and true account of all the
moneys by them received and expended for the use and benefit
of the said corporation and congregation the preceding year
which accounts shall be signed by the eldest pastor aforesaid
for the time being as well as the other trustees.

[Section IV.] (Section V, P. L.) And be it further enacted
by the authority aforesaid, That all and every the person and
persons in whom any estate real or personal whatsoever is
or shall be at the time of passing this act, vested for the use of
the regular members of the said congregation of German
Roman Catholics hereafter worshipping at the said church
called the Holy Trinity of or for any estate or interest whatsoever, shall and they are hereby enjoined and required upon the
reasonable requests and proper costs and charges of the said
trustees by good and sufficient conveyances and assurances in
the law to convey and assure, assign, transfer and set over to
the said trustees by the name aforesaid and to their successors
and assigns forever, all and every the messuages, lots, lands,
tenements, rents, hereditaments and estate, real and personal
whatsoever, whereof he or they are or shall be seized or possessed as aforesaid, to have and to hold the same to the said
trustees, their successors and assigns, to and for the use of
the society of German Roman Catholics, now or hereafter wor-

shipping at the said Church called the Holy Trinity, forever.
Provided nevertheless, That nothing in this act shall extend
to any property whatsoever which now belongs to the congregation of the religious society of Roman Catholics worshipping in the church of Saint Mary's or of the clergymen officiating in the said church of Saint Mary's. And provided, That
nothing in this act shall extend to the lot of ground bought of
James Eddy and now used as a burial ground for the Germans.

[Section V.] (Section VI, P. L.) And be it further enacted
by the authority aforesaid, That it shall and may be lawful to
and for the said trustees and their successors from time to time
as occasion shall require to meet together for the purpose of
transacting the business of the society under their care, of the
time and place of which meetings due notice shall be given
to all the said trustees at least one day before, at which meeting the eldest pastor aforesaid being present shall be president
and if five of the said trustees shall attend they shall form a
quorum or board and shall have power by a majority of votes
present to make, ordain and establish such rules, orders and
regulations for the management of the temporal business, the
government of their schools and disposing of the estate of the
said corporation, as to them shall seem proper. Provided, That
such rules, orders and regulations shall be reasonable in themselves and not repugnant to the constitution and laws of this
state. And provided also, That in the disposal or alienation of
the estate of the said congregation and corporation the consent
and concurrence of the major part of the regular members of
the said church qualified to vote as aforesaid shall be first
had and obtained.

Passed October 40, 1788. Recorded L. B. No. 8, p. 437.

CHAPTER MCCLXXXI.

AN ACT FOR THE RELIEF OF SARAH CALDWELL.

(Section I, P. L.) Whereas it appears that Sarah Caldwell on the eighteenth day of January in the year of our Lord one thousand seven hundred and eighty-eight was the holder of the following certificates, issued from the office of the comptroller-general of the state of Pennsylvania agreeable to the act of [general] assembly passed the first day of March in the year of our Lord one thousand seven hundred and eighty-six:[1] that is to say, number eight thousand four hundred and thirty-six, to Andrew Caldwell, for seven hundred and thirty-four pounds twelve shillings and sixpence; number three thousand three hundred and forty-three, to Andrew Caldwell, for six hundred and forty-nine pounds eleven shillings and two-pence; number three thousand three hundred and forty-four, five hundred and eighty-six pounds ten shillings; number three thousand three hundred and fifty-four, to Sarah Caldwell, for twenty-one pounds sixteen shillings and five pence; number three thousand three hundred and fifty-five, to Sarah Caldwell, for twenty-three pounds fifteen shillings and nine pence; number three thousand three hundred and fifty-six, to Sarah Caldwell, for sixty-six pounds eighteen shillings and eleven pence; number three thousand three hundred and fifty-seven, to Sarah Caldwell, for forty-one pounds five shillings; number three thousand three hundred and fifty-eight to Sarah Caldwell, thirty-eight pounds six shillings and eight pence; number three thousand three hundred and fifty-nine, to Sarah Caldwell, for one hundred and sixty-five pounds two shillings and six pence, number three thousand three hundred and sixty, to Sarah Caldwell, for one hundred and seventy-one pounds, twelve shillings and four pence; number three thousand three hundred and sixty one, to

[1] Chapter 1202.

Sarah Caldwell, for fourteen pounds one shilling and three pence:

And that she, the said Sarah Caldwell, on the same day, lost the said several certificates amounting in the whole to the sum of two thousand five hundred and thirteen pounds twelve shillings and six pence:

And whereas it appears probable that they have totally perished and the said Sarah Caldwell has applied to this house for relief in the premises, offering to Indemnify the state against the said certificates or any of them if they or any of them should hereafter be found to be undestroyed.

[Section I.] (Section II, P. L.) Be it therefore enacted and it is hereby enacted by the Representatives of the Freemen of the Commonwealth of Pennsylvania in General Assembly met and by the authority of the same, That upon sufficient security being given by the said Sarah Caldwell for the use of the state to his excellency the president of the supreme executive council or in his absence to the vice-president for the time being, to idemnify the state against the said certificates and on the same being duly certified to the comptroller-general for the time being, the said comptroller-general shall and hereby is authorized and directed to certify in favor of the said Sarah Caldwell or her legal representatives to the state treasurer aforesaid, the interest accrued and to accrue on the said sum of two thousand five hundred and thirteen pounds twelve shillings and sixpence, since the last payment of interest on the said certificates up to the time the first certificate of interest shall be made on the said sum of money, and from the date of such first certificate yearly and every year to certify the interest that may thereafter accrue on the said sum, which said respective certificates of the comptroller-general for the time being so to be made of the interest as aforesaid shall be sufficient authority to the state treasurer for the time being to pay the same respectively to the said Sarah Caldwell or her legal representatives. And the treasurer aforesaid is hereby enjoined and required to pay the same accordingly.

[Section II.] (Section III, P. L.) And be it further enacted by the authority aforesaid, That the said interest money so to be paid to the said Sarah Caldwell or her legal representatives shall, as often as it shall be so paid, be deemed and taken and it is hereby declared to be to the same uses as she held the said certificates immediately before the said loss thereof. And the said Sarah Caldwell and such her legal representatives who may receive such interest money shall be accountable to the person or persons respectively who had any legal or equitable interest in the said certificates or in any of them for his, her or their proportional parts of such interest money.

Passed October 4, 1788. Recorded L. B. No. 3, p. 440. See the Act of Assembly passed September 30, 1791, Chapter 1591.

CHAPTER MCCCLXXXII.

AN ACT TO ENABLE SUCH PERSONS WITHIN THIS STATE WHO ARE ENTITLED TO VOTE IN THE ELECTION OF REPRESENTATIVES OF THIS STATE IN THE HOUSE OF REPRESENTATIVES OF THE UNITED STATES AND WHO SHALL BE NECESSARILY OUT OF THEIR RESPECTIVE DISTRICTS AT THE ENSUING ELECTION, TO GIVE THEIR VOTES IN THE SEVERAL PLACES WHERE PUBLIC BUSINESS SHALL REQUIRE THEIR ATTENDANCE.

(Section I, P. L.) Whereas by an act of assembly passed the fourth day of October last past entitled, "An act for directing the time places and manner of holding elections for representatives of this state in the congress of the United States and for appointing electors on the part of this state for choosing a president and vice-president of the United States,"[1] the inhabitants of this state who are or shall be qualified as therein is mentioned are authorized to elect representatives of and for this state in the congress of the United States, at the places of holding the district elections wherein they severally reside:

And whereas the time of holding the said election is the same when the county courts of Chester and Northumberland counties are by law to be held and those persons who are bound by recognizance, summoned as jurymen, subpoenaed as wit-

[1] Chapter 1373.

nesses or have occasion to attend such courts as officers thereof or as parties to suits or otherwise, and the members of the supreme executive council and the general assembly of this commonwealth cannot go to the several places appointed for the election aforesaid and at the same time attend at the other places where their duty requires their appearance and it is reasonable to allow persons necessarily absent from the places of district elections and opportunity of giving their voices in this general election:

[Section I.] (Section II, P. L.) Be it therefore enacted and it is hereby enacted by the Representatives of the Freemen of the Commonwealth of Pennsylvania in General Assembly met and by the authority of the same, That it shall and may be lawful for every person who by law is or shall be entitled to vote under the said recited act of assembly in the choice of representatives of the state of Pennsylvania in the congress of the United States, who resides in the county of Chester or Northumberland or who shall attend either of said courts as an officer thereof or as parties or witnesses or who being a member of the supreme executive council or general assembly of this commonwealth, and who at the time of holding such election for representatives of this state in the congress of the United States shall attend at the place of holding the said county courts or either of them or at the city of Philadelphia in prosecution of public business, to give in his vote or ballot for the choice of representatives of this state in the congress of the United States at the place of holding such courts in the said counties of Chester and Northumberland and in the city of Philadelphia in the same manner and under the same regulations as if he were to deliver such vote or ballot at the place or places appointed for holding elections within the district or districts whereof he is a resident.

[Section II.] Provided always nevertheless, That every person who shall offer a vote at any of the places appointed for holding such elections and not residing within such election district shall, before such vote shall be received, make oath or affirmation (besides other oaths and affirmations requisite to entitle him to vote) that he hath not voted in such election at any other place for members of the house of representatives in the congress of the United States and that he will not afterwards vote in any other place at the election before mentioned.

Passed November [September] 13, 1788. Recorded L. B. No. 8, p. 442.

CHAPTER MCCCLXXXIII.

--

AN ACT TO SUSPEND FOR A LIMITED TIME THE COLLECTION OF ALL MILITIA FINES INCURRED UNDER LAWS PASSED BEFORE THE TWENTY-SECOND DAY OF MARCH ONE THOUSAND SEVEN HUNDRED AND EIGHTY-EIGHT.

(Section I, P. L.) Whereas complaints have been made that the collectors of militia fines incurred under the former systems frequently abuse the power given them of proceeding against delinquents by distress, whereby property far beyond the sums due is, by bad or collusive sales, lost to the owners, as much to the disreputation of government as it is to the injury of individuals, and as the strict exaction of fines long accumulating may in many cases prove highly oppressive and grievous, it is thought proper that the collection of the fines aforesaid should be discontinued until the legislature can institute an inquiry into the abuses so complained of and apply some effectual remedy thereto and also determine as to the proper subjects of exoneration from the fines now due:

[Section I.] (Section II, P. L.) Be it enacted and it is hereby enacted by the Representatives of the Freemen of the Commonwealth of Pennsylvania in General Assembly met and by the authority of the same, That from and after the passing of this act until the first day of September which will be in the year one thousand seven hundred and eighty-nine no collector or collectors or other person or persons shall proceed by distress or otherwise for the recovery of any fine or fines incurred under any of the militia laws of this commonwealth which were enacted or in force before the twenty-second day of March in the present year, anything contained in the said laws to the contrary notwithstanding.

[Section II.] (Section III, P. L.) And be it further enacted by the authority aforesaid, That all distresses, suits, process and proceedings commenced for the recovery of such fines so uncollected and unpaid shall be and they are hereby declared to be void and discontinued.

Passed November 19, 1788. Recorded L. B. No. 3, p. 442. The Act in the text was repealed by the Act of Assembly passed March 27, 1789, Chapter 1416.

CHAPTER MCCCLXXXIV.

A SUPPLEMENT TO THE ACT ENTITLED "AN ACT TO PROVIDE FOR THE PAYMENT OF THE PRINCIPAL AND INTEREST OF SUCH OF THE BILLS EMITTED PURSUANT TO RESOLUTION OF CONGRESS OF THE EIGHTEENTH DAY OF MARCH, ONE THOUSAND SEVEN HUNDRED AND EIGHTY," AND AN ACT OF THE LEGISLATURE OF THIS STATE OF JUNE THE FIRST ONE THOUSAND SEVEN HUNDRED AND EIGHTY AS SHALL REMAIN UNREDEEMED ON THE THIRTY-FIRST DAY OF DECEMBER ONE THOUSAND SEVEN HUNDRED AND EIGHTY-SIX."[1]

(Section I, P. L.) Whereas the situation of public affairs, the plighted faith of this commonwealth and the principles of natural justice and equity require that further time should be allowed for redeeming the bills of credit in and by the act to which this is a supplement mentioned and referred to, than is therein given:

[Section I.] (Section II, P. L.) Be it therefore enacted and it is hereby enacted by the Representatives of the Freemen of the Commonwealth of Pennsylvania in General Assembly met and by [the] authority of the same, That the third and fourth sections of the act to which this is a supplement and every clause, matter and thing therein and in each of them contained shall be and they are hereby repealed and made null and void.

Passed November 22, 1788. Recorded L. B. No. 3, p. 444.

1 Passed March 17, 1786, Chapter 1212.

CHAPTER MCCCLXXXV.

AN ACT FOR THE RELIEF OF HENRY CLELAND BAKER, JOSEPH RICHARD ROBESON, BENJAMIN BURTON AND ROBERT HUNTER, IN- SOLVENT DEBTORS CONFINED IN THE GAOL OF THE CITY AND COUNTY OF PHILADELPHIA.

(Section I, P. L.) Whereas Henry Cleland Baker, Joseph Richard Robeson, Benjamin Burton and Robert Hunter, prison- ers now confined in the gaol of the city and county of Phila- delphia for debts due by them to their respective creditors, have by their petitions to the house of assembly severally set forth their total inability to satisfy their respective creditors and have prayed to be discharged from further imprisonment of their persons, which from their particular circumstances cannot be done under the laws at present subsisting for the benefit of insolvent debtors without the intervention of this house:

And whereas the prayers of their petitions appear to be reasonable, as the petitioners will by such discharge be the better enabled by their industry, when at liberty, to acquire property, by which the debts now due by them may be paid to their several creditors.

[Section I.] (Section II, P. L.) Be it therefore enacted and it is hereby enacted by the Representatives of the Freemen of the Commonwealth of Pennsylvania in General Assembly met and by the authority of the same, That the county court of common pleas in and for the city and county of Philadelphia be and they are hereby authorized and required upon the sev- eral petitions of the said Henry Cleland Baker, Joseph Richard Robeson, Benjamin Burton and Robert Hunter to grant unto them and each of them relief in the like manner and upon the same terms as by the laws of this commonwealth now in force is provided for insolvent debtors who are confined in execu- tion for debt to any one person to the value of forty shillings and upwards: and the several and respective discharges there- upon to be made by the said court of the prisoners aforesaid shall be as valid and their proceedings as effectual to all intents and purposes as any discharge or proceeding in case of any

insolvent debtor under the laws of this commonwealth now in
force for the relief of insolvent debtors who severally are indebted or owe to any one creditor to the value of forty shillings
and upwards would or may be, although the said Henry Cleland
Baker, Joseph Richard Robeson, Benjamin Burton and Robert
Hunter or either of them may not have resided within this state
for the space of two years next before their or his imprisonment
or confinement aforesaid.

[Section II.] (Section III, P. L.) And be it further enacted
by the authority aforesaid, That if any creditor or creditors of
the said Henry Cleland Baker, Joseph Richard Robeson, Benjamin Burton and Robert Hunter or either of them do or shall
not reside within this state at the time of such proceeding before the said court, that the service of notice of the application
to the said court or of any rule or order of the same court in
the premises, on the known agent or attorney within this state
of such creditor or creditors shall be equally good and effectual
as if the same notice or notices were served on the person or
persons of such creditor or creditors, but if such creditor or
creditors shall have no such agent or attorney within this state,
the said court on satisfactory proof that due diligence has been
used to find out such agent or attorney and that none can be
found, shall and may, notwithstanding, proceed to discharge
any such debtor in like manner as if such notice had been actually given.

Passed November 22, 1788. Recorded L. B. No. 8, p. 444.

CHAPTER MCCCLXXXVI.

AN ACT TO INCORPORATE THE PRESBYTERIAN CONGREGATION OF TREDYFFRIN TOWNSHIP IN THE COUNTY OF CHESTER.

(Section I, P. L.) Whereas divers members of the Presbyterian
Congregation of the township of Tredyffrin in the county
of Chester have prayed that the said congregation may

be incorporated and by law enabled to recover, receive and hold bequests, legacies and donations which have or may be made to the same congregation:

And whereas it is just and right and also agreeable to the true spirit of the constitution that the prayer of their said petition be granted:

[Section I.] (Section II, P. L.) Be it enacted and it is hereby enacted by the Representatives of the Freemen of the Commonwealth of Pennsylvania in General Assembly met and by the authority of the same, That John Davis, John Christie, John Griffith, John Templeton, David Wilson, David Cloyd, John Maxwell, Robert Todd, Thomas Harris, Matthew Nearly, James Davis, Thomas R. Kennedy and their successors to be twelve in number and to be duly elected as herein after is directed, be and they are hereby made and constituted one body politic and corporate in law and in fact to have continuance forever by the name, style and title of "The Trustees of the Presbyterian Congregation of the Township of Tredyffrin in the County of Chester."

[Section II.] (Section III, P. L.) And be it further enacted by the authority aforesaid, That the said trustees and their successors by the name, style and title aforesaid, shall forever hereafter be capable [in law] as well to take, receive and hold all and all manner of lands and other real and personal estate which have at any time or times heretofore been granted, bargained, sold, enfeoffed, released, devised or otherwise given, granted or bequeathed to the said religious society and congregation. And the said trustees and their successors are hereby declared to be seized and possessed of such estate therein and for the same uses and intents as in and by the respective grant, devise or other instrument is set forth and limited. And moreover, the said trustees and their successors at all times hereafter shall be able and capable to purchase, take, hold and enjoy for the use of the said congregation any real estate in fee simple or less estate by gift, grant, alienation, devise or other act or instrument of and from any person capable to

12—XIII

make the same. And further the same trustees and their successors shall apply the rents, profits and yearly income of the said congregation for the time being for repairing and enlarging, if need be, the house of public worship and the enclosure of the burial ground of the same and to erect and repair the school house and for other pious and charitable purposes as shall be directed by the major vote of the regular members of the said society and congregation duly assembled upon public notice thereof the Sunday preceding from the pulpit or desk of the said house of worship.

[Section III.] (Section IV, P. L.) Be it further enacted by the authority aforesaid, That all and singular the powers, privileges, regulations. provisions and directions, subject to the limitations and restrictions contained in [an] act of general assembly entitled, "An act for incorporating the Presbyterian Congregation of Pequea in the county of Lancaster,"[1] enacted on the fifth day of February in the year of our Lord one thousand seven hundred and eighty-five, mutatis mutandis, shall be and the same are hereby extended and applied to the said congregation of Tredyffrin and to the twelve trustees herein before mentioned and their successors. Provided nevertheless, That no sale or alienation of the real estate of the said corporation made by the said trustees or their successors bona fide and for valuable consideration in case the possession thereof pass immediately to the purchaser thereof and continue in him or his assigns shall be impeached or called in question for want of the consent of the majority of the [regular members of the] said society and congregation given as required by the act aforesaid unless the same be done within seven years from and after the sale and delivery of possession to the said purchaser.

---

[1] Passed February 5, 1875, Chapter 1124.
Passed November 23, 1788. Recorded L. B. No. 3, p. 448.

ACTS OF THE THIRTEENTH GENERAL ASSEMBLY OF PENNSYLVANIA, SECOND SITTING.

CHAPTER MCCCLXXXVII.

AN ACT TO ENABLE ALIENS TO PURCHASE AND HOLD REAL ESTATE WITHIN THIS COMMONWEALTH.

(Section I, P. L.) Whereas the empowering of aliens to purchase and hold lands, tenements and hereditaments within this commonwealth would have a tendency to promote the public benefit not only by introducing large sums of money into this state but also by inducing such aliens as may have acquired property to follow their interest and become useful citizens:

[Section I.] (Section II, P. L.) Be it therefore enacted and it is hereby enacted by the Representatives of the Freemen of the Commonwealth of Pennsylvania in General Assembly met and by the authority of the same, That from and after the passing of this act and until the first day of January which will be in the year of our Lord one thousand seven hundred and ninety-two, it shall and may be lawful for all and every foreigner and foreigners, alien or aliens, not being the subject or subjects of some foreign state or power, which is or shall be at the time or times of such purchase or purchases at war with the United States of America, to purchase lands, tenements and hereditaments within this commonwealth and to have and hold the same to them, their heirs and assigns forever as fully to all intents and purposes as any natural born subject or subjects may or can do.

Passed February 11, 1789. Recorded L. B. No. 3, p. 449. The Act in the text was revived and continued by the Act of Assembly passed March 8, 1792, Chapter 1607; and extended by the Act of Assembly passed February 12, 1795, Chapter 1795.

CHAPTER MCCCLXXXVIII.

AN ACT TO ESTABLISH A VOLUNTEER COMPANY OF ARTILLERY IN THE CITY OF PHILADELPHIA.

(Section I, P. L.) Whereas a number of the militia artillery of the city and county of Philadelphia have uniformed, accoutred and formed themselves into a volunteer company with a view to render themselves serviceable to their country:

[Section I.] (Section II, P. L.) Be it therefore enacted and it is hereby enacted by the Representatives of the Freemen of the Commonwealth of Pennsylvania in General Assembly met and by the authority of the same, That it shall and may be lawful for the volunteers composing the aforesaid company of artillery to elect by ballot one captain, one captain lieutenant, one first lieutenant, one second lieutenant, one third lieutenant, and be commissioned in like manner as other officers of the militia artillery are and that the non-commissioned officers of the company shall be appointed in like manner as is usual in other militia and the said company may consist of one hundred privates, provided such number have joined or hereafter shall join such company, and shall be attached to and act with the battalion from which they are or shall be formed, and be subject to like rules and regulations as the other militia of this state.

Passed February 11, 1789. Recorded L. D. No. 3, p. 450.

CHAPTER MCCCLXXXIX.

AN ACT TO REPEAL AN ACT ENTITLED "AN ACT TO SUSPEND THE POWERS OF THE TRUSTEES OF WESTMORELAND COUNTY."[1]

(Section I, P. L.) Whereas a law passed on the thirteenth day of December one thousand seven hundred and eighty-five,[2] em-

[1] Passed December 27, 1786, Chapter 1257.
[2] Passed September 13, 1785, Chapter 1176.

powering certain trustees therein named to purchase a piece of
ground within certain prescribed limits and bounds and thereon to erect a courthouse and prison for the use of the county.
And in aid thereof the commissioners of said county were authorized to levy the sum of one thousand pounds, which was accordingly levied and collected for the purposes aforesaid:

And whereas the said trustees found it expedient to proceed
immediately in erecting a small wooden building to accomodate
the public business of the county as a temporary convenience
until proper materials could be procured for a substantial and
permanent court-house and prison:

And whereas by a subsequent law passed the twenty-seventh
day of December one thousand seven hundred and eighty-six
entitled, "An act to suspend the operations of the trustees of
Westmoreland,"[1] the powers of the said trustees and all further
proceedings by them intended respecting the substantial and
permanent building aforesaid were suspended until a future
legislature should further and otherwise direct concerning the
same.   And whereas the sheriff, the justices of the peace and
other officers of the county of Westmoreland have by their
petition stated the great deficiency of the small wooden building which was only intended for temporary purposes, and the
many inconveniences which the officers of the court as well as
the prisoners in confinement are subject to from the present
uncomfortable state of the small building and pray that the
said suspending law may be repealed:

And whereas it appears just and reasonable that the said
county of Westmoreland should be accommodated with decent,
sufficient and permanent buildings calculated to answer all
the important purposes of a court house and prison and that
the money which has been levied and collected for these purposes should be applied agreeably to the intentions of the law
by which it was granted:

Therefore:

[Section I.] (Section II, P. L.) Be it enacted and it is hereby
enacted by the Representatives of the Freemen of the Commonwealth of Pennsylvania in General Assembly met and by

the authority of the same, That the said suspending law by
which the powers of the trustees of Westmoreland county were
suspended is hereby repealed, made null and void to all intents
and purposes and that the said trustees are hereby authorized
and required to proceed in applying the remaining part of the
money so levied and collected to the express purposes for which
is was granted.

Passed February 14, 1789.   Recorded L. B. No. 3, p. 460.
1Ante.

CHAPTER MCCCXC.

AN ACT FOR GRANTING TO THE CORPORATION OF THE MINISTERS,
VESTRYMEN AND CHURCH-WARDENS OF THE GERMAN LUTHERAN
CONGREGATION IN AND NEAR THE CITY OF PHILADELPHIA IN THE
STATE OF PENNSYLVANIA CERTAIN LANDS THEREIN MENTIONED
FOR ENDOWING A FREE SCHOOL FOR THE USE OF THE POOR OF THE
SAID CONGREGATION.

(Section I, P. L.) Whereas it hath been represented to this
house that the corporation of "The Ministers, Vestrymen and
Church-wardens of the German Lutheran Congregation in and
near the City of Philadelphia in the state of Pennsylvania"
have at their own voluntary expense instituted a charity school
in the city of Philadelphia in which a considerable number of
poor children are educated, but the funds provided are not only
so precarious in their nature but so limited in their
amount as to render the continuance of their benevolent undertaking doubtful and uncertain without some assistance
from the legislature wherefore they have humbly prayed this
house to confer on them a grant of lands within this state:

And whereas this house in conformity to the true principles
of liberty which is more dear and valuable to men in proportion as their minds are more enlightened has always promoted
the dissemination of learning.

[Section I.] (Section II, P. L.) Be it therefore enacted and
it is hereby enacted by the Representatives of the Freemen
of the Commonwealth of Pennsylvania in General Assembly
met and by the authority of the same, That five thousand acres
of land with the usual allowance to be located, set out and surveyed within the tract of sixty thousand acres reserved by the
act of the seventh day of April one thousand seven hundred
and eighty-six entitled, "An act for the present relief and future endowment of Dickinson college in the borough of Carlisle
and county of Cumberland in this state, and for reserving part
of the unappropriated lands belonging to this state as a fund
for the endowment of public schools, agreeably to the forty-
fourth section of the constitution of this Commonwealth"[1] be
and hereby are granted to the said corporation and their successors to have and to hold the same to them and their successors forever, in trust, for the purpose of supporting and
maintaining a charity school in or near the city of Philadelphia in this state and for no other use or purpose whatever.

[Section II.] (Section III, P. L.) And be it further enacted
by the authority aforesaid, That upon the application of the
said ministers, vestrymen and church-wardens or of any person duly authorized by them to the secretary of the land office
of this state, he shall and is hereby required to grant and issue
such and so many warrants to be directed to the surveyor general requiring him to survey or cause to be surveyed for the
said ministers, vestrymen and church-wardens such and so
many tracts of land within the sixty thousand acres reserved
as aforesaid with such number of acres in each warrant as
shall be specified in each application, which shall not contain
less than five hundred acres in such application, and not otherwise appropriated by acts of assembly nor before located or
surveyed, as shall in the whole amount to five thousand acres
and the usual allowance, and the surveyor general shall receive and enter all such warrants in his office and issue copies
of them directed to his deputies and upon the execution and
return thereof and patents or grants of confirmation for the

[1] Passed April 7, 1786. Chapter 1214.

same issued and granted in like manner and form and having like force and effect as the like proceedings and patents have been, and are conducted and granted, in cases of private persons applying for and taking up lands under the laws of the commonwealth in such cases made and provided.

[Section III] (Section IV, P. L.) And be it further enacted by the authority aforesaid, That all and every tract and tracts of land hereby directed to be surveyed for the use and trust aforesaid shall be so done at the charge of the state and the president or vice-president in council is hereby authorized and empowered to draw orders on the treasurer of the state to pay and defray all the charges arising thereupon.

Passed February 14, 1789. Recorded L. B. No. 3, p. 447.

CHAPTER MCCCXCI.

AN ACT TO REPEAL SO MUCH OF AN ACT OF GENERAL ASSEMBLY OF THIS COMMONWEALTH AS PROHIBITS DRAMATIC ENTERTAINMENTS WITHIN THE CITY OF PHILDELPHIA AND THE NEIGHBORHOOD THEREOF.

(Section I, P. L.) Whereas a great number of the citizens of Philadelphia and the neighborhood thereof have petitioned this house for a repeal of so much of a certain law of this commonwealth as prohibits theatrical exhibitions and this assembly being desirous of promoting the interests of genius and literature by permitting such theatrical exhibitions as are capable of advancing morality and virtue and polishing the manners and habits of society, and it being contrary to the principles of a free government to deprive any of its citizens of a rational and innocent entertainment, which at the same time that it affords a necessary relaxation from the fatigues of business is calculated to inform the mind and improve the heart:

[Section I.] (Section II, P. L.) Be it therefore enacted and it is hereby enacted by the Representatives of the Freemen of

the Commonwealth of Pennsylvania in General Assembly
met and by the authority of the same, That so much of an act
of general assembly of this commonwealth entitled, "An act
for the prevention of vice and immorality and of unlawful
gaming and to restrain disorderly sports and dissipa-
tion,"[1] passed on the twenty-fifth day of September, which
was in the year of our Lord one thousand seven hundred and
eighty-six as restrains or prohibits any person or persons from
acting, showing or exhibiting within the city of Philadelphia
or within one mile thereof any tragedy, comedy, tragi-comedy,
farce, interlude, pantomine or other play or any scene or part
of any play whatsoever or from being concerned or employed
therein or in selling any ticket or tickets for that purpose or
as inflicts any fine, forfeiture or penalty therefor or as directs
any recognizance to be entered into on account thereof, be
and the same is hereby repealed and made null and void. Provided nevertheless, That neither this act or anything herein
contained shall bar or prevent the recovery of any fine, forfeiture, penalty or sum or sums of money which may have been
incurred, forfeited or arisen and sued or prosecuted for under
the said recited act and before the passing hereof, but that
every such indictment, suit, bill, plaint or information may
be proceeded into judgment, execution and recovery in like
manner as if this act had not been made:

And whereas many respectable citizens are apprehensive
that theatrical representations may be abused by indecent,
vicious and immoral performances being exhibited on the
stage, to the scandal of religion and virtue and the destruction ·
of good order and decency in society and the corruption of
morals:

[Section II.] (Section III, P. L.) Be it enacted by the authority aforesaid, That it shall and may be lawful for his excellency the president of the supreme executive council, the
chief justice of the supreme court or the president of the court
of common pleas for the county of Philadelphia or any or either of them for the time being and they are hereby severally

1 Chapter 1248.

authorized and empowered at all times, within three years
from and after the passing of this act to permit and license
such theatrical exhibitions or representations only as shall in
the opinion of him who shall grant such license be unexceptional and if any person or persons shall during the time aforesaid act, show or exhibit any tragedy, comedy, tragi-comedy,
farce, interlude, pantomine, or other play or any scene or part
thereof without such license or permission being first had and
obtained, he and they shall on conviction thereof severally forfeit and pay to this commonwealth any sum not exceeding two
hundred pounds and shall also be imprisoned and held to security for his, her or their good behavior during the discretion
of the court in which such conviction shall be had.

Passed March 2, 1789.   Recorded L. B. No. 3, p. 452.

CHAPTER MCCXCII.

A SUPPLEMENT TO THE ACT ENTITLED "AN ACT FOR ERECTING PART
OF BEDFORD COUNTY INTO A SEPARATE COUNTY."[1]

(Section I, P. L.) Whereas in and by an act of general assembly of this commonwealth entitled, "An act for erecting
part of Bedford county into a separate county,"[2] enacted the
twentieth day of September in the year of our Lord one thousand seven hundred and eighty-seven, part of the county of
Bedford was erected into a new county called Huntingdon, but
no provision was made therein for running and ascertaining
the boundary lines of the said county of Huntingdon:

And whereas it is reasonable and necessary that the boundary lines of said county should be run and ascertained:

Therefore:

[Section I.] (Section II, P. L.) Be it enacted and it is hereby enacted by the Representatives of the Freemen of the Com-

[1] Passed September 20, 1787, Chapter 1311.
[2] Ante.

monwealth of Pennsylvania in General Assembly met and by
the authority of the same, That the supreme executive council
shall be and they are hereby authorized to appoint three commissioners, one of whom shall reside in the county of Cumberland, one in the county of Bedford and one in the county of
Huntingdon for the purpose of running and ascertaining the
boundary lines of Huntingdon county, and the said commissioners so to be appointed or any two of them shall be and they
are authorized and directed to run and ascertain the boundary
lines of Huntingdon county or such parts thereof as by the
commissioners of said county from time to time shall be
deemed necessary.

[Section II.] (Section III, P. L.) And be it further enacted
by the authority aforesaid, That the county commissioners are
hereby authorized and required to draw orders on the county
treasurer of Huntingdon for such sums of money, to be paid
out of the county levies, as will be sufficient to discharge all
necessary expenses which shall or may accrue in consequence
of running and ascertaining the aforesaid boundary lines.

Passed March 2, 1789. Recorded L. B. No. 3, p. 463.

CHAPTER MCCCXCIII.

AN ACT TO REPEAL PART OF AN ACT ENTITLED "AN ACT TO CON-
FIRM THE ESTATES AND INTERESTS OF THE COLLEGE, ACADEMY
AND CHARITABLE SCHOOL OF THE CITY OF PHILADELPHIA AND TO
AMEND AND ALTER THE CHARTERS THEREOF CONFORMABLY TO
THE REVOLUTION AND TO THE CONSTITUTION AND GOVERNMENT
OF THIS COMMONWEALTH AND TO ERECT THE SAME INTO AN UNI-
VERSITY."[1]

(Section I, P. L.) Whereas by the constitution of this commonwealth it is declared and provided "That all religious societies or bodies of men heretofore united or incorporated for
the advancement of religion or learning or for other pious
and charitable purposes shall be encouraged and protected in

1 Passed November 27, 1779, Chapter 871.

the enjoyment of the privileges, immunities and estates which
they were accustomed to enjoy or could of right have enjoyed
under the laws and former constitution of this state:"

And whereas by two charters of incorporation granted by
the late proprietaries of Pennsylvania there existed within this
commonwealth on the twenty-seventh day of November in
the year of our Lord one thousand seven hundred and seventy-
nine an ancient corporation and body politic by the name, style
and title of "The Trustees of the College, Academy and Charitable School of Philadelphia in the province of Pennsylvania,"
which corporation at the time of passing the act herein after
mentioned was seized, possessed of and entitled unto many
rights and franchises and divers estates, real, personal and
mixed and by the constitution and laws of this state was entitled to the public protection and encouragement in the enjoyment and free use and exercise thereof in conformity to the
original design, will and intention of the founders, donors and
benefactors of the said seminary of learning in the same manner as it could of right have held, occupied and enjoyed the
same under the former laws and constitution of this state:

And whereas by the said hereinafter mentioned act which
was passed on the said twenty-seventh day of November in
the year of our Lord one thousand seven hundred and seventy-
nine the said trustees and corporation and also the provost,
vice-provost, professors and all other masters, teachers, ministers and officers of the said college, academy and charitable
school were without trial by jury, legal process or proof of
misuser or forfeiture, deprived of their said charters, franchises and estates and the said board of trustees and faculty
were declared to be dissolved and vacated and the superintendence and trust, together with all and singular the powers,
authorities and estates, real, personal and mixed of the said
college, academy and charitable school were by the said act
declared to pass to, devolve upon, and be vested in a new corporation or body politic thereby created and established by
the name, style and title of "The trustees of the University of
the state of Pennsylvania," to have, hold, use, exercise and en-

joy all the powers, authorities and advantages of the estates,
rights, claims and demands of the trustees heretofore appointed by or in pursuance of the charters of the said (ancient) corporation or either of them: all which is repugnant
to justice, a violation of the constitution of this commonwealth
and dangerous in its precedent to all incorporated bodies and
to the rights and franchises thereof.

[Section I.] (Section II, P. L.) Be it therefore enacted and
it is hereby enacted by the Representatives of the Freemen
of the Commonwealth of Pennsylvania in General Assembly
met and by the authority of the same, That so much and all
such parts of an act of general assembly of this commonwealth
passed on the said twenty-seventh day of November in the
year of our Lord one thousand seven hundred and seventy-
nine entitled, "An act to confirm the estates and interests of
the college, academy and charitable school of the city of Philadelphia and to amend and alter the charters thereof conformably to the revolution and to the constitution and government of this commonwealth and to erect the same into an university,"[1] as touch or in anywise concern or relate to the said
ancient corporation which was styled and known by the said
name and title of "The Trustees of the College, Academy and
Charitable School of Philadelphia in the province of Pennsylvania," or the said charters thereof or either of them or as
touch or in anywise concern or relate to the former rights,
franchises, immunities or estates, real, personal or mixed
thereof or as tend to disqualify or disable the said trustees to
act as a body politic under the charters aforesaid or to disqualify, deprive or disable the body and faculty of the college
and academy known and distinguished in the charter dated
the fourteenth day of May one thousand seven hundred and
fifty-five by the name, style and title of "The Provost, Vice-
Provost and Professors of the College and Academy of Philadelphia in the Province of Pennsylvania," or any of them,
from carrying on the design and purposes of the said college,
academy and charitable school or to disfranchise or deprive

[1] Ante.

them or any of them of any privileges, immunities or estates whatsoever or of any part or parcel thereof or as vests the same or purports and intends to vest the same or any part or parts thereof in "The Trustees of the University [of the State] of Pennsylvania," shall be and the same and every such part and parts thereof is and hereby are repealed and made null and void to all intents and purposes whatsoever.

[Section II.] (Section III, P. L.) And be it further enacted by the atuhority aforesaid, That the trustees of the college, academy and charitable school aforesaid who were deprived and disabled or intended so to be by and in pursuance of the said act and the survivors of them and their successors by the name, style and title of "The Trustees of the College, Academy and Charitable school of Philadelphia in the Commonwealth of Pennsylvania," and the provost, vice-provost and professors, who, as a faculty, were deprived and disabled or intended so to be by and in pursuance of the said act, and the survivors of them and their successors by the name and style of "The Provost, Vice-Provost and Professors of the College and Academy of Philadelphia in the Commonwealth of Pennsylvania," shall be reinstated and restored and they and each of them are hereby reinstated and restored to all and singular the rights, franchises, emoluments, offices, trusts and estates, real, personal and mixed which they and each of them had held and enjoyed or ought or could of right have had, held and enjoyed or were entitled unto according to the said charters and the laws and constitution of this state on the said twenty-seventh day of November in the year of our Lord one thousand seven hundred and seventy-nine and they and each of them and their successors shall and may ask, demand, sue for [recover] and receive the same and each and every part and parcel thereof and shall hold and enjoy, use and exercise the same and every part and parcel thereof in the same manner and as fully and freely as if the said act had never been passed, excepting always so much of the rents, issues and profits of the said real estate and estates as were received by the said trustees of the university before the second day of March in-

stant which shall be considered and they are hereby considered
as having been duly laid out and expended in the education
of youth and therefore no account shall be rendered thereof
and excepting also such sum or sums of money as have been
paid in discharge of the just debts, contracts and engagements
of them the trustees of the said college, academy and charitable school, entered into and subsisting on and before the
said twenty-seventh day of November in the year of our Lord
one thousand seven hundred and seventy-nine and excepting
also such bonds, mortgages and other specialties of the former
estate of the said last mentioned trustees as have been transferred, cancelled or discharged by them, the trustees of the university for the value of which only (without any account of
the interest actually received) they shall be accountable to
the trustees of the said college, academy and charitable
[school] and excepting lastly certain lots of ground in the
town of Norris and county of Montgomery which were given
for the public use and service of the said county, and certain
other lots which have been contracted for, sold and conveyed
by the said trustees of the university for the purpose of building and improving in the said town, for the value of which
lots only, as they were contracted for, sold and payment received by the said trustees, they shall be liable and accountable to the trustees of the said college, academy and charitable
school and the said lots and every of them shall be and hereby
are, confirmed to the several purchasers thereof on the payment of the purchase money and arrears thereof yet due to
the trustees of the said college, academy and charitable
[school] in the same manner as such purchase money and
arrears thereof yet due ought to have been paid to the trustees
of the said university according to the several contracts for
the sale and conveyance of the said lots, duly and bona fide
made by them before the third day of February last.

[Section III.] (Section IV, P. L.) And be it further enacted
by the authority aforesaid, That the trustees of the said college, academy and charitable school and their successors by
the name, style and title of "The Trustees of the College, Acad-

emy and Charitable school of Philadelphia in the Commonwealth of Pennsylvania," and the provost, vice-provost and professors of the said college and academy and their successors
by the name and style of "The Provost, Vice-Provost and Professors of the College and Academy of Philadelphia in the
Commonwealth of Pennsylvania," shall respectively be entitled to and shall have and pursue the like speedy, summary
and effectual means and remedies for regaining and reinstat-
ing themselves in and for having and possessing themselves
of all and singular the rights, franchises, offices, trusts and
immunities and estates, real, personal and mixed to which
they or either or any of them are in and by this act restored
or which is hereby vested in them or either or any of them, together with all books, papers and writings, touching or concerning the same or any part thereof as were given or mentioned and intended to be given in and by the said in part recited act and also in and by any other act or acts of general
assembly of this commonwealth to the trustees of the university therein mentioned or which they could thereby have
or pursue, for acquiring or possessing themselves of all or any
part or parts of the estate or estates, real, personal or mixed,
rights, franchises, offices, trusts or immunities in and by the
said in part recited act transferred to or vested in them, the
said trustees of the university aforesaid, or of any books,
papers, or writings relating thereto; and all and every person
and persons are hereby enjoined and required to govern and
demean themselves accordingly under the like pains and
penalties as are in and by the said acts mentioned.

Passed March 6, 1789.   Recorded L. B. No. 3, p. 454.

CHAPTER MCCCXCIV.

AN ACT TO INCORPORATE THE CITY OF PHILADELPHIA.

(Section I, P. L.) Whereas the intention of civil government is to provide for the order, safety and happiness of the people and where the general systems and regulations thereof are found to be ineffectual it is the duty of the legislature to remedy the defects:

And whereas the administration of government within the city of Philadelphia is in its present form inadequate to the suppression of vice and immorality, to the advancement of the public health and order and to the promotion of trade, industry and happiness and in order to provide against the [evils] occasioned thereby it is necessary to invest the inhabitants thereof with more speedy, vigorous and effective powers of government than are at present established:

[Section I.] (Section II, P. L.) Be it therefore enacted and it is hereby enacted by the Representatives of the Freemen of the Commonwealth of Pennsylvania in general assembly met and by the authority of the same, That the inhabitants of the city of Philadelphia as the same extends and is laid out between the rivers Delaware and Schuylkill be and they and their successors forever are hereby constituted a corporation and body politic in fact and in law by the name and style of "The Mayor, Aldermen and Citizens of Philadelphia," and by the same name shall have perpetual succession and they and their successors shall at all times forever be able and capable in law to have, purchase, take, receive, possess and enjoy lands, tenements and hereditaments, liberties, franchises and jurisdictions, goods, chattels and effects to them and their successors forever or for any other or less estate and the same lands, tenements and hereditaments, goods, chattels and effects to grant, bargain, sell, alien and convey, mortgage, pledge,

13—XIII

charge and encumber or demise and dispose of at their will and pleasure.

[Section II.] (Section III, P. L.) And be it further enacted by the authority aforesaid, That the said corporation by the name and style aforesaid are and forever shall be able and capable in law to sue and be sued, plead and be impleaded, answer and be answered unto, defend and be defended in all courts of record and elsewhere, in all manner of actions, suits, complaints, pleas, causes and matters whatsoever, and to do and execute all and singular other matters and things that to them as a body politic and corporate in law and in fact shall and may appertain, and for that purpose shall have and use one common seal and the same from time to time shall and may at their will and pleasure, change and alter, deface and make anew.

[Section III.] (Section IV, P. L.) And be it further enacted by the authority aforesaid, That agreeably to the desire of a majority of the freeholders of the said city expressed in their petitions to this house, it shall and may be lawful for the freeholders of the said city to meet together at the state-house in the said city or at such other place therein as shall be appointed for holding of the elections of representatives to serve in the general assembly of this commonwealth, between the hours of ten and twelve of the clock in the forenoon on the first Tuesday in April next, and on the first Tuesday in April which will be in the year of our Lord one thousand seven hundred and ninety-six and so on, on the first Tuesday in April at the end of each and every seven years forever; and then and there to choose by ballot out of the inhabitants of the said city in the manner which now is and from time to time shall be prescribed by the laws for choosing representatives to serve in the said general assembly, fifteen suitable and proper persons to serve as aldermen in and for the said city for the term of seven years.

[Section IV.] (Section V, P. L.) And be it further enacted by the authority aforesaid, That it shall and may be lawful for the freemen of the said city who are or shall be qualified

agreeably to the laws and constitution of this commonwealth
to vote for members to serve in the said general assembly, to
meet together at the place aforesaid between the hours of ten
and twelve of the clock in the forenoon on the second Tuesday
in April next and on the second Tuesday in April which will
be in the year of our Lord one thousand seven hundred and
ninety-two and so on, on the second Tuesday in April at the
end of each and every three years forever and then and there
to choose by ballot out of the inhabitants of the said city in
manner aforesaid thirty suitable and proper persons to serve
as common councilmen in and for the said city for the term
of three years.

[Section V.] (Section VI. P. L.) And be it further enacted
by the authority aforesaid, That the first and all future and
other election and elections, whether of aldermen or of common councilmen, to be had and held in pursuance of this act
shall be held and conducted by the same officers who shall
have been duly chosen or appointed and authorized to hold,
manage and conduct the election of representatives for the
said city to serve in the said general assembly, at the general
election next preceding every election to be held in pursuance
of this act, and that the said officers and the clerks who shall
be employed at the said elections and each and every of them
shall severally take a solemn oath or affirmation before entering upon the duties in and by this act enjoined them, well and
faithfully to discharge the same according to the best of their
skill and abilities.

[Section VI.] (Section VII. P. L.) And be it further enacted
by the authority aforesaid, That all elections to be had and
held in pursuance of this act shall be held and conducted
(except as to the qualifications of the voters for or electors of
aldermen and the number of persons to be voted for, elected
and chosen to serve as aldermen and common councilmen and
except that the [votes or] tickets to be given in may be either
written or printed and except also as in and by this act is
otherwise directed) in the same and like manner as in and by
the laws of this commonwealth is or shall be directed for the

holding of the general elections for representatives to serve
in the said general assembly and under and subject to the
same rules, regulations, pains and penalties and all and every
person and persons who shall be concerned in holding or conducting of the said elections or any of them who shall come
to vote thereat or be anywise concerned therein, are hereby
enjoined and required to conduct and demean him and themselves accordingly.

[Section VII.] (Section VIII, P. L.) And be it further enacted by the authority aforesaid, That when each election
to be had and held in pursuance of this act shall be closed and
the number of votes for each candidate or person voted for
shall be counted and ascertained, the judges of the said election or a majority of them shall prepare and make, under
their respective hands and seals, a return thereof containing
the names of each alderman elect or of each common councilman elect as the case may be with the number of votes in
favor of each of them, and shall, within twenty-four hours
after the closing of each of the said elections, give notice in
writing to each of the said aldermen elect or common councilmen elect of their respective elections to the office of alderman or common councilman as the case may be, and shall also
deliver or cause to be delivered the said return to the said aldermen elect or common councilmen elect as the case may be
at the times and places in and by this act appointed for them
respectively to meet and receive the same.

[Section VIII.] (Section IX, P. L.) And be it further enacted by the authority aforesaid, That the said aldermen elect
or fifteen persons having the highest number of votes for the
office of alderman shall meet together at the state house in
the said city between the hours of ten and twelve of the
clock in the forenoon on the Friday next following each and
every election of aldermen to be held in pursuance of this act
and shall then and there receive the said returns of aldermen
elect and shall forthwith proceed to examine the same and to
judge and determine thereon and for that purpose and to the
end and intent that this act or the provisions herein contained

may not be evaded, the said aldermen who shall be elected and returned as aforesaid or a majority of them shall be judges of their own elections and shall have full power and authority to approve thereof or to set aside the same and to order new elections as the law may require, to be held in the manner hereinbefore directed and at such times as shall be by them appointed, of which they shall give at least six days' previous notice in three or more of the public newspapers printed in the said city.

[Section IX.] (Section X. P. L.) And be it further enacted by the authority aforesaid, That each and every alderman who shall be elected, chosen and returned in manner aforesaid and whose election shall be so as aforesaid approved of, shall before he enters on the execution of his office take a solemn oath or affirmation before his excellency the president or the vice-president in council "well and faithfully to execute the office of alderman of the said city," and shall thereupon without any further or other commission be an alderman of the said city until the next general election of aldermen to be held in pursuance of the directions of this act and shall, during the time aforesaid be vested with all the powers and jurisdictions of a justice of the peace in and for the said city and with such other powers and jurisdictions as in and by this act are given to any alderman.

[Section X.] (Section XI, P. L.) And be it further enacted by the authority aforesaid, That the said common councilmen elect or thirty persons having the highest number of votes for the office of common councilmen shall meet together at the state house in the said city between the hours of ten and twelve of the clock in the forenoon on the Friday [next] following each and every election of common councilmen to be held in pursuance of this act and shall then and there receive the said returns of common councilmen elect and shall forthwith proceed to examine the same and to judge and determine thereon, and for that purpose and to the [end and] intent that this act or the provisions herein contained may not be ineffectual, the said common councilmen who shall be elected and

returned as aforesaid or a majority of them shall be judges
of their own elections and shall have full power and authority
to approve thereof or to set aside the same and to order new
elections as the law may require to be held in the manner
hereinbefore directed and at such times as shall be by them
appointed, of which they shall give at least six days' previous
notice in three or more of the public newspapers printed in
the said city.

[Section XI.] (Section XII, P. L.) And be it further enacted
by the authority aforesaid, That each and every common councilman who shall be elected, chosen and returned as aforesaid
and whose election shall be so as aforesaid approved of shall,
before he enters upon the execution of his office, take a solemn
oath or affirmation before the mayor of the said city for the
time being "well and faithfully to execute the office of a common councilman of the said city," and shall thereupon without
any further or other commission enter upon the duties thereof
and shall hold and exercise the same until the next general
election of common councilmen to be held in pursuance of this
act.

[Section XII] (Section XIII, P. L.) And be it further enacted by the authority aforesaid, That it shall and may be lawful for the aldermen of the said city or a majority of them
to elect and choose by ballot every year or oftener if a vacancy
shall happen by death, resignation, removal from office or
from the city, one of their own number who shall be mayor of
the said city for the ensuing year if the time for which he
shall have been elected and chosen as alderman shall so long
continue, and the said mayor [elect] shall be presented to his
excellency the president or the vice-president in council, and
shall then and there take a solemn oath or affirmation "well
and faithfully to execute the office of mayor of the said city,"
and shall thereupon enter upon and perform the duties of the
said office without any further or other commission.

[Section XIII.] (Section XIV, P. L.) And be it further enacted by the authority aforesaid, That it shall and may be lawful for the said mayor and aldermen or a majority of them to

elect and choose by ballot out of the freemen and inhabitants
of the said city a recorder of the said city who shall hold the
said office and be vested with all the powers and jurisdictions
thereof and with all the powers and jurisdictions of a justice
of the peace within the said city for the term of seven years
and the same office of recorder shall be filled and supplied in
manner aforesaid as often as a vacancy shall happen therein in
manner aforesaid and the said recorder or person who shall
be so as aforesaid chosen for that purpose shall, before he enters upon the duties of the said office, or upon any other duty
in pursuance of this act, take a solemn oath or affirmation
before the mayor of the said city for the time being "well and
faithfully to execute and perform the office of recorder of the
said city," and shall thereupon enter upon the duties thereof
without any further or other commission, Provided nevertheless, That each and every mayor, recorder or alderman who
shall be elected, chosen or appointed in pursuance of this act
and who shall misdemean himself in office shall be liable to
be impeached by the general assembly before the president
or vice-president and council and shall be removable for misconduct in office by the said general assembly.

And in order that the said common councilmen may at all
times consist of those who are not only able and capable to
perform the duties thereof but of such as shall be mindful
of and attentive to the said duties and in order also to avoid
an entire dependence which might not be politically just and
expedient of any such common councilman either on the body
of which he may be a member or on that of the aldermen:

[Section XIV.] (Section XV, P. L.) Be it further enacted
by the authority aforesaid, That if any common councilman
shall misbehave himself in his said office or shall fail or neglect well and faithfully to discharge the duties thereof, it
shall and may be lawful for the mayor or recorder, aldermen
and common councilmen or a majority of the aldermen and
also of the common councilmen if the said mayor or recorder
and two-thirds of the aldermen and also two-thirds of the common councilmen who shall be present shall agree thereto on
the petition and complaint in writing of twenty-four free-

holders of the said city and of twenty-four freemen of the said
city who shall not be freeholders but who shall nevertheless
be qualified in manner aforesaid to vote for common councilmen, to remove in a summary way any such common councilman from his said office, Provided nevertheless, That the said
petition and complaint in writing shall fully and minutely
state all the causes assigned for such removal and no other
cause whatever shall be assigned, heard or inquired into, And
provided also, That a copy of the said petition and complaint
with a notice of the time and place appointed for hearing and
inquiring into the same shall be served on such common councilman at least ten days before any such hearing or inquiring
shall take place.

[Section XV.] (Section XVI. P. L.) And be it further enacted by the authority aforesaid, That the mayor, recorder,
aldermen and common councilmen in common council assembled shall have full power and authority to make, ordain,
constitute and establish such and so many laws, ordinances,
regulations and constitutions (provided the same shall not be
repugnant to the laws and constitution of this commonwealth) as shall be necessary or convenient for the government
and welfare of the said city and the same to enforce, put in
use and execution by the proper officers and at their pleasure
to revoke, alter and make anew as occasion may require. And
in order that a knowledge of the said laws, ordinances, regulations and constitutions may at all times be had and obtained:

[Section XVI.] (Section XVII. P. L.) It is hereby further
enacted by the authority aforesaid, That such and so many
of them as shall not be published in two or more of the public
newspapers published in the said city within ten days from
and after their being severally passed, ordained and established and also recorded in the office of the master of the rolls
who shall be allowed and paid for recording thereof at the
same rate as is allowed for recording the laws of this commonwealth within thirty days from and after their being so as
aforesaid passed, ordained and established, shall be null and
void:

And in order that the publications thereof may at all times be known and ascertained:

[Section XVII.] (Section XVIII, P. L.) It is further enacted and declared by the authority aforesaid, That before any of the said laws, ordinances, regulations or constitutions shall be so as aforesaid recorded, the publications thereof respectively, with the times thereof, shall be proved by the oath or solemn affirmation of some credible person which said oath or affirmation shall be recorded therewith and at all times be deemed and taken as sufficient evidence of the time of such publication.

[Section XVIII.] (Section XIX, P. L.) And be it further enacted by the authority aforesaid, That the mayor, recorder and aldermen of the said city for the time being shall severally and respectively have all the jurisdictions, powers and authorities of justices of the peace and justices of oyer and terminer and goal delivery of and for the said city and shall act therein accordingly, jointly or severally, as fully and amply as any justice or justices of the peace or of oyer and terminer or goal delivery, of or for any county within this commonwealth may or can do, in or for such county.

[Section XIX.] (Section XX, P. L.) And be it further enacted by the authority aforesaid, That the said mayor, recorder and aldermen or any four or more of them (whereof the mayor or recorder for the time being shall be one) shall have full power and authority and they are hereby vested with full power and authority to inquire of, hear, try and determine, agreeable to the laws and constitutions of this commonwealth, all larcenies, forgeries, perjuries, assaults and batteries, riots, routs and unlawful assemblies and all other offenses which have been committed or shall be committed within the said city which would be cognizable in any county court of general quarter sessions of the peace of or for any county within this commonwealth had the same offenses or any of them been committed within any such county and to punish all persons who shall be convicted of the same offenses or any of them, agreeably to the laws of this commonwealth and also

to inquire of, hear, try and determine all offenses which shall
be committed within the said city against any of the laws,
ordinances, regulations or constitutions that shall be made,
ordained or established in pursuance of this act and to punish
the offender and offenders as by the said laws, ordinances, regulations or constitutions shall be prescribed or directed and
also to impose fines on jurymen and others according to law
and to levy the same and to award process, take recognizances
for the keeping of the peace, for being of good behavior and
for appearance or otherwise, or commit to prison as occasion
shall lawfully require, without being accountable to the commonwealth for any fines or amercements to be imposed for
the said offenses or any of them except such as are or shall
be by law made payable into the state treasury for offenses
against this commonwealth and generally to do all such matters and things within the said city as any court of general
quarter sessions of the peace, oyer and terminer and goal delivery of and for any county within this commonwealth may
or can do within any such county. And to the ends, intents
and for the purposes aforesaid and for such other ends, intents
and purposes as are in and by this act declared or mentioned,
the said mayor, recorder and aldermen or any four of them
(whereof the mayor or recorder for the time being shall be
one) shall have full power and authority and they are hereby
vested with full power and authority to hold and keep a
court of record within the said city four times in each year
by the name, style and title of "The Mayor's Court for the
City of Philadelphia," and for the inquiring, hearing, trying
and determining of the pleas and matters aforesaid and for
the punishing of those who shall be found guilty thereof and
for the causing of all encroachments in the streets of the said
city and all nuisances to be removed and for the punishing
the offenders as the law and usage shall in such case require
and for the doing and performing of all such other matters
and things as are in and by this [act] made cognizable in the
said court.

[Section XX.] (Section XXI, P. L.) And be it further

enacted by the authority aforesaid, That if any person or persons shall find him, her or themselves aggrieved by any judgment of the said court of record, it shall and may be lawful
for the party or parties so aggrieved to sue and obtain his,
her or their writ or writs of error, which shall be granted of
course in like manner as other writs of error are granted and
made returnable in the supreme court of this commonwealth
and shall be proceeded in under the same rules and regulations, Provided always, That when any writ of error shall be
granted upon any judgment to be given in the said court of
record, the said mayor, recorder and aldermen or their successors shall not be compelled thereby or by any other writ or
writs to them directed to remove, send or certify into the
[said] supreme court or elsewhere any of the indictments or
presentments, but only the tenors or transcripts thereof and
of the records touching and concerning the same and of the
proceedings thereon under their common seal and after such
judgments shall be reversed or affirmed it shall and may be
lawful for the said mayor, recorder and aldermen and their
successors to proceed to execution or otherwise as shall according to law appertain:

And to the end and intent that such persons, indicted or
outlawed for felonies or other offenses supposed by such indictments or outlawries to have been committed within the
said city, as shall dwell, remove, lurk or be received without
the bounds and limits of the said city may be brought to
justice:

[Section XXI] (Section XXII, P. L.) Be it further enacted
by the authority aforesaid, That the mayor or recorder of the
said city for the time being shall and may as often as occasion
may require, issue his writ or writs of capias to the sheriff or
sheriffs or other officer of any county or counties or town corporate within this commonwealth directed, commanding him
or them to take and bring the body or bodies of any such person or persons as shall be so as aforesaid indicted or outlawed
before him the said mayor or recorder, or either of them, to be
dealt with according to law and every sheriff and other officer
to whom any such writ or writs of capias shall be directed and

delivered is hereby enjoined and required to use due diligence to
execute the same under such pains and penalties as are by law
incurred by any sheriff or other officer for refusing or neglecting to obey and execute any capias or other process to him directed and delivered.

And to the further end and intent that there may not be a
failure of justice within the said city by reason of any person
or persons who may be charged with having committed any
offense or offenses therein lurking or being in secret or other
places in the neighborhood thereof:

[Section XXII] (Section XXIII, P. L.) Be it further enacted by the authority aforesaid, That it shall and may be lawful for any constable or constables of the said city to whom
any warrant under the hand and seal of the said mayor, recorder or aldermen or any of them shall be delivered commanding him or them to take any person or persons who shall
have been charged with having committed any offense within the said city and to bring him or them before the said mayor,
recorder and aldermen or any of them, and he and they are
hereby enjoined and required to execute the same by making
of the arrest, if the same can be done at any place within the
county of Philadelphia and also by bringing such offender
or offenders before the said mayor, recorder and aldermen, or
some of them:

And to the further end and intent that there may not be a
failure of justice within the said city by reason of any witness
or witnesses residing or being without the bounds or limits
thereof:

[Section XXIII.] (Section XXIV, P. L.) Be it further enacted by the authority of the aforesaid, That it shall and may
be lawful for the said mayor, recorder and aldermen or any
of them before whom [any] complaint, indictment, plea, matter or thing of a criminal or civil nature within his or their
jurisdiction shall be made or depending, to issue his or their
subpoena to any person or persons within this commonwealth
commanding him or them to appear and give evidence therein,
and every person to whom the same shall be directed and on
whom service thereof shall be duly made, shall attend accord-

ingly and give evidence under such pains and penalties as are
by law incurred by any person or persons refusing to attend
and give evidence when duly subpoenaed for that purpose:

And to the end and intent that the administration of justice
within the said city in matters of a civil nature in and by this
act made cognizable before the said aldermen or any of them
may be free from extortion or undue oppression and also be as
effectually as may be secured against errors happening
therein:

[Section XXIV.] (Section XXV, P. L.) Be it further enacted by the authority aforesaid, That one other court shall
be and is hereby established within the said city, by the name,
style and title of "The Aldermen's Court," and shall consist
of three of the aldermen of the said city for the time being
(any two of whom shall be a quorum) to be chosen and appointed for that purpose by the mayor and recorder four times
in each year or oftener if they shall think proper; which said
"Aldermen's Court" shall meet on the forenoon of the Monday
in each and every week and shall sit from day to day during
so many days of each week and of so much of the said days
as shall be necessary for the hearing and determining of all
the matters and things in and by this act made cognizable
therein and for carrying their judgments into full effect by
executions and otherwise, and the said "Aldermen's Court"
shall solely and exclusively have cognizance of and full power
and authority to hear, try and determine in a summary way
all such causes, matters and things within the said city as
are by law cognizable before any one justice of the peace within this state where the debt or demand amounts to forty shillings and does not exceed ten pounds, in like manner and with
the like powers and authorities and under and subject to the
like regulations, restrictions and exceptions, and to the like
relief for insolvent debtors and to the like means, process, execution and stay thereof and to the like appeal as in cases of
debts or demands of forty shillings or upwards and not exceeding ten pounds before any one justice as aforesaid.

Provided nevertheless, That in all cases where the debt or

demand shall be above forty shillings and shall not exceed
ten pounds application shall be made by the party to one of
the said aldermen who shall for the time being constitute or
be a member of the court hereby established by the name and
title of [The] "Aldermen's Court." which said alderman so
applied to is hereby authorized and empowered to issue forth
under his hand and seal any warrant or warrants of summons,
capias or attachments as the case may require, returnable into
the same court and also such and so many subpoenaes as may
be needful and necessary, all of which shall be of the like force
and effect and be obeyed in like manner and under the same
pains and penalties with any warrants or subpoenaes of a like
nature issued by any justice of the peace within this commonwealth in any matter within the jurisdiction of any such
justice.

[Section XXV.] (Section XXVI, P. L.) And be it further
enacted by the authority aforesaid, That the same and no
greater or other fees shall be taxed, allowed or taken in or for
any matter or thing in and by this act made cognizable in the
said aldermen's court than the following ones, to wit, for every
warrant of summons, capias, attachment or execution one
shilling, and for every judgment one shilling, and such other
fees and costs as are allowed and granted in and by an act of
the general assembly of the late province of Pennsylvania entitled, "An act for regulating and establishing fees,"[1] in matters cognizable before any one justice of the peace.

[Section XXVI.] (Section XXVII, P. L.) And be it further
enacted by the authority aforesaid, That the mayor of the said
city for the time being and each and every alderman thereof
shall have cognizance of and a sole and exclusive right to hear
and determine in a summary way all such matters and things
within the said city where the debt or demand shall not
amount to forty shillings as are by law cognizable before any
one justice of the peace in any county within this commonwealth and shall issue the like process in nature of a summons,
capias or attachment as the case may require and shall pro-

---

[1] Passed August 22, 1752, Chapter 392.

ceed therein in like manner for the like fees or costs and with
the like powers and authorities and under and subject to the
like rules, regulations and restrictions and to the like relief
for insolvent debtors and to the like means, process, and execution as in cases of debt or other demand under forty shillings, before any justice of the peace within this commonwealth.

(Section XXVIII, P. L.) Provided nevertheless, That if any
person or persons shall find him, her or themselves aggrieved
by any judgment or judgments of any such mayor or aldermen
in any such debt or demand under forty shillings, it shall and
may be lawful for him, her or them who shall be so aggrieved
to appeal at any time within six days from any such judgment
or judgments to the "Aldermen's Court," in and by this act
established, where the said appeal shall with all convenient
speed be heard and finally determined and execution be
awarded in the manner hereinbefore directed, and for the like
costs. And provided further, That before any such appeal
shall be allowed or admitted by the said aldermen's court, sufficient security shall be entered in the same court, by the person or persons so appealing (if he, she or they shall not be a
freeholder or freeholders) to prosecute the said appeal to effect
and to abide by and perform the order and judgment of the
said court in case judgment shall pass against him, her or
them on the said appeal. And provided further, That before
the said appeal shall be determined or heard notice in writing
of every such appeal shall be given to the adverse party.

And in order to prevent the frequent clashing of jurisdictions and the mischiefs arising therefrom:

[Section XXVII.] (Section XXIX, P. L.) Be it further enacted by the authority aforesaid, That the justices of the court
of general quarter sessions of the peace of and for the county
of Philadelphia or any or either of them shall not in any matter or thing of a civil or criminal nature have any further or
other powers of jurisdictions within the said city than the said
mayor, recorder and aldermen or any of them may or can

have in the said county of Philadelphia and without the
bounds and limits of the said city.

[Section XXVIII.[(Section XXX, P. L.) And be it further
enacted by the authority aforesaid, That from and immediately
after the fifteenth day of April next, so much of each and every
act and acts of general assembly of this commonwealth, heretofore made or enacted as directs, authorizes or regulates the
electing, choosing, nominating, [commissioning] or appointing
of any justice or justices of the peace in, of or for the said city
of Philadelphia or any ward or wards, district or districts
therein, and also so much of each and every act and acts of
general assembly as directs, authorizes or empowers any justices or justices of the peace, jointly or severally, either by
themselves or collectively with any other person or persons,
to take cognizance of or to direct, do or perform any matter
or thing whatsoever within the said city, either of a criminal
or civil nature, or otherwise, and also so much of each and
every act and acts of general assembly as directs, authorizes
or empowers the nominating, choosing, appointing or commis-
sionating of any person or persons to hold a city court or
courts in and for the said city or as directs, authorizes or empowers any such person or persons to hold any such court or
courts or to take cognizance of, hear, try or determine any
matter or thing therein, be and they and each and every of
them are hereby severally and respectively repealed and made
null and void. Provided nevertheless, That neither this act or
anything herein contained shall annul, make void or prevent
the execution of any judgment, order, sentence, decree, award
of execution or other matter or thing already passed, pronounced, awarded, ordered, issued, or done or which shall, on
or before the said fifteenth day of April next be passed, pronounced, awarded, ordered, issued or done by the said judges
or justices, or any of them, but the same shall be of the same
force and effect and be obeyed and executed as fully as if this
act had not been passed.

[Section XXIX.] (Section XXXI, P. L.) And be it further
enacted by the authority aforesaid, [That] all recognizances

which have been taken by any justice or justices of the peace
for the appearance of any person or persons in or at the said
city court, or before the justices or judges thereof and which
have not been certified and returned into the said city court
or to the justices or judges thereof, shall be returned and certified by the said justices respectively who have taken the same
to the said mayor, recorder and aldermen at the next mayor's
court, to be had and held in pursuance of this act. And that
all persons who have been so as aforesaid bound by recognizance or by recognizances entered into in the said city court to
appear at or in the said city court or before the justices or
judges thereof, shall appear before the said mayor, recorder
and aldermen, at the next mayor's court to be had and held
in pursuance of this act and the same shall be a sufficient discharge of every such recognizance and also the recognizance
or recognizances of his, her or their surety or sureties, shall be
forfeited and sued for and recovered in such manner as the law
directs.

[Section XXX.] (Section XXXII, P. L.) And be it further
enacted by the authority aforesaid, That all recognizances for
appearance which shall be taken by or before the said justices
or judges or any of them from and after the passing of this
act, shall be for the appearance of the party or parties at the
next mayor's court to be held for the city of Philadelphia, and
shall be by them respectively certified and returned to the said
court.

[Section XXXI.] (Section XXXII, P. L.) And be it further enacted by the authority aforesaid, That the judges of
the said city court shall and they are hereby enjoined and required to deliver, or cause to be delivered, to the said mayor,
recorder and aldermen at the next mayor's court to be had and
held in pursuance of this act, all recognizances for appearance
which have been taken before or certified and returned to
them and which have not been discharged by appearance or
otherwise, and also all indictments and presentments which
have been found or made or shall be found or made before
them and which shall not be ended and determined, and also

14—XIII

all papers and records, duly certified, of all such matters and things as have been or shall be begun in the said city court and as shall remain unfinished and the said mayor, recorder and aldermen or any four of them (whereof the mayor or recorder for the time being shall be one) shall proceed therein as to law and justice shall appertain, as fully and amply to all intents and purposes as they might or could have done if such indictments or presentments had been found before or made to them, or such recognizances and [sic] had been taken by them or any of them.

[Section XXXII.] (Section XXXIV, P. L.) And be it further enacted by the authority aforesaid, That so much of all and every act and acts of general assembly as directs, authorizes or requires any matters or things to be done and performed by the city wardens or by the commissioners for paving and cleansing the streets of the said city or by all or any of them, shall from and after the first day of June next be null and void and the said officers shall no longer continue in office nor shall any new appoint[ment] of such officers be made under any former law or act of assembly. Provided nevertheless, That nothing herein contained shall bar, prevent or at all impede the recovery of any sum or sums of money or of any other matter or thing for the recovery whereof the said wardens or commisisoners have instituted any suit, cause or action, but the same shall and lawfully may be carried on by the said mayor, aldermen and citizens in the names of the said wardens or of the said commissioners as the case may require, to final judgment, execution and recovery as fully and effectually as the same might or could have been done by the said wardens or commissioners had this act not been passed. And provided further, That all and every matter and thing that has been commenced, begun or entered upon by the said wardens and commissioners or either of them, in pursuance of the powers and authorities in them vested shall be of the same force and effect as if this act had not been passed and may from and after the said first day of June next be proceded in and carried into effect agreeably to the directions of this act as fully as the same might or could have been done by the said

wardens and commissioners or either of them had this act not
been made and for this purpose all contracts and agreements
made or entered into by the said wardens and commissioners
or either of them, in pursuance of the powers in them legally
vested or which they or either of them shall in manner aforesaid enter into before the said first day of June next, shall be
equally binding upon the said mayor, aldermen and citizens,
and upon the person or persons with whom the same
have been or shall be made as if the same had originally been
made and entered into by and between them.

[Section XXXIII.] (Section XXXV, P. L.) And be it further enacted by the authority aforesaid, That from and after
the said first day of June next, the mayor, recorder, aldermen
and common councilmen shall be and they are hereby fully
authorized and empowered either by themselves or by proper
persons for that purpose to be by them appointed, to do, perform and execute all such matters and things as the said wardens and street commissioners were, at and immediately before the passing of this act, respectively authorized or enabled
by law to do.

[Section XXXIV.] (Section XXXVI, P. L.) And be it further enacted by the authority aforesaid, That from and after
the said first day of June next, the mayor or recorder and four
of the aldermen shall be and they are hereby fully authorized
and empowered either by themselves or by proper persons to
be by them for that purpose appointed, to do, perform and execute all such matters and things as the said wardens and
street commissioners respectively were at and immediately
before the passing of this act authorized or enabled by law to
do and perform, in conjunction with any justice or justices of
the peace of and for the city and county of Philadelphia or [of]
either of them and for the several purposes aforesaid it shall
and may be lawful for the said mayor, recorder, aldermen and
common councilmen in common council assembled to make,
ordain and establish such ordinances, regulations and provisions concerning the same as by them shall be deemed necessary and expedient, and also to allow and make such rewards

and compensation to the several officers of the said corporation and persons to be employed in the service thereof as shall
be just and reasonable. Provided nevertheless, That the consent and approbation of the mayor or recorder and of a majority of the aldermen and also of the common councilmen who
shall from time to time be present and in common council assembled shall be necessary to the making, ordaining or establishing of any such rules, regulations, appointments, laws, ordinances and constitutions as the said mayor, recorder, aldermen and common councilmen in common council assembled
are in and by this act authorized or empowered to make, ordain or establish.

[Section XXXV.] (Section XXXVII, P. L.) And be it further enacted by the authority aforesaid, That it shall and may
be lawful for the mayor or recorder, aldermen and common
councilmen in common council assembled from time to time
to permit and license such and so many brokers within the
said city and under such rules and regulations as they may
think proper and to prohibit all other persons from using or
exercising the business of a broker therein under such pains
and penalties as shall from time to time be ordained and established in manner aforesaid.

[Section XXXVI.] (Section XXXVIII, P. L.) And be it
further enacted by the authority aforesaid, That it shall and
may be lawful for the mayor of the said city to nominate and
from time to time to appoint one or more clerk or clerks of
the markets who shall have assize of bread, wine, beer, wood
and other things within the said city and shall do and perform
all things belonging to the office of clerks of the markets
within the said city.

[Section XXXVII.] (Section XXXIX, P. L) And be it further enacted by the authority aforesaid, That for the well governing of the said city and the ordering of the affairs thereof
there shall be such other officers therein and at such salaries
or other compensation, as the mayor, recorder, aldermen and
common councilmen in common council assembled shall direct,
each and every of which said officer and officers shall nevertheless before entering on the duties of his office take a solemn

oath or affirmation before the mayor of the said city for the
time being well and faithfully to perform and execute the
same.

[Section XXXVIII.] (Section XL. P. L.) And be it further
enacted by the authority aforesaid, That all the rights of the
late corporation known by the name of "The Mayor and Com-
monalty of Philadelphia in the Province of Pennsylvania" in
and to all lands, tenements, hereditaments, ferries, wharves,
markets, stalls, landings and landing places, goods, chattels,
moneys and effects whatsoever and also all other lands, tenements and hereditaments, rights, franchises, liberties, privileges, goods, chattels, moneys and effects whereof any person
or persons or bodies politic or corporate are seized or possessed or which they or any of them hold or enjoy in trust
for or to and for the use of the citizens of the city of Philadelphia or which the said citizens are in anywise entitled to, be
and they are hereby severally and respectively vested in the
said corporation or body politic of the city of Philadelphia and
their successors in and by this act established by the name,
style and title aforesaid, to and for the use and benefit of the
said citizens and their successors for ever, saving nevertheless
to all and every person and persons and bodies politic and corporate his, her and their just rights therein:

And to the end and intent that all and singular the estate
and estates, rights, privileges and interests aforesaid may be
had and received by the said mayor, aldermen and common
councilmen and be by them and their successors faithfully applied to and for the use of the said citizens and their successors forever:

[Section XXXIX.] (Section XLI, P. L.) Be it further enacted by the authority aforesaid, That all and every person
and persons and [bodies] politic and corporate who are or shall
be seized or possessed of the same or of any part thereof, shall,
on reasonable request, deliver the same to the said mayor, aldermen and common councilmen together with all deeds, writings, evidences, books and papers touching and concerning the
same with proper assignments where the same shall be nec-

essary and just, true and fair accounts thereof, and whoever shall fail herein shall be liable to be sued for the same and shall, moreover, forfeit and pay to the said mayor, aldermen and citizens any sum of money not exceeding five hundred pounds to be sued for and recovered in any court of record.

[Section XL.] (Section XLII, P. L.) And be it further enacted by the authority aforesaid, That it shall and may be lawful for the mayor or recorder for the time being from time to time as often as they or either of them shall see occasion, to summon a common council, and that no assembly or meeting shall be deemed or accounted a common council unless the mayor or recorder and at least eight of the aldermen and sixteen of the common councilmen shall be present.

[Section XLI.] (Section XLIII, P. L.) And be it further enacted by the authority aforesaid, That the said mayor, aldermen and common councilmen shall once in every year cause to be published a just and true account of all the moneys which shall have accrued to them in their corporate capacity during the year next preceding such publication and also of the disposition thereof and shall also lay a copy thereof before the general assembly.

[Section XLII] (Section XLIV, P. L.) And be it further enacted by the authority aforesaid, That as often as any doubts shall arise concerning this act the same shall in all courts of law and equity, and elsewhere be construed and taken most favorably for the said corporation.

Passed March 11, 1789. Recorded L. B. No. 3, p. 458. See the Acts of Assembly passed December 8, 1789, Chapter 1479; April 2, 1790, Chapter 1509; March 8, 1792, Chapter 1665; April 19, 1794, Chapter 1754; April 4, 1796, Chapter 1905; April 11, 1799, Chapter 2091; March 3, 1800, Chapter 2117.

CHAPTER MCCCXCV.

A SUPPLEMENT TO AN ACT ENTITLED "AN ACT MORE EFFECTUALLY
TO PREVENT UNFAIR PRACTICES IN THE PACKING OF BEEF AND
PORK FOR EXPORTATION, AND TO REGULATE THE EXPORTATION
OF FLAXSEED, BUTTER AND BISCUITS IN KEGS."[1]

(Section I, P. L.) Whereas the commercial reputation and
general interest of this commonwealth has been greatly advanced by divers wholesome laws subjecting the produce
thereof to regular and careful inspection and it is right and
proper that the exports from this state should conform as
nearly as may be found convenient in package and value with
those of other countries which are vended from time to time in
the same foreign markets:

And whereas sundry defects in the law relating to salted
beef and pork passed the eighteenth day of August one thousand seven hundred and twenty-seven have been discovered
by observation and experience:

[Section I.] (Section II, P. L.) Be it therefore enacted and
it is hereby enacted by the Representatives of the Freemen of
the Commonwealth of Pennsylvania in General Assembly met
and by the authority of the same, That from and after the first
day of November next, every tierce, barrel or half barrel in
which salted beef or pork shall be exposed to sale within this
commonwealth or exported therefrom (except such as shall
have been brought or imported from any place or places without the bounds and limits of this commonwealth, with the
name of the state, town or place from which the same shall
have been brought or imported, branded or marked at full
length and in a plain, legible manner thereon and which shall
be sold or exported as aforesaid with the same name so as
aforesaid branded or marked thereon and not as the beef or
pork of Pennsylvania) shall be made of sound and well sea-
soned white oak timber with at least fourteen good and sub-

stantial hoops thereon, which hoops shall be fastened and secured at each end of such tierce, barrel or half barrel by iron
nails and at each bilge by wooden pins or pegs.

[Section II.] (Section III, P. L.) And be it further enacted
by the authority aforesaid, That every tierce in which salted
beef or pork (except as is before excepted) shall be exposed to
sale in this Commonwealth or exported therefrom as aforesaid shall be of the gauge of forty-two gallons of wine measure and shall contain three hundred pounds of sound and
merchantable meat, well packed and secured with salt and
pickle, and if such tierce contains beef it shall not have therein
more than three legs or shins, and if it contains pork it shall
not have therein more than three heads.

[Section III.] (Section IV, P. L.) And be it enacted by the
authority aforesaid, That every merchantable barrel of salted
beef (except as is before excepted) which shall be exposed to
sale in or exported from this Commonwealth shall be of the
gauge of twenty-eight gallons of wine measure and shall contain no more than two shins. And every merchantable barrel
of salted pork (except as is before excepted) which shall be exported from or exposed to sale in this commonwealth shall be
of the gauge of twenty-nine gallons wine measure and each
shall contain two hundred pounds of cured meat and no barrel of pork shall have more than two heads therein. And
every half barrel of beef and pork shall be of the gauge of fifteen gallons of the measure aforesaid and shall contain one
hundred pounds of cured meat and if beef not more than one
shin and if pork not more than one head. And every cask,
whether tierce, barrel or half barrel, shall be distinctly
branded with the name of the cooper or the person putting up
the same.

[Section IV.] (Section V, P. L.) And be it enacted by the
authority aforesaid, That every tierce, barrel or half barrel in
which salted beef or pork (except as is before excepted) shall
be exposed to sale within this commonwealth or exported
therefrom as aforesaid, shall, before the sale or exportation
thereof, be carefully inspected and examined by the inspector
of beef and pork for the time being, who shall pass as mer-

chantable and brand with the arms of this commonwealth
each and every tierce, barrel and half barrel being of the materials and dimensions hereinbefore directed and described and
which shall respectively contain the quantity and quality of
salted beef or pork hereinbefore mentioned and required,
packed and secured in the manner aforesaid. And the said inspector for the time being shall (with a proper instrument for
that purpose to be provided) erase, scratch out and effectually
deface the cooper's or packer's brand mark and marks of[f]
and from each and every tierce, barrel or half barrel containing salted beef or pork as aforesaid which shall not be of the
materials and dimensions hereinbefore directed and described
and in which such beef or pork shall not be of the quantity
and quality and packed and secured in the manner hereinbefore also directed and described. And if the same cannot be
rendered merchantable according to the requisitions and meaning of this act by salting, pickling, re-packing and coopering
thereof, then the said inspector for the time being shall impress
and brand a dis[tinct] mark of a cross, thus, X (each stroke
of the said cross being at least three inches long) upon one head
of every such tierce, barrel or half barrel containing beef or
pork so as aforesaid incapable of being rendered merchantable.

[Section V.] (Section VI, P. L.) And be it enacted by the
authority aforesaid, That all and every person and persons
who shall sell and deliver any tierce, barrel or half barrel of
salted beef or pork (except as is before excepted) to the purchaser or purchasers thereof before the same has been duly examined by the said inspector and branded with the arms of
this commonwealth in the manner hereinbefore directed or who
shall refuse to allow and suffer the said inspector in the cases
aforesaid to erase, scratch out and effectually deface the cooper's or packer's brand mark and marks of[f] and from any
tierce, barrel or half barrel, and if need be to impress and
brand thereon the said mark of a cross as aforesaid, shall forfeit and pay for each and every tierce, barrel or half barrel
so sold and delivered and for each and every tierce, barrel or
half barrel from which he, she or they shall refuse to allow
and suffer the said cooper's or packer's brand mark and marks

to be erased, scratched out and effectually defaced as afore-said and for each and every tierce, barrel or half barrel whereon he, she or they shall refuse to allow and suffer the said mark of a cross to be impressed and branded as aforesaid, the sum of ten shillings. And for all and every person and persons who shall by any means whatever, wilfully erase, scratch out and deface the said mark of a cross after the same has been duly impressed and branded by the said inspector upon any tierce, barrel or half barrel as aforesaid shall forfeit and pay the sum of ten pounds for each and every tierce, barrel or half barrel of[f] and from which the said mark of a cross shall be erased, scratched out and defaced, the said last two mentioned sums of money or forfeiture to be recovered and applied in the manner hereinafter provided and declared.

[Section VI] (Section VII, P. L.) And be it further enacted by the authority aforesaid, That the said inspector for the time being shall and may lawfully demand, receive and take the sum of six-pence and no more, for inspecting, examining and branding as aforesaid, each and every tierce, barrel or half barrel of salted beef or pork, which shall be sold at the port of Philadelphia or exported therefrom, whether the same be sold for ship stores or exportation, and also the further sum of one shilling and six-pence for each tierce and of one shilling for each barrel or half barrel of salted beef or pork which he, the said inspector, shall re-pack, together with such [other and] further allowance and compensation as it shall and may be reasonable and customary to allow and give for the expense and trouble of cooperage in putting the same into good and merchantable order and condition. Provided nevertheless, That it shall and may be lawful to and for the owner and owners of the said salted beef or pork to employ any person and persons other than the said inspector for the time being to do, execute and perform the cooperage necessary to put the same in good and merchantable order and condition as aforesaid and in that case the said inspector for the time being shall not be entitled to have and receive any allowance or compensation whatsoever for or on account of the said cooperage.

And whereas divers frauds and impositions have been com-

mitted in the package of sundry other commodities as well as
salted beef and pork, the frequent repetition whereof must be
equally injurious to the interest and reputation of the state
and which it is the duty and desire of the legislature as far as
may be to prevent:

Therefore:

[Section VII.] (Section VIII, P. L.) Be it enacted by the
authority aforesaid, That from and after the first day of November [next] no flaxseed shall be exported from this commonwealth into the kingdom of Ireland or into that part of
Great Britain called Scotland before the same is well cleansed
and prepared, nor in any other manner than is hereby described and directed, that is to say, the staves of each and
every cask in which flaxseed shall be exported from this commonwealth as aforesaid shall be made of sound oak and each
and every of the said casks besides a lining hoop on the outside round the chimes thereof, shall have at least twelve other
good and substantial hoops thereon and the same shall be
fastened and secured by at least three iron nails in each of the
chime hoops and by the like number of iron nails in each of the
quarter hoops and each and every of the said casks shall be
made as nearly straight as possible and there shall be two sizes
of the said casks and no more, to wit: the larger sizes thereof
shall be in length two feet and nine inches and in diameter
at each head twenty-four inches, and shall contain seven bushels of good and merchantable flaxseed; and the smaller sizes
thereof shall contain three bushels and an half bushel of like
good and merchantable flaxseed. And each and every of the
said casks shall be branded with the initial letter of the christian name and surname at full length of the person who
cleaned and prepared the flaxseed therein put up and contained. And if any cask or casks containing flaxseed shipped
with the intent to export the same as aforesaid not of the materials, make and dimensions and shall not respectively contain the quantity and quality of flaxseed hereinbefore directed
and described, or if the said cask and casks have not been first
duly branded as aforesaid, all and every person and persons
who shall ship the same as aforesaid shall forfeit and pay the

sum of twenty shillings for each and every cask which shall
not be of the materials, make and dimensions or which shall
not respectively contain the quantity and quality of flaxseed
hereinbefore directed and described, and shall also forfeit and
pay the further sum of five shillings for each and every cask
so shipped which hath not been first duly branded as aforesaid, the said two last mentioned sums of money or forfeitures
to be recovered and applied in the manner hereinafter provided
and declared.

[Section VIII.] (Section IX, P. L.) And be it further enacted by the authority aforesaid, That every cask in which butter shall be exported from this commonwealth or therein exposed to sale for exportation shall be made of good and sound
white oak staves and shall be of the following dimensions,
that is to say, in length twenty inches, in diameter at the heads
thereof twelve inches and every such cask shall have at least
fourteen hoops thereon well and sufficiently fastened and secured by iron nails in the head or chime hoops and by wooden
pegs or pins in the upper bilge or quarter hoops and all and
every person and persons who shall hereafter export butter
from this commonwealth or therein expose the same to sale
for exportation in any other or different kind of casks than is
hereby directed and described shall forfeit and pay the sum of
five shillings for every cask containing butter so exported or exposed to sale for exportation contrary to the meaning and direction of this act to be recovered and applied in the manner
herein provided and declared.

[Section IX.] (Section X, P. L.) And be it further enacted
by the authority aforesaid, That from and after the first day
of August next each and every keg in which biscuit shall be
exported from this commonwealth or therein exposed to sale
for exportation shall contain at least seven pounds of good and
merchantable biscuit, and all and every person and persons
who shall at any time from and after the said first day of
August next export biscuit from this commonwealth or therein expose the same to sale for exportation in any keg or kegs
containing a less quantity and inferior quality of biscuit than
is hereby directed shall forfeit and pay the sum of five shil-

lings for every keg so exported or exposed to sale for exportation contrary to the meaning and direction of this act, to be
recovered and applied in the manner hereinafter provided and
declared.

[Section X.] (Section XI, P. L.) And be it further enacted
by the authority aforesaid, That all and singular the forfeitures and penalties in and by this act or the act to which this
is a supplement set, declared, appointed and imposed shall be
one half thereof to the guardians of the poor in the city of
Philadelphia for the use and benefit of the poor of the said
city [and the district annexed thereto] and the other half
thereof to the informer or him, her or them who will sue for
the same to his, her or their own use and benefit and if the
said forfeitures and penalties be under the sum of ten pounds
the [same] shall and may be sued for and recovered in like
manner as debts under ten pounds may be sued for and recovered within this commonwealth, or if the said forfeitures
[and] penalties be above the [said] sum of ten pounds the
same shall and may be sued for and recovered by bill, plaint or
information in any court of record within this commonwealth
wherein no essoin protection or wager of law nor more than
one imparlance shall be allowed.

[Section XI.] (Section XII, P. L.) And be it further enacted
by the authority aforesaid, That so much and no more of the
said recited act entitled, "An act more effectually to prevent
unfair practices in the packing of beef and pork for exportation" passed the said eighteenth day of August in the year
of our Lord one thousand seven hundred twenty-seven as is by
this act altered or supplied be and the same is hereby repealed
annulled and made absolutely void any[thing] therein [con-
tained] to the contrary thereof in anywise notwithstanding.

Passed March 12, 1789. Recorded L. B. No. 9, p. 471. See the
Acts of Assembly passed November 27, 1700, Chapter 80; August 18,
1727, Chapter 295; September 24, 1789, Chapter 1440.

CHAPTER MCCCXCVI.

**AN ACT TO REPEAL ALL THE LAWS OF THIS COMMONWEALTH RE-
QUIRING ANY OATH OR AFFIRMATION OF ALLEGIANCE FROM THE
HABITANTS THEREOF.**

Whereas by several acts of the general assembly of this commonwealth sundry oaths or affirmations of allegiance, abjuration and fidelity have been from time to time required of the
citizens thereof, which, however proper and expedient they
might be during the late war when it was necessary for individuals to testify their attachment to one or the other of the
contending parties, since the restoration of peace and the establishment of government have become unnecessary:

[Section I.] (Section II, P. L.) Be it therefore enacted and it
is hereby enacted by the Representatives of the Freemen of the
Commonwealth of Pennsylvania in General Assembly met, and
by the authority of the same, That from and after the passing of
this act as well the act of Assembly entitled, "An act to alter
the test of allegiance to this commonwealth required by an act
passed the fourth day of March one thousand seven hundred
and eighty-six entitled, 'An act for securing to this commonwealth the fidelity and allegiance of the inhabitants thereof
and for admitting certain persons to the rights of citizenship' "[1]
as all other acts which require any oath or affirmation of allegiance or fidelity to this commonwealth from the subjects or inhabitants thereof or of abjuration or renunciation of any foreign power, or as impose or inflict any penalty or disability on
any person or persons by means of his or their having refused
or neglected to take and subscribe any such oath or affirmation
shall be and they are hereby repealed.

[Section II.] (Section III, P. L.) And be it further enacted
by the authority aforesaid, That from and after the passing of
this act all persons who from not having taken the said
oaths or affirmations or abjuration, allegiance or fidelity were,
by [the] force and operation of the acts of Assembly thereunto

---

[1] Passed March 29, 1787, Chapter 1294.

relating, excluded from certain privileges and exempted from
certain burdens, shall be and they are hereby restored to and
placed upon the same footing as to such privileges and burdens and in all other respects with the other citizens of this
state.

[Section III.] (Section IV, P. L.) Provided always and be it
further enacted by the authority aforesaid, That nothing herein contained shall be deemed or taken to extend to, alter or
affect the forty-second section of the plan or frame of government of this commonwealth, but that every such foreigner as
is in the said section mentioned, who shall come to settle in
this state, shall, after one year's residence therein, be entitled
to the full enjoyment of the rights and privileges therein specified upon taking and subscribing before the mayor, recorder
or some alderman of the city of Philadelphia or before some
justice of the peace within this state the following oath (or
affirmation if conscientiously scrupulous of taking an oath)
viz: "I ————do swear (or solemnly, sincerely and truly
declare and affirm) that I will be faithful and bear true allegiance to the commonwealth of Pennsylvania as a free and inde-
pendent state, and that I will not at any time wilfully and
knowingly do any matter or thing prejudicial or injurious to
the freedom and independence thereof."

[Section IV.] (Section V, P. L.) And be it further enacted
by the authority aforesaid, That the said mayor, recorder and
each and every alderman and justice of the peace before whom
such oath or affirmation shall be taken and subscribed, shall
keep a fair register of the names and additions of the persons
so sworn or affirmed and of the names and additions of their
parents and of the country, town and place of their nativity
and of that from which they shall have last arrived and of
the time of every such oath or affirmation being taken and
shall on or before the first day of October in every year transmit in writing under his or their hands and seals to the office
of recorder of deeds of his proper county a true list of such
persons as shall have so sworn or affirmed before him since
the transmitting of his last list as aforesaid, together with the
names, additions and descriptions aforesaid, for which and for

the certificate that such person hath so sworn or affirmed, the said mayor, recorder, alderman or justice shall receive from the party the sum of seven shillings and six-pence and no more.

[Section V.] (Section VI, P. L.) And be it further enacted by the authority aforesaid, That the said recorder of deeds shall record such lists with the said names, additions and descriptions in their respective counties in books kept for that purpose and shall for each person thereby certified to have taken the said oath or affirmation be paid two shillings and sixpence by the said mayor, recorder, alderman or justice who shall transmit such lists and no more.

Passed March 13, 1789. Recorded L. B. No. 3, p. 476.

CHAPTER MCCCXCVII.

AN ACT TO SUSPEND THE SALE OF LANDS FOR NON-PAYMENT OF TAXES AND FOR OTHER PURPOSES THEREIN MENTIONED.

(Section I, P. L.) Whereas the act to suspend the powers of the commissioners of the several counties within this state to make sale of unseated lands for non-payment of taxes will by its own limitation expire [on] the twenty-second day of this instant March, and as the legislature have it in contemplation to establish a mode of collecting the public taxes less burdensome and oppressive than the present, it is reasonable that the suspension aforesaid should be further continued and also be extended to all other lands.

[Section I.] (Section II, P. L.) Be it enacted and it is hereby enacted by the Representatives of the Freemen of the Commonwealth of Pennsylvania in General Assembly met and by the authority of the same, That the commissioners of the several counties within this state be and they are hereby further restricted and prohibited from making sale of any lands whatsoever in their respective counties by reason of the non-payment of taxes until the [end of the] next session of the general assembly.

[Section II.] (Section III, P. L.) And be it enacted by the authority aforesaid, That the act of assembly enacted the eleventh day of September in the year of our Lord one thousand seven hundred and eighty-six entitled, "An act to relieve the owners of unimproved lands from the inconveniences they are subjected to by the present mode of enforcing the payment of taxes assessed thereon"[1] and all powers and authorities therein given to the several officers and persons therein mentioned be and the same is and are hereby also suspended during the time aforesaid.

---

[1] Chapter 1237.

Passed March 18, 1789. Recorded L. B. No. 3, p. 477. See the Act of Assembly passed September 26, 1789, Chapter 1440.

CHAPTER MCCCXCVIII.

AN ACT IN AID OF THE CALLOWHILL MARKET IN THE TOWNSHIP OF THE NORTHERN LIBERTIES.

(Section 1, P. L.) Whereas the holding of open market at a fixed and known place where buyer and seller may at stated times meet together has been found by long experience to be beneficial to both, not only by presenting before the buyer a greater choice as to kind and quality according to his ability to purchase but also by affording to the seller a better and more steady price for his provisions according to their goodness and just value, and a more certain and expeditious sale thereof. And whereas convenient market houses have at a considerable expense been erected in the township of the Northern Liberties in the county of Philadelphia which by law are declared to be a public market-place for the buying and selling of all sorts of provisions, victuals and things of the country produce and manufacture and is commonly known by the name of Callowhill Market, and there hath been chosen

15—XIII

a clerk of the market to make essay of weights and measures and do and perform all things belonging to the office of a clerk of the market within the said township and other officers tending to the good order thereof. And whereas the practice made use of in the said township by butchers and others hawking from door to door, meat, poultry and other kinds of food for man usually sold in the city of Philadelphia in open market has in great measure defeated the good and salutory purpose for which the said market houses were erected, and thereby those victuallers and others who have hired stalls in and attended the said market-place have become great sufferers:

For remedy thereof:

[Section 1.] (Section II, P. L.) Be it enacted and it is hereby enacted by the Representatives of the Freemen of the Commonwealth of Pennsylvania in General Assembly met and by the authority of the same, That from and after the publication of this act if any victualler or butcher or other person shall hawk from door to door or by any means sell or offer to sale within the said township any beef, veal, mutton, lamb, goat, kid, pork, cheese, butter, poultry, eggs or other food for man, usually sold in the city of Philadelphia in open market, at any place or places, other than in the said Callowhill Market (vegetables only excepted) he or they shall forfeit double the value thereof, one half of the said forfeiture to the use of the said market to be paid to the superintendents thereof for the time being and the other half thereof to the person or persons who shall prosecute within one month after the offense shall be committed.

(Section II.) Provided always, That nothing herein contained shall extend to any person selling within his or her own dwelling-house or to any person not a victualler or butcher bringing any provisions aforesaid from any distance greater than five miles from the said township, or to the selling or offering to sale while alive, any cattle, calves, sheep, lambs, goats, kids or hogs, nor to any such sale made at a greater distance than two miles northward of the north side of Vine street in the city of Philadelphia.

Passed March 18, 1789. Recorded L. B. No. 3, p. 480.

CHAPTER MCCCXCIX.

AN ACT FOR THE RELIEF OF ROBERT BEATTY AND BENJAMIN MOORE, INSOLVENT COLLECTORS, CONFINED IN THE GAOLS OF CUMBERLAND AND DAUPHIN COUNTIES.

(Section I, P. L.) Whereas Robert Beatty late a collector of taxes for the township of Shippensburg in the county of Cumberland, and Benjamin Moore late a collector of taxes for the township of Lebanon, then in the county of Lancaster, but now Dauphin county, have set forth by their petitions that they are confined in goal for non-payment of moneys by them received in the collection of public taxes, which from a variety of misfortunes they are rendered unable to pay and have prayed that they may be discharged from further confinement, and it apepars to this house that the prayer of the petitionery ought to be granted:

[Section I.] (Section II, P. L.) Be it therefore enacted and it is hereby enacted by the Representatives of the Freemen of the Commonwealth of Pennsylvania in General Assembly met and by the authority of the same, That the county courts of common pleas in and for the counties of Cumberland and Dauphin respectively shall and they are hereby respectively authorized and required upon the petitions of the said Robert Beatty and Benjamin Moore respectively to grant them relief with equal and like effect, and upon like terms and conditions as to imprisonment of their persons as is by the laws of this state afforded to insolvent debtors in cases of debt by them owing to private persons. Provided always, That the discharge of the said Robert Beatty and Benjamin Moore shall not extend to exonerate the counties of Cumberland and Lancaster or either of them from any part of their quota of taxes or assessments due to this state by reason of the default of the said Robert Beatty and Benjamin Moore or either of them as collectors aforesaid. And that nothing in this act contained

shall be construed to defeat or in any wise to annul or lessen
the force and effect of any security, assumption or engagement
entered into by any person or persons for the securing or paying to the state or county the taxes or moneys collected by the
said Robert Beatty and Benjamin Moore or either of them or
for their good behavior in their appointments or duties respectively, but the said securities, assumptions or engagements
shall be as good, valid and effectual as if this act or any clause,
matter or thing therein contained had not been made and enacted.

[Section II.] (Section III, P. L.) And be it [further] enacted
by the authority aforesaid, That if the said Robert Beatty and
Benjamin Moore or either of them shall in the said courts of
common pleas or elsewhere in applying for or obtaining the
relief aforesaid be guilty of any wilfull concealment or other
fraud or perjury and be convicted thereof, he or they so offending shall be liable to such punishments as the laws for the relief of insolvent debtors have directed in like cases.

Passed March 18, 1789.   Recorded L. B. No. 3, p. 498.

CHAPTER MCD.

A SUPPLEMENT TO THE SEVERAL ACTS OF GENERAL ASSEMBLY RE-SPECTING PUBLIC AUCTIONS AND AUCTIONEERS.

(Section I, P. L.) Whereas certain public auctions are by the
laws of this commonwealth permitted and established for the
sale of estates, real and personal within the city of Philadelphia, the township of the Northern Liberties and the district
of Southwark under certain rules and regulations and all other
persons than the auctioneers duly appointed and licensed
in pursuance of the said laws (except as in and by the said
laws are excepted) are prohibited from selling at public auction within the said city, township or district any estates real
or personal under the pains and penalties in and by the said
laws mentioned:

And whereas it is necessary to amend the said laws in such a manner as to prevent evasions thereof by unlicensed auctions being opened and held in the suburbs of the said city:

[Section I.] (Section II, P. L.) Be it therefore enacted and it is hereby enacted by the Representatives of the Freemen of the Commonwealth of Pennsylvania in General Assembly met and by the authority of the same, That it shall and may be lawful for the president or vice-president in council to appoint and license as often as occasion shall require one auctioneer for the sale of estates real and personal within the township of Moyamensing who shall continue for and during the will and pleasure of the said president and council and shall give bond to the president and his successors with two sufficient sureties in the sum of two thousand pounds for the faithful discharge of his duty and for well and truly performing the terms and payments in and by this act and the several acts of general assembly to which this a supplement directed and required and the said auctioneer who shall be appointed and licensed in pursuance of this act shall have the like powers and authorities within the said township of Moyamensing and be under the like rules, regulations, provisions and directions and subject to the like pains and penalties with any auctioneer for the city of Philadelphia, the township of the Northern Liberties or the district of Southwark:

And whereas by the operation of the present laws for regulating auctions and vendues sundry inhabitants residing within the distance therein prescribed are subjected to the payment of a tax from which the other citizens of the state are exempted:

For remedy whereof:

[Section II.] (Section III, P. L.) Be it enacted by the authority aforesaid, That from and after the passing of this act no duty shall be paid on the sale of any real estate nor on the sale of any household furniture or wearing apparel which has actually been in use nor on any ship or vessel the property of any subject or subjects of the United States or any of them:

And to the end and intent that the provisions herein contained may not prove ineffectual:

[Section III.] (Section IV, P. L.) It is hereby further enacted by the authority aforesaid, That all and every act and acts of general assembly of this commonwealth respecting any auction or auctions or auctioneer or person or persons using or exercising the business thereof within the said city of Philadelphia, the township of the Northern Liberties or the district of Southwark and all the rules, regulations, provisions and directions, pains and penalties in the said acts of general assembly or in any of them contained shall extend and they are hereby extended to all and every place and places within two miles of the state house in the said city of Philadelphia and to all persons who shall within the same distance therefrom offend against or not govern themselves conformably to the directions of this act or of the said acts of general assembly to which this is a supplement or any of them.

Passed March 19, 1789. Recorded L. B. No. 3, p. 478.
See the Note to and the Act of Assembly passed December 9, 1783, Chapter 1063 and the Acts of Assembly passed March 40, 1784, Chapter 1090; February 26, 1791, Chapter 1529.

CHAPTER MCDI.

AN ACT FOR COMPENSATING EVAN OWEN FOR SUPPLIES BY HIM FURNISHED THE CIVIL OFFICERS OF NORTHUMBERLAND COUNTY IN THE YEAR ONE THOUSAND SEVEN HUNDRED AND SEVENTY-FIVE.

(Section 1, P. L.) Whereas the said Evan Owen by his petition to this house [hath] represented, That in consequence of the orders of John Penn, Esquire, late governor of Pennsylvania to enforce the execution of the laws in the county of Northumberland dated the twenty-fifth day of November one thousand seven hundred and seventy-five, be furnished sundry supplies to the persons employed to execute the said orders amounting to the sum of twenty-five pounds two shillings and three-pence for which he never received any compensation and hath prayed this house to grant him relief in the premises:

And whereas it is but just and reasonable that compensation should be made to those who advanced money for the use of the government:

Therefore:

[Section I.] (Section II, P. L.) Be it enacted and it is hereby enacted by the Representatives of the Freemen of the Commonwealth of Pennsylvania in General Assembly met and by the authority of the same, That the supreme executive council be authorized and they are hereby authorized and directed to draw their warrant on the state treasury in favor of the said Evan Owen for the sum of twenty-five pounds two shillings and three pence as a full compensation for the supplies by him furnished as aforesaid.

Passed March 21, 1789.   Recorded L. B. No. 3, p. 481.

CHAPTER MCDII.

AN ACT FOR ENLARGING THE TIME LIMITED BY THE ACT ENTITLED "AN ACT FOR FACILITATING THE REDEMPTION OF THE BILLS OF CREDIT EMITTED IN THE YEAR ONE THOUSAND SEVEN HUNDRED AND EIGHTY-ONE AND FOR REDEEMING PART OF THE FOUNDED DEBT OF THIS STATE, FOR EXTENDING THE TIME FOR PATENTING LANDS WHICH WERE LOCATED BEFORE THE DECLARATION OF INDEPENDENCY AND FOR GIVING A RIGHT OF PRE-EMPTION TO ACTUAL SETTLERS FOR PROCURING WARRANTS FOR LANDS BY THEM OCCUPIED."[1]

(Section I, P. L.) Whereas in and by the act entitled, "An act for facilitating the redemption of the bills of credit emitted in the year one thousand seven hundred and eighty-one and for redeeming part of the founded debt of this state, for extending the time of patenting lands which were located before the Declaration of Independency and for giving a right of pre-emption to actual settlers for procuring warrants for lands by them occupied," the time limited by the act lapsed the twenty-eighth day of March one thousand seven hundred and

[1] Passed March 29, 1788, Chapter 1348.
[2] Passed December 30, 1786, Chapter 1259.

eighty seven for paying or securing to the state the payments
for lands held or claimed by any citizens of this commonwealth by location or any other office right obtained before
the tenth day of December one thousand seven hundred and
seventy-six and yet remaining unpatented, was extended under
the terms and conditions therein mentioned to the tenth day
of April one thousand seven hundred and eighty-nine:

And whereas in and by the same act the time limited by the
act passed the thirtieth day of December one thousand seven
hundred and eighty-six entitled, "An act for giving during a
limited time a right of pre-emption to the actual settlers within this state" was further extended in every matter and thing
therein contained to the said tenth day of April one thousand
seven hundred and eighty-nine:

And whereas the said limitations so extended as aforesaid
will expire on the tenth day of April next and it is deemed expedient that they should be further extended:

[Section I.] (Section II, P. L.) Be it therefore enacted and
it is hereby enacted by the Representatives of the Freemen
of the Commonwealth of Pennsylvania in General Assembly
met and by the authority of the same, That the time so as aforesaid limited and extended be and they are hereby respectively
further extended to the tenth day of April in the year of our
Lord one thousand seven hundred and ninety as fully and
amply to all intents and purposes as they were by the aforesaid act extended to the [said] tenth day of April one thousand seven hundred and eighty-nine, anything to the contrary
contained in the said act or in any of the acts therein recited
and referred to notwithstanding.

Passed March 21, 1789. Recorded L. B. No. 3, p. 479. See the Act of
Assembly March 29, 1790, Chapter 1509.

CHAPTER MCDIII.

AN ACT EMPOWERING CERTAIN TRUSTEES THEREIN NAMED TO SELL
AND DISPOSE OF A CERTAIN HOUSE AND LOT OF GROUND SITUATE
IN THE TOWN OF EASTON AND COUNTY OF NORTHAMPTON AND TO
APPROPRIATE THE MONEYS ARISING FROM THE SALE THEREOF TO-
WARDS THE PURCHASE OF A PARSONAGE OR DWELLING-HOUSE FOR
THE MINISTER OF THE FOUR PROTESTANT EVANGELIC REFORMED
GERMAN CONGREGATIONS TO WIT, THAT OF EASTON, BETHLEHEM,
PLAINFIELD AND GREENWICH TOWNSHIPS, FOR THE TIME BEING.

(Section I, P. L.) Whereas the trustees, elders and deacons
of the four Protestant Evangelic Reformed German Congregations, to wit, that of Easton, Bethlehem and Plainfield townships in the county of Northampton and Greenwich township
in the county of Sussex and state of New Jersey in behalf of the said congregations by their petition have represented to this house that by virtue of a certain indenture or
deed of conveyance, bearing date the twenty-second day of
January in the year of our Lord one thousand seven hundred
and sixty-seven, Lewis Knows, Henry Rader, Peter Metz and
John Sharp and their heirs are seized of a certain house and
lot of ground situate in the town of Easton in the county
of Northampton, bounded on the north by Northampton street,
on the east by a twenty feet alley, on the south by another
twenty feet alley, and on the west by a lot late of William
Nyce containing in breadth sixty feet, and in depth two hundred and twenty feet and marked in the plan of the said town
number one hundred and sixty-nine, in trust, to and for the
sole use and behoof of the said congregations for a parsonage,
mansion or dwelling house, for the minister or pastor of the
said congregations for the time being, that the said premises
do not answer the purpose for which they were purchased and
that the members of the said congregations have unanimously
agreed that the same be disposed of and that the moneys arising therefrom be applied towards the building or purchasing
of another parsonage house or dwelling more suitable and
convenient for the use of the minister of the said congretions

for the time being, and therefore have prayed the aid of the legislature for the purpose:

[Section I.] (Section II, P. L.) Be it therefore enacted and it is hereby enacted by the Representatives of the Freemen of the Commonwealth of Pennsylvania in General Assembly met and by the authority of the same, That it shall and may be lawful to and for Philip Odewelder, the younger, Peter Sharp, Jonas Hartzell and Joseph Keller or any three of them and the survivors or survivor of them to sell and dispose of the said above described house and lot of ground with the rights, privileges and appurtenances thereto belonging as soon as the same may be conveniently done either by private or public sale for the best and highest price that can be gotten for the same and to give and execute an assurance and conveyance of the premises valid in the law (saving the rights of all other persons therein) to the purchaser, his or her heirs and assigns forever subject to the yearly ground rent, if any, that may be due for the same and to appropriate and apply the moneys arising from such a sale towards the building or purchasing of another parsonage house in the said town for the use of the minister of the said four Protestant Reformed German Congregations for the time being and for no other use and purpose whatsoever.

Passed March 21, 1789. Recorded L. B. No. 8, p. 482.

CHAPTER MCDIV.

AN ACT TO APPROPRIATE DIVERS FUNDS ACCRUING AND GROWING DUE TO THIS COMMONWEALTH TOWARDS THE PAYMENT OF THE EXPENSES OF GOVERNMENT AND TO PROVIDE A FUND FOR OTHER PURPOSES.

(Section I, P. L.) Whereas it is necessary that provision be made for the defraying the necessary expenses of the government of this state:

[Section I.] (Section II, P. L.) Be it therefore enacted and
it is hereby enacted by the Representatives of the Freemen
of the Commonwealth of Pennsylvania in General Assembly
met and by the authority of the same, That all and singular
the moneys which now are in or hereafter shall come into the
treasury of this state arising from the interest on the sum of
fifty thousand pounds directed to be loaned in the city and
several counties of this state and every part thereof by an act
of [the] general assembly of this state passed the fourth day
of April one thousand seven hundred and eighty-five and
which are not already appropriated to some other use, all and
singular the moneys which now are in or hereafter shall come
into the said treasury arising from the fees of the different
offices of the land office after payment of the salaries and other
expenses of said officers in pursuance of the act for that purpose passed the eighth day of April one thousand seven hundred and eighty-five, all and singular the moneys which now
are in or hereafter shall come into the said treasury arising
from tavern, marriage and other licenses in pursuance of an
act passed the eighteenth day of February one thousand seven
hundred and seventy-seven, after payment of the judges' salaries charged thereon by an act passed the twenty-fifth day of
March one thousand seven hundred and eighty-five and all and
singular the moneys which now are in or shall hereafter come
into the said treasury arising from the fees received by the
secretary of the supreme executive council in pursuance of
an act passed the twentieth day of March one thousand seven
hundred and eighty-three, be and they are hereby appropriated
to the sole purpose of defraying the expenses of [the] government of this state, and that the further sum of ten thousand
pounds arising from the funds accruing to the state shall be
appropriated annually to the same purpose, and the treasurer
is hereby enjoined and required to open and keep a separate
account of all the moneys by this act appropriated and to hold
the same subject to the orders of this house and of the supreme
executive council respectively according to their respective
rights under the laws of this state to draw orders for the payment of the expenses of government and shall once in

every year or oftener if thereto required render a full and true account of all his receipts and payments of the said money.

And whereas claims are frequently made upon the public which are just in themselves but from their variety cannot be ranged under any particular description and are not otherwise provided for, and the opening and improvement of public roads and the inland navigation and the encouragement of domestic manufactures frequently require the aid of this house:

[Section II.] (Section III, P. L.) Be it therefore enacted by the authority aforesaid. That the treasurer of this state shall and he is hereby enjoined and required to charge the sum of ten thousand pounds annually to the account of the general funds of this state arising and growing due under any former laws and to carry the same [sum] to the credit of a new account for that purpose to be by him opened and kept under the name of claims and improvements and that he shall hold and keep the same as a fund whereout to pay all such sums of money as this house shall by law or otherwise order and direct for all or any of the purposes aforesaid and shall once in every year or oftener if thereto required render a full and true account of all payments of the said moneys.

Passed March 26, 1789. Recorded L. B. No. 3, 514. See the Acts of Assembly passed March 26, 1789, Chapter 1407; March 27, 1789, Chapter 1408; March 3, 1790, Chapter 1487; March 27, 1789, Chapter 1422; March 28, 1789, Chapter 1423; September 28, Chapter 1446; September 28, 1789, Chapter 1447; September 29, 1789, Chapter 1459; November 20, 1789, Chapter 1466.

CHAPTER MCDV.

AN ACT TO REPEAL SO MUCH OF AN ACT ENTITLED "AN ACT FOR RAISING AND COLLECTING OF MONEY ON THE SPECIFIED ARTICLES THEREIN MENTIONED FOR THE SUPPORT OF GOVERMENT AND FOR OTHER PURPOSES THEREIN MENTIONED"[1] AS IMPOSES A TAX ON OWNERS OR POSSESSORS OF ANY ONE-HORSE TWO-WHEELED SULKY, SOLO, CHAIR OR CHAISE OR ANY COVERED FAMILY WAGON COMMONLY CALLED A CARAVAN.

(Section I, P. L.) Whereas it appears to this house that so much of the act entitled, "An act for raising and collecting of money on the specified articles therein mentioned for the support of government and for other purposes therein mentioned" passed the twentieth day of March one thousand seven hundred and eighty-three as directs the raising, levying and collecting annually from the owners or possessors of any one-horse two-wheeled sulky, solo, chair or chaise or of any covered family wagon commonly called a caravan greatly discourages the manufacturers of those useful carriages and lays a very heavy and unequal burden upon many of the citizens of this state:

[Section I.] (Section II, P. L.) Be it therefore enacted and it is hereby enacted by the Representatives of the Freemen of the Commonwealth of Pennsylvania in General Assembly met and by the authority of the same, That from and after the passing of this act so much of the above recited act as directs the raising, levying and collecting the taxes in the said recited act specified from the owners or possessors of any one-horse two-wheeled sulky, solo, chair or chaise or of any covered family wagon commonly called a caravan, be, and the same is hereby repealed and made void, anything in the said recited act to the contrary notwithstanding.

---

[1] Passed March 20, 1783, Chapter 1018.
Passed March 26, 1789. Recorded L. B. No. 3, p. 499.

CHAPTER MCDVI.

AN ACT TO ENABLE THE RECTOR, CHURCH-WARDENS AND VESTRY-
MEN OF THE PROTESTANT EPISCOPAL CHURCH OF SAINT JOHN, AT
YORKTOWN TO MORTGAGE THE PARSONAGE-HOUSE AND CERTAIN
LOTS OF GROUND.

(Section I, P. L.) Whereas the rector, church-wardens and
vestrymen of the Protestant Episcopal Church of Saint John
at Yorktown in the county of York, in the commonwealth of
Pennsylvania, have by their petition to this house represented
the necessity that they are under to raise a considerable sum
of money as well to complete the buildings which have been
began by them as to pay the workmen who have been employed in erecting the same, and have prayed that they may
be enabled to raise by mortgage on the parsonage-house belonging to the said corporation and on the two lots of ground
whereon the same is erected a sum of money not exceeding
five hundred pounds for the purposes aforesaid:

And whereas the prayer of the said petition appears to be
just and reasonable:

[Section I.] (Section II, P. L.) Be it therefore enacted and
it is hereby enacted by the Representatives of the Freemen of
th Commonwealth of Pennsylvania in General Assembly met
and by the authority of the same, That it shall and may be
lawful for the said rector, church-wardens and vestrymen and
they are hereby authorized and empowered by the name and
title aforesaid by one or more mortgage or mortgages or conditional deed or deeds in the nature of a mortgage or mortgages
duly made and executed under their common seal to mortgage
or to grant, bargain and sell in nature of mortgage to any person or persons, his, her or their heirs and assigns the parsonage house belonging to the said corporation and also the two
lots of ground whereon the same is erected or thereto belonging at Yorktown aforesaid with the appurtenances for securing
the payment of any sum or sums of money not exceeding five

hundred pounds and to be redeemed and [defeated] on the
payment thereof with lawful interest In like manner as mortgaged premises are redeemable by the laws of this commonwealth.

Passed March 26, 1789.   Recorded L. B. No. 8, p. 495.

CHAPTER MCDVII.

AN ACT TO ASSIST THE COTTON MANUFACTURERS OF THIS STATE.

(Section I, P. L.) Whereas it appears to this house that a
number of patriotic citizens of this state have subscribed sums
of money for the purpose of forming a fund to be applied to
the Institution of a manufactory in this state under the direction of certain persons styled, "The Manufacturing Committee
of the Pennsylvania Society for the encouragement of Manufactures and useful Arts," and under whom a manufactory of
cotton articles has accordingly been established with great
prospect of success in the city of Philadelphia but the sums
subscribed being inadequate to the prosecution of the plan
upon that extensive and liberal scale which it is the interest
of this state to promote:

[Section I.] (Section II, P. L.) Be it therefore enacted and
it is hereby enacted by the Representatives of the Freemen of
the Commonwealth of Pennsylvania in General Assembly met
and by the authority of the same, That the treasurer of the
state be and he is hereby authorized and directed to subscribe
in the name and for the use of the state for one hundred shares
in the manufacturing fund of the said society.

[Section II.] (Section III, P. L.) And be it further enacted
by the authority aforesaid, That the president and supreme
executive council be and they are hereby authorized and directed to draw an order on the state treasurer in favor of the
manufacturing committee aforesaid for the sum of one thousand pounds, being the amount of the said number of shares

at ten pounds each agreeably to the constitution of the said society, to be paid out of the moneys appropriated for claims and improvements by the act entitled, "An act to appropriate divers funds arising and growing due to this commonwealth towards the payment of the expenses of government and to provide a fund for other purposes."[1]

[Section III.] (Section IV, P. L.) And be it further enacted by the authority aforesaid, That the profits arising from the said shares so subscribed for shall be received and accounted for by the said treasurer.

Passed March 26, 1789. Recorded L. B. No. 3, p. 506.
[1] Passed March 26, 1789, Chapter 1404.

CHAPTER MCDVIII.

AN ACT FOR THE INCORPORATION OF THE COLLEGE OF PHYSICIANS OF PHILADELPHIA.

(Section I, P. L.) Whereas the physicians of Philadelphia, influenced by a conviction of the many advantages which have arisen from literary institutions, have associated themselves under the name and title of "The College of Physicians of Philadelphia:"

And whereas the object of this college is to advance the science of medicine and thereby to lessen human misery, by investigating the diseases and remedies which are peculiar to this country, by observing the effects of different seasons, climates and situations, upon the human body, by recording the changes which are produced in diseases by the progress of agriculture, arts, population and manners; by searching for medicines in the American woods, waters and in the bowels of the earth, by enlarging the avenues to knowledge from the discoveries and publications of foreign countries and by cultivating order and uniformity in the practice of physic:

And whereas the said College of Physicians have prayed us, the Representatives of the Freemen of the Commonwealth of

Pennsylvania, that they may be created a body politic and corporate forever with such power, privileges and immunities as may best answer the laudable purposes which the members thereof have in view:

Wherefore to assist and encourage the said College of Physicians in the prosecution and advancement of useful knowledge for the benefit of their country and of mankind:

[Section I.] (Section II, P. L.) Be it enacted and it is hereby enacted by the Representatives of the Freemen of the Commonwealth of Pennsylvania in General Assembly met and by the authority of the same, That the members of the said College of Physicians, that is to say, John Redman, John Jones, William Shippen, Junior, Adam Kuhn, John Morgan, Benjamin Rush, Samuel Duffield, Gerardus Clarkson, George Gleutworth, Thomas Parke, James Hutchinson, Robert Harris, John Carson, Benjamin Duffield, William W. Smith, John Foulke, Samuel Powel Griffits, William Clarkson, William Currie, Benjamin Say, Andrew Ross, John Morris, Nathan Dorsey, James Cunningham, Caspar Wistar, Junior, Michael Leib and John H. Gibbons be and the same persons are and shall be a body corporate and politic in deed and in name by the name and style of "The College of Physicians of Philadelphia" and by the same name they and their successors are hereby constituted and confirmed one body corporate and politic in law to have perpetual succession and to be able and capable to have hold and enjoy any goods and chattels, lands, tenements, rents, hereditaments, gifts and bequests of what nature soever in fee simple or for term of years, life or lives or otherwise and also to grant, sell, alien, assign or let the same lands, tenements, hereditaments and premises according to the grant of the respective grants and bequests made to the said corporation and of the estate of the corporation therein. Provided, That the amount of the clear yearly value of such real estate exceed not the sum of five hundred pounds [lawful] money of this commonwealth.

[Section II.] (Section III, P. L.) And be it further enacted by the authority aforesaid, That the said corporation be and

16—XIII

shall be forever hereafter able and capable in law to sue and
be sued, plead and be impleaded, answer and be answered
unto, defend and be defended in all or any courts of justice
and other places in all manner of suits, actions, complaints,
pleas, causes and matters of what nature or kind soever and
that it shall and may be lawful to and for the said corporation
forever hereafter to have and use a common seal and the same
seal at the will and pleasure of the said corporation to break,
change, alter and renew.

[Section III.] (Section IV, P. L.) And be it further enacted
by the authority aforesaid, That for the well ordering of the
said corporation and its affairs there shall be at all times hereafter the following officers of the same, that is to say, one president, one vice-president, four censors, a secretary and a treasurer, who shall be chosen annually from amongst the fellows
of the said College of Physicians on the first Tuesday in the
month of July forever hereafter or within one calendar month
after the same day in any year and that John Redman be the
present president of the said college, John Jones the present
vice-president, William Shippen, Junior, Adam Kuhn, Benjamin Rush and Samuel Duffield the present censors, Samuel
Powel Griffits the present secretary, and that the Gerardus
Clarkson be the treasurer of the said college and shall be and
remain the president, vice-president, censors, secretary and
treasurer, respectively of the said college until they are super-
seded by a new election, to be made by the fellows of the said
college, as aforesaid, and all vacancies by death, resignation
or otherwise which shall at any time hereafter happen in any
of the said offices may be filled by a special election to be held
so often as occasion shall require.

[Section IV.] (Section V, P. L.) And be it further enacted
by the authority aforesaid, That the authorities and duties of
the officers of the said corporation who are hereinbefore mentioned and of any others which the said corporation shall be
fit to appoint, the times of meeting of the said corporation,
the admission of members and the other concerns of the said
corporation, shall be regulated by the by-laws and ordinances

of the said corporation heretofore made or to be made touching the premises.

[Section V.] (Section VI, P. L.) Provided always and be it enacted by the authority aforesaid, That no by-laws nor ordinances of the said corporation hereafter made shall be binding upon the members or officers thereof unless the same shall be proposed at one regular meeting of the said corporation and enacted and received at another after the intervention of at least thirty days and that no sale or alienation or lease for above three years of any part of the real estate of the said corporation shall be valid unless the terms and nature of such sale or lease be proposed at a previous meeting of the said corporation.

Passed March 26, 1789.   Recorded L. B. No. 3, p. 490.

CHAPTER MCDIX.

AN ACT TO AMEND AN ACT ENTITLED "AN ACT FOR AMENDING THE PENAL LAWS OF THIS STATE."[1]

(Section I, P. L.) In order to remedy several abuses arising from certain defects in the act entitled "An act for amending the penal laws of this state," and to render the provisions therein contained more beneficial and effectual:

[Section I.] (Section II, P. L.) Be it enacted and it is hereby enacted by the Representatives of the Freemen of the Commonwealth of Pennsylvania in General Assembly met and by the authority of the same, That the county commissioners of the several counties of this state except the county of Philadelphia shall and they are hereby enjoined and required as soon as conveniently may be after the passing of this act to cause to be set apart and prepared in their respective county gaols and in the yards thereof suitable and sufficient places and apartments for the accommodation of such persons as are or may be con-

[1] Passed September 15, 1786, Chapter 1241.

fined therein on account of debt or [upon] civil process and also
as witnesses in cases of criminal prosecutions, which places and
apartments shall be exclusively appropriated to the reception
and accommodation of the foregoing description of prisoners
and no felon charged or convicted shall be permitted to have
access to the same or any communication with any person of
the description aforesaid.

[Section II.] (Section III, P. L.) And be it further enacted
by the authority aforesaid, That all persons who shall be confined in the gaol of the city and county of Philadelphia upon
civil process or as witnesses in criminal prosecutions or
charged with or convicted of misdemeanors only, shall upon
[due] notice from the persons hereinafter mentioned to the
sheriff of the said city and county that the workhouse in the
said city is altered and prepared for their reception in the
manner hereinafter directed, be removed to the said workhouse, and that so much thereof as shall be necessary together
with the east yard to the same belonging shall be set apart and
appropriated to the reception and safekeeping of such persons
only, which shall be and remain under the care and custody
of the sheriff of the said city and county, and shall and is
hereby declared to be the gaol of the city and county of Philadelphia.

[Section III] (Section IV, P. L.) And be it further enacted
by the authority aforesaid, That the mayor, aldermen and citizens of Philadelphia together with the commissioners for the
county of Philadelphia shall as soon as conveniently may be
cause such alterations to be made in the said workhouse and
yard as shall be necessary for the safe and comfortable keeping of such prisoners and when the same shall be completed
give notice thereof to the said sheriff for the purpose aforesaid.

[Section IV.] (Section V, P. L.) And be it further enacted
by the authority aforesaid, That the residence of the said work
house with the west yard thereto belonging shall be reserved
for the uses to which it is at present applied, and if the present building shall be found upon experience to be too small
for the purpose of safely keeping, accommodating and employ-

ing the number of persons who are or shall be confined there-
[in] it shall and may be lawful for [the] said mayor, aldermen, citizens and commissioners, to cause such additional
buildings to be erected contiguous thereto as they shall find
necessary and expedient for the purposes aforesaid.

[Section V.] (Section VI, P. L.) And be it further enacted
by the authority aforesaid, That the mayor and any three
[of the] aldermen of the said city and any four justices of the
peace of the county of Philadelphia shall be and they are
hereby authorized and required to fix and regulate from time
to time the fees of the keeper of the said workhouse and for
securing the payment thereof from the vagrants and other
disorderly persons who shall be committed to the same, the
said keeper shall have power notwithstanding any rule or order to the contrary to detain any such person in confinement
until payment or satisfaction thereof shall be made.

[Section VI.] (Section VII, P. L.) And be it further enacted
by the authority aforesaid, That the said mayor, aldermen, citizens and commissioners shall as soon as conveniently may be
cause to be prepared, separated and set apart such parts of
the present gaol of the city and county of Philadelphia as may
be necessary for the reception and safe keeping of all persons
charged with or convicted of felonies or other crimes to which
the provisions hereinafter contained do not extend, and that
the residue of the said gaol shall be reserved for the reception,
safe keeping and employment of all felons sentenced to hard
labor and confinement, and that the said mayor, aldermen, citizens and commissioners shall cause the rooms [and] apartments thereof and such parts of the yard as shall be so reserved from the last mentioned purposes to be divided from
the rest, and cells, sheds and other suitable buildings to be constructed for the purpose of separating, confining and keeping
employed at hard labor all felons of the last mentioned description and that as well such apartments, cells and sheds as
the residue of the said gaol where necessary shall be properly walled up and secured to prevent all communication
among the same felons and with the persons abroad and that
the [same] gaol from and after the passing of this act shall

be called and styled the common prison of the city and county of Philadelphia.

[Section VII.] (Section VIII, P. L.) And be it further enacted by the authority aforesaid, That all felons convicted in any county in this state of any felony or felonies for which he, she or they shall be sentenced to hard labor for the space of twelve months or upwards may at the discretion of the justices of the court in which such felon shall be convicted within three months after such sentence shall have been given, be removed at the expense of the said county under safe and [secure] conduct to the said prison and be therein confined, fed, clothed and put to hard labor in the manner by the act entitled "An act for amending the penal laws of this state,"[1] and by this act directed for the remaining space of time for which by such sentence they shall be liable to imprisonment.

[Section VIII.] (Section IX, P. L.) And be it further enacted by the authority aforesaid, That it shall and may be lawful for the said mayor and aldermen of the said city in the mayor's court for the said city and for the justices of the peace of the several counties in their general [courts of] quarter sessions of the peace and they are hereby enjoined and required to appoint annually or oftener if necessary six suitable and discreet persons within the said city and the respective counties as inspectors of the said prison and the several gaols and workhouses within the said city and the respective counties, whose powers and duties shall be as follows:

First. To provide a proper quantity of suitable raw materials and to see that the same is duly distributed by the prison keeper or his deputies among the felons sentenced to hard labor as aforesaid.

Secondly. To receive and dispose of the produce of their labor and apply the same in the manner hereinafter directed.

Thirdly. To examine into all breaches and neglects of duty on the part of the prison keepers and their deputies and of all keepers of gaols and workhouses and report in writing the special instances thereof to the said mayor and aldermen and to the said justices at their courts aforesaid quarterly if occasion be.

¹ *Ante.*

Fourthly. To inquire into and report to the mayor, aldermen or justices of the peace such repairs, alterations or additions to the buildings provided for the purposes aforesaid as
may be necessary and expedient.

[Section IX.] (Section X, P. L.) And be it further enacted
by the authority aforesaid, That it shall and may be lawful
for the said mayor and aldermen annually to appoint a suitable and proper person to be keeper of the said common prison
in the city of Philadelphia who shall however be liable to
be removed by the said mayor and aldermen when occasion may require, in which case another such person shall be
appointed in the manner aforesaid, who, besides the care and
custody of the prisoners, shall superintend the felons employed
at hard labor; that it shall be the duty of the said keeper to
prevent all communication between the men and woman felons and to separate the men felons from each other as much
as the construction of the buildings and the nature of their
employment will admit of; to admit no persons whatever except officers and ministers of justice or counsellors or attorneys at law employed by the prisoners, ministers of the gospel
or persons producing a written license from one of the said inspectors to enter within the walls where such felons shall be
confined. To suffer no spirituous liquors to be conveyed to the
said prisoners unless in cases of sickness and with the consent
of one of the said inspectors in writing first obtained. To
punish the obstinate and refractory and to reward those who
shall show signs of reformation by lightening or increasing
their tasks and by increasing or lessening their food, as occasion may require. To prevent profligate or idle conversation
and demeanor and to preserve the utmost possible cleanliness
in the persons and apartments of the prisoners.

[Section X.] (Section XI, P. L.) And be it further enacted
by the authority aforesaid, That such keeper shall have power
with the approbation of the said mayor and aldermen to appoint a suitable number of deputies and assistants for whose
faithful execution of their offices he shall be accountable and
he shall also be punishable at the discretion of the court hav-

ing cognizance thereof for all escapes wilfully or negligently assistants so much per annum as shall be allowed and agreed assistants, and neither he, his deputies or assistants shall ask, demand or receive any fee, emolument or reward of any kind except the salaries hereafter mentioned.

[Section XI] (Section VII. P. L.) And be it further enacted by the authority aforesaid, That the said keeper of the said prison shall receive as a full compensation for his services including the expense of hiring and retaining his deputies and assistants so much per annum as shall be allowed and agreed on by the said mayor, aldermen, citizens and commissioners, which shall be paid to him quarterly by orders to be drawn in his favor on the treasurer of the county of Philadelphia by the mayor of the said city for the time being and he shall moreover receive from the said inspectors of the prison a commission or allowance of ten per centum on the moneys arising from the labors of the said prisoners

[Section XII.] (Section XIII, P. L.) And be it further enacted by the authority aforesaid, That before such prison keeper, his deputies or assistants shall exercise any part of the said office he shall give bond with two sufficient sureties to the said mayor, aldermen and citizens in the sum of five hundred pounds upon condition that he, his deputies and assistants, will well and faithfully perform the trust and duty in them reposed, according to the form and effect of the several acts of assembly of this state thereto relating, which bond, the due execution thereof being proved [before] and certified by any one of the aldermen of the said city, shall be recorded in the office of the recorder of deeds for the city and county of Philadelphia and copies thereof exemplified by the said recorder of deeds, shall be good evidence in all courts of law [in any suit brought] against such prison keeper or his sureties.

[Section XIII.] (Section XIV, P. L.) And be it further enacted by the authority aforesaid, That if any felon sentenced to hard labor and confinement shall escape, he shall on conviction thereof suffer such additional confinement at hard labor agreeably to the directions of this and of the said recited act

and shall also suffer such corporal punishment as the
court in their discretion shall adjudge and direct. And
if any such felon or felons shall after his or their escape
be guilty of any offense for which on conviction he
she or they would have been sentenced to death under
the law as it stood before the passing the act entitled "An
act for amending the penal laws of this state,"¹ he, she or they
shall suffer death accordingly as if no such act had been
passed.

[Section XIV.] (Section XV, P. L.) And be it further enacted by the authority aforesaid, That if any felon or felons
who may have served or shall hereafter serve out the term or
time for which he, she or they was or were or shall be sentenced agreeably to the terms of the act entitled "An act for
amending the penal laws of this state,"² or of this act, or hath
or have been or shall hereafter be pardoned for the offenses
or crimes of which he, she or they hath or have been or shall
hereafter be convicted agreeably to the said act or of this
act, provided the offense or offenses for which he, she or they
was or were or shall be convicted was or were by the former
laws of the late province or of this commonwealth declared
capital and is, are or shall be convicted of a second offence
which was by the laws of the late province or of this commonwealth made capital, he, she or they being duly convicted of
such second offense shall suffer death on such conviction without benefit of clergy.

[Section XV.] (Section XVI, P. L.) And be it further enacted by the authority aforesaid, That it shall and may be
lawful for the commissioners for the county of Philadelphia
with the assent and concurrence of the mayor, recorder and
any three aldermen of the city of Philadelphia and any three
of the justices of the peace for the county of Philadelphia, and
they are hereby required to assess and levy in the manner directed by the acts of assembly for raising county rates and levies so much money as they shall judge necessary for the pur-

¹Ante.
²Ante.

poses of altering, accomodating and enlarging the said [gaol] prison and workhouse in manner aforesaid and also so much per annum as shall be necessary for the payment of the salary of the said prison keeper and for providing the materials, tools and implements for the labor of the said felons.

[Section XVI.] (Section XVII, P. L.) And be it further enacted by the authority aforesaid, That the charges of clothing, feeding and maintaining the said felons sentenced to hard labor as aforesaid, of providing the necessary materials, tools and implements for labor [and the profits of such labor] shall be equally and annually apportioned and divided by the said inspectors of the said common prison among the said city and the several counties in proportion to the number of criminals from each of them respectively who shall be so confined at hard labor in the said common prison, in which settlement and distribution the city and county of Philadelphia shall be allowed the sum of one hundred pounds annually as a compensation for the additional expenses arising from the provisions of this act. Provided always, That it shall and may be lawful for the commissioners of any such county to appeal from such settlement and distribution to the supreme executive council who shall upon examination and due notice to the parties, revise, alter or confirm the same as shall be just and reasonable. And provided also, That nothing herein contained shall alter, lessen or defeat the estate and interest of the city and county of Philadelphia in the said common prison [or] lot of ground thereunto belonging and their appurtenances.

[Section XV.] (Section XVIII, P. L.) And be it further enacted by the authority aforesaid, That if the expenses attending the necessary alterations of the said [common prison] and employment of the said felons shall be found to exceed the profits arising from their labor it shall and may be lawful for the supreme executive council and they are hereby required upon the application of a majority of the inspectors of the said prison of the said city and county to draw orders upon the treasurer of the respective counties for such sums of money to be paid to the commissioners of the county of Philadelphia or their orders as upon and equal rate and [apportion]ment of

such expenses according to the principles aforesaid such counties may be severally liable to.

[Section XVIII.] (Section XIX, P. L.) And be it further enacted by the authority aforesaid, That if any keeper of the
said common prison of the city and county of Philadelphia
or any of his deputies or assistants shall suffer any spirituous
liquors, except as is before excepted, to be introduced into the
places so reserved for the employment of felons at hard labor
or shall willingly suffer any communication between the men
and women felons so confined or shall ask, demand or receive
of or from any person whatsoever by color of his office or under
any pretence whatever any sum or sums of money or other
fee, gratuity or reward other than the salaries and allowances
hereinbefore mentioned, he or they on conviction thereof shall
be liable to a fine of ten pounds to be applied to the purchase
of materials, tools and implements for the labor and employment of the said felons in the manner by this act directed for
the support and maintenance of such felons.

Passed March 27, 1789. Recorded L. B. No. 3, p. 500.

The Act in the text was repealed by the Act of Assembly passed April
5, 1790, Chapter 1516.

CHAPTER MCDX.

AN ACT FOR THE MORE EFFECTUAL COLLECTION OF THE POOR TAX
IN THE CITY OF PHILADELPHIA, THE DISTRICT OF SOUTHWARK
AND THE TOWNSHIPS OF MOYAMENSING AND THE NORTHERN LIB-
ERTIES AND TO PROVIDE IN A MORE CONVENIENT AND SALUTARY
MANNER FOR THE CONFINEMENT OF DISORDERLY PERSONS,
FOUND AND APPREHENDED IN THE SAID CITY, DISTRICT AND
TOWNSHIPS.

(Section I, P. L.) Whereas by the eventual operation of an
act entitled "An act to amend an act entitled 'An act for the
better employment of the poor of the city of Philadelphia, the
district of Southwark, the townships of Moyamensing, Pas-
sayunk and the Northern Liberties,' and to revive and perpetu-

ate an act entitled 'An act for the relief of the poor and for re-
pealing two other acts herein mentioned,' [1] the overseers of the
poor of the city of Philadelphia, district of Southwark and
townships of Moyamensing and of the Northern Liberties by
the corporate style and name of "The Guardians of the Poor in
the City of Philadelphia" have become invested with all and
singular the powers, authorities, rights, claims, demands, interest and estate, real and personal and mixed which were of
a certain corporation heretofore known by the name of "The
Contributors to the relief and employment of the Poor in the
City of Philadelphia":

And whereas the said guardians of the poor in the city of
Philadelphia are by the said recited act required and directed
half-yearly to appoint six of their members to superintend the
almshouse and house of employment and to exercise and perform all the authorities of the former managers of the said institution. And it is further therein declared that the said six
persons so appointed shall, during their continuance as managers aforesaid, be exempted from all other duties of the offices
of overseer of the poor and that the whole duties thereof shall
be performed by the rest of the overseers.

And whereas it hath been represented that in consequence
of the additional duties thus imposed upon the said overseers
of the poor the business of their appointment hath been rendered burdensome and oppressive and the collection of the poor
tax hath become difficult, precarious and inefficient:

And whereas it is expedient and reasonable that an adequate
remedy should be provided for the evil complained of:

Therefore:

[Section I.] (Section II. P. L.) Be it enacted and it is hereby
enacted by the Representatives of the Freemen of the Commonwealth of Pennsylvania in General Assembly met and by
the authority of the same, That it shall and may be lawful
for the said guardians of the poor in the city of Philadelphia
from time to time to nominate, appoint, employ and pay one
or more fit person or persons to be collector or collectors of

[1] Passed March 25, 1762, Chapter 962.

the poor tax and taxes, assessed or imposed or hereafter to be assessed or imposed upon the inhabitants of the said city of Philadelphia, the district of Southwark and the townships of Moyamensing and the Northern Liberties for the use and benefit of the poor thereof, which said collector or collectors so to be nominated, appointed and employed shall with at least one surety to be with him or them joined, severally and respectively make and execute a bond or bonds unto the said guardians of the poor in a sum equal to double the amount of his or their duplicates with a condition or conditions thereunto severally annexed and underwritten for the true and faithful performance of all and singular the duties and services which shall or may lawfully be imposed upon and required from such collector or collectors respectively.

Provided nevertheless, That the compensation to be received for such collections by such collector or collectors shall not exceed five pounds per centum on the sums by them respectively received.

[Section II.] (Section III, P. L.) And be it enacted by the authority aforesaid, That the collector or collectors to be appointed as aforesaid shall and may from time to time levy and raise from and upon all and every the said inhabitants of the said city of Philadelphia, the district of Southwark, the townships of Moyamensing and Northern Liberties and of and from their respective estates, chattels and effects, all such sum and sums of money as shall be lawfully assessed and imposed [upon] the said inhabitants respectively or their respective estates, chattels and effects for the use and benefit of the poor aforesaid in like manner and with like powers, jurisdiction and authority as they the said overseers of the poor of the city of Philadelphia heretofore might or could do and subject to all and singular the rules, regulations, proceedings, appeals, penalties and forfeitures to which the said overseers of the poor were by any law or laws heretofore subject in the business of levying and raising the said poor tax and taxes in manner aforesaid.

[Section III.] (Section IV, P. L.) And be it further enacted by the authority aforesaid, That the said guardians of the poor in the city of Philadelphia shall nominate and appoint one of their board to act as treasurer under the like form and penalties with the treasurer to the house of employment, to whom the collector or collectors shall [pay over] once in every week, render an account of and concerning all such sums of money as they shall have respectively received for or on account of the said poor tax or taxes and the said treasurer shall give a receipt or receipts to the said collector or collectors for the sum or sums of money which he or they shall from time to time bring in and pay unto him as aforesaid which said receipt or receipts shall be good and sufficient discharge unto the said collector or collectors for so much money as may be herein respectively acknowledged and expressed to have been received by the said treasurer.

And whereas it hath been further represented that the commitment of disorderly persons found in the city of Philadelphia, the district of Southwark, the townships of Moyamensing and Northern Liberties, to the almshouse or house of employment is inconvenient, improper and pernicious inasmuch as the said almshouse or house of employment is calculated for the accommodation of the poor and infirm and not for the reformation of the idle and profligate and the intermixture of persons who are sent thither as subjects of punishment with those who are admitted as objects of charity may be the means of extending the depravity of morals and manners which is ever fatal to the well being of society and the peace and order of government:

And whereas the laws of this commonwealth have provided for the establishment of a suitable workhouse in the county of Philadelphia for the confinement of disorderly persons of the said county other than those found in the said city of Philadelphia, the district of Southwark, the townships of Moyamensing and the Northern Liberties and it is not only expedient but also just that the maintenance and charge of disorderly persons found in the [said] last mentioned places should likewise be borne and defrayed by the said county of Philadelphia and that the said workhouse should be employed as the com-

mon receptacle of all vagabonds and disorderly persons found
in the said county and therein duly apprehended and committed:

Therefore:

[Section IV.] (Section V, P. L.) Be it further enacted by the
authority aforesaid, That all and every disorderly person and
persons found and apprehended in the said city of Philadelphia,
the district of Southwark, the townships of Moyamensing and
Northern Liberties shall and may be from time to time lawfully
committed to the said workhouse of the county of Philadelphia,
by the like authority and shall be there kept and maintained in
the same manner and the charge and expense thereof shall be
borne and defrayed by the same means as are allowed, declared
and provided in the case of disorderly persons, found and apprehended in any other place within the said county of Philadelphia.

[Section V.] (Section VI, P. L.) And be it further enacted
by the authority aforesaid, That from and after the passing
of this act it shall not be lawful to commit any disorderly person or persons whatsoever unto the said house of employment
and all such disorderly person or persons as have been at any
time heretofore committed to the said house of employment
and are now therein kept and maintained shall and they are
hereby ordered and directed as soon as conveniently may be
to be delivered by the said guardians of the poor unto the
keeper of the said workhouse of the county of Philadelphia
to be by him there kept and maintained in manner aforesaid.

[Section VII.] (Section VIII, P. L.) And be it further enacted by the authority aforesaid, That so much and no more
of any law or laws of this commonwealth as is by this act
altered and supplied shall be and the same is hereby repealed,
annulled and made absolutely void.

Passed March 27, 1789. Recorded L. D. No. 3, p. 483, etc.

CHAPTER MCDXI.

A SUPPLEMENT TO THE SEVERAL ACTS OF ASSEMBLY FOR THE RE-
LIEF OF INSOLVENT DEBTORS.[1]

(Section I. P. L.) Whereas by the laws of this commonwealth
no person is entitled to the benefit of the several acts of assembly made for the relief of insolvent debtors, unless he or
she shall have resided therein for the space of two years next
before his or their imprisonment; and it is thought expedient
to alter the same under certain limitations and restrictions, in
order to prevent the necessity of frequent applications to the
legislature by persons who may be unable to make payment
and who are nevertheless without relief under the existing
laws.

[Section I.] (Section II, P. L.) Be it therefore enacted and
it is hereby enacted by the Representatives of the Freemen of
the Commonwealth of Pennsylvania in General Assembly met
and by the authority of the same, That so much of the laws of
this commonwealth as deprives any person or persons by reason of his her or their not having resided therein for the
space of two years next before his, her or their imprisonment,
of the benefit of or relief under all or any of the acts of
general assembly made for the relief of insolvent debtors, shall,
as against him, her or them at whose suit or suits any such
person or persons is, are or shall be imprisoned and so far as
relates or shall relate to the debt or debts due to such plaintiff or plaintiffs, if the same shall not in the whole exceed the
sum of one hundred pounds, be, and they are hereby repealed
and made null and void.

[Section II.] (Section III, P. L.) And be it further enacted
by the authority aforesaid, That at all times from and immediately after the passing of this act the like benefit and relief

------

[1] See original act for relief of insolvent debtors passed February 14,
1729-30, Chapter 315.

which, by the laws of this commonwealth made for the relief
of insolvent debtors may or can be afforded to any of the inhabitants thereof who have resided therein for the space of two
years next before his, her or their imprisonment, shall be extended and afforded under the same rules, regulations, exceptions and restrictions and on the same terms and conditions
to all and every such person and persons as are in and by the
said acts of general assembly or any of them mentioned, notwithstanding he, she or they has or have not resided or shall not
have resided within this commonwealth for any time before
his, her or their imprisonment. Provided nevertheless, That
nothing herein contained shall extend to or operate against
any other creditor or creditors of any such insolvent debtor or
debtors than him, her or them at whose suit or suits such insolvent debtor or debtors is, are or shall be imprisoned. And
provided further, That the provisions herein contained shall not
extend to any person who is or shall be imprisoned at the suit
or suits of one or more person or persons for any debt or debts
exceeding one hundred pounds in the whole:

And whereas it has been found on experience that the long
confinement for small debts, fines or forfeitures of those who
are incapable of making satisfaction tends to the distress of
their families as well as to the public injury by the burdens
created and idle habits contracted thereby:

For remedy thereof:

[Section III.] (Section IV, P. L.) Be it further enacted by
the authority aforesaid, That every person who now is or
hereafter shall be confined in any gaol within this commonwealth in execution or otherwise for any debt or debts, sum or
sums of money, or fine or fines, forfeiture or forfeitures, none
of which do or shall exceed the sum of five pounds exclusive
of costs and has or shall have remained so confined for the
space of thirty days shall be discharged from such confinement
and not be liable to be again imprisoned for the same and the
sheriff, gaoler or keeper of the gaol in which such person is or
shall be confined shall upon application to him by the person

17—XIII

so confined, discharge him or her out of custody if detained
for such debt or debts, sum or sums of money, fine or forfeiture
only and for no other cause.

Passed March 27, 1789. Recorded L. B. No. 3, p. 491. See the note to
the Act of Assembly passed February 14, 1729-30, Chapter 315.

CHAPTER MCDXII.

AN ACT FOR GRANTING TRIALS AT NISI PRIUS IN THE COUNTY OF PHILADELPHIA.

(Section I, P. L.) Whereas the periods for holding the several
terms of the supreme court at Philadelphia have by experience been found too short for the dispatch of and expediting
the business of the said court owing partly to the great length
of time necessary to the discussion of many important and com-
plex cases which have been there determined, whereby many
other trials have been unavoidably postponed and partly to
a portion of each term being necessarily allotted for arguments
of points of law and motions in actions removed from the several counties in the state, and it is conceived that a power in
the said court to hold courts of nisi prius for the trial of such
issues in fact as are or shall be depending in the said supreme
court either by removal or otherwise from the city or county of
Philadelphia would greatly expedite the determination of the
business in the said supreme court and be a great relief to
such suitors as should not be able from want of time to procure trials at bar.

[Section I.] (Section II, P. L.) Be it therefore enacted and it
is hereby enacted by the Representatives of the Freemen of
the Commonwealth of Pennsylvania in General Assembly met
and by the authority of the same, That from and after the passing of this act the justices of the said supreme court in term
time or a majority of them in vacation shall be empowered and
they are hereby enjoined when occasion shall require to direct

the holding of courts of nisi prius in the city of Philadelphia for
the city and county of Philadelphia before them or any one or
more of them on such days and times as they shall nominate
and appoint and for that purpose to direct the usual process
to issue returnable at such times during the sitting of the
same courts of nisi prius as they shall see fit for the trial of
all such issues in fact as are or shall be depending in the said
supreme court in pleas either civil or criminal, originally instituted in the said supreme court or brought thither by writs
of removal, appeals or otherwise from any civil or criminal ·
jurisdiction in the city or county of Philadelphia already
erected or hereafter to be erected, and generally to do, execute
and perform all and every such 't s, matters and things and
put in practice all such powers, authorities, jurisdictions and
privileges as by the present existi;.g laws relative to courts
of nisi prius for other counties within this commonwealth
or which in any manner respect the same are enjoined and required of or are given and granted to the said justices of the
said supreme court or to any one of the same justices:

And whereas rules for the striking of special juries are often
taken by defendants in the said court for the mere purpose
of delaying the recovery of undisputed debts, which practice
has also a tendency to postpone the determination of litigated
causes:

[Section II.] (Section III, P. L.) It is therefore enacted by
the authority aforesaid, That no rule on the defendants application for a trial by special in the [said] supreme court or
at nisi prius of any issue in any of the said civil actions except
in cases [where] the title to real estate shall be in question
shall hereafter be granted unless the defendant, or some person
for him shall previously make and file an affidavit in the said
court that he conceives there is a just ad legal cause of defence
against the plaintiff's demand in the said action or against
some part thereof.

[Section III.] (Section IV, P. L.) And be it further enacted
by the authority aforesaid, That so much of an act of general
assembly entitled "An act for the better regulation of juries" [1]

------

[1] Passed March 19, 1785, Chapter 1139.

as provides or enacts "that every special jury shall be struck
thirty days at least before the day of the return of the process
for summoning such jury to attend and that the party entering a rule for such special jury shall forthwith serve a copy
thereof on the attorney of the other party together with a
copy of the list of jurors so to be struck and due notice to attend, to strike the same at the office of the prothonotary or
clerk of the court," shall be and the same is hereby repealed
and made null and void.

Passed March 27, 1789. Recorded L. B. No. 8, p. 495.

CHAPTER MCDXIII.

AN ACT TO PREVENT THE GRANTING OF SPECIAL COURTS ON THE PLAINTIFF'S APPLICATION.

(Section I, P. L.) Whereas the granting of special courts on
the application of plaintiffs under pretence of their sudden departure out of this commonwealth has been found on experience to be attended with much injury to the good people
thereof by giving to foreigners an undue preference in the decision of causes:

For remedy thereof:

[Section I.] (Section II, P. L.) Be it enacted and it is hereby
enacted by the Representatives of the Freemen of the Commonwealth of Pennsylvania in General Assembly met and by the
authority of the same, That so much of an act of general assembly of this commonwealth entitled "A supplement to an act entitled 'An act for establishing courts of justice in this province,' " as authorizes or requires the justices of the supreme
court or of any court of common pleas within this commonwealth to grant to any plaintiff or plaintiffs a special court or
courts or to hear and determine any suit cause or action without the usual imparlances be and the same is hereby repealed.

Passed March 27, 1789. Recorded L. B. No. 8, p. 494.
[1] Passed April 10, 1782, Chapter 966.

CHAPTER MCDIV.

AN ACT TO PREVENT THE IMPORTATION OF CONVICTS INTO THIS
COMMONWEALTH.

(Section I, P. L.) Whereas it hath been represented to this
house by the United States in congress assembled that
a practice prevails of importing felons convict into this
state, under various pretences which said felons convict
so imported have been sold and dispersed among the people
of this state whereby much injury hath arisen to the
morals of some and others have been greatly endangered in
their lives and property:

For remedy whereof:

[Section I.] (Section II, P. L.) Be it enacted and it is hereby
enacted by the Representatives of the Freemen of the Commonwealth of Pennsylvania in General Assembly met and by
the authority of the same, That from and after the third day of
May next no captain or master of any vessel or any other person
or persons shall knowingly or willingly import, bring or send
or cause or procure to be imported, brought or sent or be aiding
or assisting therein into this commonwealth by land or water
any felon convict or person under sentence of death or any
other legal disability incurred by a criminal prosecution or who
shall be delivered or sent to him or her from any prison or
place of confinement in any place out of the United States.

[Section II.] (Section IV, P. L.) And be it further enacted
by the authority aforesaid, That every captain or master of
a vessel or any other person who shall so as aforesaid, import
bring or send or cause or procure to be imported, brought or
sent or be aiding and assisting therein, into this commonwealth
by land or water or who shall as factor or agent of the person
or persons so offending or as consignee sell or offer for sale
any such person as above described knowing him or her so to
be, shall suffer three months imprisonment without bail or

mainprize, and shall forfeit and pay over and beyond the costs of prosecution for every such person so brought, imported or sent or caused or procured so to be or sold or offered for sale, fifty pounds lawful money of Pennsylvania, one half thereof to the commonwealth and the other half to him or her who shall sue or prosecute for the same, which said penalty shall be recovered by action of debt or information in any court of record, and the defendant or person sued or impleaded therefor shall be ruled to give special bail in like manner and under the same rules as is usual in actions of debt founded on contract.

[Section III.] (Section V, P. L.) And be it further enacted by the authority aforesaid, That every person who shall offend against this act or anything herein contained shall on conviction thereof be adjudged and ordered to enter into a recognizance with sufficient sureties to convey and transport within such reasonable time as shall be ordered and directed by the court to some place or places without the bounds, limits and jurisdiction of the United States every such felon convict or other person of the description aforesaid which he or she shall have been convicted of having brought, imported or sent or having been aiding or assisting therein into this commonwealth against the true intent and meaning of this act or of having so as aforesaid sold or offered for sale, and in default of entering into such recognizance with sufficient sureties as aforesaid he or she shall be committed to gaol there to remain without bail or mainprize until he or she shall enter into such recognizance with such sureties as aforesaid or until he or she shall cause every such person so as aforesaid by him or her imported, brought or sent or cause or procured to have been imported, brought or sent or that he or she shall have been aiding or assisting in the importing, bringing or sending into this commonwealth against the true intent and meaning of this act or that he or she shall have been convicted of having so as aforesaid sold or offered for sale.

Passed March 27, 1789. Recorded L. B. No. 3, 497. See Act of Assembly passed February 14, 1729-30, Chapter, 314.

The Act in the text was repealed by the Act of Assembly passed March 31, 1860, P. L. 452.

CHAPTER MCDXV.

AN ACT TO REPEAL SO MUCH OF ANY ACT OR ACTS OF ASSEMBLY
OF THIS COMMONWEALTH AS DIRECTS THE PAYMENT OF THE NEW
LOAN DEBT OR THE INTEREST THEREOF BEYOND THE FIRST DAY
OF APRIL NEXT, AND FOR OTHER PURPOSES THEREIN MENTIONED.

(Section I, P. L.) Whereas by an act of the General Assembly
of this state passed the first day of March, in the year of our
Lord one thousand seven hundred and eighty-six and by a
supplement thereto passed the twenty-eighth day of March
one thousand seven hundred and eighty-seven the comptroller-
general of this commonwealth was authorized and directed to
receive on loan in behalf of the state such certificates of the
debts due from the United States as in the said act and supplement thereto are particularly described and to issue and deliver in lieu thereof to the person or persons who should before
the first day of March which should be in the year of our Lord
one thousand seven hundred and eighty-eight voluntarily make
such loan or loans, a certificate or certificates (in the said first
recited act before described) to the amount or value of the sum
and sums due as principal money on the certificate or certificates which he should so receive on loan, expressing the period
from which the said principal sum is entitled to draw interest
according to the tenor and terms of the certificate or certificates so received on loan and by the said act divers other provisions are made for preserving as exact a conformity in the
relative value and periods of payment of interest between the
said certificates to be received on loan and the certificates to
be issued in lieu thereof as the nature and circumstances thereof would reasonably admit and to mark thereon respectively
such reference to each other as would as plainly as possible
ascertain upon the face of each of them what certificates were
given and received in lieu of each other:

And whereas in and by the said recited act and supplement
thereto the treasurer of the state for the time being was auth-

orized and required twice in every year to pay with and out of
the aggregate fund provided by the act of the sixteenth day
of March one thousand seven hundred and eighty-five the interest for six months accrued on all such debts due from this
state as should be ascertained and established by certificates
which payments of interest should commence on the first days
of April and October respectively in each year and to be made
to the holders or possessors of such certificates respectively.
And whereas by an act of assembly passed the twenty-second
day of September one thousand seven hundred and eighty-five
it is enacted that all such officers, soldiers and seamen of the
late continental army of the Pennsylvania line or navy militia
of this state or Pennsylvania state navy who during the time
of their actual service therein had been wounded, maimed or
otherwise disabled so as to prevent their obtaining a livelihood
by their industry, should during the time of such disability
be entitled to receive from the state a pension proportionate
thereof transmitted to and lodged in the comptroller-general's
office and the comptroller-general was to report quarterly or
oftner to the supreme executive council the sums due to those
pensioners respectively and the council were to draw orders on
the state treasurer for the payment thereof out of the moneys
appropriated to discharge the requisitions of the United States
within the year and by the same act the supreme executive
council were authorized and empowered from time to time to
form so many as they should think proper of the invalids provided for by that act into a corps to be employed in guarding
the offices where the public records and military stores of the
state were kept, or such uses as might be necessary, provided
the number so taken into service did not exceed two officers and
twenty-five men, at one time who should be entitled to rations
whilst so employed in addition to the provisions therein before
made and the said rations to be contracted for or supplied by
directions from the said council.

And whereas the congress of the United States "have power
to lay and collect taxes, duties, imposts, and excises, to pay
the debts and provide for the common defence and the general

1789]   *The Statutes at Large of Pennsylvania.*

welfare of the United States and no State can without the consent of Congress lay any imposts or duties on imports or exports except what may be absolutely necessary for executing
its inspection laws and the net produce of all duties and imposts laid by any state on imports or exports shall be for the
use of the treasury of the United States and all such laws shall
be subject to the revision and control of Congress," as by the
constitution of the United States appears. And whereas the
said congress having full power to provide for the payment of
the debts of the United States no doubt can be entertained but
they will with all convenient speed make due provision for the
same and as that part of the said aggregate fund created by
the said act of the sixteenth day of March one thousand seven
hundred and eighty-five which arises from the duties and imposts on importation therein mentioned will shortly cease to
come into the treasury of this state it is reasonable and just
that the temporary relief which by the said recited acts was
granted to the persons therein described should also cease and
that payment of public debts due to the said creditors should
be provided for out of the treasury of the United States and
that the alterations of the said recited laws hereinafter mentioned should be made.

[Section I.] (Section II, P. L.) Be it therefore enacted and it
is hereby enacted by the Representatives of the Freemen of
the Commonwealth of Pennsylvania in General Assembly met
and by the authority of the same, That the interest due and to
become due and payable upon all and every the certificates
issued by the comptroller-general in pursuance of the said recited acts or either of them shall be paid up so as to complete
the payment of interest to four years and that so much of
every act or acts of general assembly as directs or secures the
payment of the principal sum or sums in the said certificates
or any of them mentioned or of the interest thereof beyond the
term of four years shall be and the same is hereby repealed and
made null and void.

And whereas many who have exchanged the certificates of
the United States for certificates issued by this state in lieu
thereof as aforesaid may be desirous of taking back the same

gross abuses have been committed in the levying and collecting
of militia fines, whereby many individuals, as well as families
have been greatly aggrieved and oppressed. And as such
abuses may still be continued unless better provision than now
subsists, be made for the hearing of appeals and granting exonerations.

[Section I.] (Section II, P. L.) Be it therefore enacted and it
is hereby enacted by the Representatives of the Freemen of
the Commonwealth of Pennsylvania in General Assembly met
and by the authority of the same, That within each of the counties of this state there shall be constituted and established and
there is hereby constituted and established a board consisting
of the commissioners of the several counties in this state, who
or any two of them shall have power to receive all appeals from
persons charged in the several counties with militia fines who
may consider themselves aggrieved thereby and also to receive
the applications of such persons so charged [who] may pray
relief on account of peculiar hardship or inability and the said
board shall have full power and authority to determine on such
appeals and applications and to give relief and grant exonerations according to their judgment and discretion and as justice and humanity may require and shall also give certificates
of such relief or exonerations which shall be available to the
appellants against the payment of the amount to the collecting officer.

[Section II.] (Section III, P. L.) And be it further enacted
by the authority aforesaid, That for the purposes aforesaid it
shall and may be lawful for the said board or any two of them
to meet together for the purposes aforesaid at such times and
places, in their respective counties as to them may appear
proper and as best calculated to give opportunities for the appeals and applications of all such persons as may think themselves so aggrieved or oppressed.

[Section III.] (Section IV, P. L.) And be it further enacted
by the authority aforesaid, That the said board shall severally
be entitled to receive the sum of ten shillings for each and every
day, they and each of them shall be employed in performing
the duties enjoined by this act.

[Section V.] (Section V, P. L.) And be it further enacted
by the authority aforesaid, That an act entitled "An act to
suspend for a limited time, the collection of all militia fines,
incurred under laws passed before the twenty-second day of
March one thousand seven hundred and eighty-eight,"[1] shall
from and after the first day of May next be and the same hereby
is repealed and made void.

[1] Passed November 19, 1788, Chapter 1383.
Passed March 27, 1789. Recorded L. B. No. 8, p. 515. See the Act
of Assembly passed April 5, 1790, Chapter 1513.

CHAPTER MCDXVII.

A SUPPLEMENT TO AN ACT ENTITLED "AN ACT TO ESTABLISH A
BOARD OF WARDENS FOR THE PORT OF PHILADELPHIA AND FOR
OTHER PURPOSES THEREIN MENTIONED."[1]

(Section I, P. L.) Whereas an act of this commonwealth entitled "An act to establish a board of wardens for the port of
Philadelphia and for other purposes therein mentioned," hath
in the operation thereof proved in some respects defective and
therefore requires to be amended:

[Section I.] (Section II, P. L.) Be it enacted and it is hereby
enacted by the Representatives of the Freemen of the Commonwealth of Pennsylvania in General Assembly met and by
the authority of the same, That all and every certificate and
certificates heretofore granted unto any pilot and pilots by any
board of wardens prior to the passing of the said recited act
and not vacated by any board of wardens shall and the same
are hereby declared to be of the like force and effect for the
time and term of six months and no longer to be computed
from the day of the passing of said recited act as if the said
certificate and certificates were granted in pursuance of the
said recited act, anything therein contained to the contrary
thereof in any-wise notwithstanding. Nor shall it be lawful to
and for the collector of tonnage or to and for any other person

or persons whomsoever, to ask, demand, enforce, exact or collect
any forfeiture or forfeitures, penalty or penalties which hath or
have accrued or which could or might accrue in pursuance of
the said recited act in the case aforesaid for and during the
said term and time of six months, and if the said collector of
tonnage or any other person or persons whomsoever hath or
have heretofore enforced, collected and received any such forfeiture, the said collector of tonnage or such other person and
persons is and are hereby authorized, required and enjoined
to repay, restore and deliver the same and every part and
parcel thereof unto the pilot or pilots respectively from whom
the same shall or may have been enforced, collected and received as aforesaid, anything in the said recited act to the contrary thereof in anywise notwithstanding.

[Section II.] (Section III, P. L.) And be it further enacted
by the authority aforesaid, That whenever and as often as
the master warden shall be incapable of attending and discharging the duties of his office by reason of sickness or other
disability or shall be necessarily absent, it shall and may be
lawful to and for the wardens of the said port of Philadelphia,
and they are hereby required to meet at the warden's office and
then to choose some fit person of their own number to perform
and discharge the duties required of the said master warden
for and during the continuance of such sickness or other disability or such necessary absence and no longer.   And the
person so chosen shall during the period aforesaid be vested
with all the powers and authorities and do and perform all the
duties which are by the said recited act or by this supplement
vested in or required from the said master warden.

[Section III.] (Section IV, P. L.) And be it enacted by the
authority aforesaid, That any number not less than three of
the wardens shall constitute a board competent to the business
from time to time of examining any person or persons offering
himself or themselves to serve as pilot or pilots to and from
the port of Philadelphia or to grant a certificate or certificates
to such person and persons according to the provision, true
intent and meaning of the fifth section of the said recited act.

[Section IV.] (Section V, P. L.) And be it enacted by the
authority aforesaid, That from and after the passing of this
supplement it shall not be lawful to and for the said master
warden or to and for any other person or persons whatsoever
under his authority to sell or expose to sale any cable or cables,
anchor or anchor-stock found and taken up within the said bay
or river Delaware and delivered unto the said master warden
according to the directions of the said recited act until the full
end and term of four months from and after the date of the
first advertisement directed by the twentieth section of the said
recited act to be made and published concerning the finding of
such cable and cables, anchor or anchor-stock, anything in the
said recited act to the contrary thereof in anywise notwithstanding:

And whereas many matters and things are unnecessarily
introduced into the eleventh section of the said recited act,
provision being made touching the same in other parts and
clauses thereof:

[Section V.] (Section VI, P. L.) Be it enacted by the authority aforesaid, That so much of the eleventh section of the
said recited act as imposes a forfeiture on the master, owner
or merchant of any ship or vessel of not more than one hundred
tons burden that shall be carried from the port of Philadelphia
by any person or persons not having the certificate by the said
recited act directed, if a qualified pilot may be had or procured,
or which directs the collector of tonnage to pay the money arising from such forfeiture to the wardens or master warden of
the port of Philadelphia for the time being, before the same
is delivered to the pilot for whose use it was originally imposed, or which excepts the making of contracts or disposing
of moneys and declares that the same shall only be done by
the wardens at their monthly meetings or by a majority of
them when specially convened in the manner therein before
directed as far as the aforesaid several matters and things are
contained and set forth in the said eleventh section, but no
further, together with each and every other clause and clauses,
section and sections, part and parts of clauses and sections of
the said recited act, as is and are by this supplement altered

the exemptions of vessels under fifty tons from the necessity
of making entry at the tonnage office may afford an opportunity
for vessels of a greater burden to evade the duties of tonnage
imposed by the laws of this commonwealth and thereby considerably diminish the revenues thereof.

Therefore:

[Section VI.] (Section VII. P. L.) Be it further enacted by
the authority aforesaid, That from and after the passing of this
act all and every vessel and vessels of whatsoever burden the
same may be which shall come from any port or ports to the
southward of Senapuxent or from any port or ports to the
Northward of Little Egg Harbor shall be reported and entered
and the masters, owners and merchants thereof are hereby required to report and enter the same or to cause the same to be
reported and entered before the tonnage-officer of the said port
of Philadelphia in the same manner and within the same time
and subject to the same forfeitures and penalties for the neglect or refusal to do so to the same uses with like remedy for
the recovery thereof as are directed, declared, imposed and provided in and by the said recited act to which this is a supplement in the case of any vessel or vessels of more than fifty tons
burden. Provided always nevertheless, That if such vessel
and vessels so reported and entered as aforesaid shall not exceed the burden of fifty tons, then and in every such case, the
same shall be allowed and receive all and every discharge, exemption, freedom from duty, benefit and advantage whatsoever which before the passing of this act any vessel not exceeding the said burden of fifty tons could have claimed or
to which the same would have been entitled by virtue of the
said recited act to which this is a supplement, anything herein
contained to the contrary thereof in anywise notwithstanding.

And whereas complaints have been made by the masters and
owners of vessels against the pilots piloting the same in the
said bay and river Delaware for and on account of the negligence, inattention or intoxication of such pilots, by means
whereof vessels are unnecessarily delayed in their passage to
and from the said port of Philadelphia and are exposed to many
injuries and losses in their tackle, rigging, boats and anchors:

And whereas complaints have also been made by pilots against the masters of vessels for that such masters without any reasonable cause have wantonly and capriciously discharged and dismissed such pilots and taken others in their place and stead and have sometimes compelled them to depart in their pilot boats at unseasonable and inclement times or have set them on shore at inconvenient and improper places to the manifest discredit and great injury of such pilots:

And whereas the laws of this commonwealth have not provided any adequate remedy for the two several cases hereinbefore immediately recited and it is expedient and just that the same should be entitled to a speedy and summary consideration and redress:

Therefore:

[Section VII.] (Section VIII, P. L.) Be it enacted by the authority aforesaid, That it shall and may be lawful to and for the said master warden or wardens of the port of Philadelphia at their monthly meetings or when specially convened according to the powers and directions for that purpose given in the said recited act to which this is a supplement and he or they are hereby required to receive and hear all and every such complaint or complaints and the evidence and proof in support thereof respectively and upon due consideration of the circumstances and merits of each and every case to decide and give judgment thereupon, that is to say: if such complaint or complaints shall be made by any master or masters, owner or owners of any vessel or vessels against the pilot or pilots employed in piloting the same in the said bay and river Delaware and such complaint or complaints shall upon consideration as aforesaid be deemed just and well founded then and in every such case the said master warden or wardens shall and he or they are hereby authorized and empowered to fine the said pilot or pilots in any such sum not exceeding the whole of his or their pilotage as they the said master warden or wardens shall think a sufficient compensation for the injury done by the neglect, inattention, intoxication or other misconduct of such pilot or pilots, for the use of the party aggrieved and also shall the authority aforesaid, That the president or vice president in council be and they are hereby authorized to apply the further sum of one hundred and fifty pounds out of the moneys provided and set apart for the improvements of roads etc. for the completing the road aforesaid in such manner as they may direct and the president or vice president in council is hereby impowered to draw orders on the state treasurer for the several sums before mentioned according to the directions of this act.

And whereas the inhabitants of York and Franklin counties have by their petitions prayed this house to grant a sum of money for opening and repairing a road through Black's Gap between Chambersburg and Yorktown and it is but just and reasonable that the prayer of the petition be granted:

[Section III.] (Section IV, P. L.) Be it therefore enacted by the authority aforesaid, That the president or vice-president in council be and they are hereby authorized to apply the sum of one hundred and fifty pounds out of the moneys provided and set apart for the improvement of roads etc. for the completing the road through Black's Gap aforesaid in such manner as they may direct and the president or vice-president in council is hereby authorized and empowered to draw an order or orders on the state treasurer for the sum herein last mentioned.

Passed March 27, 1789. Recorded L. B. No. 3, p. 513.

CHAPTER MCDXIX.

AN ACT FOR RAISING BY WAY OF LOTTERY THE SUM OF EIGHT THOUSAND DOLLARS FOR DEFRAYING THE EXPENSE OF ERECTING A COMMON HALL IN THE CITY OF PHILADELPHIA AND TWO THOU-SAND DOLLARS FOR THE USE OF DICKINSON COLLEGE IN THE BOR-OUGH OF CARLISLE.

(Section I, P. L.) Whereas the buildings already erected on the public (or State House) Square are not only ornamental to the city but have heretofore been found very convenient and useful for the accommodation of the congress of the United States, and for holding the sessions of the general assembly

council, conventions and such other bodies as the exigencies of
this state [have] from time to time required:

And whereas the city of Philadelphia is possessed of a lot
on the northeast corner of the said square sufficient for the
erecting of a city hall of the same dimensions and form with
the county court house lately built, which, when completed,
will add considerably to the elegance and usefulness of the
whole:

And whereas the taxes levied upon the inhabitants of the
said city (for state and city uses) are exceedingly heavy and
it would be improper at this time to lay any additional burden
on them for building the same and a number of [the] citizens
being desirous of having a lottery instituted for the purpose:

And whereas the funds of Dickinson College in the borough
of Carlisle have been found inadequate for the purposes by
them intended:

Therefore:

[Section I.] (Section II, P. L.) Be it therefore enacted and
it is hereby enacted by the Representatives of the Freemen of
the Commonwealth of Pennsylvania in General Assembly met
and by the authority of the same, That the mayor, aldermen
and citizens of Philadelphia in common council assembled shall
be and they are hereby authorized and empowered to appoint
[six] managers and directors of the lottery hereby instituted
and directed to be drawn for the preparing and disposing of
tickets, to oversee the drawing of the lots and to order and
perform all such other matters and things as are hereinafter
directed and appointed to be done and performed: and that the
said managers or any six of them shall meet together at some
convenient place by them to be appointed for the execution of
the powers and trust reposed in them by this act and shall
cause proper books to be prepared in which each leaf shall be
divided into three columns, upon the innermost of which shall
be printed twelve thousand five hundred tickets numbered one,
two, three and so onwards in arithmetical progression where
the common excess is to be one, until they rise to the number
of twelve thousand five hundred; upon the outside column

there shall be printed the like number of tickets of the same breadth and form and numbered in like manner and in the middle column shall be printed a third set of tickets of the same numbers with those of the other two columns, which tickets shall be joined with oblique lines or devices in such manner as the said managers shall direct, and every of the last mentioned tickets shall have written or printed thereupon (besides the number of such ticket and the year of our Lord) the following words, viz. "City Hall and Dickinson College Lottery."

"This ticket entitles the bearer to such prize as may be drawn against its number if demanded in nine months after the drawing is finished, subject to a deduction of twenty per cent."

[Section II.] (Section III, P. L.) And be it further enacted by the authority aforesaid, That the said managers shall have full power and authority to sell and dispose of to such person or persons as shall choose to adventure in the said lottery the tickets of the middle column aforesaid at the rate of four dollars each for ready money and not otherwise, and upon the receipt of such sum of four dollars shall deliver to the said adventurer one of the said tickets signed by one of the managers and cut out of the said books through the said oblique lines and devices, indentwise, to be kept and used for the better ascertaining and securing his or her or their interest in the said ticket in case it should be fortunate.

[Section III.] (Section IV, P. L.) And be it further enacted by the authority aforesaid, That for the greater security of the adventurers and punctual payment of the prizes that shall be drawn in the said lottery, the said managers shall pay weekly into the Bank of North America all the moneys arising from tickets by them sold, for which they shall receive from the said bank such acknowledgment in behalf of the city and college aforesaid for the purposes in this act mentioned as are usually given by the said bank for other moneys deposited therein.

[Section IV.] (Section V, P. L.) And be it further enacted by the authority aforesaid, That for enabling the said managers

to pay off the prizes as they are severally drawn and for discharging the incidental expenses attending the management
and drawing of the said lottery, orders shall be drawn by the
said managers or any four or more of them on the said bank in
checks provided for that purpose expressing that such drafts
are upon account of the said lottery.

[Section V.] (Section VI, P. L.) And be it further enacted
by the authority aforesaid, That as soon as the tickets of the
middle column shall be sold the said managers or any four
or more of them shall cause all the tickets of the extreme
column in the said books, the same being cut out indentwise
through the said oblique lines or devices, to be carefully rolled
up, and made fast with silk or thread and shall cause them to
be put into a box to be prepared for that purpose, marked
with the letter A, and to be immediately after sealed with the
several seals of the said managers until the said tickets are to
be drawn as is hereinafter mentioned, but the tickets of the
innermost column shall remain in the said books for the discovering any mistake or fraud if such should happen to be
committed contrary to the meaning of this act.

[Section VI.] (Section VII, P. L.) And be it further enacted
by the authority aforesaid, That the said managers or any four
or more of them shall also prepare or cause to be prepared
three thousand eight hundred and sixty-seven prize tickets on
which shall be written or expressed as well in figures as in
words at length as follows: that is to say, upon one of them
three thousand dollars, upon one other of them two thousand
dollars, upon two others of them severally one thousand five
hundred dollars, upon three others of them severally one thousand dollars, upon ten other of them severally five hundred
dollars, upon twenty other of them severally two hundred dollars, upon thirty other of them, severally one hundred dollars;
upon fifty other of them severally fifty dollars, upon one hundred other [of them] severally twenty dollars, upon one hundred and fifty other of them severally ten dollars, and upon
three thousand five hundred other of them severally six dollars
which principal sums so to be expressed upon the said tickets
will amount in the whole to fifty thousand dollars, out of which

the said managers are hereby authorized and required to deduct twenty per centum and no more amounting in the whole
to ten thousand dollars, the sum intended to be raised by this
act for the purposes therein mentioned and specified.

[Section VII.] (Section VIII, P. L.) And be it further enacted by the authority aforesaid, That the said managers or
any four or more of them shall cause the said prize tickets
written upon as aforesaid to be carefully rolled up and fastened
with silk or thread and put into another box to be prepared
for that purpose marked with the letter "B" and sealed up
with the several seals of the said managers to be by them
carefully kept until the tickets shall be drawn in a manner
hereinafter directed.

[Section VIII.] (Section IX, P. L.) And be it further enacted
by the authority aforesaid. That the said managers or any
four or more of them shall cause the said boxes with all the
tickets therein to be carried to some public and convenient
room in the city of Philadelphia by ten o'clock in the forenoon
on some certain day to be by them appointed and placed on
a stage or table and shall then and there severally attend this
service and cause the two boxes to be unsealed and opened
and the tickets or lots in the said boxes being in the presence
of the managers and such of the adventurers as shall think
proper to attend well shaken and mixed together in each box,
some one indifferent and fit person to be appointed and directed
by the said managers shall draw one ticket from the box A
in which the said numbered tickets shall have been put as
aforesaid and one other indifferent and fit person appointed
and directed in like manner shall at the same time draw one
ticket or lot from the box B in which the said three thousand
eight hundred and sixty-seven prize tickets shall have been
promiscuously put as aforesaid and the tickets so drawn shall
be immediately opened and the number of ticket drawn from
the box A and the value of the prize drawn out of the box B
shall be called aloud and the number and prize shall be filed
together and entered in books by clerks whom the managers
are hereby authorized and empowered to employ and oversee
for this purpose, and so the drawing to continue by taking one

ticket at a time out of each box and opening, calling aloud
filing and entering the same as is before mentioned until the
whole three thousand, eight hundred and sixty-seven prize
tickets shall be completely drawn from the box B, and if the
drawing aforesaid cannot be performed in one day, the said
managers shall cause the said boxes to be sealed up in manner
aforesaid and adjourn until the next day and so from day to
day (Sundays excepted) until the drawing shall be finished
and completed as aforesaid, and the tickets so drawn shall
remain in the custody of the managers.

[Section IX.] (Section X, P. L.) And be it further enacted
by the authority aforesaid, That as soon as the drawing is
finished the books of the several clerks compared and lists
made out there from, the managers shall cause a list of the
fortunate numbers to be published in two English and one
German newspaper printed in the city of Philadelphia and
immediately thereafter proceed to the payment of the prize
money, and if any dispute shall arise in adjusting the property of any of the said fortunate numbers, the managers shall
determine to whom it doth or ought to belong.

[Section X.] (Section XI, P. L.) And be it further enacted
by the authority aforesaid, That if any of the fortunate adventurers shall neglect to apply to the said managers for the sum
due on his or her or their tickets respectively within the space
of nine months after the publication of the prize list, such sum
or sums of money so due to him, her or them shall be applied
to the uses, intents and purposes to which the sum hereby
intended to be raised is ordered to be appropriated and applied.

[Section XI.] (Section XII, P. L.) Provided always and be
it enacted by the authority aforesaid, That before any of the
said managers shall take upon himself the duties and offices
hereby enjoined or any clerk employed by the said managers
shall act in such employment, they and each of them shall
respectively before the mayor or one of the aldermen of the
city of Philadelphia take the following oath or affirmation, viz.
"I A. B. do swear or affirm that I will faithfully execute the
trust reposed in me and that I will not use or permit or direct
any person to use any indirect arts or means to obtain a prize

or fortunate ticket either for myself or any other person whatsoever: And that I will to the best of my judgment declare
to whom any prize lot or ticket of right does belong according
to the true intent and meaning of the act of assembly entitled
"An act for raising by way of lottery the sum of eight thousand dollars for defraying the expense of erecting a common
hall in the city of Philadelphia and two thousand dollars for
the use of Dickinson College in the borough of Carlisle."

[Section XII.] (Section XIII, P. L.) And be it further enacted
by the authority aforesaid, That the moneys arising from the
lottery hereby instituted shall be and hereby are appropriated
to the building a common hall in the city of Philadelphia and
to and for the use of Dickinson College in the proportions herein directed and to no other use, purpose or intent whatsoever.

[Section XIII.] (Section XIV, P. L.) And be it further enacted by the authority aforesaid, That the said managers shall
from time to time when thereunto required lay before the
mayor, alderman and citizens of Philadelphia in common council assembled a true state of the lottery, and shall also, when
the drawing of the same is finished and the prizes and incidental charges are paid settle their accounts with and pay
over the moneys in their hands to the said mayor, aldermen
and citizens who are hereby authorized and empowered to contract with proper persons for carrying into effect the purposes
intended by this act and shall pay to the trustees of Dickinson
College one fifth of the net proceeds of the said lottery.

Passed March 27, 1789. Recorded L. B. No. 8, p. 509. See the Act
of Assembly passed September 29, 1789, Chapter 1460.

CHAPTER MCDXX.

AN ACT TO ENABLE THE JUSTICES OF THE ORPHANS' COURT TO
AUTHORIZE AND EMPOWER FRANCES BUDDEN TO SELL AND CON-
VEY SO MUCH OF THE LANDS [AND] TENEMENTS OF HER LATE
HUSBAND JAMES BUDDEN, DECEASED, AS SHALL BE NECESSARY
FOR THE PAYMENT OF HIS DEBTS AND FOR OTHER PURPOSES
THEREIN MENTIONED.

(Section I, P. L.) Whereas it appears to this house that James
Budden late of the city of Philadelphia, merchant, now deceased, was at the time of making his testament and last will
in writing on the twentieth day of October in the year of our
Lord one thousand seven hundred and eighty-three and for a
long time before largely indebted in divers sums of money to
different persons in Europe, which at the time of making his
will he had reason to believe had been paid off and discharged,
as he had placed sufficient funds for that purpose in the hands
of his late partner William Stricker who is also dead, with
directions to apply the same accordingly:

And whereas it further appears that the said funds or any
parts thereof were not applied by the said William Stricker in
discharge of the said debts, by reason whereof the same still
remain due and payable and said Frances Budden hath made
it appear to this house that she hath not in [her] hands sufficient of the goods and chattels which were of the said James
Budden to discharge the said debts and hath prayed that she
may be enabled by a sale or mortgage of the lands and tenements whereof the said James Budden died seized to raise
sufficient moneys for the purpose aforesaid and for the other
purposes hereinafter mentioned.

[Section I.] (Section II, P. L.) Be it therefore enacted and it
is hereby enacted by the Representatives of the Freemen of the
Commonwealth of Pennsylvania in General Assembly met and
by the authority of the same, That it shall and may be lawful
for Frances Budden, administratrix, of all and singular the

for Frances Budden, administrator, of all and singular the
goods and chattels, rights and credits which were of the said
James Budden at the time of his decease, with the will of the
said James Budden annexed, to sell and convey or to mortgage
or to grant, bargain and sell by one or more conditional deed
or deeds in nature of a mortgage or mortgages such part
or parts of the lands and tenements whereof the said James
Budden died seized or entitled unto, for defraying the just
debts of the said James Budden, the maintenance of his children and for putting them apprentices and teaching them to
read and write and for improvement of the residue of the estate
if any be, to their advantage, as the orphans' court of the
county where such estate lies shall think fit to allow, order
and direct from time to time, subject nevertheless to such rules
and regulations and on such terms and conditions as are by
the laws of this commonwealth provided respecting the sales
of lands by administrators for the purposes in this act mentioned. Provided nevertheless, That so much of the said rules,
regulations, terms and conditions as relate to the advertising,
or to the form and manner of selling and conveying of lands
and tenements and are inapplicable to the case of a mortgage
shall not be required on the making or executing of any mortgage in pursuance of this act.

Passed March 27, 1789. Recorded L. B. No. 3, p. 604.

CHAPTER MCDXXI.

AN ACT TO INCORPORATE THE NEWTOWN LIBRARY COMPANY IN BUCKS COUNTY.

(Section I, P. L.) Whereas the members of the Newtown
Library Company in the county of Bucks by their petition have
prayed to be incorporated and vested with such powers and
privileges as are enjoyed by corporations of a similar nature
within this commonwealth:

And whereas public libraries by diffusing useful knowledge are beneficial to the commonwealth as well as to individuals and merit the encouragement of the legislature:

Therefore:

[Section I.] (Section II, P. L.) Be it enacted and it is hereby enacted by the Representatives of the Freemen of the Commonwealth of Pennsylvania in General Assembly met and by the authority of the same, That all those who now are or hereafter shall or may become members of the said Library Company agreeably to the laws and constitution thereof be and they hereby are made and constituted a corporate and body politic in law and in fact to have continuance forever by the name, style and title of "The Newtown Library Company."

[Section II.] (Section II, P. L.) And be it further enacted by the authority aforesaid, That all and singular the goods and chattels heretofore given, granted or devised to said Library Company, or to any person or persons for the use thereof or that have been purchased for or on account of the same be and the said goods and chattels are hereby vested in and confirmed to the said corporation. And further, That the said corporation may take and receive any sum or sums of money or any goods, chattels, or other effects of what kind or nature soever which shall or may hereafter be given, granted or bequeathed unto them by any person or persons bodies politic or corporate capable of making such gift or bequest, such money goods, chattels or other effects to be laid out and disposed of for the use and benefit of the said corporation agreeably to the inuse and benefit of the said corporation agreeably to the intentions of the donors.

[Section III.] (Section IV., P. L.) And be it further enacted by the authority aforesaid, That the said corporation by the name, style and title aforesaid are hereby declared and made able and capable in law at all times hereafter to purchase, have, hold, receive and enjoy in fee simple or of any less estate or estates any lands, tenements, rents, annuities, liberties, franchises and other hereditaments not exceeding the clear yearly value of five hundred pounds by the gift, grant, bargain, sale, alienation, enfeoffment, release, confirmation or devise of

any person or persons, bodies politic or corporate able and capable to make the same, and also to give, grant, let, sell and
convey or assign the same lands, tenements, rents, annuities,
liberties, franchises and hereditaments as to the said corporation shall seem meet and convenient.

[Section IV.] (Section V, P. L.) And be it further enacted
by the authority aforesaid, That the said corporation by the
name, style and title aforesaid be and shall be forever hereafter
able and capable in law to sue and be sued, plead and be impleaded, answer and be answered unto, defend and be defended in any court or courts or other places and before any
judge or judges, justice or justices or other persons whatsoever
within this commonwealth or elsewhere in all and all manner
of suits, actions, complaints, pleas, causes, matters and demands of whatever kind or nature they may be in as full and
effectual a manner as any other person or persons, bodies
politic and corporate may or can do.

[Section V.] (Section VI, P. L.) And be it further enacted
by the authority aforesaid, That the said corporation shall
have full power and authority to make, have and use one common seal with such device and inscription as they shall think
proper and the same to break, alter and renew at their pleasure.

[Section VI.] (Section VII, P. L.) And be it further enacted
by the authority aforesaid, That there shall be a general meeting of the members of the said corporation held on the last
Saturday of October in every year hereafter forever at such
convenient and suitable place as the directors from time to
time shall appoint, at which time and place the members or
such of them as are or shall be present shall yearly and in
every year elect and choose by ballot five directors and a treasurer to serve for one year next after such election, which directors shall appoint a secretary and librarian and at their pleasure remove him or them from office and appoint another in
his or their place, when, and as often as they shall see fit and
also do and transact all business and matters appertaining to
said corporation agreeably to the rules, ordinances, regulations
and by-laws thereof for and during their continuance in office.

And they are hereby authorized and empowered to consider, treat of and determine upon and concerning all and every the matters and things relating to the prudent management, good order and government of said corporation and also to make and ordain such rules, ordinances, regulations and by-laws for the purposes aforesaid as a majority of them from time to time shall see needful and convenient and the same to put in execution or to revoke, disannul, alter or amend at their pleasure, which rules, ordinances, regulations and by-laws shall be valid in law and binding on the parties concerned in as full and effectual a manner as if herein particularly expressed. Provided always, That the said rules ordinances, regulations and by-laws be not repugnant to or inconsistent with the laws of this commonwealth. And provided also, That none of the rules, ordinances, regulations or by-laws to be made and agreed to as aforesaid shall extend to a dissolution of said corporation or shall give power to dissolve the same or to divide or make distribution of the books or other property thereof unless the free consent of nine-tenths of all the members thereunto belonging be first had and obtained.

And whereas the said Library Company at their last general meeting on the eighteenth day of November last past did elect and choose Henry Wynkoop, Thomas Jenks, Francis Murray, Samuel Benezet, and Abraham Du Bois, directors, and William Linton, treasurer, for the present year or until the last Saturday in October next:

[Section VII.] (Section VIII, P. L.) Be it therefore enacted by the authority aforesaid, That the said Henry Wynkoop, Thomas Jenks, Francis Murray, Samuel Benezet, and [Abraham] Du Bois, the present directors and William Linton, the present treasurer, shall hold and continue in their respective offices and use and exercise all the authorities, rights and privileges which are necessary for the good order and government of said Library Company until the said last Saturday in October next, at which time a new election for directors and a treasurer is to take place agreeable to the directions of this act.

Passed March 27, 1789. Recorded L. B. No. 3, p. 492.

CHAPTER MCDXXII.

AN ACT TO ENABLE JOHN HEWSON TO ENLARGE AND CARRY ON THE
BUSINESS OF CALICO PRINTING AND BLEACHING WITHIN THIS
STATE.

(Section I, P. L.) Whereas it appears to this general assembly
that John Hewson of the Northern Liberties of the city of
Philadelphia in the county of Philadelphia, calico printer and
bleacher, is sufficiently qualified to carry on that business and
that it will be of great public utility to have those manufactures carried on in this country:

And whereas the said John Hewson hath by his petition
prayed this house to lend him a sum of money to enable him to
enlarge and carry on his business aforesaid and it [is] reasonable and proper that the prayer of his petition should be
granted:

[Section I.] (Section II, P. L.) Be it therefore enacted and
it is hereby enacted by the Representatives of the Freemen of
the Commonwealth of Pennsylvania in General Assembly met
and by the authority of the same, That the president or vice-
president in council be and they are hereby authorized and
empowered to draw an order or orders on the treasurer of
this state for the sum of two hundred pounds to be advanced
and paid to the said John Hewson for the purpose of assisting
and enabling him to enlarge and carry on the business of calico
printing and bleaching within this state, the said sum of two
hundred pounds to be paid unto the said John Hewson or his
attorney out of the moneys appropriated by an act entitled
"An act to appropriate divers funds accruing and growing due
to this commonwealth towards the payment of the expenses
of the government and to provide a fund for other purposes,"[1]
in four equal installments, the first shall be made on the fifteenth day of April next and the second installment on the fifteenth day of July thereafter and the third on the fifteenth
day of October following and the fourth and last installment

[to be paid] on the fifteenth day of December next.

[Section II.] (Section III, P. L.) Provided always and be it enacted by the authority aforesaid, That previously to the granting any of the orders aforesaid, the said John Hewson shall give sufficient security as well for the application of the money to the use and purpose for which it is lent as for the repayment of the same to the treasurer of this state for the use of the commonwealth without interest at the expiration of seven years from and after the date of such obligation.

Passed March 27, 1789. Recorded L. B. No. 3, p. 512.
1 Passed March 26, 1789, Chapter 1404.

CHAPTER MCDXXIII.

AN ACT FOR THE APPOINTMENT OF A REGISTER-GENERAL FOR THE PURPOSE OF REGISTERING THE ACCOUNTS OF THIS STATE.

(Section I, P. L.) Whereas the settlement and adjustment of the accounts of this state in a clear and accurate manner and the keeping the same in a fair, regular and intelligible mode, so as to show in a short and comprehensive view a general state of them is of great importance to the community and the mode at present pursued does not answer those useful purposes:

[Section I.] (Section II, P. L.) Be it therefore enacted and it is hereby enacted by the Representatives of the Freemen of the Commonwealth of Pennsylvania in General Assembly met and by the authority of the same, That there be and by this act there is erected and established within this state an office to be called the office for registering the public accounts which shall be kept in some part of the state-house in the city of Philadelphia to be assigned for the purpose by the supreme executive council and that the officer who shall superintend the same and execute the duties thereof shall be appointed

19—XIII

from time to time by the general assembly of this commonwealth and shall be called the register-general of the public
accounts of the state of Pennsylvania, which officer shall be
entitled to have and receive in full for his services the sum of
five hundred pounds per annum out of the moneys appropriated
by an act entitled "An act to appropriate divers funds accruing
and growing due to this commonwealth towards the payment
of the expenses of government and to provide a fund for other
purposes."[1] enacted the twenty-sixth day of March instant to
be paid to him quarterly, by virtue of orders to be drawn by
the supreme executive council on the state treasurer, besides
all his reasonable charges for books, [stationery] and the hire
of such and so many clerks as in the opinion of council shall
be necessary for his assistance in performing the services by
this act required.

[Section II.] (Section III, P. L.) And it is hereby further
enacted by the authority aforesaid, That the comptroller-
general of this commonwealth shall and he is hereby enjoined
and required to submit all accounts which he shall hereafter
adjust between this commonwealth and the United States or
any one or more states or any one or more individuals, before
he shall finally settle the same in pursuance of any law or
laws now in force, to the inspection and examination of the
said register-general and shall take his advice and assistance
in making such settlements, and that all and every statement
and settlements to be so made of any public accounts by the
said comptroller-general with the aid and assistance of the
said register-general shall be laid before the supreme executive
council of this commonwealth in the same manner and for
the same purposes as is provided by the laws now in being as
to accounts to be settled by the said comptroller-general.

[Section III.] (Section IV, P. L.) And it is hereby enacted by
the authority aforesaid, That the said register-general shall
and he is hereby enjoined and required to provide suitable
books for the purpose aforesaid and therein open a fair set of
accounts with and for all and every person and persons and

---

1 Passed March 26, 1789, Chapter 1404.

bodies politic whatsoever with whom any accounts now are or shall hereafter be depending with this state or who have received or shall receive of the public moneys belonging to the state and shall transfer unto such accounts all and every the balances which shall appear to be due to or from any persons or bodies politic at the time of the passing of this act, and where any account or accounts cannot be finally settled and balanced up to the time of the passing of this act, so much thereof as can be settled or ascertained shall be transferred to and entered in such books and the residue thereof shall be brought forward and entered therein when and so soon as the same can by and with the aid of the said register-general be ascertained.

[Section IV.] (Section V. P. L.) And it is hereby further enacted by the authority aforesaid, That in all and every warrants and orders whatsoever hereafter to be drawn and issued by the supreme executive council or by the general assembly from and after the tenth day of April next for any public moneys which they respectively have or shall have right by any laws now or hereafter to be in force to draw and issue, shall be carried to the said office of the said register-general and there be countersigned by him and entered in the proper accounts to which such warrants or orders shall be respectively chargeable before the same shall be allowed or charged to the public in the office of the comptroller-general.

[Section V.] (Section VI, P. L.) And be it hereby enacted by the authority aforesaid, That the said register-general shall and he is hereby authorized and required when and so often as the supreme executive council of this commonwealth shall order and direct to inspect and examine all such part and parts of the transactions and accounts of the said comptroller-general as the said council shall judge necessary and proper and to make fair and just reports thereof to them for their information.

[Section VI.] (Section VII, P. L.) And it is hereby further enacted by the authority aforesaid that John Donaldson Esquire be and is hereby appointed to the office of register-general herein above mentioned and shall forthwith after the passing of this act enter upon the duties of the said office and continue to hold and exercise the same during the pleasure of the general assembly.

[Section VII.] (Section VIII, P. L.) And it is hereby further enacted by the authority aforesaid, That so much of an act of assembly passed the fourth day of April Anno Domini one thousand seven hundred and eighty-five as authorized the appointment of the present or any future comptroller-general for the term of seven years if he shall so long behave himself well shall be and the same is hereby repealed and made void and that from and after the passing of this act the comptroller-general shall hold his said office during the pleasure of the supreme executive council.

Passed March 28, 1789. Recorded L. B. No. 3, p. 516 See the Acts of Assembly passed September 30, 1789, Chapter 1463; April 1, 1790. Chapter 1506.

CHAPTER MCDXXIV.

A SUPPLEMENT TO THE ACT ENTITLED "A SUPPLEMENT TO THE ACT ENTITLED 'AN ACT TO ENFORCE THE DUE COLLECTION AND PAYMENT OF TAXES WITHIN THIS COMMONWEALTH.'"[1]

[Section I.] Whereas the provisions contained in an act entitled "A supplement to the act entitled 'An act to enforce the due collection and payment of taxes within this commonwealth,'" do not extend to any sheriffs or constables who have received or shall receive any moneys for taxes in virtue of their respective offices, and have refused or neglected or shall refuse or neglect to pay the same to the treasurer of the proper county and it is just and right that the like speedy and effectual means which are in and by the act to which this is a supplement afforded against any delinquent collector, treasurer or justice of the peace should be extended to all and every delinquent sheriffs and constables:

[1] Passed October 4, 1788, Chapter 1374.

[Section I.] (Section II, P. L.) Be it therefore enacted and it is hereby enacted by the Representatives of the Freemen of the Commonwealth of Pennsylvania in General Assembly met and by the authority of the same, That if any sheriff or sheriffs constable or constables, who has or have received or who shall receive any money or moneys for taxes in virtue of their respective offices and the laws in such cases provided, shall neglect or refuse within twenty days after demand made by the treasurer or treasurers of the proper county to render a just and true account thereof or to pay the same to such treasurer or treasurers, a warrant or warrants shall be issued against such delinquent sheriff or sheriffs, constable or constables in like manner as [is] in and by the act to which this is a supplement directed for proceeding against delinquent collectors, and such proceedings shall thereon be had to final judgment, execution and sale as are in and by the said act to which this is a supplement directed respecting delinquent collectors, with this difference only, that if such delinquent sheriff or sheriffs shall, at the time or times of the commencement of such proceedings against him or them, continue to be in office, the warrant or warrants to be issued against him or them in pursuance hereof shall be directed to the coroner or coroners of the proper county who shall in all respects proceed thereon in like manner as any sheriff or sheriffs may or can do under the recited act in the cases therein mentioned.

[Section II.] (Section III. P. L.) And be it further enacted by the authority aforesaid, That if any such delinquent collector or collectors, treasurer or treasurers, justice or justices, sheriff or sheriffs, constable or constables, as is or are in the said recited act or in this act mentioned, has or have removed or shall remove into any other county or counties within this commonwealth or has or have or shall have any estate, real or personal in any such other county or counties or shall at the time or times of his or their death or deaths have left any estate which may be found in any such other county or counties and which shall not have been bona fide and for a valuable consideration disposed of, any process to be issued in pursuance of this act or of the act to which this is a supplement may be directed to the sheriff or sheriffs, coroner or coroners of any such other county or counties and shall be proceeded on as in and by the said act is directed in the case therein mentioned.

Passed March 28, 1789. Recorded L. B. No. 3, p. 517.

THIRD SITTING OF THE FIFTEENTH ASSEMBLY.

CHAPTER MCDXXV.

AN ACT TO ENABLE THE OWNERS AND POSSESSORS OF A CERTAIN TRACT OF MARSH AND MEADOW LAND THEREIN DESCRIBED SITUATE IN THE COUNTY OF CHESTER TO KEEP THE BANKS, DAMS, SLUICES AND FLOODGATES IN REPAIR AND TO RAISE A FUND TO DEFRAY THE EXPENSE THEREOF.

(Section I, P. L.) Whereas there is a certain tract of marsh and meadow land situated in the township of Tinicum in the county of Chester bounded by the river Delaware, Darby Creek and the fast land, which said tract or parcel of marsh and meadow hath been and now is embanked, but inasmuch as the banks, dams, sluices and flood-gates made for the stopping out the tide waters from the same and for preventing the overflowing thereof cannot be equitably and sufficiently maintained without a law.

[Section I.] (Section II, P. L.) Be it enacted and it is hereby enacted by the Representatives of the Freemen of the Commonwealth of Pennsylvania in General Assembly met and by the authority of the same, That the owners, occupiers and possessors of the said tract or district of meadow land shall be henceforth called and named "the Darby Creek Company," and that Philip Price, John Pearson, Hugh Lloyd, John Hunt, Jun., and Isaac Serrill, gentlemen, or any three of them are hereby nominated, authorized and appointed within three months after the publication of this act, to divide the banks which surround and include the said tract or piece of meadow land and allot

and appoint how many perches of the said bank each owner or
possessor shall hereafter make, repair, maintain and support
in proportion to the number of acres he now holds or hereafter shall hold therein having an equitable regard to the
quality, situation and circumstances of the bank so to be
allotted, all which said allotments and divisions so made and
signified by an instrument in writing under the hands and
seals of any three of them and recorded in the office for recording deeds for the county of Chester shall be the proper shares,
parts, proportions and quantities of bank for the several owners or possessors of the said meadows to repair and support at
their own proper charge and expense.

[Section II.] (Section III, P. L.) And be it enacted by the
authority aforesaid, That the owners, occupiers or possessors
of the said tract of meadow land whose allotments, shares or
parts of the bank are in anywise defective shall within three
months after the allotments made in pursuance of this act
cause them to be put in good and substantial repair and make
up or cause their respective parts of the banks so
as aforesaid allotted to be made up of a sufficient breadth and
level on the top and sufficiently strong and secure to defend the
said meadows from all inundations, for which end the said
banks shall always be kept at least six inches higher than any
tide that hath been known, by each or any of the said owners
possessors or occupiers on their and each of their parts so
as aforesaid to them respectively allotted, under the penalty
of ten shillings for every perch of bank not made, repaired
and supported as aforesaid, which fine shall be recovered in the
manner hereinafter directed and added to the common stock
of the said company, and the owners or occupiers of lands of
which the banks are shall sow the said banks with grass seed
and mow and keep them clean from time to time when necessary and at such times as a major part of the managers shall
order and direct and upon the neglect or refusal of any of the
respective owners or possessors of any meadow lands in the
said district after ten days notice being given him, her or them
by a major part of the managers for the time being to sow with
grass seed, mow and keep clean their respective parts of the

said bank, it shall and may be lawful to and for the major part of the said managers from time to time to employ a sufficient number of workmen to mow, keep clean and sow with grass-seed the banks so neglected and charge the owners, possessors or occupiers respectively with the whole cost arising thereupon and upon their or any of their neglect or refusal to defray the same it shall and may be lawful for the treasurer of the said district by the order of the major part of the managers to recover the money so expended in the manner hereinafter directed.

[Section III.] (Section IV, P. L.) And be it enacted by the authority aforesaid, That after the banks shall be made and repaired as aforesaid the costs and charges of maintaining and amending the dams, sluices and floodgates at all future times shall be paid by all the owners, occupiers, or possessors of the meadow land in the said district according to the number of acres that they and each of them shall hold, possess and occupy, the same to be maintained, supported and amended by the managers of the said district and in such manner as they or a majority of them hereafter to be chosen shall direct.

[Section IV.] (Section V, P. L.) And be it enacted by the authority aforesaid, That it shall and may be lawful for the said company or as many of them as shall think fit to meet together on the second Monday in September yearly and every year at the school house in the said township or such other convenient place as shall hereafter be appointed by the managers of the said company or any two of them to be chosen by virtue of this act, of which place and time of meeting the treasurer of the said company shall by advertisement notify the owners or occupiers ten days before the day appointed for such meeting and then and thereby a majority of those met shall choose by ticket in writing three fit persons, owners or possessors of land in the said company to be managers and one fit person to be treasurer of the said company for the year then next ensuing.

[Section V.] (Section VI, P. L.) And be it enacted by the authority aforesaid, That if any of the owners or pos-

sessors elected managers as aforesaid on due notice given in
writing of his election by some of the company present at the
said election shall refuse or afterwards neglect to do the duty
required of him or them by this act, he or they so refusing or
neglecting his duty shall severally forfeit and pay to the treasurer for the time being the sum of three pounds to be added to
the common stock of the said company unless he or they have
served two years successively in the said office next before his
or their said appointment, which fine shall be recovered in the
manner hereinafter directed for the recovery of other moneys
payable to the treasurer of the said company and the other
managers shall proceed in the execution of their office without
him or them or if they think fit may choose others of the said
owners or possessors to be manager or managers in the place
of him or them so refusing or neglecting, and if the person so
elected treasurer shall refuse or neglect to do the duties or to
give the securities required by this act, or shall misbehave himself or by death or otherwise be rendered incapable to execute
the said office, in any of these cases the manager for the time
being shall choose another fit person to be the treasurer for
that year.

[Section VI.] (Section VII, P. L.) And be it further enacted
by the authority aforesaid, That every treasurer hereafter to
be chosen shall before he takes upon him the execution of his
office enter into an obligation to the said Darby Creek Company
with at least one sufficient surety in double the value of the
money that may probably come into his hands during the continuance of his office as near as can be estimated by the managers, conditioned that he will once in every year or oftener
if required render his accounts to the said managers or a
majority of them and well and truly account, adjust and settle
with them when required for and concerning all moneys that
are or shall come to his hands by virtue of this act, or that
belong to the said company and shall well and truly pay the
balance that shall appear on such settlement to be in his hands
to such person and to such services as any two of the managers
for the time being shall order and appoint and not otherwise,

and that he will do and execute all other matters and things
as treasurer to the said company according to the true intent
and meaning of this act and that he will at the expiration
of his office well and truly pay or cause to be paid and delivered
all the money then remaining in his hands together with the
books of accounts concerning the same and all other papers
and writings in his keeping belonging to the said company unto
his successor in the said office.

[Section VII.] (Section VIII, P. L.) And be it enacted by
the authority aforesaid, That it shall and may be lawful for
the said managers or any two of them as often as they shall see
occasion, to meet together and lay such assessments and taxes
on every acre of land in the said district as they shall judge
to be necessary for the benefit and security of the same, and
the said managers or any two of them for the time being shall
have the power of disposing of all moneys paid to the said
treasurer by virtue of this act and of hiring and appointing
at the expense of the company, if they see occasion, any person or persons from time to time to inspect the condition of
all the banks, dams, sluices and floodgates within the bounds
of the said district and to offer and pay such rewards as they
think necessary out of the common stock for the destruction
of such vermin as usually damage the banks and dams as well
as for all other general services of the said company.

[Section VIII.] (Section IX, P. L.) And be it enacted by the
authority aforesaid, That the major part of the managers of
the said company for the time being shall at least three times
in each year at such times as they think necessary by written
or printed advertisements published in two or more places in
the township of Tinicum and at two or more places in the township of Ridley at least ten days before the time therein to be
appointed, require the owners or occupiers of all meadow lands
within the bounds of the said company to cut all ransted,
elders, poke, thistles, burdock and other weeds growing therein which may be injurious to the said meadows, and should the
owner or owners or occupiers of the [lands] or any of them
neglect to cut or mow the same at such times as they shall be
so required, it shall and may be lawful for the said managers

and they are hereby enjoined and required to hire and employ
a sufficient number of workmen to cut or mow the same and
to fine the said owner or occupier for their neglect in any sum
not exceeding the cost of the said cutting or mowing and recover the money so expended in hiring men and the fine so
imposed in like manner as other sums of money are by this
act directed to be recovered, which fines shall be applied to
the benefit of the said company.

[Section IX.] (Section X, P. L.) And be it enacted by the
authority aforesaid, That all creeks or ditches which now are
or hereafter shall be made in the said district of the width of
nine feet and [the] depth of three feet shall be deemed and
considered in law as lawful fences and enclosures and if any
owner or occupier shall find on his or her land within the said
district so enclosed as aforesaid any swine or hogs, it shall
and may be lawful for the said owner or occupier to seize and
take all such swine or hogs whether yoked and ringed or not
and it being legally proved before the next justice of the peace
that such swine or hogs were taken in his or her meadow land
so enclosed, the said justice shall forthwith order and direct
the treasurer of the said company to advertise the same and
within five days sell at public auction all such swine and, after
deducting all reasonable cost, divide the remainder equally
between the treasurer for the use of the company and the person so taking them up.

[Section X.] (Section XI, P. L.) And be it enacted by the
authority aforesaid, That the orders of any two of the managers for the time being on the treasurer shall be complied
with by the said treasurer and shall be good vouchers to indemnify him for the payment and delivery of the money and
effects committed to his care by virtue of this act, and that all
bonds, mortgages, deeds and conveyances in trust for the use
of the said owners shall be taken in the name of the treasurer
of the said company and be payable to him and his successors
and shall be mentioned to be for the use of the owners thereof
and with or without assignment shall be good and available
in law to his successor or successors in the said trust for the
use of the owners as aforesaid and shall be recoverable in any

court of record in this commonwealth where the same may
be cognizable as fully and effectually to all intents and purposes as if the same were private property and the receipts
and discharges of such succeeding treasurer or treasurers for
any such sums of money paid to him or them shall be effectual
in law.

And whereas the cutting or making drains or ditches in suitable place and scouring those now made or which may hereafter be made will greatly conduce to the better improvement
of the said meadows:

[Section XI.] (Section XII, P. L.) Be it therefore enacted
by the authority aforesaid, That the major part of the managers of the said district shall at such times and so often as
they see occasion direct and order that new drains and ditches
be made where necessary or those which are already made
scoured, and proportion the cost of making or scouring the
same among those benefited thereby or order such compensation to those who may be injured as shall appear to them just
and reasonable and compel payment in the manner hereinafter directed.

[Section XII.] (Section XIII, P. L.) And be it enacted by the
authority aforesaid, That if any owner or occupier shall think
him, her or themselves aggrieved by any act, order, account
proceeding or neglect of any of the said managers, such owner
or occupier shall, if he or they think proper, choose two fit and
disinterested persons and the said managers or any two of
them shall choose two other fit and disinterested persons, who,
if occasion be, shall choose a fifth person alike disinterested
and the person so chosen or any three of them shall finally
settle the same and all matters and things in dispute that shall
be referred to them by the parties.

[Section XIII.] (Section XIV, P. L.) And be it enacted by
the authority aforesaid, That if any person or persons shall
wickedly and maliciously cut through, break down or damage
any of the banks, dams, sluices or floodgates to the said district belonging, or shall let in any creek or water to annoy,
injure or overflow any of their neighbor's lands in the said
district and shall thereof be convicted before the justices of

the quarter sessions for the county of Chester, in all such cases the person or persons so offending shall be fined treble the value of the damages, one-third part of which fine shall be paid to the informer and the remaining two-thirds thereof shall be added to the common stock of the said company for the general use and benefit thereof.

[Section XIV.] (Section XV, P. L.) And be it enacted by the authority aforesaid, That If any of the said owners, oc-cupiers or possessors of meadow land within the said district shall neglect or refuse to pay the several sums of money that shall from time to time be rated, assessed or imposed by the major part of the managers of the said company for paying and discharging their respective proportions for maintaining the dams and sluices to the said district belonging or for making and scouring drains or ditches when thereunto required as aforesaid, or fines incurred, for the space of twenty days after demand made by the treasurer of the said company, it shall and may be lawful to and for the said treasurer by the direction of the major part of the managers for the time being in his own name to sue for and recover the fines and sums of money so charged or assessed in the same manner as debts not exceeding ten pounds are by law recoverable and give this act and the said assessment or the said account in evidence. Provided, always, That such delinquent owner, occupier or possessor shall not be entitled to stay of execution for any longer time than ten days, or it shall and may be lawful to and for the said treasurer by the direction of the managers as aforesaid in his own name to apply to some justice of the peace of the county for his warrant of distress for levying the said sums of money, so neglected or refused to be paid directed to the constable of the said township, which said warrant the said justice of the peace is hereby empowered and directed to grant accordingly to be by the said constable levied on the tract or piece of marsh meadow belonging to such owner, occupier or possessor so neglecting or refusing and deliver the same over unto the managers for the time being, who, or a major part of them, are hereby empowered, authorized and directed to let the same on rent or any part thereof as may

be sufficient, belonging to such delinquent owner or occupier
so neglecting as aforesaid from time to time for so long time
as until the rent or rents arising therefrom shall as nearly as
may be computed pay such sum or sums of money so assessed,
charged or imposed, together with all costs and reasonable
expenses arising thereon for his, her or their neglect or refusal
to pay the same as aforesaid and no longer. Provided always,
That in letting out the said meadow land the said managers
shall for the space of ten days previous to letting the same
publicly notify the leasing thereof and let the same to the
highest bidder at public sale.

[Section XV.] (Section XVI, P. L.) And be it enacted by
the authority aforesaid, That the said managers or any two
of them for the time being in every year are hereby empowered,
authorized and required to enter upon and inspect at least four
times in each year in the condition of all the said banks, dams,
sluices, floodgates and other conveniences for stopping out the
tides or draining the waters from the said meadows and upon
such inspection any allotment shall appear to be defective,
damaged or unfinished, they, the said managers or a majority
of them, shall give notice to and require the said owners, possessors or their guardians (if minors) forthwith to amend their
and each of their parts and allotments in such manner as by
this act is directed and if any of the said owners
or possessors of the land in the said tract of meadows or any
guardian of a minor, owner thereof, so warned by the said managers or a majority of them shall refuse or neglect after such
warning (notice thereof being given in writing) to amend and
repair their respective parts agreeable to the directions of the
said managers, or if any of the said owners or guardians are not
known or readily to be found at the time aforesaid, that then
and as often as it shall so happen, it shall and may be lawful
to and for the said managers or any of them together with such
workmen, horses, carts, barrows and tools as they shall think
necessary, to enter into and upon the lands of him, her or them
where such breach or defect shall happen to be and then and
there to dig, with the least damage to the owner thereof and
carry earth or purchase suitable materials to make amend

and repair the said banks, dams, sluices, floodgates and all
other conveniences necessary for stopping out the tides or for
draining the waters off the said meadows in such manner and
by such ways and means as they shall think fit and reasonable,
any law of this commonwealth, usage or custom to the contrary
in anywise notwithstanding, and they, the said managers or
some of them shall deliver to the said owners, possessors or
guardians of the said meadow land on whose allotments such
repairs shall be made or to as many of them as shall be found
their respective bills of [the charges] of repairing the part
of the bank to them before allotted and shall order payment
accordingly, and in case of their or any of their refusal or
delay of payment they shall order the treasurer for the time
being to recover the several sums of money so expended in the
manner hereinbefore directed for the recovery of fines and
moneys due to the said company.

[Section XVI.] (Section XVII, P. L.) And be it enacted by
the authority aforesaid, That the managers of the said district shall each of them have and receive seven shillings and
six pence per day for each day that they shall be employed in
the several duties required of them and the treasurer shall
have such compensation for his services as a major part of the
said managers shall think adequate.

[Section XVII.] (Section XVIII.) And be it further enacted
by the authority aforesaid, That the owner or occupier of
the ferry across Darby creek shall maintain and support that
part of the bank in the said district which adjoins the highway on which they land their passengers and of the breadth
of the said highway and should [the] owner or occupier of
the said ferry neglect to maintain and support the said piece
of bank when thereunto required by the managers of the said
company or any two of them, it shall and may be lawful for the
said managers or either of [them to] cause the said piece of
bank to be amended and repaired sufficiently and compel the
owner or occupier of the said ferry to pay the expense thereof
in the manner hereinbefore directed.

Passed September 4, 1789. Recorded L. B. No. 3, p. 518.

CHAPTER MODXXVI.

AN ACT TO ERECT WYOMING TOWNSHIP AND THAT PART OF CATA-
WISSA AND MAHONING TOWNSHIPS HEREINAFTER DESCRIBED IN
THE COUNTY OF NORTHUMBERLAND INTO A SEPARATE ELECTION
DISTRICT.

(Section I, P. L.) Whereas the freemen of Wyoming township
and part of the freemen of Catawissa and Mahoning townships
in the county of Northumberland have by their petitions set
forth that they labor under very great inconveniences on account of the distance many of them live from the place of
holding the annual election as well as on account of the bad
roads they are obliged to pass over in their way to their said
elections:

For the remedy whereof:

[Section I.] (Section II, P. L.) Be it enacted and it
is hereby enacted by the Representatives of the Commonwealth of Pennsylvania in General Assembly met and
by the authority of the same, That all the freemen living
within the following bounds, viz:, beginning at a place
known by the name of Bear Gap of Roaring creek, thence
down the same creek about three miles, thence with a
straight line to the head branch of Little Roaring creek,
thence down the same to the northeast branch of the
river Susquehanna, thence down the same to the lower
end of James Cochran's plantation, thence across the river by
a north line to be run through [the] township [of] Mahoning
to the northern boundary thereof including all Wyoming township and all those parts of Catawissa and Mahoning townships
that are north and east of said lines in the county or Northumberland aforesaid, shall from and after the passing of this
act be struck off and separated from the first and second districts in the said county and established and erected into a
separate district called the seventh district in the county of
Northumberland aforesaid and that the freemen of the said

seventh district now erected as aforesaid shall hold their elections at the house of Samuel Boon, near the mouth of Fishing creek, anything in a former law obliging the inhabitants of this last erected district to attend their elections at the county town or at the town of Northumberland notwithstanding.

Passed September 7, 1789. Recorded L. B. No. 3, p. 525.

CHAPTER MCDXXVII.

AN ACT TO ALTER THE TIMES OF HOLDING THE COURTS OF GENERAL QUARTER SESSIONS OF THE PEACE AND GAOL DELIVERY IN THE SEVERAL COUNTIES WITHIN THIS COMMONWEALTH.

(Section I, P. L.) Whereas the opening and commencing of the courts of general quarter sessions of the peace and gaol delivery in the several counties within this commonwealth on the Tuesdays of the weeks appointed by law for the holding of the same respectively have on experience been found to be highly inconvenient by reason [of the remainder of the] week being insufficient to dispatch the business thereof and of the other courts which are opened and held at the same time:

For remedy whereof:

[Section I.] (Section II, P. L.) Be it enacted and it is hereby enacted by the Representatives of the Freemen of the Commonwealth of Pennsylvania in General Assembly met and by the authority of the same, That from and after the first day of November next the county courts of general quarter sessions of the peace and gaol delivery of and for each and every county within this commonwealth shall begin, open, commence and be held by the justices of the said courts respectively and they are hereby severally and respectively enjoined to begin, open, commence and hold the same and every future sessions thereof on the first Monday of each and every week appointed by the law for holding of the said courts respectively

20—XIII

pose of holding the general elections and that part of the county aforesaid beginning at the north line of the state of Pennsylvania and extending down including both sides of the river
Susquehanna to a line drawn east and west across the county,
at Wyalusing falls shall be an election district by the name
of the Tioga district and the freemen thereof shall meet at
the house now occupied by Simon Spalding and hold their
elections. From the line last mentioned to a line drawn from
the mouth of the Falling spring easterly on the Lackawanna
mountain, to the northerly part of Providence township, thence
east to the east line of the county, and a line drawn from the
said Falling spring west to the west line of the county shall
be an election district by the name of Tunkhannock district
and the freemen thereof shall meet at the house now occupied
by Gideon Osterhout and hold their elections from the Falling
Spring down the Susquehanna river on the east side so far as
to include Newport township, thence east to the east line of
the county, thence northerly on the said line to the Tunkhannock district, thence westerly on the line of Tunkhannock
to the place of beginning shall be an election district by the
name of Wilkes-Barre district, and the freemen thereof shall
meet and hold their elections at the court-house in Wilkes-
Barre. From a point on the west side of Susquehanna river
opposite the Falling Spring down the said river to Henlock's
creek, thence up said creek to the head thereof, thence west
to the west line of the county, thence northerly on said line
to the Tunkhannock district, thence east on the line of Tunkhannock district to the point the place of beginning shall be
an election district by the name of Kingston district and the
freemen thereof shall meet at the house now occupied by Lawrence Meyers and hold their elections. And all the lands within the county aforesaid between the southerly lines of the two
last mentioned districts and the southerly line of the county
shall be an election district by the name of Salem district and
the freemen thereof shall meet at the house now occupied by
Nathan Beach and hold their elections, anything to the contrary hereof in any former law contained notwithstanding.

　　Passed September 7, 1789. Recorded L. B. No. 3, p. 527.

CHAPTER MCDXXX.

AN ACT TO GRANT AND SECURE TO ROBERT LESLIE FOR A LIMITED
TIME THE SOLE AND EXCLUSIVE RIGHT AND BENEFIT OF CON-
STRUCTING, MAKING AND SELLING WITHIN THIS COMMONWEALTH
THE IMPROVEMENTS BY HIM LATELY INVENTED ON CLOCKS AND
WATCHES.

(Section I, P. L.) Whereas it appears to this house that
Robert Leslie of the city of Philadelphia, clock and watch
maker, hath invented and discovered sundry improvements
upon clocks and watches which are described as follows, that
is to say: three methods of communicating the motion from
the movements of a clock to the pendulum in such manner
that no change or action of the weather can increase or diminish its swing or vibration.

A scapement for clocks which gives both beats the same
power and advantage.   An improvement upon horizontal
watches by which both beats are inside of the cylinder, which
reduces the friction and gives a greater motion to the balance.

A balance wheel and cylinder which have every advantage
of the last above mentioned improvement.

A balance wheel and verge with spiral wings or pallets which
give a large motion to the balance, And,

A cycloid curb which causes all the vibrations of the balance
whether long or short to be performed in the same space of
time.   Draughts or drawings of all which he hath deposited in
the prothonotary's office for the city and county of Philadelphia.   And the said Robert Leslie by his said petitions did
pray this house to grant him, his executors, administrators and
assigns the exclusive right and benefit of constructing, making
and vending his said inventions and improvements for a certain
term of years:

And whereas it is just and right to reward the inventors of
useful improvements:

Therefore:

[Section I.] (Section II, P. L.) Be it enacted and it is hereby enacted by the Representatives of the Freemen of the Commonwealth of Pennsylvania in General Assembly met and by the authority of the same, That from and after the passing of this act the said Robert Leslie, his executors, administrators and assigns shall have the sole and exclusive right and benefit of constructing, making and selling within this Comwealth all and every the invention and improvements or any of them made thereto for and during the full space and term of fourteen years from thence next ensuing.

[Section II.] (Section III, P. L.) And be it further enacted by the authority aforesaid, That if any person or persons shall make, sell or use or cause to be made, sold or used within this commonwealth, any clock or clocks, watch or watches, or any other time piece by any other name or description which shall have the inventions or improvements before described or any of them during the said term of fourteen years without the consent of the said Robert Leslie, his executors, administrators or assigns in writing first had and obtained, he, she, or they so offending shall forfeit unto the said Robert Leslie, his executors, administrators or assigns, all and every such clock and clocks, watch or watches and other timepiece by any other name or description so made or sold or used or caused to be made, sold or used which shall have the said inventions and improvements or any of them made thereto as aforesaid. And moreover shall forfeit and pay unto the said Robert Leslie his executors, administrators or assigns for every such clock, watch or timepiece so made, sold or used or caused to be made, sold or used, respectively, which shall have the said inventions and improvements or any of them made thereto as aforesaid contrary to the true intent and meaning of this act, the sum of twenty pounds lawful money of Pennsylvania to be recovered by the said Robert Leslie, his executors, administrators or asigns with costs of suit by action of debt, bill, plaint or information in any court of record within this commonwealth or elsewhere, wherein no essoign, protection or wager of law nor more than one imparlance shall be allowed.

[Section III.] Provided always nevertheless, That if any

person or persons shall at any time hereafter within the term
aforesaid claim to have Invented or used the same improvements or any or either of them before the said Robert Leslle,
it shall be lawful for him or them so claiming or for his or their
executors or administrators to sue forth and prosecute one or
more writ or writs of scire facias returnable before the justices
of the supreme court of this commonwealth to be devised or
approved by the chief justice or one of the justices of the said
court, warning the said Robert Leslle, his executors, administrators or assigns then having the sole and exclusive right
aforesaid, to be and appear before the said justices at the next
supreme court to be held for the said commonwealth to show
cause why the grant of the said sole and exclusive right and
benefit of constructing, making and selling such invention, improvement or improvements should not be repealed and made
void, and upon such writ the proceedings shall be such as in
other suits of scire facias in the said court shall be used and
accustomed and if judgment shall thereupon be rendered by default, confession or upon verdict or demurrer for the plaintiff,
judgment shall be entered that so much of the grant herein contained as shall be alleged by the plaintiff and so confessed or
found against the defendant shall be repealed and made null
and void, and thenceforth so much of the said grant shall be
and the same is hereby repealed and made null and void to all
intents and purposes whatsoever and the said court shall
award such and the same costs to be recovered in the like manner as in other suits or actions brought and determined in the
said court.   And provided also, That in all suits or actions to
be brought by the said Robert Leslie, his executors or assigns
for any penalty or forfeiture in pursuance of this act it shall
and may be lawful for the defendant or defendants to plead the
general issue and give this act (and any special matter whereof
notice shall be given to the plaintiff or his attorney at least
sixty days before the trial) in evidence and if upon the trial it
shall be made to appear to the satisfaction of the court and
jury that the defendant or any other person whatsoever
than the said Robert Leslie was the true and original inventor
of the improvement or invention in question or had used the

same before the first day of January in the year of our Lord one thousand seven hundred and eighty-seven, the verdict shall be found and judgment entered for the defendant and he shall be acquitted of all the penalties and forfeitures demanded against him and shall recover his costs and charges by him expended in defending such suit or action in the same manner as in other suits or actions determined in the same court.

Passed September 7, 1789. Recorded L. B. No. 3, p. 528.

CHAPTER MCDXXXI.

AN ACT FOR THE RELIEF OF JAMES PETTIGREW AN INSOLVENT DEBTOR IN THE COUNTY OF NORTHAMPTON CONFINED IN THE GAOL OF SAID COUNTY.

(Section I, P. L.) Whereas James Pettigrew late collector of excise of the county of Northampton hath set forth by his petition that he is confined in the gaol of the said county under execution at the suit of this commonwealth for arrearages due by him as the late collector of excise in the said county, which from a variety of misfortunes he is rendered unable to pay and hath prayed that an act may be passed extending to him the benefit of the insolvent laws and it appears to this house [that] the prayer of the petitioner ought to be granted:

[Section I.] (Section II, P. L.) Be it therefore enacted and it is hereby enacted by the Representatives of the Freemen of the commonwealth of Pennsylvania in General Assembly met and by the authority of the same, That the county court of common pleas of the county of Northampton upon the petition of James Pettigrew is hereby authorized and empowered to grant [him] relief with equal and like effect and upon the like terms and conditions as to the imprisonment of his person as is by the laws of this state afforded to insolvent debtors in cases of debts by them owing to private persons.

[Section II.]   Provided, That the discharge of the said James Pettigrew shall not extend to exonerate, annul or lessen

the force and effect of any security or engagement entered into
by any other person for securing the payment of the moneys
collected by him or for his good behavior in the duties of his
office.

Passed September 11, 1789. Recorded L. B. No. 3, p. 530, etc.

CHAPTER MCDXXXII.

AN ACT TO AUTHORIZE GEORGE FREY OF MIDDLETOWN IN THE
COUNTY OF DAUPHIN TO SUPPORT A MILL-DAM ACROSS SWATARA
CREEK, AND TO OBLIGE HIM TO MAINTAIN A FREE NAVIGATION
FOR BOATS AND OTHER CRAFT ALONG HIS MILL-RACE INTO HIS
MILLDAM.

(Section I, P. L.) Whereas George Frey of Middletown in
the county of Dauphin, hath at a great expense erected a mill
near the mouth of Swatara creek which is bound to be public utility.

And whereas the navigation of the said creek may be facilitated by means of the race, dam and other works constructed by the said George Frey and it is reasonable and just
that he should be obliged to keep the same in repair, on condition of his being permitted to support a dam across the creek
aforesaid.

[Section I.] (Section II, P. L.) Be it therefore enacted and it
is hereby enacted by the Representatives of the Freemen of the
Commonwealth of Pennsylvania in General Assembly met and
by the authority of the same, That from and after the passing
of this act it shall and may be lawful for the said George Frey,
his heirs, executors, administrators and assigns to support and
maintain the tumbling dam which he has already built on Swatara creek, in such manner nevertheless as to enable the fish at
all times to pass and re-pass into, out of and over the same with
as little obstruction as may be, provided that the water of the
said dam (when not raised or swelled by flood or freshes) shall
not be more than three feet higher than it would have

from whence the same shall be intended to be exported and before the same shall be inspected, approved and adjudged by the said inspector, his deputies (or three persons to be appointed by one of the magistrates in the manner by the said recited act directed as to merchantable flour) to be of a due degree of fineness and quality to be exported as middlings and the said inspector or his deputy shall try and search the same and plug up the holes he shall make in the same manner and shall receive the same reward for inspecting the same as by the said act is directed concerning merchantable flour.

[Section II.] (Section III, P. L.) And be it further enacted by the authority aforesaid, That if the said inspector or his deputies or the three persons to be appointed by a magistrate as aforesaid shall adjudge and determine that any such flour of wheat so to be branded "middlings" shall not be of a due fineness and quality to be exported as and for middlings, he or they shall cause the said word "middlings" so branded to be scratched out and obliterated and the owner of such middlings or the person or persons offering or intending the same for sale or exportation shall pay for the inspection thereof the same reward as if the same had been adjudged to be fit for exportation.

[Section III.] (Section IV, P. L.) And it is hereby further enacted by the authority aforesaid, That all and every the regulations, fines, penalties and forfeitures in and by the said recited act and the several supplements thereto and by this act made, imposed and inflicted on any person or persons who should or shall grind, bolt, make casks for, pack, brand after the same shall have left [the mill or] bolting-house, transport, export or other ways have anything to do with common or superfine flour and who should or shall offend against the said recited act or the supplements thereto or against this act, shall from and after the said first day of November next extend and be construed to extend to such persons and offences as to the species of wheat flour called middlings as fully and effectually as if the article "middlings" was inserted with flour in the said acts, or as if the said regulations, fines penalties and forfeitures were herein repeated.

And whereas the packing of wheat flour in half casks containing ninety-eight pounds neat weight although not warranted by the said recited act or its supplements has been practised and is found to be beneficial in the stowage of ships and vessels:

[Section IV.] (Section V. P. L.) It is therefore enacted by the authority aforesaid, That it shall and may be lawful for millers and bolters to pack any flour of wheat for exportation in casks made of staves of the length of twenty-three inches and of the diameter at each head of twelve inches and an half, such miller and bolter complying with all and every the directions of the said recited acts of assembly as to the casks No. 1, 2, and 3 therein mentioned and subject to the same regulations, fines, forfeitures and penalties and branding the [said] smaller casks No. 4-98 after the said first day of November next.

And whereas one of the reasons for requiring all casks wherein flour intended for exportation shall be packed to be made of certain dimensions is to prevent the loss of space in stowing the same in ships or vessels and the non-compliance with the said requisition is of material disadvantage to the merchants and owners of ships:

And whereas the price of the casks (which under the said recited act was the measure of penalty for such non-compliance) is by the general practice of selling flour by the barrel sunk and confounded therewith.

[Section V.] (Section VI, P. L.) It is therefore hereby enacted by the authority aforesaid, That whenever any flour of wheat sold for exportation shall be offered to the view and examination of the said inspectors or his deputies, he or they shall and each and every of them is hereby enjoined and required to view and measure each and every cask and casks thereof and if they or any of them shall be found to vary from the dimensions in the said act and in this act contained, the person or persons who shall have sold the same for exportation as aforesaid shall forfeit and pay for every cask thereof which shall be found to vary as aforesaid the sum of one shilling and sixpence, to be sued for and recovered by the said inspector or his deputy or deputies, in like manner as other debts of the

like amount may or can be sued for and be recovered by the
laws of this commonwealth together with costs of suit which
with all other the fines, forfeitures and penalties imposed and
directed to be levied by this act shall be applied in like manner
as is directed by the act to which this is a supplement.

Passed September 12th, 1789.　Recorded L. B. No. 8, p. 582.

See note to the Act of Assembly passed April 5, 1781.　Chapter
986.

CHAPTER MCDXXXIV.

AN ACT TO CEDE TO THE UNITED STATES THE RIGHT TO EXERCISE
EXCLUSIVE LEGISLATION OVER SUCH DISTRICTS AS MAY BECOME
THE SEAT OF GOVERNMENT THEREOF WITHIN THIS COMMON-
WEALTH.

(Section I, P. L.) It being directed and established by the
constitution of the United States that the "congress thereof
shall have power to exercise exclusive legislation in all cases
whatsoever over such district (not exceeding ten miles square)
as may by cession of particular states and the acceptance
of congress become the seat of government of the United
States:" And the same appearing to be just and reasonable
and this house being willing to make such cession as aforesaid over such district as may be chosen within this state for
the purpose aforesaid.

[Section I.] (Section II, P. L.) Be it enacted and it is hereby
enacted by the Representatives of the Freemen of the Commonwealth of Pennsylvania in General Assembly met and by
the authority of the same, That the right and power to exercise
exclusive legislation in all cases whatsoever over such district
or part of this state not exceeding ten miles square as shall be
accepted and located by the congress of the United States
and become the seat of Government thereof shall so soon as
such district shall be accepted located and become the seat of
the said Government be and the same hereby is ceded to and
vested in the said United States and this state shall thereupon
be to all intents and purposes irrevocably divested thereof.

‑<!‑‑ ‑‑>

[Section II.] (Section III, P. L.) Provided nevertheless and it is hereby enacted and declared by the authority aforesaid, That the power of exercising exclusive legislation in and over the city of Philadelphia and the district of Southwark and that part of the Northern Liberties included within a line running parallel with Vine street at the distance of one mile northward thereof from the river Schuylkill to the southern side of the main branch of Cohocksink creek, thence down the said creek till it falls into the Delaware (other than the marsh land and so much of the adjoining bank or fast land on the same side of the said creek as shall be necessary for docks and dock yards and the erecting any dams or works to command the water of the said creek) shall be and the same are hereby excepted out of this grant and cession and retained by this commonwealth.

Passed September 14, 1789. Recorded L. B. No. 3, p. 534.

CHAPTER MCDXXXV.

AN ACT FOR ANNEXING PART OF THE COUNTY OF WASHINGTON TO THE COUNTY OF ALLEGHENY.

(Section I, P. L.) Whereas the inhabitants of that part of the county of Washington which is included in the boundaries hereinafter mentioned have by their petition represented to this house their remote situation from the seat of justice and prayed to be annexed to the county of Allegheny and the prayer of the petitioners appearing just and reasonable:

[Section I.] (Section II, P. L.) Be it enacted and it is hereby enacted by the Representatives of the Freemen of the Commonwealth of Pennsylvania in General Assembly met and by the authority of the same, That all that part of Washington county included by the following lines, viz., beginning at the river Ohio where the boundary line of the state crosses the said river, from thence in a straight line to White's mill on Raccoon creek, from thence by a straight line to Armstrong's mill on

Miller's run, and from thence by a straight line to the Monongahela river opposite the mouth of Perry's run where it strikes the present line of the county of Allegheny be immediately after the running of said lines and the same is hereby annexed to the said county of Allegheny and to all intents and purposes constituted a part of the same.

[Section II.] (Section III, P. L.) And be it further enacted by the authority aforesaid, That the inhabitants of all that part of Washington county by this act annexed to the said county of Allegheny shall at all times hereafter have and enjoy all and singular the jurisdictions, powers, rights, liberties and privileges whatsoever which the inhabitants of Allegheny county or the inhabitants of any other county within this state do, may or ought to enjoy by the laws of this state.

[Section III.] (Section IV, P. L.) And be it further enacted by the authority aforesaid, That Peter Kidd and John Beaver be and they or either of them are and is hereby authorized and directed to survey and mark the lines agreeable to the directions of this act for which service they shall be severally allowed twenty-five shillings per day each and no more and the charges so incurred shall be defrayed by the said county of Allegheny and for that purpose levied and raised by the inhabitants thereof in like manner with other public money by law raised and levied for the use of the said county.

[Section IV.] (Section V, P. L.) And be it further enacted by the authority aforesaid, That should it so happen that any of the election districts heretofore established within the county of Washington shall be separated and divided into parts by the running of the said lines, then and in such case or cases all such parts of such districts as shall be and remain within the county of Washington shall be and they are hereby annexed to such other election districts within the said county of Washington as shall be next adjoining to such parts of any such separated and divided districts and the freemen of such parts thereof shall vote at their elections at the same places appointed by law for the holding of the elections of such districts to which they shall be so as aforesaid annexed.

Passed September 17, 1789. Recorded L. B. No. 3, p. 535.

CHAPTER MCDXXXVI.

AN ACT FOR ERECTING CERTAIN PARTS OF CUMBERLAND AND NORTHUMBERLAND COUNTIES INTO A SEPARATE COUNTY.

(Section I, P. L.) Whereas it hath been represented to the general assembly of this state by the inhabitants of those parts of Cumberland and Northumberland counties which are included within the lines hereinafter mentioned that they labor under great hardships by reason of their great distance from the present seats of justice and the public offices for the said counties:

For remedy whereof:

[Section I.] (Section II, P. L.) Be it enacted and it is hereby enacted by the Representatives of the Freemen of the Commonwealth of Pennsylvania in General Assembly met and by the authority of the same, That all and singular the lands lying within the bonds and limits hereinafter described and following, shall be and are hereby erected into a separate county by the name of "Mifflin County," namely, beginning at Susquehanna river where the Turkey hill extends to the said river, then along the said hill to Juniata where it cuts Tuscarora mountain, thence along the summit of the said mountain to the line of Franklin county, thence along the said line to Huntingdon county line, thence along the said line to Juniata river, thence up the said river to Jack's narrows, thence along the line of Huntingdon county to the summit of Tussey's mountain, thence along the lines of Huntingdon and Northumberland counties so as to include the whole of Upper Bald Eagle township in the county of Northumberland to the mouth of Buck creek where it empties into the Bald Eagle creek, thence to Logan's Gap in Nittany mountain, thence to the head of Penn's creek, thence down the said creek to Sinking creek, leaving George McCormick's in Northumberland county, thence to the top of Jack's mountain at the line between Northumberland county and Cumberland, thence along the said line to Montour's spring at the heads of Mahantango creek, thence down the said creek to Susquehanna river and thence down the said river to the place of beginning.

[Section II.] (Section III, P. L.) And be it enacted by the authority aforesaid, That the inhabitants of the said county shall at all times hereafter have and enjoy all and singular the privileges and jurisdictions which the inhabitants of any other county within this state do, may or ought to enjoy by the constitution and laws of this state.

[Section III.] (Section IV, P. L.) And be it further enacted by the authority aforesaid, That the justices of the peace commissioned at the time of passing this act and residing within the bounds and limits of the said county herein and hereby erected and constituted shall be justices of the peace for the said county during the time for which they were so commissioned, and they or any three of them shall and may hold courts of general quarter sessions of the peace. And the justices of the common pleas in like manner commissioned and residing or any three or more of them shall and may hold courts of common pleas in the said county during the time they were so commissioned, and the said courts of general quarter sessions of the peace and of common pleas shall have all and singular the powers and authorities, rights and jurisdictions to all intents and purposes which any other counties of this state may, can or ought to have in their respective counties, and the said courts of common pleas shall sit and be held for the said county of Mifflin on the second Tuesdays in the months of December, March, June and September in each year at the house now occupied by Arthur Buchanan until a court-house shall be built as hereafter directed and the courts of quarter sessions of and for the said county shall open and commence on the days next preceding the opening of the said courts of common pleas in each of the said months in each year as aforesaid until the time aforesaid and then shall sit and be holden and kept at the said court-house on the days and times before mentioned.

[Section IV.] (Section V, P. L.) And be it further enacted by the authority aforesaid, That all taxes and arrears of taxes

laid or directed to be laid or which have become due within
the said county of Mifflin before the passing of this act shall
be levied and collected by the same persons and in like manner
as if this act had not been passed, and the collector of excise
for the counties of Cumberland and Northumberland respectively shall have authority in like manner to demand, recover
and collect within the said county of Mifflin all sums of money
which have or shall become due to this commonwealth for excise on or before the second Tuesday in October next and all
sums of money due to this commonwealth for militia fines
within said county of Mifflin shall be collected and recovered
as if this act had not been made.

[Section V.] (Section VI, P. L.) Be it further enacted by
the authority aforesaid, That the inhabitants of each township
for the county hereby erected, qualified by law to elect, shall
at the usual places in their respective districts as heretofore
laid off from the counties of Cumberland and Northumberland
and which may now fall in the county hereby erected at the
ships and districts of other counties in the state, meet and
choose justices of the peace, inspectors, judges of elections for
representatives in general assembly, a councillor and other
elective county officers agreeably to the constitution and laws
of this state for the time being. Provided always nevertheless,
That that part of Northumberland county which is contained
within the bounds of the said county of Mifflin be and the same
hereby is erected into an election district and that the freemen
of the said district meet at the house occupied by Enoch Hest-
ing and hold their election.

[Section VI.] (Section VII, P. L.) And be it further enacted by the authority aforesaid, That the sheriff, treasurer,
prothonotary, collector of excise and all such other officers
as have heretofore given security for the faithful performance
of and discharge of their several offices in the other counties of
this state and who shall hereafter be appointed or elected in
the said county, before they or any of them shall enter upon
the execution of their respective offices, duties and trusts, shall
give sufficient security in the like sums and in the like manner and forms and for the same uses, trusts and purposes as

such officers and persons elected and appointed for the like offices, duties and trusts are obliged by law to give in the county of Cumberland for the time being.

Whereas by the act to appoint a representation for the city and county of Philadelphia and the several counties of this commonwealth in proportion [to the number] of taxable inhabitants for the ensuing seven years the county of Cumberland is entitled to choose four representatives in general assembly.

[Section VII.] (Section VIII, P. L.) Be it further enacted by the authority aforesaid, That the said county of Cumberland shall elect three members only and the county of Mifflin shall elect one member to represent them respectivly in the general assembly of this commonwealth from and after the passing of this act until the same shall be altered agreeable to the constitution and laws of this state, one councillor, two fit persons for sheriffs, two fit persons for coroners and three commissioners in the same manner and under the same rules, regulations and penalties as by the constitution and laws of this state is directed in respect to other counties, and the said representatives, councillor and other officers, when chosen as aforesaid, and duly qualified, shall have and enjoy all and singular such powers, authority and privileges in and for their county as such officers elected in and for any other county of this state may, can or ought to have. Provided nevertheless, That no councillor shall be elected by the freemen of the said county of Mifflin to serve for the said county before the term for which the present councillor for the county of Cumberland was elected shall expire or till his death, resignation or removal from office.

[Section VIII.] (Section IX, P. L.) And be it further enacted by the authority aforesaid, That John Oliver, William Brown, David Beale, John Stewart, David Bole and Andrew Gregg of said county be and they are hereby appointed trustees for the county aforesaid with full authority for them or a majority of them to purchase or take and receive by grant, bargain or otherwise any quantity or quantities of land not exceeding one hundred and fifty acres on the north side of Juniata river and within one mile from the mouth of Kishicoquillas creek for the

use, trust and benefit of said county, and to lay out the same
into regular town lots and to dispose of so many of them as
they or any four of them may think best for the advantage of
said county and they or any four of them are hereby authorized
to sell and convey so many of them as they may think proper
and with the moneys so arising from the sale of such lots and
with other moneys assessed, levied and collected within the
said county of Mifflin for that purpose which it is hereby declared it shall and may be lawful for the commissioners thereof
to do or cause to be done, to build and erect a court house and
prison suitable and convenient for the public on the public
and such other square as shall be reserved for that purpose
and the said trustees shall from time to time render true and
faithful accounts of the expenditures of the same not only to
the commissioners but to the grand jury for inspection, adjustment and settlement of the accounts of said county.

[Section IX.] (Section X, P. L.) Be it further enacted by the
authority aforesaid, That the justices of the supreme court and
of the courts of oyer and terminer and general gaol delivery of
this state shall have the like powers, jurisdictions and authorities within the said county of Mifflin as by law they are vested
with and entitled to have and exercise in other counties of this
state, and they are hereby authorized and empowered from
time to time to deliver the gaol of the said county of capital
and other offenders, in the same manner as they are authorized
and empowered to do in any other counties of this state.

[Section X.] (Section XI, P. L.) Provided always and be
it further enacted by the authority aforesaid, That no action
or suit, indictment or prosecution now commenced or depending in any of the courts of the counties of Cumberland, Northumberland or either of them or which shall be commenced in
the same on or before the fifth day of November next in the
due and usual forms of the law shall be delayed, discontinued
or affected by this act, but the same shall be proceeded to judgment and execution shall be issued and awarded upon all such
judgments to the sheriff or coroner of the said county of Cumberland or Northumberland as the case may be, as if this act
had not been made, and it shall and may be lawful for the

justices of the counties of Cumberland or Northumberland respectively aforesaid for the carrying on and obtaining the effects of such suits, to issue any necessary process for such purpose to be directed to the sheriff or coroner of said counties of Cumberland or Northumberland as the case may be, which said sheriffs and coroners are hereby commanded to obey the said process and to make the necessary and usual returns thereof before the court issuing such process as if the party or parties defendant were residing in the same county.

Passed September 19, 1798. Recorded L. B. No. 3, p. 536. See the Acts of Assembly passed April 5, 1790, Chapter 1515; April 9, 1791, Chapter 1561.

CHAPTER MCDXXXVII.

AN ACT TO DIVIDE THE COUNTY [OF] BERKS INTO ELECTION DISTRICTS.

(Section I, P. L.) Whereas the freemen of the county of Berks have by their petitions to this house prayed that the said county may be divided into election districts and it is conceived that [the] same would contribute to their ease in attending their general elections:

[Section I.] (Section II, P. L.) Be it therefore enacted and it is hereby enacted by the Representatives of the Freemen of the Commonwealth of Pennsylvania in General Assembly met and by the authority of the same, That from and after the passing of this act the county of Berks shall be and the same is hereby divided into five election districts for the purpose of holding the general elections of which the borough of Reading and the townships of Alsace, Cumru, Exter, Heidelberg, Brecknoch, Maiden-creek, Carnarvon, Oley, Robinson, Ruscombmanor and the lower part of Bern (the township of Bern to be divided as follows, beginning at a black oak tree standing on the eastern bank of Tulpehocken creek in said township, being a corner of Anthony Shomo and Abraham Stout's land, thence by [a] straight line to John Noecker's mill on the river Schuylkill) shall be the first, and the freemen thereof shall hold their elections at the court-house in the said borough of Reading, and the townships of Maxatawney, Longswamp, Hereford district, Richmond, Rockland and Greenwich shall be the second, and the freemen thereof shall hold their elections at the house now occupied by Philip Gehr in Kutztown in the township of Maxatawney, and the townships of Windsor, Brunswick, [Albany] and the upper part of Bern shall be the third and freemen thereof shall hold their elections at the house now occupied by John Moyer in the town of Hamburg in the township of Windsor and the townships of Tulpehocken, Bethel and Pine Grove shall be the fourth and the freemen thereof shall hold their elections at the house now occupied by Godfrey Roehrer in the township of Tulpehocken, and the townships of Earl, Amity, Union, Colebrookdale and Douglass shall be the fifth and the freemen thereof shall hold their elections at the house now occupied by William Witman in the township of Amity, anything to the contrary hereof in any former law contained notwithstanding.

Passed September 21, 1789.   Recorded L. B. No. 3, p. 539.

CHAPTER MCDXXXVIII.

AN ACT FOR ERECTING THE TOWN OF EASTON IN THE COUNTY OF NORTHAMPTON INTO A BOROUGH AND FOR OTHER PURPOSES THEREIN MENTIONED.

(Section I, P. L.) Whereas the inhabitants of the town of Easton have represented by their petition to the assembly that the said town is advantageously situated on the conflux of the rivers Delaware and Lehigh and is greatly improving and increasing in the number of buildings and inhabitants and that the courts of justice for the county are held there, and for these reasons have prayed that the said town may be erected into a borough.

[Section I.] (Section II, P. L.) Be it therefore enacted and it is hereby enacted by the Representatives of the Freemen of the Commonwealth of Pennsylvania in General Assembly met and by the authority of the same, That the said town of Easton, out-lots and commons thereto belonging, shall be and the same are hereby erected into a borough which shall be called "The Borough of Easton," forever, the extent of which borough is and shall be comprised within the following boundaries, to wit; beginning at a black oak on the west bank of the river Delaware, being a corner of land of Andrew Kroup, running thence west five hundred and sixty-three perches to a post in the line of George Messinger's land, thence by the line of land late of Barnett Walter and others south four hundred and fifty-three perches to a birch on the north-west bank of Lehigh river, thence down the same river by several courses thereof to the mouth thereof, and thence up the river Delaware by the several courses thereof, crossing the mouth of Bushkill creek to the place of beginning.

[Section II.] (Section III, P. L.) And be it further enacted by the authority aforesaid, That Peter Kachlein, Henry Barnet, Jacob Weygand, William Raup and John Protsman be and they are hereby appointed the present burgesses and the said Peter Kachlein shall be the chief burgess within the same borough and Frederick Barthold shall be high constable and Samuel Sitgreaves shall be town-clerk, to continue burgesses, high constable and town-clerk until the first Monday in the month of May in the year of our Lord one thousand seven hundred and ninety and from thence until others shall be duly elected and qualified in their place as hereinafter is directed.

[Section III.] (Section IV, P. L.) And be it further enacted by the authority aforesaid, That the said burgesses, freeholders and inhabitants within the borough aforesaid [and their successors forever hereafter] shall be one body corporate and politic in deed and name and by the name of "The Burgesses and Inhabitants of the Borough of Easton in the County of Northampton," one body corporate and politic in deed and in name, are hereby fully created and constituted and confirmed and by the same name of "The Burgesses and Inhabitants of

the Borough of Easton in the County of Northampton," shall
have a perpetual succession and they and their successors by
the name of "The Burgesses and Inhabitants of the Borough
of Easton in the County of Northampton," shall at all times
hereafter be persons able and capable in law to have, get, receive and possess lands, tenements, rents, liberties, jurisdictions, franchises and hereditaments to them and their successors in fee simple or for term of life, lives, [years] or otherwise, and also goods and chattels and other things of what
nature or kind soever, and also to give, grant, let, sell and assign the same lands, tenements, hereditaments, goods and chattels and to do and execute all other things about the same by
the name aforesaid, and they shall forever hereafter be persons
able and capable in law to sue and be sued, plead and be impleaded, answer and be answered unto, defend and be defended
in all or any of the courts within this commonwealth or other
places, and before any judges, justices or other persons within
this commonwealth in all manner of actions, suits, complaints,
pleas, causes and matters whatsoever and that it shall and
may be lawful to and for the said burgesses and inhabitants of
Easton aforesaid and their successors forever hereafter to have
and use one common seal for the sealing of all business whatsoever touching the said corporation and the same from time
to time at their will to change and alter.

[Section IV.] (Section V, P. L.) And be it further enacted
by the authority aforesaid, That it shall and may be lawful
for the burgesses, constable and freeholders together with such
inhabitants, housekeepers within the said borough, as shall
have resided therein at least for the space of one year next
preceding any such election as is hereinafter directed, on the
first Monday in the month of May in the year of our Lord one
thousand seven hundred and ninety and in every year thereafter publicly to meet at the court-house within the said borough and then and there to elect and choose by ballot five fit
and suitable men of the inhabitants of the said borough to be
burgesses, one to be constable and one to be town-clerk of the
said borough, which election shall be taken by the high constable of the preceding year and of which election the said

high constable shall give at least ten days' public notice by
advertisements fixed up in at least six of the most public places
within the said borough and the names of the persons so
elected shall be certified under his seal to the president of the
supreme executive council for the time being within fifteen
days next after such election, and the burgess who shall have
a majority of votes shall be called the chief burgess of the said
borough, but in case no one of the persons so elected shall have
a majority of votes then the same shall be decided by lot between those who are equal and highest in votes, which lot shall
be taken by the high constable and certified as aforesaid; which
said burgesses, constable and town-clerk so elected shall be
and continue the burgesses, constable and town-clerk of the
said borough until the next day of election and until others
shall be elected and qualified in their stead as herein is directed.

[Section V.] (Section VI, P. L.) And be it further enacted
by the authority aforesaid, That the said burgesses for the
time being shall be and are hereby empowered and authorized
by themselves and upon their own view or in other lawful
manner to remove all nuisances and encroachments on the
streets, lanes, alleys and highways within the said borough as
they shall see occasion.

[Section VI.] (Section VII, P. L.) And be it further enacted
by the authority aforesaid, That before any of the said burgesses, constable, town-clerk or other officers shall take upon
them their respective offices, they shall take and subscribe
such oath or affirmation of allegiance and fidelity as by the laws
of this commonwealth are or shall be in such cases provided,
together with an oath or affirmation for the due execution of
their respective offices. And every chief burgess so elected and
appointed from year to year as aforesaid shall within two
weeks immediately after his election take the oaths or affirmations aforesaid, before a justice of the peace of the county
aforesaid, unless disabled by sickness or other reasonable
cause. And the chief burgess having qualified himself in manner aforesaid shall enter upon his office, and the other burgesses, constable, town-clerk and other officers shall and may

qualify themselves for their respective offices by taking and
subscribing the oaths or affirmations aforesaid before the said
chief burgess or before one of the justices of the peace for the
said county who are hereby authorized and empowered to administer the same.

[Section VII.] (Section VIII, P. L.) And be it further enacted by the authority aforesaid, That it shall and may be lawful for the burgesses, freeholders and inhabitants, housekeepers aforesaid, and their successors to have, hold and keep
within the said borough two markets in each week, that is to
say, one market on Wednesday and one market on Saturday
in every week of the year forever in the great square in the said
borough and two fairs in the year, the first to begin on the
fourth Tuesday of April and the other of said fairs to begin
on the fourth Tuesday of October in every year, each fair to
continue two days; together with free liberties, customs, profits
and emoluments to the said markets and fairs belonging and
In anywise appertaining forever; and that there shall be a
clerk of the market of the said borough who shall have the assize of bread, wine, beer, wood, hay and all other provisions
brought for the use of the inhabitants and who shall and may
perform all things belonging to the office of a clerk of the
market within the said borough, which said clerk of the market shall be nominated and from time to time appointed by the
burgesses of the said borough or any two of them, whereof
the chief burgess to be one and shall be removable by them as
they shall find necessary, and that Henry Sparing shall be the
present clerk of the market of the said borough.

[Section VIII.] (Section IX, P. L.) And be it further enacted by the authority aforesaid, That if any of the inhabitants
of the said borough shall hereafter be elected to the office of
burgess or constable and having notice of his or their election
shall refuse to undertake and execute that office to which he
is chosen, it shall and may be lawful for the burgesses then
acting to impose such moderate fines on the person or persons
so refusing as to them shall seem meet, so always that the fines
imposed on a burgess [elect] do not exceed ten pounds and the
fine on a high constable elect do not exceed the sum of five
pounds, to be levied by warrant under the hands and seals of

the burgesses who shall impose the said fine or fines, or by any other lawful ways or means whatsoever for the use of the said corporation, and in any such case the said acting burgesses shall issue their process directed to the high constable requiring him to hold an election for the choice of some fit person or persons in the stead of such who shall so refuse.

[Section IX.] (Section X, P. L.) And be it further enacted by the authority aforesaid, That it shall and may be lawful for the burgesses, freeholders and inhabitants, housekeepers aforesaid of the said borough, to assemble in town meeting as often as occasion may require, at which meetings they may make such ordinances and rules not repugnant to or inconsistent with the laws of this commonwealth as to the greatest part of the inhabitants assembled as aforesaid shall seem necessary and convenient for the good government of the said borough and the same to revoke, alter and make anew as occasion shall require, which rules and ordinances so made as aforesaid, the said burgesses and high constable shall execute and enforce, and at such town meetings to impose such mulcts and amercements upon the breakers of the said ordinances as to the makers thereof shall be thought reasonable, to be levied by warrant under the hand and seal of one of the burgesses or in other lawful manner and also at the said meetings to mitigate the said fines or wholly to release them on the submission of the parties, which said town meetings shall be assembled by the burgesses aforesaid at their discretion, who shall require the high constable of the said borough to give at least five days' public notice of any such intended town meeting by advertisements fixed up in at least six of the most public places within the said borough notifying the time and place, and as far as is possible the object of such intended [town meeting].

[Section X.] (Section XI, P. L.) And be it further enacted by the authority aforesaid, That where any doubts shall arise touching this act the same shall in all courts of law and equity be construed and taken most favorably for the said corporation.

Passed September 23, 1789. Recorded L. B. No. 3, p. 540.

CHAPTER MCDXXXIX.

AN ACT TO GRANT TO THE CORPORATION OF THE MINISTER, TRUS-
TEES, ELDERS AND DEACONS OF THE GERMAN REFORMED CON-
GREGATION IN THE CITY OF PHILADELPHIA IN THE STATE OF
PENNSYLVANIA CERTAIN LANDS THEREIN MENTIONED FOR EN-
DOWING A FREE SCHOOL FOR THE USE OF THE POOR OF THE SAID
CONGREGATION.

(Section I, P. L.) Whereas it hath been represented to this
house that the corporation of "The Minister, Trustees, Elders,
and Deacons of the German Reformed Congregation in the
City of Philadelphia in the State of Pennsylvania" have at
their own voluntary expense instituted a charity school in the
city of Philadelphia in which a number of poor children are
educated, but the funds provided are not only so precarious in
their nature, but so limited in their amount as to render the
continuance of their benevolent undertaking doubtful and uncertain without some assistance from the legislature, wherefore they have prayed this house to confer on them a grant of
part of the unappropriated lands within this state:

And whereas this house in conformity to the true principles
of liberty which is the more dear and valuable to men in proportion as their minds are more enlightened, has always promoted the dissemination of learning:

[Section I.] (Section II, P. L.) Be it therefore enacted and
it is hereby enacted by the Representatives of the Freemen of
the Commonwealth of Pennsylvania in General Assembly met
and by the authority of the same, That five thousand acres of
land with the usual allowance, to be located, set out and conveyed within the unappropriated lands of this state be and
hereby are granted to the said corporation and their successors to have and to hold the same to them and their successors
forever in trust for the purpose of supporting and maintaining
a charity school for the education of the youth of the said congregation or others at the option of the said minister, trustees,
elders and deacons or their successors, in and near the city of
Philadelphia, and for no other purpose whatever.

[Section II.] (Section III, P. L.) And be it further enacted by the authority aforesaid, That upon the application of the said minister, trustees, elders and deacons or of any person duly authorized by them to the secretary of the land office of this state, he shall and hereby is required to grant and issue such and so many warrants to be directed to the surveyor-general requiring him to survey or cause to be surveyed for the said minister, trustees, elders and deacons such and so many tracts of land with such number of acres in each warrant as shall be specified in each application and not otherwise appropriated by acts of assembly nor before located or surveyed, as shall in the whole amount to five thousand acres and the usual allowance, and the surveyor-general shall receive and enter all such warrants in his office and issue copies of them directed to his deputies and upon the execution and return thereof, patents or grants of confirmation for the same shall be issued and granted in like manner and form and have the like force and effect as patents granted to private persons can or may have.

[Section III.] (Section IV, P. L.) And be it further enacted by the authority aforesaid, That all and every tract and tracts of land hereby directed to be surveyed for the use and trust aforesaid, shall be so done at the charge of the state and the president or vice-president in council is hereby authorized and empowered to draw orders on the treasurer of this state to pay and defray all charges arising thereupon.

Passed September 22, 1789. Recorded L. B. No. 8, p. 543.

CHAPTER MCDXL.

AN ACT TO REMEDY THE DEFECTS OF AN ACT ENTITLED "A SUPPLE-
MENT TO AN ACT ENTITLED 'AN ACT MORE EFFECTUALLY TO
PREVENT UNFAIR PRACTICES IN THE PACKING OF BEEF AND PORK
FOR EXPORTATION AND TO REGULATE THE EXPORTATION OF
FLAXSEED, BUTTER AND BUSCUIT IN KEGS' " [1]

(Section I, P. L.) Whereas by the act entitled "A supplement to an act entitled 'An act more effectually to prevent unfair

[1] Passed March 12, 1789, Chapter 1895.

practices in the packing of beef and pork for exportation and
to regulate the exportation of flaxseed, butter and biscuit in
kegs,' " it is enacted that salted beef and pork which shall have
been brought or imported from any place or places without
the bounds and limits of this commonwealth and which shall
have been branded in the manner therein described, shall be
excepted from the regulations of the said act:

And whereas the said exception from its extent may be injurious to the reputation of the salted provisions of this state:

[Section I.] (Section II, P. L.) Be it therefore enacted and
it is hereby enacted by the Representatives of the Freemen of
the Commonwealth of Pennsylvania in General Assembly met
and by the authority of the same, That the exception contained
in the act aforesaid shall not be deemed to extend to any salted
beef or pork unless the same shall be brought into this commonwealth by water from some place without and beyond the
Capes of Delaware.

And in order that such beef and pork as shall be exported
from this commonwealth may be the better known in foreign
parts and estimated according to the qualities thereof:

[Section II.] (Section III, P. L.) Be it further enacted by
the authority aforesaid, That all such tierces, barrels and half
barrels as are in and by the said recited act directed and required to be branded with the arms of Pennsylvania shall instead thereof be branded with the word "Philadelphia" at full
length and in a plain and legible manner.

Passed September 24, 1789. Recorded L. B. No. 3, p. 545.

CHAPTER MCDXLI.

AN ACT TO REPEAL CERTAIN PARTS OF AN ACT ENTITLED "AN ACT
FOR INCORPORATING THE PRESBYTERIAN CONGREGATION OF NEW
LONDON IN THE COUNTY OF CHESTER. [1]

(Section I, P. L.) Whereas certain parts of the act entitled
"An act for incorporating the Presbyterian congregation of

[1] Passed March 28, 1787, Chapter 1289.

New London in the County of Chester" have on experience been found to be disagreeable to many of the members thereof and they have thereupon prayed that every part of the said recited act, except so much as relates to the recovering, receiving and appropriating bequests and donations by the present trustees and their successors may be repealed:

In order therefore to ease the minds of the said members and to restore harmony amongst them:

[Section I.] (Section II, P. L.) Be it enacted and it is hereby enacted by the Representatives of the Freemen of the Commonwealth of Pennsylvania in General Assembly met and by the authority of the same, That all and every part and parts of the said recited act, except so much thereof as concerns the recovering, receiving and appropriating of bequests and donations, the electing, choosing or appointing trustees or as relates to the alienation, disposition or application of the property of the corporation or any part thereof shall be and the same hereby is repealed and made null and void.

Passed September 24, 1789.   Recorded L. B. No. 3, p. 546.

CHAPTER MCDXLII.

AN ACT FURTHER TO CONTINUE AN ACT ENTITLED "AN ACT TO SUS PEND THE SALE OF LANDS FOR NON-PAYMENT OF TAXES AND FOR OTHER PURPOSES THEREIN MENTIONED."[1]

(Section I, P. L.) Whereas the act passed on the eighteenth day of March last "to suspend the sale of lands for non-payment of taxes" will by its own limitation expire on the rising of this house:

And whereas at the time of passing the said act "the legislature had it in contemplation to establish a mode of collecting the public taxes less burdensome and oppressive than the present," but by reason of other urgent affairs of the state have not yet been able to devise and establish such mode of collec-

---

[1] Passed March 18, 1789, Chapter 1397.

tion and it is therefore reasonable that the suspension aforesaid should be further continued:

[Section I.] (Section II, P. L.) Be it therefore enacted and
it is hereby enacted by the Representatives of the Freemen of
the Commonwealth of Pennsylvania in General Assembly met
and by the authority of the same, That the act entitled "An
act to suspend the sale of lands for non-payment of taxes and
for other purposes therein mentioned," be and the same is
hereby declared to be continued and to remain in full force
and effect until the first day of April which shall be in the year
of our Lord one thousand seven hundred and ninety.

Passed September 26, 1789. Recorded L. B. No. 3, p. 651   See the
act of Assembly passed April 6, 1790, Chapter 1519.

CHAPTER MCDXLIII.

AN ACT FOR DIVIDING THE COUNTY OF CHESTER, AND TO ERECT PART THEREOF INTO A SEPARATE COUNTY.

(Section I, P. L.) Whereas the inhabitants of the borough
of Chester and the south-eastern parts of the county of Chester
have by their petitions set forth to the general assembly of this
state that they labor under many and great inconveniences
from the seat of justice being removed to a great distance from
them and have prayed that they may be relieved from the said
inconveniences, by erecting the said borough and south-eastern
parts of the said county into a separate county:

And as it appears but just and reasonable that they should
be relieved in the premises.

[Section I.] (Section II, P. L.) Be it enacted and it is hereby
enacted by the Representatives of the Freemen of the Commonwealth of Pennsylvania in General Assembly met and by
the authority of the same, That all that part of Chester county
lying within the bounds and limits hereinafter described shall
be and the same is hereby erected into a separate county, that

22—XIII

is to say, Beginning in the middle of Brandywine river where the same crosses the circular line of New Castle county, thence up the middle of the said river to the line dividing the lands of Elizabeth Chads and Caleb Brinton, at or near the ford commonly called or known by the name of Chads' ford and from thence on a line as nearly straight as may be so as not to split or divide plantations, to the great road leading from Goshen to Chester where the Westtown line intersects or crosses the said road, and from thence along the lines of Edgemont, Newtown and Radnor so as to include those townships to the line of Montgomery county and along the same and Philadelphia county line to the river Delaware and down the same to the circular line aforesaid and along the same to the place of beginning, to be henceforth known and called by the name of "Delaware County."

[Section II.] (Section III, P. L.) And be it further enacted by the authority aforesaid, That all that part of the township of Birmingham which by the line of division aforesaid shall fall within the county of Chester shall be one township and retain the name of Birmingham and all that part of the said township which by the division line aforesaid shall fall within the county of Delaware shall be one township and shall retain the name of Birmingham and that all such part of the township of Thornbury which by the division line aforesaid shall fall within the county of Chester shall be one township and shall retain the name of Thornbury and that all such part of the same township which by the line of division aforesaid shall fall within the county of Delaware shall be one township and shall retain the name of Thornbury, until the same shall be altered by the courts of general quarter sessions of the peace for the said counties respectively.

[Section III.] (Section IV, P. L.) And be it further enacted by the authority aforesaid, That the inhabitants of the said county of Delaware shall at all times hereafter enjoy all and singular the jurisdictions, powers, rights, liberties and privileges whatsoever which the inhabitants of any other county of this state do, may or ought to enjoy by the constitution and laws of this state.

[Section IV.] (Section V, P. L.) And be it further enacted
by the authority aforesaid, That the elections for the said
county of Delaware shall be held at the old court-house in the
county of Delaware to elect or choose a councillor for the same
borough of Chester where the freemen of the said county shall
elect at the times and under the regulations directed by the
officers elected in and for any other county may, can or ought
to have, and the said elections shall be conducted in the same
manner and form, and agreeably to the same rules and regulations as now are or hereafter may be in force in the other
counties of this state. Provided always, That nothing herein
contained shall authorize or empower the electors of the
constitution and laws of this state a councillor, representatives
to serve them in general assembly, censors, sheriffs, coroners
and commissioners, which said officers, when duly elected and
qualified, shall have and enjoy all and singular such powers,
authorities and privileges with respect to their county as such
county until the term for which the present councillor for
Chester county was elected shall by law expire or until his
death, resignation or removal from office.

[Section V.] (Section VI, P. L.) And be it further enacted
by the authority aforesaid, That the freemen of the said county
of Delaware shall at all future general elections elect two members and the freemen of the county of Chester at all future general elections shall elect four members to represent them respectively in the general assembly of this commonwealth until
the same shall be altered agreeably to the consitution and laws
of this state.

[Section VI.] (Section VII, P. L.) And be it further enacted
by the authority aforesaid, That the justices of the supreme
court and of the courts of oyer and terminer and general gaol
delivery of this state shall have like powers, jurisdictions and
authorities in the said county of Delaware as in the other
counties of this state and they hereby are authorized and empowered to deliver the gaols of the said county of Delaware of
capital and other offenders in like manner as they are authorized to do in other counties of this state.

[Section VII.] (Section VIII, P. L.) And be it further enacted by the authority aforesaid, That the justices of the courts
of quarter sessions and common pleas now commissioned within the limits of the county of Delaware and those that may
hereafter be commissioned, or any three of them, shall and may
hold courts of general quarter sessions of the peace and gaol
delivery and county courts of common pleas for the said county
of Delaware and shall have all and singular such powers,
rights, jurisdictions and authorities to all intents and purposes
as other justices of the courts of general quarter sessions and
justices of the county courts of common pleas in the other
counties of this state may, can or ought to have in their respective counties, which said courts of common pleas shall
open, commence and be held for the said county of Delaware at
the court-house in the said borough of Chester on the second
Tuesday in the months of November, February, May and August in each year, for the dispatch of public business and the
said courts of general quarter sessions of the peace shall open,
commence and be held at the same place and for the same
county on the Mondays next preceding the second Tuesday in
each of the said months yearly.

And whereas it is represented to this assembly by the petitioners, that they have contracted and agreed with the present
owner of the old courthouse, prison and workhouse in the
said borough of Chester for the purchase thereof at a price far
beneath what such buildings could be erected for, which they
are willing and desirous should be conveyed for the use of the
county on re-payment of the sum agreed upon:

[Section VIII.] (Section IX, P. L.) Be it therefore enacted
by the authority aforesaid, That it shall and may be lawful to
and for Henry Hale Graham, Richard Reilly, Josiah Lewis, Edward Jones and Benjamin Brannan, or any three of them, to
take conveyances and assurances to them and their heirs of the
said old courthouse, and of the prison and workhouse in the
said borough of Chester, with the lots of ground thereunto belonging, in trust and for the use of the inhabitants of the said
county of Delaware to accommodate the public service of the
said county.

And in order to defray the charge of purchasing the said old court-house, prison and workhouse and the lot of ground thereunto belonging:

[Section IX.] (Section X. P. L.) Be it further enacted by the authority aforesaid, That it shall and may be lawful to and for the commissioners and township assessors of the said county of Delaware or a majority of them to assess and levy and they are hereby required to assess and levy in the manner directed by the act for raising county rates and levies, so much money as the said trustees or any three of them shall judge necessary to lay out in the purchase and repairing of the said old court-house, prison and workhouse and the lot of ground thereunto belonging:

Provided always, That the sum so to be raised does not exceed the sum of seven hundred and fifty pounds, clear of the charges in assessing, levying and collecting thereof.

[Section X.] (Section XI, P. L.) And be it further enacted by the authority aforesaid, That no action or suit, indictment or prosecution already commenced or depending in the county courts of Chester county or in any of them against any person or persons living within the bounds of the county of Delaware shall be stayed or discontinued by this act or by anything in the same contained, but that the same actions, suits, indictments and prosecutions may be prosecuted to final judgment and execution in like manner as if this act had not been made. And it shall be lawful for the justices of Chester county to issue process to the sheriff of the county of Chester for carrying on and obtaining the full and legal effect of such suits, indictments and prosecutions in the same manner as if the parties resided in the same county of Chester or as if this act had not been made.

[Section XI.] (Section XII, P. L.) And be it further enacted by the authority aforesaid, That the sheriff, coroner and public officers of the county of Chester other than the justices of the peace, oyer and terminer, gaol delivery and of the court of common pleas, shall continue to exercise the duties of their respective offices within the county of Delaware until similar officers shall be appointed agreeably to law within the said county of

Delaware, and that all arrearages of excise and public taxes shall be paid into the hands of the present collectors to be by them accounted for in manner and form as if this act had never been passed. Provided nevertheless, That the commissioners of Chester county shall ascertain all the just debts due by the said county (before the passing of this act) and deliver a true and certified account thereof to the before mentioned trustees of Delaware county within three months after the passing of this act and if the taxes assessed and laid in Chester county before the passing of this act for county uses shall be more than sufficient to pay all the just debts of the said county when the said taxes shall be collected and paid to the treasurer of Chester county, he, the said treasurer, shall pay unto the said trustees of Delaware county their full proportion or part of such overplus money agreeably to the taxes the said two counties have respectively paid, the same to be ascertained by the commissioners of Chester county, and also that the said county of Delaware shall be liable and accountable for its due and proper proportion of all public taxes due from the said county of Chester before the division thereof in like manner as if this act had not been made.

[Section XII.] (Section XIII, P. L.) And be it further enacted by the authority aforesaid, That the sheriffs, coroners, treasurers and collectors of excise hereafter to be appointed or elected in the said county of Delaware, before they or any of them shall enter upon the execution of their respective offices, shall give security for the faithful execution of their respective offices, that is to say the sheriff in the sum of one thousand five hundred pounds, the coroner seven hundred and fifty pounds, the treasurer in the sum of one thousand five hundred pounds, the collector of excise in the sum of two hundred pounds.

[Section III.] (Section XIV, P. L.) And be it further enacted by the authority aforesaid, That John Sellers, Thomas Tucker and Charles Dilworth or any two of them shall be commissioners to run and mark the county line dividing the said counties of Chester and Delaware, in the manner hereinbefore described, which line and when so run and marked shall be the boundary line between the counties aforesaid and that the said commis-

sioners shall receive for their services at the rate of twenty-
five shillings per day each, including the expenses of chain-
carriers and markers and no more, to be paid half by the
county of Chester and half by the county of Delaware by
draughts from the commissioners of the respective counties on
the treasurers of the same, which the said commissioners are
hereby authorized and directed to grant.

Passed September 26, 1789.   Recorded L. B. No. 3, p. 551.

CHAPTER MCDXLIV.

AN ACT TO ENABLE THE OWNERS AND POSSESSORS OF A CERTAIN
TRACT OF MEADOW LAND SITUATED IN THE PRECINCT OF RICH-
MOND IN THE TOWNSHIP OF THE NORTHERN LIBERTIES TO KEEP
THE BANK, DAMS, SLUICES AND FLOOD-GATES IN REPAIR.

(Section I, P. L.) Whereas great damages and controversies
frequently arise by the neglect of owners of marsh meadows
keeping their banks, dams, sluices and flood-gates in repair and
the labor and expenses of the generality of a neighborhood may
be rendered ineffectual by the default of an individual:

And whereas there is a certain contiguous tract of banked
and improved meadow lying on the river Delaware in the precinct of Richmond in the township of the Northern Liberties, Philadelphia county, contained within the bounds following, to wit, Beginning at the fast land of Frederick Pigou
(late Abel James) thence southeastward along and including a
bank lately made (at the joint expense of the owners of the
said tract of meadow) on the south-west side of the said Pigou's
meadow, to his front bank on Delaware, thence up the said
river the several courses thereof to the north-east end of
Thomas Lloyd Moore's (late William Moore, Esquire's) meadow
adjoining to his fast land and thence along the said fast land
belonging to several owners of said meadow the several courses
thereof to the place of beginning. But inasmuch as the banks,
dams, sluices and flood-gates, and the side bank made cannot

be equitably and sufficiently maintained for stopping the tides and overflowing of the waters without an act incorporating the owners thereof:

[Section I.] (Section II, P. L.) Be it therefore enacted and it is hereby enacted by the Representatives of the Freemen of the Commonwealth of Pennsylvania in General Assembly met and by the authority of the same, That the present and all future owners of the said tract of banked and improved meadow within the limits aforesaid shall be called the "Richmond Company."

[Section II.] (Section III, P. L.) And be it enacted by the authority aforesaid, That it shall and may be lawful for the said company or as many of them as shall think fit by themselves or their attorneys or agents duly constituted and appointed to meet together within fifteen days after the publication of this act at the court-house in Philadelphia, of which place and time of meeting notice shall be given to the owners or possessors of the said meadow by advertisements in two or more of the newspapers published in the city of Philadelphia for at least ten days before the day appointed for such meeting and then and there by a majority of those met shall choose by ballot in writing three fit persons owners, possessors or the attorneys in fact of owners of the said meadows to be managers and one fit person to be treasurer until the first Monday in March next. At which time, ten days' previous notice having been given as aforesaid, by the treasurer and so yearly and every year, an election shall be held on the first Monday in March at the courthouse of such other convenient place as the managers may hereafter appoint, for the choice of three managers and a treasurer as aforesaid.

[Section III.] (Section IV, P. L.) And be it enacted by the authority aforesaid, That if any of the owners, occupiers, possessors or attorneys in fact elected managers as aforesaid on due notice given in writing of his election by some of the company present at the said election shall refuse or afterwards neglect to do the duty of him or them required by this act, he or they so refusing or neglecting his duty shall forfeit and pay to the treasurer for the time being the sum

of three pounds, to be added to the common stock of
the company, unless he or they shall have served two years
successively in the said office next before his or their appointment, which fine shall be recovered in the manner hereinafter directed for the recovery of other moneys payable to
the treasurer and the other managers shall proceed in the
execution of their office without him or if they think fit may
choose other managers out of the said owners, possessors,
occupiers or attorneys in fact to be a manager in the place
of him so refusing, and if the person so elected treasurer
shall refuse or neglect to take upon him the duties or give
the securities required by this act or shall misbehave himself or by death or otherwise be rendered incapable to execute the said office, in any of these cases the managers for
the time being shall choose another fit person to be the treasurer for that year.

[Section IV.] (Section V, P. L.) And be it enacted by the
authority aforesaid, That the treasurer hereafter to be chosen,
shall, before he takes upon him the execution of his office, enter
into an obligation to the said company and their successors
with one sufficient security in double the value of the money
that doth or may probably come into his hands during the continuance in his office as near as can be estimated by the managers, conditioned that he will once in six months, or oftener if
required, render his accounts to the said managers or a majority of them, and well and truly account, adjust and settle with
them, when required, for and concerning all moneys that are or
shall come into his hands by virtue of this act, or belonging to
the said Richmond Company, and pay the balance, that shall
appear on such settlement to be in his hands, to such person
and for such services as any two of the managers for the time
being, shall order and appoint and not otherwise; and that he
will at the expiration of his office well and truly pay or cause
to be paid and delivered, all the moneys then remaining in his
hands, together with the books of accounts concerning the
same, and all other papers and writings in his keeping, belonging to the said Richmond Company unto his successor in the
said office.

[Section V.] (Section VI, P. L.) And be it enacted by the authority aforesaid, That the banks, dams, sluices and flood-gates which belong to the said Richmond Company shall hereafter be maintained and supported at the expense of the owners in common, for which purpose it shall and may be lawful for the said maangers or any two of them as often as they shall see occasion to meet together and lay such assessments and taxes on every acre of land within the limits of the said meadow as they shall judge to be necessary for the benefit and security of the same and for the defraying the expenses thereof. Provided always, That previous to such reparation and maintenance in common those banks, dams, sluices and floodgates which are now deficient shall be put into equal good order with the best, by and at the expense and cost of the respective owners to which they belong and that within fifty days from the publication hereof.

[Section VI.] (Section VII, P. L.) And be it enacted by the authority aforesaid, That if any of the owners or possessors within the limits aforesaid shall neglect or refuse to put his or their banks, dams, sluices and floodgates in good state and condition and within the time mentioned in the foregoing proviso, being warned by the said managers at least fifteen days so to do, which good state and condition shall be viewed and adjudged of by five men indifferently chosen by the said managers, the judgment of any three of which persons so chosen shall be conclusive on the owners or possessors respectively, each and every of such delinquent owner or possessor shall forfeit and pay to the treasurer for the time being the sum of ten pounds for the use and benefit of the said company to be recovered as other moneys by this act are directed to be recovered and paid. And moreover, that it shall and may be lawful for the said managers or any two of them for the time being to proceed and lay a tax on the meadow of the said delinquent owner or owners, possessor or possessors and to recover the same in the manner hereinafter directed, sufficient to defray the expense of putting his or their respective banks, dams, sluices and flood gates in the good order and condition herein first before described and to apply it for that purpose.

[Section VII.] (Section VIII, P. L.) And be it enacted by the authority aforesaid, That the managers for the time being or any two of them shall have the power of disposing of all moneys paid to the treasurer by virtue of this act and of hiring and appointing at the expense of the company any person or persons from time to time to inspect. the condition of all banks, dams, sluices and floodgates belonging to the same and to offer and pay such rewards as they shall think necessary out of the common stock for the destruction of such vermin as usually damage the banks and dams as well as for all other general services of the said banks, dams, sluices and floodgates.

[Section VIII.] (Section IX, P. L.) And be it enacted by the authority aforesaid, That the major part of the managers for the time being shall at least three times in each year hereafter by advertisements published in two or more newspapers in the said city at least ten days before the time therein to be appointed, require the owners or occupiers of all banks belonging to the company to cut all ranstead, elders, poke, thistles, burdock and other weeds which may be injurious to the said banks and should the owners or occupiers of the said banks or any of them neglect to cut or mow the same at such times as shall be required, it shall and may be lawful for the said managers and they are hereby enjoined and required to hire and employ a sufficient number of men to cut and mow the same and fine the owner or occupier for their neglect in any sum not exceeding the cost of said cutting or mowing, and recover the money so expended and the fines so imposed in like manner as other sums of money are by this act directed to be recovered, which fine shall be applied to the benefit of said company.

And whereas the cutting or making drains or ditches in suitable places near the front bank and scouring those that are now in order or may be made will greatly conduce to the better improvement of said banks:

[Section IX.] (Section X, P. L.) Be it therefore enacted by

the authority aforesaid, That the major part of the managers
shall at such times and as often as they see occasion, direct
and order that new drains near the front banks shall be
made when necessary, or those which are already made,
scoured, and apportion the cost of making and scouring the
same among those in whose land they are respectively made
or to be made or order such compensation to those who may
be injured as shall appear just and reasonable and compel
payment in the manner hereinafter directed.

[Section X.] (Section XI, P. L.) And be it further enacted by the authority aforesaid, That if any owner or occupier shall think him, her or themselves aggrieved by any act,
order, account, proceeding or neglect of any of the managers, such owner or occupier shall if he or they think proper,
choose one fit and disinterested person and the said managers
in such cases are hereby enjoined to choose one other fit and
disinterested person, which two persons so chosen, if there
be occasion, shall choose a third person like disinterested
and the persons thus chosen or any two of them shall finally
settle the same and all matters referred to them.

[Section XI.] (Section XII, P. L.) And be it enacted by
the authority aforesaid, That the orders of any two of the
managers on the treasurer for the time being shall be complied with by the treasurer and shall be good vouchers to
indemnify him for the payment and delivery of the money
committed to his care by virtue of this act.

[Section XII.] (Section XIII, P. L.) And be it enacted by
the authority aforesaid, That if any of the said owners, occupiers or possessors of meadow land within the limits aforesaid shall neglect or refuse to pay the several sums of money
that shall from time [to time] be rated, assessed and imposed by the major part of the managers for paying and discharging their respective proportions, for maintaining the
front banks, dams, sluices and floodgates and for the money
expended in making the said side bank and also for maintaining the same, in common required as aforesaid, for the
space of thirty days after demand made by the treasurer,
it shall and may be lawful to and for the said treasurer by

the direction of the major part of the managers for the time
being in his own name to sue for and recover the several
sums of money so charged and assessed in the manner
debts not exceeding ten pounds are by law recoverable and
give this act and the assessment or the said account in evidence. Provided always, That such delinquent owner, occupier or possessor shall not be entitled to stay of execution
for any longer time than ten days or it shall and may be lawful to and for the said treasurer by the directions of the managers as aforesaid in his own name to apply to some justice
of the peace of the said county for his warrant of distress
for levying the said sums of money so neglected or refused
to be paid, directed to the constable of the township, which
said warrant the said justice is hereby empowered and directed to grant accordingly, to be by the said constable levied on the tract belonging to or possessed by the person or
persons so neglecting and deliver the same over to the managers for the time being, who or a majority of them are
hereby empowered and authorized to let the same on rent
or any part thereof that may be sufficient from time to time
and for so long a time as the rent or rents arising therefrom
shall as nearly as may be computed pay all sum or sums of
money so assessed, charged or imposed together with all costs
and reasonable expenses arising thereon for his, her or their
neglect or refusal to pay the same as aforesaid and no
longer. Provided always, That in letting out the said meadow
land the said managers do publicly notify the leasing
thereof for at least ten days previous thereto and let the same
to the highest bidder.

[Section XIII.] (Section XIV.) And be it further enacted
by the authority aforesaid, That it shall and may be lawful
for the said managers to meet together as often as they shall
see occasion to direct the necessary repairs and the said managers or a majority of them for the time being are hereby
empowered and authorized to enter upon and inspect at least
four times in each year the condition of all the said front
banks and side banks, dams, sluices and floodgates and other
conveniences necessary for stopping out the tides and drain-

ing the water from the meadows and shall and may be lawful to and for the said managers or any of them together with such workmen, horses, carts, barrows and other tools as they shall think necessary, to enter into and upon any lands where the breach or defect now is or shall hereafter happen to be and then and there dig [and] carry earth or purchase suitable materials to make and repair the said front banks and side banks, dams, sluices and floodgates and all other conveniences necessary for stopping out the tide or draining the waters off the meadows, in such manner and by such ways as they the said managers or a majority of them shall think fit and reasonable, any law, usage or custom of this commonwealth to the contrary in anywise notwithstanding. Provided always nevertheless, That if any damage shall hereafter be sustained by any new ditches or holes to be made or any other injury or injuries whatsoever to be done to any meadow or [sic] meadows for the purpose of making or repairing of the said side bank, the managers for the time being shall order such compensation to be made as they or indifferent men to be chosen as aforesaid to judge thereof shall conclude to be just and reasonable.

[Section XIV.] (Section XV, P. L.) And be it enacted by the authority aforesaid, That the managers shall each of them have and receive ten shillings per day for each day they shall be employed in the several duties required of them and the treasurer shall have such compensation for his services as a major part of the managers shall think adequate.

[Section XV.] (Section XVI, P. L.) And be it further enacted by the authority aforesaid, That if any person or persons shall wilfully or maliciously cut through, break down or injure any part of the front bank, stone walls thereof or the side bank, dams, sluices or floodgates or cut down or destroy any willow or other trees which now or may be hereafter planted for the security or protection of the said banks and shall be convicted before the justices of the court of quarter sessions of the said county of Philadelphia, in all such cases the person or persons so offending shall forfeit to the said company treble value of the damages, which shall be assessed by the jury which

shall convict him or them thereof, to be added to the common
stock for the general use and benefit thereof.

[Section XVI.] (Section XVII, P. L.) And be it further
enacted by the authority aforesaid, That an act of assembly
of the province of Pennsylvania entitled "An act to enable
the owners and possessors of the meadows at Point No Point
in the precinct of Richmond in the county of Philadelphia
and to keep the banks, sluices and floodgates in repair and to
raise a fund to defray the expenses thereof"[1] so far as relates
to the meadow land or any part thereof contained within the
limits herein described shall be and is hereby repealed and
made null and void.

Passed September 24, 1789. Recorded L. B. No. 3, p. 546.
See the Act of Assembly passed March 16, 1791, Chapter 1534.

CHAPTER MCDXLV.

A SUPPLEMENT TO THE SEVERAL LAWS OF THIS COMMONWEALTH
RESPECTING ATTACHMENTS.

(Section I, P. L.) Whereas the laws of this commonwealth
respecting attachments have been found defective, inasmuch
as no adequate provision is therein made for obtaining and
compelling a disclosure of the goods, chattels, moneys, effects
and credits of the defendant and defendants in the custody,
possession and charge or due and owing from any garnishee or
garnishees, upon whom such writs of attachment are respectively served, so that many honest creditors have been unable
to recover their just debts, and the wholesome regulations of
the said laws have often been defeated:

For remedy thereof:

[Section I.] (Section II, P. L.) Be it enacted and it is hereby
enacted by the Representatives of the Freemen of the Commonwealth of Pennsylvania in General Assembly met and
by the authority of the same, That it shall and may be law-

[1] Passed April 12, 1760, Chapter 454.

ful to and for any and every plaintiff and plaintiffs in any and every writ and writs of attachment already issued or to be issued by and out of any court or courts within this commonwealth, after judgment hath been duly obtained against the defendant and defendants therein respectively named, to prepare and exhibit in writing all and singular such interrogatories upon which the said plaintiff and plaintiffs is, are or shall be desirous to obtain and compel the answer and answers of any and every garnishee and garnishees in whose hands the said writ or writs of attachment hath or have been or shall or may be respectively laid and served touching the goods, chattels moneys, effects and credits of the said defendant and defendants in his or their possession, custody and charge or from him or them respectively due and owing at the time of the service of such writ or writs of attachment or at any other time. And the said interrogatories so prepared and exhibited the said plaintiff or plaintiffs shall file or cause to be filed in the proper court by or out of which the said writ or writs of attachment respectively hath or have issued or shall or may issue.

[Section II.] (Section III, P. L.) And be it enacted by the authority aforesaid, That each and every such garnishee and garnishees respectively to whom a copy of such interrogatories shall be delivered is and are hereby required and enjoined to be and appear before the justices of the same court on a day and time by them for that purpose to be named and then and there in writing exhibit and file under his or their oath or oaths, affirmation or affirmations (which the prothono-'ary of the proper court is hereby authorized and required to administer) full, direct and true answers to all and singular the interrogatories by the said plaintiff and plaintiffs respectively prepared, exhibited and filed in the manner hereinbefore directed and described. And if any garnishee or garnishees shall neglect or refuse so to do, then and in every such case it shall and may be lawful to and for the justices of the proper court and they are hereby required to adjudge that such garnishee or garnishees so neglecting or refusing as aforesaid hath or have in his or their possession, custody and charge goods, chattels, moneys and effects of the said defendant or defendants in such writ or writs of attachment respectively named or is and are indebted unto such defendant or defendants to an amount and value sufficient to pay and satisfy the debt, claim or demand of the said plaintiff or plaintiffs together with all legal costs and charges of suits. And the said justices of the proper court shall thereupon award and issue a writ or writs of execution against the person or persons or against the goods and chattels, lands and tenements of such garnishees so refusing or neglecting as aforesaid, and therein shall proceed in like manner as if such writ or writs of execution had been awarded and issued by reason of any judgment in such court regularly pronounced and entered in pursuance of the verdict of a jury or by virtue of the confession of the party.

And whereas it frequently happens that garnishees in writs of attachment have in their hands and possession goods and chattels belonging to the defendant which cannot be found by the officer serving such writs to be taken and secured by him and others are indebted in large sums of money which they refuse to pay or in anywise to secure:

For remedy thereof:

[Section III.] (Section IV, P. L.) Be it [further] enacted by the authority aforesaid, That if any plaintiff in any writ of attachment to be issued within this commonwealth or any person for him shall upon oath or solemn affirmation declare that he or she verily believes that any person or persons upon whom any writ of attachment shall be directed to be served as garnishee hath or have any goods, chattels or effects belonging to the defendant or defendants in his, her or their hands or possession or under his, her or their care or is or are indebted to the defendant or defendants in any sum of money, although the same shall not then be due and shall also in manner aforesaid declare that the person or persons upon whom such writ of attachment shall be directed to be served as garnishee is or are not an inhabitant or inhabitants of the county within which the same shall issue or that he or she verily be-

23—XIII

lieves that there is just cause to fear that such person or persons is or are about to depart and remove from the same, it shall and may be lawful for the plaintiff to cause to be inserted in the body of the writ of attachment a clause of capias against all such person and persons as aforesaid, upon whom the same shall be directed to be served as garnishee and he, she or they shall thereupon be held to sufficient sureties to appear at court and to make answers as by this act is required and further render his, her or their bodies to the prison of the proper county or to pay the condemnation money if judgment shall pass against him, her or them.

Passed September 26, 1789. Recorded L. B. No. 3, p. 557. See the Acts of Assembly passed October 21, 1791, Chapter 108; January 12, 1705 6, Chapter 142

--- ...

CHAPTER MCDXLVI.

AN ACT TO APPROPRIATE THE SUM OF FIVE THOUSAND POUNDS AN-
NUALLY FOR THE PURPOSE THEREIN MENTIONED.

(Section I, P. L.) This house having set apart out of the aggregate funds of the state the sum of ten thousand pounds annually for the purposes mentioned in an act entitled "An act to appropriate divers funds accruing and growing due to this commonwealth towards the payment of the expenses of government, and to provide a fund for other purposes,"[1] but no specific designation of the particular parts of the said sum having been made, declarative of the special purpose to which such parts shall be exclusively applied, and it being necessary to make such designation as well to prevent disorders in accounts as to preserve a due regard to the objects of the appropriation, so that one shall not be injured or neglected while the moneys are applied to others, and it being of the highest consequence to the prosperity of this commonwealth that the transportation of produce, commodities and merchandise should by every practicable means be facilitated by an atten-

[1]Passed March 26, 1789, Chapter 1404.

tion to the improvement of roads and inland navigation, and as
it is the truest economy to provide money to pay all expenses
incurred on this account so that no difficulties may occur in
payments, delays in such cases raising prices and obstructing
the execution of the measures:

[Section I.] (Section II, P. L.) Be it enacted and it is hereby
enacted by the Representatives of the Freeman of the Commonwealth of Pennsylvania in General Assembly met and by the
authority of the same, That the treasurer of this state be and he
is hereby directed and enjoined yearly and every year to set
apart the sum of five thousand pounds [part of the sum of ten
thousand pounds] appropriated by an act entitled "An act to
appropriate divers funds accruing and growing due to this commonwealth towards the payment of the expenses of government
and to provide a fund for other purposes,"[1] for claims and improvements, and the said treasurer shall keep a distinct account
of this fund and always take care that so much be reserved in
his hands ready to answer all drafts directed by law to be
drawn for the purposes of roads and navigation to which it
is hereby solely and exclusively appropriated. And that in the
first instance a sum, part of the said sum hereby appropriated
not exceeding twenty-five hundred pounds, shall be expended
and laid out under the direction of council for clearing and
making navigable such parts of the river Susquehanna above
Wright's ferry and the Juniata and their waters as the supreme executive council shall judge most proper and necessary, the sum of one thousand pounds under the like circumstances for clearing and making navigable the Schuylkill and
its waters, and the sum of fifteen hundred pounds under the
like circumstances and direction for clearing and making navigable the Delaware, Lehigh and their waters.

And whereas the time for which the members of this house
are elected is so nearly expired that it is impracticable to ma-
ture and finally enact any proper system on a subject so important, but to the end that sufficient information may be
possessed by the succeeding house of assembly on this subject:

---

[1] Ante.

[Section II.] (Section III, P. L.) Be it enacted by the authority aforesaid, That the supreme executive council be and they
are hereby authorized and empowered to appoint a sufficient
number of ingenious and discreet persons commissioners to
view the navigable waters in this state, confining their in-
vestigations in the first instance to those of the Delaware,
Schuylkill and Susquehanna and the various streams running
into the said rivers respectively or capable of being connected
therewith, marking places where locks or canals are necessary,
the distances between the waters capable of navigation, all
falls, obstructions and all other matters and things requisite
and necessary as well for the information of the assembly of
this state so as to enable them to form and enact a proper law
on the subject as to afford materials, plans, maps and estimates for facilitating the execution [of] the important design
herein mentioned. And the said commissioners or any convenient number of them at the direction of the supreme executive council shall also view such and so many of the roads and
highways already laid out within this commonwealth or the
places and parts of the state through which roads generally useful should pass, having regard to the general purposes of commerce and transportation most interesting to the state at large
and pointing out the necessary improvements in the said roads
already laid out and also such others as may be deemed [re-
quisite] for the purposes aforesaid, noting everything properly
falling under the subject and returning their plans, estimates,
maps and observations to the supreme executive council, to
be laid before the general assembly of this commonwealth.
And the supreme executive council are hereby authorized and
empowered to give such instructions to the said commissioners
as they shall deem necessary for effectuating the purposes
aforesaid. And the supreme executive council are hereby authorized and empowered to draw orders from time to time for
the moneys as appropriated herein or any part or parts thereof
on the treasurer of this state for the time being for the purpose
herein directed and no other.

Passed September 28, 1789. Recorded L. B. No. 4, p. 4. **See the
Acts of Assembly passed March 14, 1761, Chapter 465; April 17, 1795,
Chapter 1849.**

CHAPTER MCDXLVII.

AN ACT TO AUTHORIZE THE SUPREME EXECUTIVE COUNCIL TO DRAW
ON THE STATE TREASURER FOR AN ADDITIONAL SUM OF MONEY
FOR DEFRAYING THE EXPENSE OF PURCHASING OF THE INDIANS
LANDS ON LAKE ERIE.

(Section I, P. L.)   Whereas the sum of twelve hundred
pounds granted and appropriated by the act entitled "An act
to authorize the supreme executive council to draw on the
state treasurer for a sum of money for defraying the expense
of purchasing of the Indians lands on Lake Erie" falls eight
hundred and sixty-five pounds fifteen shillings and four pence
short of perfecting the said purchase and the necessary ex-
expenses attending the same:

[Section I.] (Section II, P. L.) Be it therefore enacted and it
is hereby enacted by the Representatives of the Freemen of the
Commonwealth of Pennsylvania in General Assembly met, and
by the authority of the same, That the supreme executive council of this state be and the same are hereby authorized and directed to draw an order or orders on the state treasurer for the
said sum of eight hundred and sixty-five pounds fifteen shillings and four-pence, which sum shall be paid by the state
treasurer out of the ten thousand pounds appropriated by the
act entitled "An act to appropriate divers funds accruing and
growing due to this commonwealth towards the payment of
the expenses of government, and to provide a fund for other
purposes" ² enacted the twenty-sixth day of March one thousand seven hundred and eighty-nine.

Passed September 28, 1789. Recorded L. B. No. 4, p. 6.
¹Passed October 3, 1788, Chapter 1367.
²Passed March 26th, 1789, Chapter 1404.

CHAPTER MCDXLVIII.

AN ACT IN FAVOR OF JOHN HOUSTON.

(Section I, P. L.) Whereas by a petition presented to this house by John Houston it is set forth that he was appointed surveyor of one of the districts in the late purchase, that after he had carried out one of his division lines and a considerable part of another and before he had executed one warrant, he received orders from the supreme executive council to desist, by means of which he has been subjected to very considerable expense and as the running of said lines is rendered useless, he hath prayed for relief in the premises, and it is just and reasonable that the expenses aforesaid be paid:

Therefore:

[Section I.] (Section II, P. L.) Be it enacted and it is hereby enacted by the Representatives of the Freemen of the Commonwealth of Pennsylvania in General Assembly met and by the authority of the same, That the supreme executive council be and they are hereby authorized to draw an order on the treasurer of this state for the sum of eighty-eight pounds ten shillings in favor of John Houston, being the balance due him.

Passed September 28, 1789. Recorded L. B. No. 3, p. 557.

CHAPTER MCDXLIX.

AN ACT EMPOWERING MARY PINE TO DISPOSE OF BY WAY OF LOTTERY A CERTAIN LOT AND THE BUILDINGS THEREON ERECTED TOGETHER WITH A COLLECTION OF PAINTINGS AND PRINTS LATELY THE PROPERTY OF HER DECEASED HUSBAND ROBERT EDGE PINE.

(Section I, P. L.) Whereas it has been represented to this house, that Robert Edge Pine, now deceased, did in the year one thousand seven hundred and eighty-four remove with his family from London in the kingdom of Great Britain to the city of Philadelphia and brought with him a large and valuable collection of original historical paintings, drawings and designs, that the said Robert Edge Pine purchased a lot of ground in Eighth Street, between Market and Arch Streets and erected a building thereon for the purposes of exhibiting the said collection and of carrying on his business as a painter, that the expenses incident to such an undertaking involved him in debts and difficulties from which he was prevented by death from extricating himself by the exertions of his abilities and industry:

And whereas Mary Pine widow and executrix of the said Robert Edge Pine is under the necessity of selling not only the said lot and buildings but also the said collection of paintings, engravings and designs by way of lottery for the purpose of paying off and satisfying the demands against her as executrix of her late husband:

And whereas it is as well the wish of this house as of a number of respectable citizens that said collection of paintings should not be sent from this continent in order to be sold but that the same should be disposed of in the United States:

Therefore:

[Section I.] (Section II, P. L.) Be it enacted and it is hereby enacted by the Representatives of the Freemen of the Commonwealth of Pennsylvania in General Assembly met and by the authority of the same, That John Jones, Francis Hopkinson, George Meade, Walter Stewart, Charles Heatly, John Vaughan and Temple Franklin shall be and they are hereby nominated and appointed managers and directors of a lottery hereby instituted and directed to be drawn, for the preparing and disposing of tickets, and to oversee the drawing of the same and to order and perform all such other matters and things as are hereinafter directed and appointed by such managers and directors to be done and performed. And that the said managers or any three of them shall meet together at tion of the adventures in the said lottery as soon as the draw-cution of the powers and trust reposed in them by this act and shall cause a set of books to be prepared for the purpose of keeping the accounts, which books shall be open to the inspection of the adventures in the said lottery as soon as the drawing of the same shall be finished and completed, and they shall cause to be printed off eleven hundred tickets, numbered one, two, three and so onwards in arithmetical progression to the number of [eleven hundred] and that every of the last mentioned tickets shall be signed by at least two of the managers aforesaid and shall have written or printed thereupon, beside the number of such ticket and the year of our Lord, the following words, viz: "Pine's Lottery, this ticket entitles the bearer to such prize as may be drawn against its number, if demanded within nine months after the drawing is finished."

[Section II.] (Section III, P. L.) And be it further enacted by the authority aforesaid, That the said managers shall have full power and authority to sell and dispose of to such person or persons as shall choose to adventure in the said lottery the said tickets at the rate of ten Spanish milled dollars for each ticket. And the said managers shall cause to be published in at least two of the public newspapers of Philadelphia the plan of said lottery and the number and appraised value of the respective prizes to which the fortunate adventurers may become entitled.

[Section III.] (Section IV, P. L.) And be it further enacted by the authority aforesaid, That the said managers or a majority of them shall cause duplicates of the tickets to be carefully rolled up and fastened with silk or thread and to be put into a box, prepared for that purpose, which box shall be sealed with the several seals of the said managers, and on a day and hour to be appointed, of which days' public notice shall be given in at least two of the public newspapers of this city, they shall cause the said box to be unsealed and opened and the tickets in the said box being in the presence of the said managers and such of the said adventurers as shall think proper to attend well shaken and mixed, some one indifferent and fit person to be appointed and directed by the said managers or a majority of them shall draw out and take the tickets from the said box which shall be handed to the said managers who shall read the same aloud and immediately

after shall in like manner pronounce the prize to which each
ticket shall be entitled, according to the plan to be published
by the said managers, which said tickets so drawn shall be
filed and the same entered in the book of the said managers,
and if any dispute shall arise in adjusting the property of the
said fortunate tickets, the said managers or a majority of
them shall adjudge to whom it doth or ought to belong, and the
said managers and all other persons concerned in conducting
or drawing the said lottery, in buying or selling tickets or in
any other manner promoting the same, are hereby declared
free and exonerated from all fines and penalties inflicted by
any law of this state on any person or persons who shall draw,
promote, or encourage any lottery within this commonwealth,
any law, usage, or custom to the contrary in anywise notwithstanding.

Passed September 28, 1789. Recorded L. B. No. 3, p. 555.

CHAPTER MCDL.

AN ACT FOR VESTING IN JAMES RUMSEY, ESQUIRE, THE EXCLUSIVE
RIGHT AND PRIVILEGE OF MAKING, USING AND VENDING DIVERS
ENGINES, MACHINES AND DEVICES BY HIM INVENTED OR IMPROV-
ED, FOR A TERM OF YEARS THEREIN MENTIONED.

(Section I, P. L.) Whereas James Rumsey of Berkley county
in Virginia hath represented to this house that he hath invented or improved divers engines, machines and devices hereinafter particularly mentioned upon principles and construc-
tions not before used and by actual experiments hath demon-
strated the practicability and utility thereof, which engines,
machines and devices are called by the following names and
known by the following distinguishing characters, viz:

Rumsey's boilers, for the more ample and easy generating
of steam by enclosing a small quantity of water in incurvated
tubes or in several connected receivers or projections placed
in a furnace, whereby the action of fire is communicated to the

water and steam in all its passage from the entrance to the
exit and which kind of boilers can be easily adapted to every
species of fire or steam engine.

Rumsey's boilers, for the more ample and easy generating
engine, whereby water may be raised in great quantities to
any reasonable height for the turning of mills or for agri-
cultural or other purposes.

Rumsey's improvement upon Doctor Barker's mill, a mode
by which mill stones and other machinery requiring a circular
or retrograde motion may be turned by or worked with a
smaller quantity of water than by any plan yet exhibited to
the public and entirely free from the difficulties which prevented Doctor Barker's invention from coming into use.

Rumsey's double piston machine with two connected cylinders for applying the force of steam immediately to the forcing of water without the intervention of any mechanical power
to a great distance horizontally, obliquely or perpendicularly
with or without air vessels through one or more tubes.

Rumsey's pendulum mill for working mill saws or any other
machinery requiring an alternately opposite motion whether
perpendicular or horizontal, constructed on the principle of
Doctor Barker's mill.

Rumsey's cylindric saw mill or a mode by which mill saws
and all other machinery requiring an alternately opposite motion, whether perpendicular or horizontal, may be worked
without the loss of the weight or force of any part of the water
used.

Rumsey's steam and pump cylinders engine, with two or
more connected pistons for the purpose of forcing water in
any direction or to any required height:

And whereas it is highly proper that ingenious men who
by their labors and study contrive and invent improvements in
arts and sciences should be rewarded by the community in
proportion to the advantages resulting from the usefulness
of their inventions, and as the most proper mode of ascertaining the utility of any new invention or improvement must be
experience, and as the exclusive right and privileges of making, using and vending to others such newly invented engines,

machines and inventions is not only the most cheap and frugal
but the most certain way of rewarding inventors according to
their several merits:

[Section I.] (Section II, P. L.) Be it therefore enacted and
it is hereby enacted by the Representatives of the Freemen of
the Commonwealth of Pennsylvania in General Assembly met
and by the authority of the same, That from and after the
passing of this act the said James Rumsey, his executors, administrators and assigns, shall have the sole and exclusive
right, liberty and privileges within this state of making, using
and vending to others the said boilers for generating steam
called "Rumsey's boilers;" the said improvement of Savery's
engine for raising water for the turning of mills or for agri-
cultural or other purposes called "Rumsey's improvement
upon Savery's machine, or steam engine;" the said mode for
turning mill stones and other machinery requiring a circular
or retrograde motion called "Rumsey's improvement upon Doctor Barker's mill;" the said mode of raising water called·
"Rumsey's double piston machine for raising water;" the said
mode of working saw mills and other machines requiring an
alternately opposite motion, perpendicular or horizontal,
called "Rumsey's cylindric saw-mill;" the said mode of working saw mills or other machines requiring an alternately opposite motion called "Rumsey's pendulum mill;" and the said
double cylinders engine with two or more connected pistons
called "Rumsey's steam and pump cylinder engine."

[Section II.] (Section III, P. L.) And be it further enacted
by the authority aforesaid, That no person or persons whomsoever shall make, use or vend to others to be used any or
either of the inventions or improvements so as aforesaid described or defined in this act or in the plans or explanations
thereof to be filed of record in the office of the prothonotary
of the court of common pleas for the county of Philadelphia
and hereby referred unto, under the penalty of forfeiting to
the said James Rumsey, his executors, administrators or assigns the sum of one hundred pounds lawful money of this
state and moreover forfeiting to him and them [all and every
such engine, machine and device] so as aforesaid to be con-

trived, made, used or vended within this state and the said
penalty to be recovered by action of debt founded upon this
act wherein no [session] protection or wager of law, nor more
than one imparlance, shall be allowed, and in the execution to
be issued upon any judgment obtained in pursuance of this
act, a clause shall be inserted commanding the sheriff or other
proper officer to deliver the said engine, device or machine
to the plaintiff if it can be conveniently removed, but if not,
that then and in such case the said sheriff or other proper
officer shall cause the same to be prostrated, destroyed and rendered useless.

[Section III.] (Section IV, P. L.) And be it further enacted
by the authority aforesaid, That the sole exclusive right and
privileges for making, using and vending the engines, machines and devices aforesaid by this act granted to the said
James Rumsey his executors, administrators and assigns shall
continue for the term of fourteen years from the time of
passing this act and no longer, and that all actions to him or
them accrued or accruing within the said term shall remain
in full force during and after the expiration of this act. Provided that the said James Rumsey or his certain attorney
shall within four months after the passing of this act file of
record in the office of the said prothonotary such specimens,
draughts or models of the above mentioned engines, machines
and devices as shall clearly and fully distinguish and ascertain their form and the principles upon which they operate.
Provided likewise, if any person or persons shall at any time
hereafter within the said term of fourteen years claim to have
invented or used the aforesaid inventions or improvements or
either of them before the said James Rumsey, it shall be lawful for him or them so claiming to sue forth and prosecute
one or more writ or writs of scire facias returnable before the
justices of the supreme court of this commonwealth to be devised or approved by the chief justice or one of the justices
of the said court, warning the said James Rumsey, his executors, administrators or assigns then having the sole and
exclusive right aforesaid to be and appear before the said justices at the next supreme court to be held for the said com-

monwealth to show cause why the grant of the said sole and
exclusive right and benefit of constructing, making, using and
selling such inventions, improvement or improvements should
not be repealed and made void, and upon such writ the proceeding shall be such as in other writs of scire facias in the
said court shall be used and accustomed and if judgment
shall thereupon be rendered by default, confession or upon
verdict or demurrer for the plaintiff, judgment shall be entered that so much of the grant herein contained as shall be
alleged by the plaintiff and so confessed or found against the
defendant shall be repealed and made null and void and
thenceforth so much of the said grant shall be and the same
is hereby repealed and made null and void to all intents and
purposes whatsoever, and the said court shall award such and
the same costs to be recovered in the like manner as in other
suits or actions brought and determined in the said court.

[Section IV.] (Section V, P. L.) And provided also, That in
all suits or actions to be brought by the said James Rumsey, his
executors, administrators or assigns for any penalty or forfeiture in pursuance of this act, it shall and may be lawful
for the defendant or defendants to plead the general issue
and give this act (and any special matter whereof notice shall
be given to the plaintiff or his attorney at least sixty days
before the trial) in evidence and if upon the trial it shall be
made to appear to the satisfaction of the said court and jury
that the defendant or any other person whatsoever than the
said James Rumsey was the true and original inventor of the
inventions and improvements in question, the verdict shall
be found and judgment entered for the defendant and he shall
be acquitted of all the penalties and forfeitures demanded
against him and shall recover his costs and charges by him
expended in defending such suit or action in the same manner
as in other suits or actions determined in said court.

Passed September 26, 1789. Recorded I. B. No. 4, p. 1.

CHAPTER MCDLI.

AN ACT FOR THE INSPECTION OF SHINGLES.

(Section I, P. L.) Whereas the inspection laws of this state have been found beneficial to commerce and productive of fair dealing between individuals but the same are not sufficiently extensive:

Therefore:

[Section I.] (Section II, P. L.) Be it enacted and it is hereby enacted by the Representatives of the Freemen of the Commonwealth of Pennsylvania in General Assembly met and by the authority of the same, That no shingles shall be exported from this state unless the same shall be of one of the kinds hereinafter mentioned and described, viz:

Shingles of the first kind shall be two feet nine inches at least in length, five and an half inches at least in width and of [such] thickness that when dressed they may remain at least half an inch thick at every place between the butt end and a distance of ten inches from the same.

Shingles of the second kind shall be twenty-four inches at least and not more than twenty-six inches in length, five inches at least in width and of such thickness that when dressed they may remain at least half an inch thick at every part between the butt end and a distance of seven inches therefrom.

Shingles of the third kind shall be at least eighteen inches and not more than twenty inches long, nor less than four inches wide and of thickness sufficient to remain when dressed three eighth parts of an inch [thick] at every place between the butt end and a distance of six inches from the same.

And every of the same kinds of shingles shall be made of sound wood, free from splits and in other respects of merchantable quality, and every exporter of shingles shall previously to lading the same on board any vessels submit them to the inspection of an officer for such purpose legally appointed.

[Section II.] (Section III, P. L.) And be it further enacted
by the authority aforesaid, That the officer who now is or
hereafter may be appointed to inspect staves and heading
shall be the officer for inspecting shingles in conformity to the
directions of this act and shall be authorized to appoint deputies, and the said officer and his deputies shall respectively
have all the powers and authorities respecting the culling and
inspecting shingles, which the officer or his deputies for [the]
culling and inspecting staves and heading now by law have
with respect to staves and heading. And if the determination
of any such officer shall be disputed a like review shall be allowed and on the like terms as by the laws in force are directed with respect to staves and heading and like penalties
shall be adjudged, inflicted and recovered for offenses against
this act as would legally be adjudged, inflicted and recovered
for similar offenses against the laws for the inspection of
staves and heading and all fines shall be applied and appropriated in like manner.

[Section III.] (Section IV, P. L.) And be it further enacted
by the authority [aforesaid,] That the said officer or his deputies when thereunto required shall inspect, count and cull conformably to the directions of this act all shingles intended to
be exported and shall keep a like record thereof as is required
by law with respect to staves and heading to which recourse
may in like manner be had for similar fees and allowances,
and the following fees shall be allowed for inspecting, culling
and counting of shingles, viz: for the first and second kinds
eighteen pence per thousand, for the third kind one shilling
per thousand, which fees shall be paid by the exporter or
purchaser provided the shingles shall be adjudged merchantable and by the seller provided the same shall be deemed unmerchantable, and whenever shingles are offered for inspection in bundles which require to be opened by the officer, the
expense of putting up the same again (if so wanted) shall be
borne by the seller.

[Section IV.] (Section V, P. L.) And be it further enacted
by the authority aforesaid, That before the said officer or any
deputy shall proceed to the execution of this act he shall take

an oath or affirmation "faithfully and impartially to perform his duty or trust according to the directions of this act to the best of his judgment," which oath shall be administered to him and a record thereof kept as is by law directed respecting the inspectors of staves and heading, the expense whereof shall be paid by such officer.

[Section V.] (Section VI, P. L.) And be it further enacted by the authority aforesaid, That this act shall take effect and be in force from and immediately after the first day of March next.

Passed September 29, 1789. Recorded L. B. No. 4, p. 16.
See the Acts of Assembly passed April 5, 1790, Charter 1514.

CHAPTER MCDLII.

AN ACT RELATING TO SHERIFFS AND CORONERS.

(Section 1, P. L.) Whereas doubts have arisen whether the powers and authority of sheriffs do not expire at the end of one year from and after their respective elections, although another person should not be commissioned as sheriff at the end of such term and inconveniences have ensued and are likely to ensue from the want of a suitable provision in this behalf:

[Section I.] (Section II, P. L.) Be it therefore enacted and it is hereby enacted by the Representatives of the Freemen of the Commonwealth of Pennsylvania in General Assembly met and by the authority of the same, That the present and all future sheriffs of the city and county of Philadelphia and of every county within this commonwealth shall continue in office and execute the same and all things thereunto belonging until another sheriff shall be duly commissioned and notice thereof given to the first sheriff, notwithstanding the term for which he and they shall have been chosen and commissioned shall have expired and notwithstanding he and they shall have held and exercised the office of sheriff for the term of three years, and that the execution of the said office and of all matters and things thereunto belonging shall be of the like force and effect as if the term for which such sheriff was elected or commissioned had not expired, anything to the contrary hereof in any former law or laws notwithstanding.

[Section II.] (Section III, P. L.) And be it further enacted by the authority aforesaid, That the late and all former sheriffs of the city and county of Philadelphia and of each and every county within this commonwealth and their respective deputies shall be and the same are hereby indemnified and saved harmless against all and all manner of suits, actions and prosecutions which is, are or may be brought or commenced against them or any of them by reason of their or any or either of their execution of any legal process issued an ddirected to the said sheriffs respectively after the time for which they were respectively commissioned had expired and before another sheriff had been commissioned in the place and stead of any such sheriff and notice thereof given to the sheriff executing such process and that all such execution of legal process shall be and is hereby declared to be of the same force and effect as if the same had been executed by the sheriff or his deputies during the continuance of his commission. Provided always, That nothing herein contained shall extend to make good such process or execution of process or such acts of the same sheriff or of his deputies as would have been illegal or void had the same taken place during the continuance of his said commission.

And whereas sufficient provision is not made by the laws of this commonwealth for obliging the coroners of the several counties within the same to give sufficient security for the faithful discharge of their respective offices:

For remedy whereof:

[Section III.] (Section IV, P. L.) Be it further enacted by the authority aforesaid, That before any coroner of the city and county of Philadelphia or of any county within this commonwealth hereafter to be elected, chosen or appointed shall receive his commission or exercise any part of his said office,

24—XIII

he shall put in sufficient sureties in one half of the sum which is or shall be by law required from the sheriff of the same county that he will well and faithfully perform his duty and trust in the said office of coroner, which said sureties shall be taken in like manner and be of the like force and effect respecting the said office of coroner and the duties thereof as any sureties directed by law to be given by any sheriff respecting his office and the duties thereof and shall be in trust for and to and for the use of this commonwealth and of all persons concerned and the like proceedings for remedy and relief by the commonwealth and by all persons aggrieved shall thereon be had and obtained.

[Section IV.] (Section V, P. L.) And be it further enacted by the authority aforesaid, That if any sheriff of the city and county of Philadelphia or of any other county within this commonwealth shall be legally removed from his office or happen to die before the expiration of the term for which he shall have been commissioned, the coroner of the proper county shall execute the office of sheriff and all things thereunto appertaining until another sheriff shall be duly commissioned and notice thereof given as aforesaid, and the security and pledges given by every coroner in pursuance of this act shall be a security to the commonwealth and to all persons whatsoever for the faithful discharge and due performance of all the duties as well in and by this act [required] as by any other or former laws required from any such coroner and coroners.

And whereas the process by distringas is dilatory and expensive and it is necessary to provide some adequate remedy therein to prevent the delays of sheriffs and others in the duties of their respective offices:

[Section V.] (Section VI, P. L.) Be it therefore further enacted by the authority aforesaid, That the court out of which any writ of distringas, vicecomitem, distringas nuper vicecomitem or other writ of distringas proceeds may by a rule for that purpose made, order and direct that the issues levied from time to time shall be sold and the money arising thereby be applied in the first instance to pay such costs to the plaintiff as the said court shall think just under all circumstances, to order and to

have the remainder thereof in court to be retained till the defendant shall have appeared or other purpose of the writ be
answered or to be rendered to the plaintiff for his debt, damages and costs where the same shall be ascertained. Provided
always, That where the purpose of a writ is answered the said
issues shall be returned, or, if sold, what shall remain of the
money arising by such sale shall be repaid to the party dis-
trained upon.

Passed September 29, 1789. Recorded L. B. No. 4, p. 13.

CHAPTER MCDLIII.

AN ACT TO CEDE TO AND VEST IN THE UNITED STATES THE LIGHT-
HOUSE AT CAPE HENLOPEN AND ALL THE BEACONS, BUOYS AND
PUBLIC PIERS, TOGETHER WITH THE LANDS AND TENEMENTS
THEREUNTO BELONGING AND TOGETHER WITH THE JURISDICTION
OF THE SAME.

(Section I, P. L.) Whereas by an act of the senate and house
of representatives of the United States in congress assembled,
approved the seventh day of August in the year of our Lord
one thousand seven hundred and eighty-nine by the president
of the United States entitled "An act for the establishment
and support of light-houses, beacons, buoys and public piers,"
provision is made "That all expenses which shall accrue from
and after the fifteenth day of August one thousand seven hundred and eighty-nine in the necessary support, maintenance
and repairs of all light-houses, beacons, buoys and public
piers erected, placed or sunk before the passing of the said act
at the entrance of or in any bay, inlet, harbor or port of the
United States for rendering the navigation thereof easy and
safe, shall be defrayed out of the treasury of the United
States," under this proviso nevertheless, "That none of the
said expenses shall continue to be so defrayed by the United
States after the expiration of one year from the day aforesaid, unless such light-houses, beacons, buoys and public piers

shall in the meantime be ceded to and vested in the United States by the state or states respectively in which the same may be, together with the lands and tenements thereunto belonging and together with the jurisdiction of the same:"

And whereas by the constitution of the United States the congress thereof are vested with the power of regulating the commerce of the Union and it is necessary that the jurisdiction, property and control of the light-houses, beacons, buoys and public piers should be ceded and vested in them for the purpose of carrying such power into complete effect:

[Section I.] (Section II, P. L.) Be it therefore enacted and it is hereby enacted by the Representatives of the Freemen of the Commonwealth of Pennsylvania in General Assembly met and by the authority of the same, That all the right, title, property and interest of this commonwealth in and to the lighthouse at Cape Henlopen and all the beacons, buoys and public piers now erected, placed or sunk in the bay and river Delaware for the improvement and safety of the navigation thereof and for rendering the same more easy and convenient, together with all the lands and tenements thereunto belonging shall be and hereby are ceded to and vested in the United States of America as fully, absolutely and to the same extent as this commonwealth now holds and is entitled [in and] to the same, together with the jurisdiction thereof so far as this commonwealth hath or had right to exercise jurisdiction over the whole or any part of the same. Provided nevertheless, That nothing in this act contained shall be construed, deemed or taken to extend to or include Mud Island in the river Delaware or any part thereof or the wharves or any of them which are built out and extended therefrom.

Passed September 28, 1789. Recorded L. B. No. 4, p. 20.

CHAPTER MCDLIV.

AN ACT RELATING TO DRAWBACKS AND DISCOUNTS.

(Section I, P. L.) Whereas by several acts of the general

assembly of this commonwealth divers duties were imposed on
goods, wares and merchandise to be paid on the importation
thereof into this state, and by the said act it is provided, that
in all cases where any goods, wares or merchandise charged
with an impost or duty by any acts of the general assembly
of this state and imported after the twenty-fifth day of September one thousand seven hundred and eighty-three should
be exported within the time and under the conditions in the
said acts expressed, "the whole of the said duty (if before paid)
should be returned within one month after exportation or if
bonded it should be allowed out of such bond:"

And whereas Sharp Delany, Esquire, was by an act of the
general assembly of this state appointed collector of the imposts and duties by the said several acts imposed:

And whereas by an act of the senate and house of representatives of the United States of America entitled "An act
for laying a duty on goods, wares and merchandise imported
into the United States" the duties and imposts laid by the several acts of assembly of this state ceased to be due and payable
from and after the first day of August last past, and the merchants of the port of Philadelphia are in possession of divers
goods, wares and merchandise imported before that day for
which the duties and imposts then payable to the collector
have been paid or secured and the said merchants are daily
exporting the same in the course of their trade, but doubts
have been entertained whether the said Sharp Delany continues to be the collector of the said duties and imposts on
goods, wares and merchandise imported into this state before
the said first day of August last and whether he is bound to
pay or discount the said duties paid or secured on such of the
same goods, wares and merchandise as have been or shall be
exported since that day:

[Section I.] (Section II, P. L.) Be it therefore enacted and
it is hereby enacted by the Representatives of the Freemen of
the Commonwealth of Pennsylvania in General Assembly met
and by the authority of the same, That the said Sharp Delany
is and continues to be the collector of the duties and imposts
upon goods, wares and merchandise imported into this state

before the said first day of August [last] imposed by the several acts of the general assembly of this commonwealth upon the importation thereof and that he or his successor in the said office is and are bound to collect and receive the duties and imposts aforesaid upon all goods, wares and merchandise imported into this state on or before the said first day of August last, and to account for the same and to pay and discount the drawbacks upon exportation thereof in the same manner and upon the same terms and conditions as in the several acts of assembly in such case provided are mentioned and contained. And also that Frederick Phile, Esquire, is and continues to be the naval officer of this state so far as concerns any such goods, wares and merchandise aforesaid.

[Section II.] (Section III, P. L.) And be it further enacted by the authority aforesaid, That all export entries which have been offered to the said Sharp Delany, Esquire, since the said first day of August last conformably to the aforesaid impost acts, shall upon being sworn or affirmed to and the other requisites of the said laws being complied with be of equal avail and effect as if the same had been received by the said collector at the time of offering the same.

Passed September 29, 1789.   Recorded L. B. No. 4 p. 17.

CHAPTER MCDLV.

AN ACT FOR REGULATING CERTAIN ELECTION DISTRICTS IN THE COUNTIES OF WESTMORELAND AND ALLEGHENY.

(Section I, P. L.) Whereas the boundary lines of the county of Allegheny which have been lately run and marked so far as they have extended through the county of Westmoreland have divided several of the election districts in such manner that the places appointed for holding the elections in said districts are included within the boundaries of the said county of Allegheny and those parts of the said districts which remain within the county of Westmoreland are left without any

known place where the people can legally vote at their general
elections:

For remedy whereof:

[Section I.] (Section II, P. L.) Be it enacted and it is hereby
enacted by the Representatives of the Freemen of the Commonwealth of Pennsylvania in General Assembly met and by
the authority of the same, That all that part of the county of
Allegheny comprehended within the forks of the rivers Monongahela and Youghiogany and the boundary line of the
said county is hereby erected into a separate election district,
and it shall and may be lawful for the freemen of [the] said district to meet at the house of David Robison and there give in
their votes at the general election, to be distinguished and
known by the name of the second election district.

And whereas the inhabitants of Plumb and Versailles townships in the said county of Allegheny have by their petitions
stated the great difficulty of attending the general elections at
the town of Pittsburgh and prayed to be erected into a separate
district:

[Section II.] (Section III, P. L.) Therefore be it enacted
and it is hereby enacted by the authority aforesaid, That the
said townships of Plumb and Versailles in the county aforesaid are hereby erected into a separate election district to be
known by the name of the third district, and it shall and may
be lawful for the freemen of the said district to meet at the
house now occupied by Matthew Simpson and there give in
their votes at the general election.

[Section III.] (Section IV, P. L.) And be it enacted by the
authority aforesaid, That all that part of Restraver township
which remains within the county of Westmoreland is hereby
erected into a separate election district known by the name of
the fourth district and that it shall and may be lawful for the
freemen of the said district to meet at the house occupied by
Samuel Wilson and there give in their votes at the general
election.

[Section IV.] (Section V, P. L.) And be it further enacted
by the authority aforesaid, That such parts of Huntingdon and
Franklin townships as remain within the county of Westmore-

land are hereby annexed to the fifth election district, and that it shall and may be lawful for the freemen of those townships which so remain within the county of Westmoreland to meet at the town of Greensburgh and there give in their votes at the general election.

And whereas the inhabitants of Derry township are subject to great difficulties in crossing waters and attending the place of their election at so great a distance and have expressed a desire of being erected into a separate district:

Therefore:

[Section V.] (Section VI, P. L.) Be it enacted by the authority aforesaid, That the said township of Derry is hereby erected into a separate election district and that it shall and may be lawful for the freemen of said township to meet at the house now occupied by Moses Donald and there give in their votes at the general election.

[Section VI.] (Section VII, P. L.) And be it further enacted by the authority aforesaid, That so much of an act of general assembly entitled "An act for dividing Westmoreland county into election districts,"¹ as directs and requires the people of the several townships and parts of townships herein named and described to attend at any other place or places of election within the said county of Westmoreland is hereby repealed and made null and void.

Passed September 29, 1769.   Recorded L. B. No. 4, p. 22.
¹ See the Act of Assembly passed September 13, 1785, Chapter 1175.

CHAPTER MCDLVI.

AN ACT RELATING TO SEVERAL ELECTION DISTRICTS IN THE COUNTIES OF BEDFORD AND MIFFLIN.

(Section I, P. L.) Whereas it has been found very inconvenient for the freemen of Londonderry township in the county of Bedford to attend at Bedford town for the purpose of holding their annual elections as the law directs: •

For remedy whereof:

[Section I.] (Section II, P. L.) Be it enacted and it is hereby enacted by the Representatives of the Freemen of the Commonwealth of Pennsylvania in General Assembly met and by the authority of the same, That the township of Londonderry in the county of Bedford be and the same hereby is severed from the first election district in said county and erected into a new and separate district to be called the fourth election district in Bedford county. And that the freemen of the said township of Londonderry shall hereafter hold their general elections at the house now occupied by John Bright in the said township of Londonderry according to the constitution and laws in such [case] made and provided and shall make return of such elections in the same manner as the laws of this commonwealth direct the other districts in said county to make their returns, anything in the election laws of this commonwealth contained to the contrary in anywise notwithstanding.

And whereas the freemen of Air and Dublin townships in Bedford county have by their petition set forth that they labor under very great inconveniences in attending at their elections as the place where Dublin township formerly elected is now in Huntingdon county, occasioned by the division of Bedford county:

[Section II.] (Section III, P. L.) Be it therefore further enacted by the authority aforesaid, That the townships of Air and Dublin in the county of Bedford be and the same are hereby erected into a new and separate district to be called the fifth election district in Bedford county and the freemen of said two townships shall hereafter meet and hold their elections at the house now occupied by Daniel McConnel in Air township in said county and in all other matters and things conduct themselves as is directed by the constitution and laws of this commonwealth respecting elections.

And whereas the freemen of that part of Greenwood township now lying in the county of Mifflin are separated from their usual place of election by the division of Cumberland county and it is inconvenient for the freemen of the township of Lack in the said county of Mifflin to attend at the house of Thomas Wilson for the purpose of holding their annual elections:

[Section III.] (Section IV, P. L.) Be it enacted by the authority aforesaid, That that part of the township of Green wood lying in the county of Mifflin be and the same is hereby erected into a separate district and the freemen of the said district shall hereafter meet on the day appointed by the constitution of this commonwealth for holding the general election at the house now occupied by Henry McConnel in said district and then and there elect members of assembly and other elective officers for the said county according to the laws and constitution of this commonwealth.

[Section IV.] (Section V, P. L.) And be it enacted by the authority aforesaid, That the township of Lack in the said county of Mifflin be and the same is hereby enacted into a new and separate district and the freemen of the said township of Lack shall hereafter meet at the house lately occupied by James Stackpole in the said township of Lack on the day appointed by the constitution of this commonwealth for holding the general election and then and there elect members of the general assembly and other elective officers for said county of Mifflin according to the constitution and laws of this state and the freemen of said districts of Greenwood and Lack shall severally make return of such elections at the same time and in the same manner as the laws of this commonwealth direct in the like cases.

Passed September 29, 1789.   Recorded L. B, No. 4, p. 18.

CHAPTER MCDLVII.

AN ACT TO ESTABLISH AND CONFIRM THE BOUNDARY LINE BETWEEN THIS STATE AND THE STATE OF NEW YORK.

(Section I, P. L.) Whereas the honorable John Penn, Esquire, then governor of the late province, now state, of Penn-

one thousand seven hundred and seventy-four nominate and
appoint David Rittenhouse, Esquire, on the part of Pennsylvania to fix in conjunction with any person to be appointed on
the part of the then province of New York the beginning
of the forty-third degree of north latitude on the Mohawk
or western branch of Delaware river, which is the north-east
corner of Pennsylvania, and to proceed westward in fixing and
marking the boundary line between the said provinces of
Pennsylvania and New York:

And whereas the honorable Cadwallader Colden, Esquire,
then governor of the late province, now state, of New York
with the advice of the then council did on the eighth day of
November in the same year nominate and appoint Samuel Hol-
land, Esquire, on the part of New York to fix in conjunction
with the said David Rittenhouse the same corner and to proceed in running and marking the said line:

And whereas by virtue of an act of the general assembly,
of the state of Pennsylvania the supreme executive council
of this commonwealth by commission under the hand of
Charles Biddle, Esquire, and the great seal, bearing date the
sixteenth day of June one thousand seven hundred and eighty-
six, did constitute and appoint Andrew Ellicot, Esquire, commissioner on the part of the said commonwealth of Pennsylvania to run and mark the northern boundary line of this
commonwealth:

And whereas the said David Rittenhouse and Samuel Hol-
land in pursuance of their said respective appointments did
proceed on the said business and made return thereof under
their hands, bearing date at Philadelphia the fourteenth day
of December in the same year, by which it appears that they
ascertained and fixed the beginning of the forty-third degree
of north latitude on the said Mohawk or western branch of
Delaware and there in a small island of the said river planted
a stone marked with the letters NEW YORK 1774, cut on the
north side thereof and the letters and figures Lat. 42° Var. 4°
20' cut on the top thereof, and in a direction due west from
thence on the west side of the said branch of Delaware, collected and placed a heap of stones at the water mark and pro-

ceeding further west four perches planted another stone in the said line marked with the letters and figures PENNSYL- VANIA 1774 cut on the south side thereof and the letters and figures Lat. 42° Var. 4° 20' cut on the top thereof and at the distance of eighteen perches due west from the last mentioned stone marked an ash tree, but that the rigor of the season prevented them from proceeding further in running the said line as by the said return remaining of record fully appears.

And whereas by virtue of an act of the general assembly of the state of New York entitled "An act for running out and marking the jurisdiction line between this state and the com- monwealth of Pennsylvania, passed the twenty-sixth day of February in the year one thousand seven hundred and eighty- six, James Clinton and Simeon Dewitt, Esquires, were duly appointed commissioners on the part of the state of New York to join with such person or persons as should be appointed on the part of Pennsylvania to run out, mark and ascertain the said line, beginning at the place so fixed and ascertained by the said commissioners as above mentioned on the Mohawk or western branch of Delaware river:

And whereas the said Andrew Ellicot on the part of this commonwealth and the said James Clinton and Simeon Dew- itt on the part of the state of New York did in the year of our Lord one thousand seven hundred and eighty-six and seven in pursuance of the powers so as aforesaid vested in them, run, fix and ascertain the said boundary line beginning at the first mentioned stone marked as is hereinabove recited, and extending thence due west by a line of mill-stones marked with the number of mile and miles which each stone is distant from the said first mentioned stone planted in the said small island, to the bank of Lake Erie, at the distance of two hun- dred and fifty-nine miles and eighty-eight perches from the said first mentioned corner stone, and the said commissioners did accordingly return a draught or plot of the said line under their hands to the supreme executive council of this common- wealth, in which said draught or plot are noted and laid down the several principal waters, mountains and other remarkable places through and over which the said boundary line runs,

sylvania, did on the twenty-fourth day of October in the year
which said boundary line is and ought to be forever hereafter
deemed and taken as the true boundary of territory and jurisdiction between this state and the state of New York so far
as the state of New York is bounded thereby.

[Section 1.] (Section II, P. L.) It is therefore hereby declared and enacted by the Representatives of the Freemen of
the Commonwealth of Pennsylvania in General Assembly met
and by the authority of the same, That the said boundary line
so as aforesaid run, marked and returned by the said Andrew
Ellicott, commissioner on the part of this state and the said
James Clinton and Simeon Dewitt, commissioners on the part
of the state of New York, beginning at the first mentioned
corner stone planted in the said small island in the Mohawk
or west branch of Delaware river and thence extending due
west by marked stones aforesaid, so far westward as to meet
the meridian line which is hereafter to be fixed and established
as the western boundary of the state of New York, shall be
and forever hereafter shall be deemed and taken to be and is
hereby declared to be the true and just line of boundary and
partition both of territory and jurisdiction between the state
of Pennsylvania and the state of New York, and that this
commonwealth of Pennsylvania doth not nor at any time hereafter shall or will claim to have, hold or exercise any right,
power or jurisdiction in or over the soil or inhabitants dwelling
northward of the said line hereby established, eastward of
the said meridian line or western boundary of New York.
Provided always nevertheless, That nothing in this act contained shall be deemed to bind the commonwealth of Pennsylvania until the legislature of New York shall establish
and confirm the said boundary line on their part as fully and
effectually as the same is by this act established and confirmed.

And in order that the knowledge of the said boundary line
may be rendered permanent and extensive:

[Section II.] (Section III, P. L.) It is hereby further enacted by the authority aforesaid, That it shall and may be
lawful for the supreme executive council of this common-

wealth to cause and procure the draught or plot of the said
line and of the reports of the commissioners who completed
the same, together with such notes and observations of the
said commissioners as in the opinion of the said council may
be necessary to be preserved, to be engraved on plates of cop-
per and such number of copies to be printed from such plates
as will be sufficient to perpetuate the memory of the said line,
not exceeding in the first instance two hundred copies and to
preserve the said plates for any future use or purpose to
which they may be applied by the legislature of Pennsylvania
and to issue any order or orders on the treasurer of this state
for the payment of the expenses of engraving and printing the
same, to be charged with the contingent expenses of government on the fund provided therefor.

Passed September 29, 1789.   Recorded L. B. No. 4, p. 33.

CHAPTER MCDLVIII.

AN ACT TO PROVIDE FOR THE PAYMENT OF THE DEMANDS OF
JOSEPH PERKINS, ABRAM MORROW AND JOHN NICHOLSON UPON
THIS COMMONWEALTH.

(Section I, P. L.) Whereas it appears that this state is indebted to Joseph Perkins, Abram Morrow and John Nicholson for repairing the public arms by order of the supreme executive council, which debts are legally chargeable upon the fund
established by the laws for regulating the militia:

And whereas the said fund is at present inadequate to discharge the claims thereon:

Therefore:

[Section I.] (Section II, P. L.) Be it enacted and it is hereby
enacted by the Representatives of the Freemen of the Commonwealth of Pennsylvania in General Assembly met and by
the authority of the same, That the president or vice-president
in council be and they hereby are authorized and required to
issue their warrants directed to the state treasurer requiring

him to pay to Joseph Perkins, Abram Morrow and John
Nicholson respectively the amount of their several accounts as
the same have been or shall be settled and ascertained according to law, out of the fund for "claims and improvements" established by the act entitled "An act to appropriate divers
funds accruing and growing due to this commonwealth towards the payment of the expenses of government and to provide a fund for other purposes,[1] the said Joseph Perkins,
Abram Morrow and John Nicholson re-delivering to be cancelled all warrants by them received hitherto on the account
aforesaid previously to their receiving the new warrants hereby
directed to be issued in their favor.

[Section II.] (Section III, P. L.) And be it further enacted by
the authority aforesaid. That whenever and so soon as the fund
established by the laws for the regulation of the militia, usually
called the militia fund, shall become sufficiently productive to
reimburse the payments to be made as aforesaid, a sum equiva-
lent to the amount of the warrants to be issued in pursuance
of the directions of this act shall be charged on the same and
the fund for claims and improvements be credited therefor.

---

[1] Passed March 26, 1789, Chapter 1404.
Passed September 29, 1789.   Recorded L. D. No. 4, p. 13.

CHAPTER MCDLIX.

AN ACT FOR THE RELIEF OF ROBERT ROSS AND FRANCIS WHITE.

(Section I, P. L.) Whereas it appears to this house that
Francis White and Robert Ross, two prisoners now confined
in the gaol of the county of Philadelphia have been severally
adjudged bankrupts by the commissioners named in certain
commissions of bankrupt issued against them severally, that
the said commissioners having adjudged that the said Francis
White had not by his answers made a full and fair disclosure of his estate and effects have for that cause committed him

to gaol, there to remain until he should make such full and fair disclosure, that the said Robert Rose not having in the opinion of the said commissioners made a full and fair disclosure of his estate and effects they have refused to grant him a certificate of his conformity as the law in such case provides, and he hath been since taken in execution by virtue of several writs of capias ad satisfaciendum at the suit of sundry creditors, and the said Francis and Robert have since, by their respective petitions, humbly sought the aid of the legislature in their behalf, representing that the existing laws for the relief of insolvent debtors do not extend to the particular circumstances of their cases, and it appears reasonable that some relief should be extended to them:

[Section I.] (Section II, P. L.) Be it therefore enacted and it is hereby enacted by the Representatives of the Freemen of the Commonwealth of Pennsylvania in General Assembly met and by the authority of the same, That it shall and may be lawful for the said Francis White and Robert Rose respectively to present their petitions to the next supreme court to be held for this commonwealth or to any two justices of the said court (whereof the chief justice to be one) in vacation, praying that [the] commissioners named in the commissions of bankruptcy against them respectively issued and also the creditors of the said Robert and Francis respectively be warned to appear before the said court or the said two justices in vacation at a day to be by them appointed and show cause if any they have why the said Francis White and Robert Rose should not be discharged from their respective imprisonments. Whereupon it shall and may be lawful to and for the said court or the said justices thereof in vacation to issue such process and cause such proceedings to be had thereon as the nature of the case shall be by them found to require. And after a due examination of the proofs and allegations of the said petitioners and of the said commissioners and creditors or of such of them as shall attend to make such decree confirming the proceedings of the said commissioners in this behalf or reversing and annulling the same in whole or in part as to them shall appear consistent with law and justice.

[Section II.] (Section III, P. L.) And be it further enacted
by the authority aforesaid, That if upon due examination the
said court or two of the justices thereof in vacation shall adjudge that the said Francis White and Robert Ross or either
of them have or hath conformed agreeably to the laws of this
commonwealth touching bankrupts and the disclosure of their
estate and effects, it shall be lawful for the said court or two
justices thereof in vacation to adjudge and order that the like
relief be afforded and extended to the said Robert Ross and
Francis White or either of them and under the same regulations, exceptions and restrictions and upon the same terms
and conditions as by the laws of this commonwealth is provided for bankrupts conforming agreeably to the laws of this
commonwealth touching and concerning bankrupts and disclosure of their estate and effects.

Passed September 29, 1789. Recorded L. B. No. 4, p. 21.

CHAPTER MCDLX.

A SUPPLEMENT TO AN ACT ENTITLED "AN ACT FOR RAISING BY WAY
OF LOTTERY THE SUM OF EIGHT THOUSAND DOLLARS FOR DEFRAY-
ING THE EXPENSE OF ERECTING A COMMON HALL IN THE CITY OF
PHILADELPHIA AND TWO THOUSAND DOLLARS FOR THE USE OF
DICKINSON COLLEGE IN THE BOROUGH OF CARLISLE.[1]

(Section I, P. L.) Whereas the act entitled "An act for raising by way of lottery the sum of eight thousand dollars for
defraying the expense of erecting a common hall in the city
of Philadelphia and two thousand dollars for the use of Dickinson College in the borough of Carlisle," is not likely to answer
the good ends thereby intended:

For remedy whereof:

[Section 1.] (Section II, P. L.) Be it enacted and it is hereby
enacted by the Representatives of the Freemen of the Commonwealth of Pennsylvania in General Assembly met and by
the authority of the same, That the managers of the said lot-

[1] Passed March 27, 1789, Chapter 1419.
25—XIII

tery or any four of them shall instead of the prize tickets directed by the said recited act to be prepared, prepare or cause to be prepared five thousand and thirty-six prize tickets on which shall be written or expressed as well in figures as in words at length as follows, that is to say, upon one of them three thousand dollars, upon one other of them two thousand dollars, upon two other of them severally one thousand dollars, upon six other of them severally five hundred dollars, upon ten other of them severally three hundred dollars, upon twenty other of them severally two hundred dollars, upon thirty other of them severally one hundred dollars, upon sixty other of them severally fifty dollars, upon [one] hundred other of them severally thirty dollars, upon [one] hundred and eighty-five other of them severally twenty dollars, and upon four thousand six hundred and twenty-one other of them severally eight dollars, which principal sums so to be expressed upon the said tickets will amount in the whole to sixty-six thousand six hundred and sixty-eight dollars out of which the said managers are hereby authorized and required to deduct fifteen per centum and no more, amounting in the whole to ten thousand dollars and two tenths of a dollar, the sum intended to be raised for the purposes in the said act mentioned and specified.

[Section II.] (Section III, P. L.) And be it further enacted by the authority aforesaid, That it shall and may be lawful for the managers of the said lottery and they are hereby enjoined and required to prepare eleven thousand six hundred and thirty-one pieces of blank paper of equal dimensions and of the size of the papers upon which the prizes are to be written conformably to the directions of the act to which this is a supplement, and the said blanks so prepared shall cause to be rolled up and tied in the same manner and as much as possible to resemble the said prize tickets, which blanks shall be put into the wheel containing the prizes and being well mixed with the said prizes shall be drawn with them, anything in the act to which this is a supplement to the contrary notwithstanding.

And in order to promote the sale of the said tickets:

[Section III.] (Section IV, P. L.) Be it further enacted by the authority aforesaid, That the managers of the said lottery shall [be] and they are hereby authorized and empowered to place in the hands of such persons as they judge safe such parcels of tickets from time to time for sale on account of the said lottery as they may suppose to be necessary to forward the designs of the lottery.

[Section IV.] (Section V, P. L.) And be it further enacted by the authority aforesaid, That the said managers shall have and receive one half per centum on the gross amount of the sales of the tickets to be equally divided amongst them in full satisfaction for their care, attention and trouble in managing, directing and drawing the said lottery.

Passed September 29, 1789.   Recorded L. B. No. 4, p. 15&c.

CHAPTER MCDXLI.

AN ACT FOR INCORPORATING THE SOCIETY FORMED FOR THE RELIEF OF DISTRESSED AND DECAYED PILOTS, THEIR WIDOWS AND CHILDREN.

(Section I, P. L.) Whereas by an act of general assembly passed the fourth day of October in the year of our Lord one thousand seven hundred and eighty-eight entitled "An act to establish a board of wardens for the port of Philadelphia and for other purposes therein mentioned,"[1] it was enacted that all and singular the sums of money which should be paid to the collector of the tonnage by virtue of the said act for one fourth part of the pilotage of all ships or vessels brought or navigated up to the port of Philadelphia or carried from thence without a pilot and all fines to be recovered from pilots for any breach of the said act should be kept as a fund by the said collector for the use of distressed and decayed pilots, their widows and children, to be distributed by a society of pilots to be formed for that purpose and that so soon as a society should be formed by the said pilots consisting of two thirds of the whole number of first rate certificate pilots at least and

[1] Chapter 1365.

having a board of managers, treasurer and clerk, the said collector should pay to them or their orders all the said moneys
to be by them kept, managed and distributed as aforesaid and
also should once in every half year pay over to the said managers for the uses aforesaid all the moneys by him to be
received from time to time for such one fourth part of pilot-
ages and the fines which may be recovered from pilots by
virtue of the said act.

And whereas more than two thirds of the whole number of
such first rate certificate pilots have formed themselves into
a society for the relief of distressed and decayed pilots, their
widows and children and by their articles for forming the said
society bearing date the tenth day of November in the year of
our Lord one thousand seven hundred and eighty-eight did
appoint Henry Fisher, Aaron Bennet, Richard Howard, William Ross, Andrew Higgins, Samuel Thompson, James Art,
Henry Stephens, William West, John Barnes, Aaron Edmonds
and John Snyder to be managers; Isaac Roach to be treasurer
and Nathaniel Galt to be clerk of the said society, to continue
in office until the second Monday in October in this present
year one thousand seven hundred and eighty-nine:

[Section I.] (Section II, P. L.) Be it therefore enacted and it
is hereby enacted by the representatives of the Freemen of
the Commonwealth of Pennsylvania in General Assembly met
and by the authority of the same, That all and every person
and persons who have heretofore subscribed the said articles
and each and every person serving as a pilot to and from
the port of Philadelphia who shall be furnished with a certificate according to the directions of the said act of assembly,
who shall hereafter pay and contribute any sum of money not
less than three shillings and nine pence and the further sum of
six shillings annually to the treasurer hereinafter mentioned to
and for the uses and purposes in this act specified and who shall
be admitted into the said society by the ballots of a majority of
the members who shall have met at any general meeting of
the said society to be held in manner and at the times hereinafter mentioned, shall be and they are hereby declared to be
members of the said society and are hereby made a body politic

and corporate in law to all intents and purposes and shall have
perpetual succession and may sue and be sued, plead and be
impleaded by the name of "The Society for the Relief of Distressed and Decayed Pilots, their Widows and Children," in all
courts of judicature within this commonwealth, and by that
name shall and may purchase any lands, tenements and estates,
and also receive and take any lands, tenements or hereditaments not exceeding the value of ten thousand pounds of the
gifts, alienation or devise and any goods or chattels of the
bequest of any person or persons whatsoever, and shall and
may lend on interest any sum or sums of money belonging to
the said contributors to such person or persons, bodies politic
or corporate as may be willing to borrow the same in the
manner and on such real and other securities as they shall
think proper and sufficient and the said corporation are hereby empowered to have and use one common seal in all their
affairs.

[Section II.] (Section III, P. L.) And be it enacted
by the authority aforesaid, That the said Henry Fisher, Aaron
Bennet, Richard Howard, William Ross, Andrew Higgins,
Samuel Thompson, James Art, Henry Stephens, William West,
John Barnes, Aaron Edmonds and John Snyder shall be and
continue managers of the said society until the second Monday
in October next and until others shall be chosen in their room
which said managers and all other managers to be hereafter
chosen by virtue of this act or a majority of them are hereby
authorized and empowered to provide a seal for the said society
and to change and alter the same if they shall see occasion
and also to take in, place out, secure and improve the stock and
to dispose of the interest, profits and produce thereof together
with the yearly payments of six shillings which shall be made
or have been made since the said tenth day of November in
the year one thousand seven hundred and eighty-eight for and
towards the relief and support of poor distressed and decayed
pilots, their widows and children and for and towards no other
use, intent and purpose whatsoever. And that all future subscriptions, donations, gifts, bequests and devises shall be adjudged and deemed capital stock unless the same shall be other-

quired to see duly given and executed and recorded in the office for recording deeds for the county of Philadelphia before he shall receive any of the said moneys, securities, deeds, writings, and other effects as aforesaid.

[Section VI.] (Section VII, P. L.) And be it further enacted by the authority aforesaid, That the said managers shall meet when and where and as often as they shall think proper and being a majority at least shall and may enter upon, order and direct and dispatch all such matters and things as shall properly come before them and such their proceedings shall be good and valid in all the affairs of the society aforesaid, done and performed in pursuance of this act or that shall be committed to their management by the contributors aforesaid from time to time at their general or special meetings.

[Section VII.] (Section VIII, P. L.) And be it further enacted by the authority aforesaid, That the said managers shall keep fair and exact accounts of all their transactions and proceedings and a true and fair list of all donations, subscriptions and payments which shall from time to time be made to and for the uses and purposes in this act mentioned and shall yearly and every year publish the same together with an account of moneys expended in some of the newspapers printed in the city of Philadelphia and shall at all times when required submit the books, minutes, accounts, affairs and economy of the said society to the inspection and free examination of such committee of the general assembly as may from time to time be appointed for inspecting and examining the same.

Passed September 29, 1789. Recorded L. B. No. 4, p. 7.
See the Act of Assembly passed February 27, 1789, Chapter 1969.

CHAPTER MCDLXII.

AN ACT FOR INCORPORATING THE GERMAN LUTHERN CONGREGATION WORSHIPPING AT THE CHURCH CALLED S. PETER'S IN PIKELAND OWNSHIP IN THE COUNTY OF CHESTER.

(Section I, P. L.) Whereas the congregation of the German Lutheran Church, worshipping at the church called St. Peter's

in Pikeland township in the county of Chester have prayed
that their said congregation may be incorporated and by
law enabled as a body politic and corporate to receive and
hold such charitable donations, bequests, grants and enfeoffments as have been or that hereafter may be made to their
said society and vested with such powers and privileges as are
enjoyed by other religious societies who are incorporated in
this state:

And whereas this house is disposed to exercise the powers
vested in the legislature of the commonwealth for the encouragement of pious and charitable purposes:

[Section I.] (Section II, P. L.) Be it therefore enacted and it
is hereby enacted by the Representatives of the Freemen of the
Commonwealth of Pennsylvania in General Assembly met and
by the authority of the same, That the Reverend Ludwig Voigt,
the present minister of the same congregation, Jacob Dann-
efelser, George Deric and Zachariah Reis the present trustees,
Valentine Orner, John King, Valentine Fuss, Charles Stell,
Jacob Ludwig and Conrad Henry the present elders, Michael
Hallman, Frederick Stranck and Lawrence King the present
deacons and their successors duly elected and appointed in
such manner as hereinafter is directed be and they are hereby
made, declared and constituted to be a corporation and body
politic and corporate in law and in fact to have continuance
forever by the name, style and title of "The Minister, Trustees,
Elders and Deacons of the German Lutheran Congregation
worshipping at the church called St. Peter's in Pikeland township in the county of Chester."   Provided always nevertheless,
That the number of ministers may be increased and again diminished from time to time according to the circumstances or
desire of the said congregation, in which case the name, style
and title of the said corporation shall be "The Ministers, Trustees, Elders and Deacons of the German Lutheran congregation worshipping at the church called St. Peter's in Pikeland
Township in the county of Chester."

[Section II.] (Section III, P. L.) And be it further enacted
by the authority aforesaid, That the said corporation and their
successors by the name, style and title aforesaid shall forever

hereafter be persons able and capable in law as well to take,
receive and hold all and all manner of lands, tenements, rents,
annuities, franchises and other hereditaments which at any
time or times heretofore have been granted, bargained, sold,
enfeoffed, released, devised or otherwise conveyed to the said
congregation and church now under the pastoral care of the
Reverend Ludwig Voigt or to any other person or persons to
their use or in trust for them, and the same lands, tenements,
rents, annuities, liberties, franchises and other hereditaments
are hereby vested and established in the said corporation and
their successors forever according to the original use and intent   for   which   such   devises,   gifts   and   grants
were respectively made, and the said corporation and their successors are hereby declared to be seized and possessed of such
estate or estates therein as in and by the respective grants,
bargains, sales, enfeoffments, releases or other devises and
conveyances thereof is or are declared, limited or expressed,
as also that the said corporation and their successors at all
times hereafter shall be capable and able to purchase, have,
receive, take, hold and enjoy in fee simple or of less estate
or estates any lands, tenements, rents, annuities, liberties, franchises and other hereditaments by the gift, grant, bargain, sale,
alienation, enfeoffment, release, confirmation or devise of any
person or person, bodies politic and corporate capable and able
to make the same, and further that the said corporation and
their successors may take and receive any sum or sums of money
and any portion of goods and chattels that have been or hereafter shall be given or bequeathed unto them or to the said
church by any person or persons, bodies politic or corporate
able and capable to make a bequest or gift thereof, such
money, goods or chattels to be laid out and disposed for the
benefit of the aforesaid congregation agreeably to the intention
of the donors.

[Section III.] (Section IV, P. L.) And be it further enacted
by the authority aforesaid, That no misnomer of the said
corporation and their successors shall defeat or annul any gift,
grant, devise or bequest to or from the said corporation provided the intent of the party or parties shall sufficiently appear

upon the face of the gift, grant, will or other writing whereby any estate or interest was intended to pass to or from the said corporation.

[Section IV.] (Section V, P. L.) And be it further enacted by the authority aforesaid, That the rents, profits and interest of the said real and personal estate of the said congregation and corporation shall by the said corporation and their successors from time to time be applied and laid out for the maintenance and support of the Gospel ministry in said congregation, for repairing and maintaining their church or churches (in case any more should be added to that already built) places of public worship, lots of land, burial grounds, parsonage houses, school houses or other houses, and buildings which now do or hereafter shall belong to the said congregation and corporation and such pious and charitable uses as shall be thought proper by the said corporation and their successors or a quorum of them.

[Section V.] (Section VI, P. L.) And be it further enacted by the authority aforesaid, That the said corporation and their successors shall not by deed or otherwise grant, alien, convey or otherwise dispose of any part or parcel of the estate, real or personal in the said corporation vested or to be vested or charge or encumber the same to any person or persons whatsoever except by and with the consent of a majority of the regular contributing members of the said congregation convened for that purpose.

[Section VI.] (Section VII, P. L.) And be it further enacted by the authority aforesaid, That the said corporation and their successors shall have full power and authority to make, have and use one common seal with such device and inscription as they shall think fit and proper and the same to break, alter and renew at their pleasure.

[Section VII.] (Section VIII, P. L.) And be it further enacted by the authority aforesaid, That the [said] corporation and their successors by the name of "The Minister, Trustees, Elders and Deacons of the German Lutheran Congregation worshipping at the church called St. Peters in Pikeland Township in the County of Chester" or in case there shall be more than one minister belonging to the same congregation, by the name of "The Ministers, Trustees, Elders and Deacons of the German Lutheran Congregation worshipping at the church called St. Peter's in Pikeland Township in the County of Chester" shall be able and capable in law to sue and be sued, plead and be impleaded in any court or before any judge or justice in all and all manner of suits, complaints, pleas, matters and demands of whatsoever kind, nature and form they may be and in all and every matter and thing therein to do in as full and effectual a manner as any other person body politic or corporate within this commonwealth may or can do.

[Section VIII.] (Section IX, P. L.) And be it further enacted by the authority aforesaid, That the said corporation shall at all times hereafter consist of the minister or ministers of the said congregation duly chosen from time to time and of three trustees, six elders and three deacons and that the said trustees, elders and deacons shall be and continue until removed in manner following, that is to say, one third part in number of the trustees, being the one first named, one third part in number of the elders, being the two first named and one third part in number of the deacons, being the one first named, shall cease and discontinue and their appointment determine on Whitsun Monday which will be in the year of our Lord one thousand seven hundred and ninety, at which time a new election shall be had and held of an equal number in their stead and places by a majority of votes of the members met and qualified to vote and elect according to the purport, true intent and meaning of the fundamental articles of said congregation and of this act, and on Whitsun Monday which will be in the year of our Lord one thousand seven hundred and ninety-one the second third part in number of the remaining elders, and deacons shall in like manner cease and discontinue and their appointment determine and new election be had and held in like manner of an equal number in their stead and places and on Whitsun Monday which will be in the year of our Lord one thousand seven hundred and ninety-two the last third part in number of the said remaining trustees, elders and deacons aforesaid, shall cease and discontinue and their ap-

pointment determine and a new election be had and held of
an equal number in their places and stead in like manner, and
that in the same manner by the same mode of rotation one third
part in number of the said trustees, of the elders and of the
church-wardens shall cease and discontinue and their appointments determine and a new election of the said third part
be had and held in manner aforesaid on the Whitsun Monday in
every year forever, so that no person or persons shall continue to be a trustee, elder or deacon for any longer time than
three years without being re-elected, but that the members of
the said congregation qualified to vote as aforesaid shall and
may be at liberty to re-elect any one or more of the trustees,
elders and deacons whose time shall have expired on the day
of the said annual election whenever and so often as they shall
think fit.

[Section IX.] (Section X, P. L.) And be it further enacted
by the authority aforesaid, That whenever a vacancy shall
happen by death, refusal to serve or removal from office of
any one or more of the trustees, elders or deacons the said
corporation shall have power at their discretion to appoint
the time and place for electing others in their stead whereof
they shall give public notice to the congregation on the preceding Sunday, and that at the time and place so appointed
some fit person or persons shall be elected in the place of him or
them so dying, refusing or being removed as aforesaid, and that
the person or persons so elected to the office in the place and
stead of a trustee, elder or deacon shall be remain and continue in office so long as the person or persons in whose place
or stead he or they shall have been so elected would or might
have continued.

[Section X.] (Section XI, P. L.) And be it further enacted
by the authority aforesaid, That no person or persons shall
be entitled to elect or be elected to office who is not a regular
member of said congregation and otherwise qualified thereto
agreeably to the fundamental articles of the said congregation,
excepting the minister or ministers who from time to time
be chosen or elected by a majority of the trustees, elders and

deacons and regular members of the said congregation to officiate in said congregation.

[Section XI.] (Section XII, P. L.) And be it further enacted
by the authority aforesaid, That whenever any circumstance
or concurrence of circumstances shall happen to prevent the
holding an election at the periods in this act before mentioned
for trustees, elders and deacons instead and place of those
whose appointment shall have ceased and determined, an
election shall be held as soon as conveniently can be done in
the same manner as before directed and that the remaining
members of the said corporation have power to call a meeting
of the electors of said congregation for such purposes.

[Section XII.] (Section XIII, P. L.) And be it further enacted by the authority aforesaid, That such and so many of
the fundamental articles tending to the orderly and good government of the said church which now are in force and duly
entered and registered in their church books as are not altered
and repealed by this act and are not repugnant to the laws
of this commonwealth shall be, remain and continue forever
valid and effectual, unless the same be altered by the consent
for [sic] a majority of the members of the said congregation
qualified to vote at elections according to the purport and meaning of said fundamental articles and this act.

[Section XIII.] (Section XIV, P. L.) And be it further enacted by the authority aforesaid, That the members of the
said corporation shall and may from time to time as often as
occasion may require elect by vote or ballot from amongst
their own number a president and vice-president agreeably
to the fundamental articles aforesaid as they now are or shall
be made pursuant to the foregoing section, that they may elect
by vote or ballot a treasurer and secretary and may remove
them at pleasure, that the president or vice-president for the
time being or any three members of the said corporation shall
be empowered to call a meeting of the corporation when and
so often as he or they shall find it to be necessary or shall be
requested to do so by any six regular members of said congregation, that the said corporation and their successors or
a majority of seven in number of them met and convened upon

due notice given either in the church on the preceding Sunday
after divine service and before the congregation is dismissed
or in any other convenient manner (which seven shall be a
quorum) shall be authorized and empowered and they are
hereby authorized and empowered to make by-laws and ordinances and do everything needful for the support and government of the said congregation.

Provided always, That the said by-laws, rules, ordinances
or any of them be not repugnant to the laws of this commonwealth; and be duly published in the said church on the
succeeding Sunday after they have been made and not dissented to by a majority of the regular contributing members
of the said congregation within one week after such publication, and also that all their laws and proceedings be fairly and
regularly entered in the books of records of the said congregation.

[Section XIV.] (Section XV, P. L.) And be it further enacted by the authority aforesaid, That the said corporation
shall and may be empowered at any time or times hereafter
to build one or more church or churches or places of public
worship in addition to the one already built, and that the clear
yearly value of the messuages, houses, lands, tenements, rents,
annuities and other hereditaments and real estate of the said
corporation shall and may be of any amount not exceeding the
sum of five hundred pounds gold or silver money at the present
current value thereof in the commonwealth of Pennsylvania
for each and every of the said churches or places of public
worship, the said yearly value or amount to be taken and computed exclusive of the moneys arising, from the letting of the
pews of the said church or churches or for opening the ground
for burials in the church yards belonging to them, and also
exclusive of the voluntary contributions of the members for
the support of their minister or ministers duly officiating in
the said congregation, which yearly income of the said real
estate ascertained and limited as aforesaid shall be disposed
of by the said corporation for the purposes hereinbefore described and directed.

Passed September 29, 1789.   Recorded L. B. No. 4, p. 34.

CHAPTER MCDLXIII.

SUPPLEMENT TO AN ACT ENTITLED "AN ACT FOR THE APPOINTMENT
OF A REGISTER-GENERAL FOR THE PURPOSE OF REGISTERING THE
ACCOUNTS OF THIS STATE." [1]

(Section I, P. L.) Whereas the method of arranging the accounts of this state adopted by the register-general appointed by the act to which this act is a supplement has appeared to a committee of the legislature appointed to examine the same to be judicious and the object of the said act of rendering a complete view of the accounts of the commonwealth at all times practicable may be attained by some additional regulations and by an explanation of some clauses in the said recited act to which this is a supplement:

Therefore:

[Section I.] (Section II, P. L.) Be it enacted and it is hereby enacted by the Representatives of the Freemen of the Commonwealth of Pennsylvania in General Assembly met and by the authority of the same, That it shall be the duty of the comptroller-general of this commonwealth to state and adjust and strike the balance of all and every the account and accounts between this commonwealth and the United States or any one or more states or any one or more individuals or body or bodies corporate and to examine the vouchers for all debits and credits therein contained and to report his opinion thereon together with the vouchers thereof to and to take the advice and assistance of the register-general in settling the same before the final allowance thereof and after such settlement and allowance the same shall be laid before the supreme executive council in the manner and for the purposes mentioned in the third section of the said act.

[Section II.] (Section III, P. L.) And it is hereby enacted by the authority aforesaid, That it is and shall be the duty of the said comptroller-general forthwith to furnish to the said register-general an account of all and every the balance and

[1] Passed March 26, 1789, Chapter 1423.

balances which on the twenty-eighth day of March last past
were due to or from any person or persons or bodies politic
with whom accounts were then depending with this
state and to submit to the examination of the said register-
general his books containing all entries which have relation
thereto and such papers, accounts, documents and vouchers
as shall be necessary [and sufficient] to prove the justice of
such balances to the end that said register-general may be
enabled to open the accounts in his books required by the
fourth section of [the] said act.

[Section III.] (Section IV, P. L.) And it is hereby [further]
enacted by the authority aforesaid, That it shall be the duty
of the comptroller-general forthwith to furnish the register-
general with an exact account of all and every the continental
and state usually called new loan certificates which in pursuance of an act of this general assembly passed the twenty-
seventh day of March last have been exchanged for each other,
containing the dates, numbers, sums, names of the persons in
whose favor they have been issued and the amount of interest
paid thereon, with such other particulars as the case shall
require and of the payments or receipts of indents for equaliz-
ing the balance of interest respectively due thereon, together
with the vouchers to support the same, and upon all applications hereafter to be made for the exchange of such certificates the comptroller-general shall before the exchange shall
be made furnish to the register-general an account of each
certificate offered and of the certificate or certificates intended
to be given in exchange of the interest due to and from the
state thereon and the register-general shall after examination
and approbation of such certificates and accounts cause the
same to be registered in his books accordingly.

[Section IV.] (Section V, P. L.) And it is hereby further enacted by the authority aforesaid, That the said comptroller-
general shall forthwith furnish to the register-general a just
and true account supported by vouchers of all and every the
certificate and certificates which have been granted by the
comptroller-general since the twenty-eighth day of March last

26—XIII

to any person or persons or body politic for any debt due by and from this commonwealth, and the said comptroller-general shall from and after the passing of this act before granting any certificate for any debt due by and from this commonwealth submit the accounts and vouchers of such debts not already examined by the said register-general together with the certificates intended to be granted for the same to the examination and approbation of the register-general who shall thereupon cause the same to be registered in the books by him kept and indorse the registry thereof on such certificates.

And to the end that a complete state of the receipts and payments for and on account of the commonwealth may be always ready for the inspection of the general assembly or supreme executive council to the last day of any preceding month:

[Section V.] (Section VI, P. L.) It is hereby further enacted by the authority aforesaid, That the treasurer of this state shall and he is hereby enjoined and required to furnish to the register-general on the first day of every month (unless the same shall happen on Sunday and in such case on the next day following) from and after the time directed for the next rendering of his annual account an account of all moneys by him received for the use of the commonwealth and of all interest paid by him upon any securities of the commonwealth during the preceding month, and the register [general] is hereby required to transfer all such receipts and payments to the proper accounts in his books.

[Section VI.] (Section VII, P. L.) And it is hereby further enacted by the authority aforesaid, That the register shall and he is hereby enjoined and required to prepare a general statement of all the accounts of this commonwealth ending on the thirtieth day of September in every year on or before the twenty-first day of October following and to lay the same before the general assembly of the commonwealth within the first week after a house shall be convened in the first session of every year and shall make additional statements as often afterwards in the course of each year as the general assembly shall order and direct and that the register-general shall at any and all times submit his books to the inspection

and examination of the general assembly and supreme executive council or either of them and of any committee or committees of them or either of them which shall or may be appointed to view the same.

Passed September 30, 1789. Recorded L. B. No. 4, p. 36. See the
Act of Assembly passed April 1, 1790, Chapter 1506.

CHAPTER MCDLXIV.

AN ACT FOR INCORPORATING THE GERMAN LUTHERAN CONGREGA-
TION WORSHIPPING AT THE CHURCH CALLED ZION IN PIKELAND
TOWNSHIP IN THE COUNTY OF CHESTER.

(Section I, P. L.) Whereas the congregation of the German
Lutheran church worshipping at the church called Zion in
Pikeland township in the county of Chester have prayed that
their said congregation may be incorporated and by law enabled as a body politic and corporate to receive and hold such
charitable donations, bequests, grants and enfeoffments as
have been or hereafter may be made to their said society and
vested with such powers and privileges as are enjoyed by other
religious societies who are incorporated in this state:

And whereas this house is disposed to exercise the powers
vested in the legislature of the commonwealth for the encouragement of pious and charitable purposes:

[Section I.] (Section II, P. L.) Be it therefore enacted and it
is hereby enacted by the Representatives of the Freemen of the
Commonwealth of Pennsylvania in General Assembly met and
by the authority of the same, That the Reverend Ludwig Voigt,
the present minister of the said congregation, John Hass, John
Walter and Henry Christmen the present trustees, Nicholas
Schneider, Conrad Herleman, Stephen Heilman, George Christ-
man, Philip Miller and Henry Knerr, the present elders, John
Fertich, Nicholas Lahr and George Emrich, the present deacons
and their successors duly elected and appointed in such manner
as hereinafter is directed, be and they are hereby made, declared

and constituted to be a corporation and body politic and corporate, in law and in fact to have continuance forever by the name, style and title of "The Minister, Trustees, Elders and Deacons of the German Lutheran Congregation worshipping at the church called Zion in Pikeland Township in the county of Chester." Provided always nevertheless, That the number of ministers may be increased and again diminished from time to time according to the circumstances or desire of the said corporation in which case the name, style and title of the said corporation shall be "The Ministers, Trustees, Elders and Deacons of the German Lutheran congregation worshipping at the church called Zion in Pikeland Township in the County of Chester."

[Section II.] (Section III, P. L.) And be it further enacted by the authority aforesaid, That the said corporation and their successors by the name, style and title aforesaid shall forever hereafter be persons able and capable in law as well to take receive and hold all and all manner of lands, tenements, rents, annuities, franchises and other hereditaments which at any time or times heretofore have been granted, bargained, sold, enfeoffed, released, devised or otherwise conveyed to the said congregation and church now under the pastoral care of the Reverend Ludwig Voigt or to any other person or persons to their use or in trust for them, and the same lands, tenements, rents, annuities, liberties, franchises and other hereditaments are hereby vested and established in the said corporation and their successors forever according to the original use and intent for which such devises, gifts and grants were respectfully made, and the said corporation and their successors are hereby declared to be seized and possessed of such estate and estates therein as in and by the respective grants, bargains, enfeoffments, releases, devises or other conveyances thereof is or are declared, limited or expressed. As also that the said corporation and their successors at all times hereafter shall be capable and able to purchase, have, receive, take, hold and enjoy in fee simple or of lesser estate or estates any lands, tenements, rents, annuities, liberties, franchises and other hereditaments by the gift, grant, bargain, sale, alienation, enfeoffment, release,

confirmation or devise of any person or persons, bodies politic
and corporate, capable and able to make the same and further
that the said congregation and their successors may take and
receive any sum or sums of money and any portion of goods
and chattels that have been or hereafter shall be given or bequeathed unto them or to the said church by any person or
persons, bodies politic or corporate able and capable to make
a bequest or gift thereof, such money, goods or chattels to be
laid out and disposed for the use and benefit of the aforesaid
congregation agreeably to the intention of the donors.

[Section III.] (Section IV, P. L.) And be it further enacted
by the authority aforesaid, That no misnomer of the said corporation and their successors shall defeat or annul any gift,
grant, devise or bequest to or from the said corporation, provided the intent of the party or parties shall sufficiently appear upon the face of the gift, grant, will or other writing
whereby any estate or interest was intended to pass to or
from the said corporation.

[Section IV.] (Section V, P. L.) And be it further enacted
by the authority aforesaid, That the rents, profits and interests
of the said real and personal estate of the said congregation
and corporation shall by the said corporation and their successors from time to time be applied and laid out for the maintenance and support of the Gospel Ministry in said congregation, for maintaining and repairing their church or churches
(in case any more should be added to that already built) places
of public worship, lots of land, burial grounds, parsonage
houses, school houses or other houses and buildings which now
do or hereafter shall belong to the said congregation and corporation and such pious and charitable uses as shall be thought
proper by the said corporation and their successors or a quorum
of them.

[Section V.] (Section VI, P. L.) And be it further enacted by
the authority aforesaid, That the said corporation and their
successors shall not by deed or otherwise grant, alien, convey
or otherwise dispose of any part or parcel of the estate, real
or personal in the said corporation vested or to be vested or
charge or encumber the same to any person or persons whatso-

ever except by and with the consent of a majority of the regular contributing members of the said congregation convened for that purpose.

[Section VI.] (Section VII, P. L.) And be it further enacted by the authority aforesaid, That the said corporation and their successors shall have full power and authority to make have and use one common seal with such device and inscription as they shall think fit and proper and the same to break, alter and renew at their pleasure.

[Section VII.] (Section VIII, P. L.) And be it further enacted by the authority aforesaid, That the said corporation and their successors by the name of "The Minister, Trustees, Elders and Deacons of the German Lutheran Congregation worshipping at the church called Zion in Pikeland township in the county of Chester" or in case there shall be more than one minister belonging to the said congregation by the name of "The Ministers, Trustees, Elders and Deacons of the German Lutheran Congregation worshipping at the church called Zion in Pikeland township in the county of Chester," shall be able and capable in law to sue and be sued, plead and be impleaded in any court or before any judge or justice in all and all manner of suits, complaints, pleas, matters and demands of whatsoever kind, nature and form they may be and all and every matter and thing therein to do in as full and effectual a manner as any other person, bodies politic or corporate within this commonwealth may or can do.

[Section VIII.] (Section IX, P. L.) And be it further enacted by the authority aforesaid, That the said corporation shall at all times hereafter consist of the minister or ministers of the said congregation duly chosen from time to time and of three trustees, six elders, and three deacons, and that the said trustees, elders and deacons shall be and continue until removed in the manner following that is to say, one third part in number of the trustees being the one first named, and one third part in number of the elders being the two first named and one third part in number of the deacons being the one first named, shall cease and discontinue and their appointment determine on Easter Monday which will be in the year of our Lord

one thousand seven hundred and ninety, at which time a new
election shall be had and held of an equal number in their
stead and places by a majority of votes of the members met
and qualified to vote and elect according to the purport, true
intent and meaning of the fundamental articles of the said
congregation and of this act, and on Easter Monday which will
be in the year of our Lord one thousand seven hundred and
ninety one the second third part in the number of the said remaining trustees elders and deacons shall in like manner cease
and discontinue and their appointment determine and a new
election be had and held in like manner of an equal number
in their places and stead, and on Easter Monday which will
be in the year of our Lord one thousand seven hundred and
ninety-two the last third part in number of the said remaining trustees, elders and deacons shall cease and discontinue and their appointment determine and a new election be
had and held of an equal number in their places and stead in
like manner, and that in the same manner and by the like
mode of rotation one third part in number of the trustees of
the elders and of the deacons shall cease and discontinue and
their appointment determine and a new election of the said
third part be had and held in manner aforesaid on the Easter
Monday in every year forever, so that no person or persons
shall continue to be trustee, elder or deacon any longer time
than three years without being re-elected, but that the members of the said congregation qualified to vote as aforesaid shall
and may be at liberty to re-elect one or more of the trustees,
elders and deacons whose time shall have expired on the day
of the said annual election whenever and so often they shall
think fit.

[Section IX.] (Section X, P. L.) And be it further enacted
by the authority aforesaid, That whenever a vacancy shall
happen by the death, refusal to serve or removal from office
of any one of the trustees, elders or deacons, the said corporation shall have power at their discretion to appoint the time
and place for electing others in their stead, whereof they shall
give public notice to the congregation on the preceding Sunday
and that at the time and place so appointed some fit person

or persons shall be elected in the place and stead of him or them so dying, refusing or being removed as aforesaid, and that the person or persons so elected to the office or in the place and stead of any trustee, elder or deacon, be, remain and continue in office so long as the person or persons in whose place or stead he or they shall have been so elected would or might have continued.

[Section X.] (Section XI, P. L.) And be it further enacted by the authority aforesaid, That no person or persons shall be entitled to elect or be elected to office who is not a regular member of the said congregation and otherwise qualified thereto agreeably to the fundamental articles of said congregation excepting the minister or ministers who may from time to time be chosen or elected by a majority of the trustees, elders, deacons and regular members of the said congregation to officiate in the said congregation.

[Section XI.] (Section XII, P. L.) And be it further enacted by the authority aforesaid, That whenever any circumstances or concurrence of circumstances shall happen to prevent the holding of an election at the periods in this act before mentioned for trustees, elders and deacons in stead and place of those whose appointment shall have ceased and determined, an election shall be held as soon as conveniently can be done in manner before directed and that the remaining members of the said corporation have power to call a meeting of the electors of the said congregation for such purposes.

[Section XII.] (Section XIII, P. L.) And be it further enacted by the authority aforesaid, That such and so many of the fundamental articles tending to the orderly and good government of the said church which now are in force and duly entered and registered in their church books as are not altered and repealed by this act and are not repugnant to the laws of this commonwealth shall be, remain and continue forever valid and effectual unless the same be altered by the consent of a majority of the members of the said congregation qualified to vote at elections according to the purport and meaning of said fundamental articles and this act.

[Section XIII.] (Section XIV, P. L.) And be it further en-

acted by the authority aforesaid, That the members of the
aforesaid corporation shall and may from time to time as
often as occasion may require elect by vote or ballot from
among their own number a president and vice-president agreeably to the fundamental articles aforesaid, as they now are
or shall be made pursuant to the foregoing section; that they
may elect by vote or ballot a treasurer and secretary and
may remove them at pleasure, that the president or vice-president for the time being or any three members of the said corporation shall be empowered to call a meeting of the corporation when and so often as he or they shall find it to be necessary or shall be requested so to do by any six regular members
of the said congregation, that the said corporation and their
successors or a majority of seven in number of them met and
convened upon due notice given either in the church on the
preceding Sunday after divine service and before the congregation is dismissed or in any other convenient manner
(which seven shall be a quorum) shall be authorized and empowered to make by-laws and ordinances and do everything
needful for the support and government of the said congregation. Provided always, That the said by-laws, rules and ordinances or any of them be not repugnant to the laws of this commonwealth and be duly published in the said church on the succeeding Sunday after they have been made and not dissented
to by a majority of the regular contributing members of the
said congregation within one week after such publication and
also that all their laws and proceedings be fairly and regularly
entered in the books of records of the said congregation.

[Section XIV.] (Section XV. P. L.) And be it further enacted
by the authority aforesaid, That the said congregation shall
and may be empowered at any time or times hereafter to build
one or more church or churches or places of public worship
in addition to the one already built and that the clear yearly
value of messuages, houses, lands, tenements, rents, annuities
and other hereditaments and real estate of the said corporation shall and may be of any amount not exceeding the sum
of five hundred pounds gold or silver money at the present
current value thereof in the commonwealth of Pennsylvania for

each and every of the said churches or places of public worship,
the said yearly value or amount to be taken exclusive of the
moneys arising from the letting of the pews of the said church
or churches or for opening the ground for burials in the church
yards belonging to them and also of the voluntary contributions of the members for the support of their minister or ministers duly officiating in the said congregation, which yearly
income of the said real estate ascertained and limited as aforesaid shall be disposed of by the said corporation for the purposes hereinbefore described and directed.

Passed September 30, 1789.   Recorded L. B. No. 4, p. 28.

CHAPTER MCDLXV.

AN ACT TO ASCERTAIN THE SECURITY TO BE GIVEN BY THE TREASURER OF THE STATE FOR THE TIME BEING.

(Section I, P. L.) Whereas it is expedient from the large
sums of money intrusted to the treasurer of the state that
adequate security should be given for the faithful performance of the duties of his office.

[Section I.] (Section II, P. L.) Be it therefore enacted and
it is hereby enacted by the Representatives of the Freemen of
the Commonwealth of Pennsylvania in General Assembly met
and by the authority of the same, That the treasurer of the
state already appointed and every treasurer of the state hereafter to be appointed before he shall enter upon the duties of
his office shall become bound in an obligation with two or
more sufficient sureties to be approved by the speaker of the
house of general assembly for the time being in the sum of
thirty thousand pounds lawful money of Pennsylvania conditioned for the true and faithful performance of the trusts
and duties enjoined and required by law to be performed by
such treasurer, and that all such obligations shall be taken in
the name of the commonwealth and the execution thereof being
the first duly proved shall be entered of record in the office of

the master of the rolls for this state, and copies of such obligations being duly authenticated under the seal of the said office shall be admitted as legal evidence in any suit or suits that may or shall be brought against such treasurer or his sureties.

[Section II.] (Section III, P. L.) And be it further enacted by the authority aforesaid, That an act of general assembly passed the eighteenth day of February one thousand seven hundred and sixty-nine entitled, "An act for ascertaining the securities to be given by the provincial treasurer for the time being for the faithful performance of his trust,"[1] shall be and it is hereby repealed.

Passed November 19, 1789.   Recorded L. B. No. 4, p. 38.
1 Chapter 586.

CHAPTER MCDLXVI.

AN ACT FOR GRANTING PRESENT RELIEF TO THE WOUNDED AND DISABLED SOLDIERS WHO HAVE RECEIVED PENSIONS FROM THIS STATE.

(Section I, P. L.) Whereas in pursuance of the several recommendations of the congress of the United States pensions have been granted to the wounded and disabled soldiers of the late continental army resident in this state:

And whereas by an act of the senate and house of representatives of the United States in congress assembled passed on the twenty-ninth day of September one thousand seven hundred and eighty-nine it is enacted that the military pensions which have been granted and paid by the states respectively in pursuance of the acts of the United States in congress assembled to the invalids who were wounded and disabled during the late war shall be continued and paid by the United States from the fourth day of March last for the space of one year under such regulations as the president of the United States may direct; and it appears that by the directions of the president of the United States such pensions are to be paid at the treasury of the United States on the fifth day of March one thousand seven hundred and ninety:

And whereas there are a considerable number of such wounded and disabled pensioners who, without any present means of support and incapable of procuring subsistence by their labor, are in danger of perishing for want unless some speedy relief should be extended to them:

[Section I.] (Section II. P. L.) Be it therefore enacted and it is hereby enacted by the Representatives of the Freemen of the Commonwealth of Pennsylvania in General Assembly met and by the authority of the same, That the president or vice-president and supreme executive council of this state shall be and they are hereby authorized and requested to borrow on behalf of this state for the space of four months the sum of nine hundred pounds or so much thereof as shall be necessary for the immediate relief of the said wounded and disabled soldiers and to cause the same or so much thereof as may be necessary to be distributed amongst them in monthly payments proportioned to the amount of their respective pensions.

[Section II.] (Section III, P. L.) And be it further enacted by the authority aforesaid, That the president or vice-president and supreme executive council be and they are hereby requested to take effectual measures for insuring the repayment of the moneys so borrowed on or before the fifth day of March next by receiving or causing to be received from such soldiers at the time of distributing such proportionate parts of their respective pensions, regular and sufficient transfers and assignments of an equal amount of their respective pensions payable at the treasury of the United States on the said fifth day of March next, but in case repayment of such advances shall not be made by the United States on or before the fifth day of March next, the president or vice-president and supreme executive council shall be and they are hereby authorized and required to draw orders on the treasurer of this state, in favor of the person or persons lending such moneys for the said sum of money or such part thereof as shall be so lent to this state and shall not be reimbursed by the United States on or before the fifth day of March next, which orders shall be payable out of the fund specially appropriated for claims and improvements by virtue of the act entitled, "An act to appropriate divers

funds accruing and growing due to this Commonwealth towards the payment of the expenses of government and to provide a fund for other purposes,"[1] passed the twenty-sixth day
of March one thousand seven hundred and eighty-nine.

[Section III.] Provided, That the payment of such orders
shall not interfere with the appropriation of part of the fund
as directed by an act entitled "An act to appropriate the sum
of five thousand pounds annually for the purposes therein
mentioned."[2]

Passed November 20, 1789. Recorded L. B. No. 4, p. 39.
[1] Chapter 1404.
[2] Passed September 28, 1789, Chapter 1446.

CHAPTER MCDLXVII.

AN ACT TO REPEAL SO MUCH OF AN ACT OR ACTS OF THE GENERAL
ASSEMBLY OF THIS STATE AS AUTHORIZES AND DIRECTS THE RE-
CEIVING OF CERTIFICATES OF THE UNITED STATES IN PAYMENT OF
LANDS PURCHASED OR TO BE PURCHASED OF THIS STATE.

(Section I, P. L.) Whereas by virtue of sundry acts of the
general assembly of this state certificates granted by the
United States are receivable in payment for lands belonging
[to] and sold by this state:

And whereas this state being indebted to its own citizens
and others it is reasonable and expedient that the property
belonging to it should be applied in satisfaction of such debts
and it cannot be douted that the wisdom and justice of the
congress of the United States will, from the ample funds now
in their power, make a proper provision for the debts due from
the United States:

[Section I.] (Section II, P. L.) Be it therefore enacted and
it is hereby enacted by the Representatives of the Freemen of
the Commonwealth of Pennsylvania in General Assembly met
and by the authority of the same, That so much of any act or
acts of the general assembly of this state as authorizes or di-

rects the receiving of any certificates issued or granted by the
United States in payment of any lands purchased or to be purchased of this commonwealth shall be and is hereby repealed.

Passed November 20, 1789. Recorded L. B. No. 4, p. 40.

CHAPTER MCDLXVIII.

AN ACT TO LIMIT THE TIME OF EXHIBITING CLAIMS AGAINST THE
STATE FOR SUPPLIES FURNISHED OR SERVICES RENDERED DURING
THE LATE WAR.

(Section I, P. L.) For the purpose of establishing a due limitation of the time of exhibiting claims against the state for
supplies furnished or services rendered during the late war.

[Section I.] (Section II, P. L.) Be it enacted and it is hereby
enacted by the Representatives of the Freemen of the Commonwealth of Pennsylvania in General Assembly met and by
the authority of the same, That from and after the first day
of January which will be in the year of our Lord one thousand
seven hundred and ninety-one, no claims or demands not
already liquidated and adjusted by the proper officers of this
state for articles or suplies of any kind furnished by individuals
for the use of this state or for services of any kind rendered to
this state during the late war between the United States and
the King of Great Britain shall be received or admitted nor
shall this state be held or deemed liable to satisfy any such
claim not preferred before the said first day of January which
will be in the year of our Lord one thousand seven hundred and
ninety-one.

And in order that sufficient notice may be given to all persons concerned:

[Section II.] (Section III, P. L.) Be it further enacted by
the authority aforesaid, That the prothonotaries of the respective county courts of common pleas for the several counties
of this state shall cause one or more printed copies of this act
to be affixed to the door of the respective court houses of such

counties and shall also cause this act to be publicly read in open
court at least once in each term for the four terms next ensuing
the enacting hereof.

Passed November 21, 1789. Recorded L. B. No. 4, p. 40.

CHAPTER MCDLXIX.

AN ACT TO DEFRAY THE EXPENSES OF HOLDING THE STATE CON-
VENTION.

(Section I, P. L.) Whereas it is necessary to determine the
allowance to be made to the members of the state convention
which is to be held for the purpose of reviewing and if they see
occasion altering and amending the constitution of this state
and also to provide for the same together with the incidental
expenses of the said convention:

[Section I.] (Section II, P. L.) Be it therefore enacted and
it is hereby enacted by the Representatives of the Freemen of
the Commonwealth of Pennsylvania in General Assembly met
and by the authority of the same, That the same allowances
shall be made of wages and mileage to attending members of
the state convention as is now made to the members of the
General Assembly and that the same together with the incidental expenses of the convention be paid by warrant or
warrants on the state treasurer, drawn by the president or
chairman of the said convention and countersigned by the
comptroller and register general.

Passed November 25, 1789. Recorded L. B. No. 4, p. 41.

CHAPTER MCDLXX.

AN ACT TO LIMIT THE TIME FOR EXCHANGING AND REDEEMING CERTAIN BILLS OF CREDIT AND CERTIFICATES THEREIN MENTIONED.

(Section I, P. L.) Whereas the legislature did by sundry votes or resolutions in the years one thousand seven hundred and seventy-five and one thousand seven hundred and seventy-six and by an act of general assembly passed on the twentieth day of March in the year of our Lord one thousand seven hundred and seventy-seven entitled, "An act for emitting the sum of two hundred thousand pounds in bills of credit for the defence of this state and providing a fund for sinking the same by a tax on the estates real and personal and on all taxables within the same,"[1] emit and issue certain bills of credit amounting in the whole to the sum of four hundred thousand pounds:

And whereas by one other act of general assembly passed on the seventh day of April in the year of our Lord one thousand seven hundred and eighty-one entitled, "An act for emitting the sum of five hundred thousand pounds in bills of credit for the support of the army and for establishing a fund for the redemption of the same and for other purposes therein mentioned,"[2] all the said bills of credit not emitted and issued by and in pursuance of the said last recited act:

And whereas a reasonable and sufficient time hath been afforded and allowed for making the exchange directed as aforesaid and it is now proper and expedient that some limitation of the period for making thereof should be ascertained and fixed:

Therefore:

[Section I.] (Section II, P. L.) Be it enacted and it is hereby enacted by the Representatives of the Freemen of the Commonwealth of Pennsylvania in General Assembly met and by the

[1] Chapter 752.
[2] Chapter 939.

authority of the same, That all the said bills of credit emitted
and issued in pursuance of any vote or resolution of the general
assembly of Pennsylvania in the years one thousand seven hundred and seventy-five and one thousand seven hundred and seventy-six or in pursuance of the said recited act passed on the
twentieth day of March one thousand seven hundred and seventy-seven, which shall not be brought in and exchanged as
aforesaid on or before the first day of January one thousand
seven hundred and ninety-one shall not afterwards be exchanged but the same shall be and are hereby declared to be from
thenceforth irredeemable, anything contained in the said votes
or resolutions or in the said act by which the said bills of credit
were made current or in any other act whatsoever to the contrary thereof in anywise notwithstanding.

And whereas by virtue of an act of general assembly passed
on the first day of June in the year of our Lord one thousand
seven hundred and eighty entitled, "An act for procuring an
immediate supply of provisions for the federal army in its
present exigency,"[1] the supreme executive council did appoint
and authorize certain commissioners to purchase horses, provisions and other articles for the use of the army of the United
States in consideration whereof certificates bearing interest
at six per centum were given by the said commisisoners unto
the persons respectively from whom the same were purchased
and which said certificates were also exchanged for the bills
of credit issued and emitted by and in pursuance of the above
recited act of general assembly passed on the seventh day of
April in the year of our Lord one thousand seven hundred and
eighty-one.

And whereas there still remains a great number of the said
certificates unexchanged notwithstanding a reasonable and
sufficient time hath been afforded and allowed for exchanging
thereof and it is proper and expedient that some limitation
of the period for so doing should be ascertained and fixed:

Therefore:

[Section II.] (Section III, P. L.) Be it further enacted by

---

[1] Chapter 913.

27—XIII

the authority aforesaid, That all the said certificates which
shall not be brought in and exchanged as aforesaid on or before the first day of January one thousand seven hundred and
ninety-one shall not afterwards be exchanged but the same
shall be and the same are hereby declared to be from henceforth irredeemable anything in the said recited act by virtue
whereof the said commissioners were appointed or in any
other act whatsoever to the contrary thereof in any wise notwithstanding.

Passed December 4, 1789. Recorded L. B. No. 4, p. 41.

CHAPTER MCDLXXI.

AN ACT TO CONTINUE AN ACT ENTITLED "AN ACT FOR OPENING AND
AMENDING THE PUBLIC ROADS AND HIGHWAYS WITHIN THIS PRO-
VINCE." [1]

(Section I, P. L.) Whereas the act of general assembly entitled "An act to continue the act of general assembly entitled
'An act for opening and better amending and keeping in
repair the public roads and highways within this province,'"[2]
enacted on the twenty-ninth day of September which was in the
year of our Lord one thousand seven hundred and eighty-seven
will soon expire by its own limitation and it is proper that the
same should be continued:

[Section I.] (Section II, P. L.) Be it enacted and it is hereby
enacted by the Representatives of the Freemen of the Commonwealth of Pennsylvania in General Assembly met and by
the authority of the same, That the act entitled "An act for
opening and better amending and keeping in repair the public
roads and highways within this province," and everything in
the same act contained (the clause of limitation thereof only
excepted) shall be and the same hereby is continued for and
during the term of seven years from and after the enacting
hereof and from thence until the end of the next session of the
general assembly and no longer.

Passed December 4, 1789. Recorded L. B. No. 4, p. 43.
[1] Passed March 21, 1772, Chapter 653.
[2] Chapter 1320.

CHAPTER MCDLXXII.

AN ACT TO PROVIDE FOR THE CUSTODY OF PRISONERS COMMITTED UNDER THE AUTHORITY OF THE UNITED STATES.

(Section I, P. L.) Whereas by a resolution of the senate and house of representatives of the United States in congress assembled it hath been recommended to the legislatures of the several states to pass laws making it expressly the duty of the keepers of their gaols to receive and safe keep therein all prisoners committed under the authority of the United States until they shall be discharged by the due course of the laws thereof under the like penalties as in the case of prisoners committed under the authority of such states respectively, the United States to pay for the use and keeping of such gaols at the rate of fifty cents per month for each prisoner that shall under their authority be committed thereto during the time such prisoners shall be therein confined and also to support such of said prisoners as shall be committed for offences:

And whereas it is just and reasonable to aid the United States herein on the terms aforesaid until other provision shall be made by law in the premises.

[Section I.] (Section II, P. L.) Be it therefore enacted and it is hereby enacted by the Representatives of the Freemen of the Commonwealth of Pennsylvania in General Assembly met and by the authority of the same, That all sheriffs, gaolers, prison-keepers and their and every of their deputies within this commonwealth to whom any person or persons shall be sent or committed by virtue of legal process issued by or under the authority of the United States shall be and they are hereby enjoined and required to receive such prisoners into custody and to keep the same safely until they shall be discharged by due course of law and that all such sheriffs, gaolers and prison-keepers and their deputies offending in the premises shall be liable to the same pains and penalties and the parties aggrieved shall be entitled to the same remedies against them or any

of them as if such prisoners had been committed to their custody by virtue of legal process issued under the authority of
this state.

[Section II.] (Section III, P. L.) Be it further enacted by
the authority aforesaid, That a calendar of such prisoners shall
on the first day of January in every year be made out by the
respective gaolers and prison-keepers in each county upon
oath or affirmation to be administered by the president of the
court of common pleas of the respective county specifying
particularly the names of such prisoners the time of their commitment and discharge and whether upon civil or criminal
process together with the expense of subsisting such of the said
prisoners as shall have been committed for offences, which
calendar shall be transmitted to the president and supreme executive council of this state to the end that order may be taken
for the payment of the allowances and expenses on the part
of the United States in and by the said resolution assumed.

Passed December 5, 1789.   Recorded L. B. No. 4, p. 43.

CHAPTER MCDLXXIII.

AN ACT TO SUSPEND FOR THE TIME THEREIN MENTIONED PART OF
AN ACT ENTITLED "AN ACT FOR FURNISHING THE QUOTA OF THIS
STATE TOWARDS PAYING THE ANNUAL INTEREST OF THE DEBTS
OF THE UNITED STATES AND FOR FUNDING AND PAYING THE
INTEREST OF THE PUBLIC DEBTS OF THIS STATE." [1]

(Section I, P. L.) Whereas in order to provide a sufficient
fund for the immediate relief of the creditors of the United
States of certain descriptions the sum of seventy-six thousand
nine hundred and forty-five pounds seventeen shillings and six
pence was by an act entitled, "An act for furnishing the quota
of this state towards paying the annual interest of the debts
of the United States and for funding and paying the interest of
the public debts of this state," enacted the sixteenth day of
March one thousand seven hundred and eighty-five directed to

[1] Passed March 16, 1785, Chapter 1137.

be annually levied and raised upon the persons and property
of the inhabitants of this state:

And whereas by an act entitled "An act to repeal so much
of any act or acts of assembly of this state as directs the payment of the new loan debt or the interest thereof beyond the
first day of April next and for other purposes therein mentioned,"[1] enacted the twenty-seventh day of March one thousand seven hundred and eighty-nine it was enacted that the
interest upon the certificates issued by the comptroller-general
of this state in pursuance of certain acts in the last mentioned
act recited and commonly called new loan certificates should
be paid up so as to complete the payment of interest to four
years:

And whereas it appears to this house that the sum of three
hundred and eleven thousand pounds and upwards is in arrear
and unpaid on the account of the said annual tax and of other
general taxes laid by the authority of this state since the year
one thousand seven hundred and eighty and it is not only unjust to continue to impose the said tax annually upon those
who have paid their respective contributions without collecting the arrearages from those who are deficient but contrary
to the interests of the state to omit collecting debts which the
length of time renders it more difficult to recover:

And whereas this house have it in contemplation to provide
adequate measures for compelling the payment of such arrearages in a manner the least burdensome to the persons deficient
whereby the state will be the better enabled to pay the proportion of interest on the said certificates in and by the act
last mentioned assumed and equal justice in this respect will
be administered to the people and it is therefore necessary to
suspend for one year so much of the act hereinbefore mentioned
as directs an assessment to be made in each county and in the
city of Philadelphia on the first Tuesday of January annually.

[Section I.] (Section II, P. L.) Be it enacted and it is hereby
enacted by the Representatives of the Freemen of the Commonwealth of Pennsylvania in General Assembly met and by
the authority of the same, That so much of the act entitled,

[1] Chapter 1415.

"An act for furnishing the quota of this state towards paying
the annual interest of the debts of the United States and for
funding and paying the interest of the public debts of this
state,"³ enacted the sixteenth day of March one thousand seven
hundred and eighty-five as requires the commissioners of the
city and county of Philadelphia and of the other counties of this
state respectively to issue their warrants as therein is directed
and the assessors of or in the county of Philadelphia and of each
respective county to make return of property as is therein
directed or as requires an assessment or apportionment of the
said tax to be made for the year ensuing in the city or any of
the counties aforesaid shall be and is hereby suspended for one
year from and after the first day of January next and no longer.

Passed December 8, 1789. Recorded L. D. No. 4, p. 44.

CHAPTER MCDLXXIV

AN ACT TO REPEAL SO MUCH OF AN ACT ENTITLED " AN ACT TO PRO·
VIDE FOR A CONTINUATION OF THE SALARIES OF THE OFFICERS
OF THE LAND OFFICE AND TO ASCERTAIN AND PROVIDE THE SAL·
ARY FOR THE JUDGE OF THE ADMIRALTY AND FOR OTHER PUR·
POSES THEREIN MENTIONED,"¹ AS RELATES TO THE SALARY OF
THE JUDGE OF THE ADMIRALTY.

(Section 1, P. L.) The district court of the district of Penn·
sylvania erected under the authority of the United States
having exclusive jurisdiction of admiralty causes within this
state it is inexpedient to continue a salary after the duties of
the office have ceased:

Therefore:

[Section I.] (Section II, P. L.) Be it enacted and it is here·
by enacted by the Representatives of the Freemen of the Com·
monwealth of Pennsylvania in General Assembly met and by
the authority of the same. That so much of an act of assembly

---

³See Ante.
¹ Passed September 29, 1787, Chapter 1322.

entitled, "An act to provide for a continuation of the salaries of the officers of the land office and to ascertain and provide the salary for the judge of the admiralty and for other purposes therein mentioned," passed the twenty-ninth day of September one thousand seven hundred and eighty-seven as relates to the salary of the judge of the admiralty of this state shall be and is hereby repealed.

Passed December 7, 1789. Recorded L. D. No. 4, p. 45.

CHAPTER MCDLXXV.

AN ACT TO PROVIDE FOR THE SALARIES OF OFFICERS OF THE LAND OFFICE.

(Section I, P. L.) Whereas so much of the provisions contained in the act entitled "An act to provide for a continuation of the salaries of the officers of the land-office and to ascertain and provide the salary for the judge of the admiralty and for other purposes therein mentioned," enacted on the twenty-ninth day of September one thousand seven hundred and eighty-seven as related to the salaries of the officers of the land office expired by the limitation in the said act contained on the first day of May last and it is expedient that proper salaries should be allowed them:

[Section I.] (Section II, P. L.) Be it therefore enacted and it is hereby enacted by the Representatives of the Freemen of the Commonwealth of Pennsylvania in General Assembly met and by the authority of the same, That the secretary of the land office shall be allowed the yearly sum of five hundred pounds lawful money of Pennsylvania, the surveyor general the yearly sum of five hundred pounds lawful money of Pennsylvania and the receiver general the yearly sum of five hundred pounds lawful money of Pennsylvania. And that each of the said officers shall also be allowed a yearly sum not exceeding two hundred and fifty pounds lawful money of Penn-

sylvania for his clerk or clerks besides a reasonable allowance
for stationery consumed in his respective office, all which salaries and allowances shall commence from and after the enacting hereof.

[Section II.] (Section III, P. L.) And be it further enacted
by the authority aforesaid, That the said salaries and allowances shall be paid to each of the said officers quarterly upon
orders to be drawn by the president or vice president in council
on the treasurer of the state out of the fees of the said offices
which shall have been paid into the treasury.

Passed December 8, 1789.   Recorded L. B. No. 4, p. 46.   See the
Act of Assembly passed February 19, 1790, Chapter 1480.

CHAPTER MCDLXXVI.

AN ACT TO INCORPORATE A SOCIETY BY THE NAME OF "THE PENN-
SYLVANIA SOCIETY FOR PROMOTING THE ABOLITION OF SLAVERY
AND FOR THE RELIEF OF FREE NEGROES UNLAWFULLY HELD
IN BONDAGE AND FOR IMPROVING THE CONDITION OF THE AFRI-
CAN RACE."

(Section I, P. L.) Whereas a voluntary society has for some
years subsisted [in this state] by the name and title of "The
Pennsylvania Society for promoting the abolition of slavery and
the relief of free negroes unlawfully held in bondage," which
has evidently co-operated with the views of the legislature expressed in the act of the general assembly of the commonwealth passed the first day of March in the year of our Lord
one thousand seven hundred and eighty entitled, "An act for
the gradual abolition of slavery,"[1] and a supplement thereto
passed the twenty-ninth day of March in the year of our Lord
one thousand seven hundred and eighty-eight entitled, "An
act to explain and amend an act entitled an act for the gradual
abolition of slavery:"[2]

[1] Chapter 881.
[2] Chapter 1345.

And whereas the said society have lately extended their plan so far as to comprehend within their intentions the improving the condition as well of those negroes who now are or hereafter shall become free by the operation of said acts or otherwise and their posterity, and have by their petition to this house prayed to be created and erected into a body politic and corporate for the purpose of increasing their ability to be useful in the several matters aforesaid:

[Section I.] (Section II, P. L.) Be it therefore enacted and it is hereby enacted by the Representatives of the Freemen of the Commonwealth of Pennsylvania in General Assembly met and by the authority of the same. That the present members of the said society, to wit, Dr. Benjamin Franklin, James Pemberton, Jonathan Penrose, Thomas Harrison, James Starr, William Lippincott, John Thomas, Benjamin Horner, Samuel Richards, John Evans, John Todd, James Whiteall, Edward Brooks, Thomas Armat, John Warner, Samuel Davis, Thomas Bartow, Robert Evans, Robert Wood, Seymour Hart, Richard Humphreys, Robert Towers, Joseph Moore, Joseph Russell, William Zane, Israel Whelen, Samuel Baker, Richard Price, Charles Jervis, Israel Hallowell, Clement Biddle, Amos Wickersham, Pattison Hartshorn, Nathan Sellers, David Sellers, Isaac Parrish, Zacariah Jess, Dr. Benjamin Rush, John Field, Richard Jones, William Poyntell, Andrew Carson, Philip Price, John Hunt, Junior, Norris Jones, John Norton, Thomas Penrose, Thomas Poultney, Thomas Eddy, Isaac Weaver, Junior, Caleb Attmore, Joseph Budd, Abraham Sharpless, Isaac Massey, James Lewis, Thomas Shoemaker, Robert Morris, Jeremiah Paul, Thomas Savery, Francis Bailey, Thomas Shields, George Eddy, John Morrison, John Morris, Joseph Clark, Zachariah Poulson, Junior, Thomas Parker, William Graham, Thomas Rodgers, John Poultney, Isaac Bonsall, Joseph Cruckshank, John Jacobs, Nathan Boys, William Ashby, Jacob Trasel, William Jackson, Charles Crawford, Ellis Yarnall, John Olden, Touch Coxe, Jonathan Pugh, Reece John, Jacob Shoemaker, Junior, William McIlhenny, Caleb Lownes, John Letchworth, William West, Isaac Peason, Burton Wallace, Francis John-

ston, Joseph Sharpless, Thomas Wistar, Joseph Lownes, Dr.
Benjamin Say, Joseph Anthony, Caspar W. Haines, Joseph
Bacon, George Rutter, David Lownes, Bartholomew Wistar,
George Fox, William T. Franklin, William Rawle, James
Trenchard, Conrad Hanse, Samuel Coates, Richard Wells,
Sharp Delaney, Johnathan Willis, Junior, Joseph Gibbons,
Samuel Pancoast, Junior, Kearney Wharton, Dr. James Hutchinson, Charles Williams, John Claypole, John Dowers, Hilary
Baker, George Latimer, Andrew Geyer, James Read, Peter
Woglom, John Haghn, John Todd, Junior, Philip Benezet,
Joseph James, Dr. Caspar Wistar, Junior, Dr. Samuel P. Griffiths, Thomas Fitzgerald, Stephen Maxfield, Philip Price, Junior, Israel Pleasants, Mordicai Churchman, Thomas Annesly,
Benjamin W. Morris, John McCree, George Richie, James
Olden, John Huntchinson, George Wilson, Jacob Parke,
Thomas Lawrence, Dr. John Foulke, Jesse Waterman, James
Trimble, Dr. William Rogers, Dr. Nicholas Collin, Samuel M.
Fox, Benjamin Shoemaker, Joseph Parker Norris, George
Roberts, Jeremiah Parker, Abraham Liddon, John Bleakley,
Joseph Inskeep, Robert Wuln, Richard Parker, John Starr,
Nathan Allen Smith, Thomas Norton, Robert Taggart, Samuel
Emlen, Junior, William Kidd, Dr. John Andrews, Zebulon
Potts, Samuel Kingsley, Nathan Field, Daniel Trotter, Benjamin Taylor, James Smith, Junior, Caleb Carmalt, Robert
Roberts, William Chancellor, Thomas Forrest, Jonathan
Jones, Ebenezer Breed, George Ashton, Thomas Proctor,
George Davis, John Smilie, Thomas Palmer, Anthony Felix
Wuibert, Matthew Hale Richard Peters, Joseph Thomas,
Thomas Ross, Isaac Buckbee, Joshua Gilpin, Dr. Amos Gregg,
Gerard Vogels, Richard Riley, Samuel Claphamson, Zacchens
Collins, Henry Hale Graham, John Ely, Richard H. Morris,
John Stapler, Junior, Daniel May, Andrew Johnston, S. Barnett, William Welsh, Isaiah Ham, Charles Lukins, James
Smith, S. Morris, Ambrose Updegraff, Peter Monderf, Thomas
Fisher, Robert Kummersly, John Smith, William Webb, John
Roberts, John Kittere, William Brisband, William Gibbons,
Samuel Updegraff, Caleb Johnston, Robert Veree, Dr. John
Chapman, Alexander Anderson, Samuel Redwood, Rees Cad-

wallader, Samuel Jackson, Dr. John Luther, Dr. John Story, Benjamin Wright and Eli Lewis, all of the state of Pennsylvania,

Joseph Shotwell, Junior, David Cooper, Samuel Allison, Thomas Redman, Thomas Stokes, John Wistar, Thomas Clemens, Joseph Sloan, Ebenezer Howell, Clement Hall, James Jess, Benjamin Wright, Richard Waln, Stacy Biddle, Hezekiah Hughes, Thomas Githen, all of the state of New Jersey,

The Honorable John Jay, and Matthew Clarkson of the state of New York,

John Boggs, Caleb Kirk and Warner Mifflin of the state of Delaware,

Zebulon Hollingsworth, John Richardson, Woolman Hickson, John Feigle, Joseph Wilkinson and John Needles of the state of Maryland.

Samuel Hopkins, Benjamin Foster, Enos Hitchcock, Benjamin West, Moses Brown, William Patton, Samuel Vinson, Thomas Robinson and Jonathan Easton of the state of Rhode Island,

John Saunders, George Tegal and George Corbyn of the state of Virginia,

Noah Webster, Thomas Gain and Benjamin West of the state of Massachusetts,

Capel Loft, David Barclay, Granville Sharpe, Dr. Richard Price, James Philips, Thomas Day, Dr. Thomas Clarson, The Right Honorable William Pitt, Dr. John Okely Lettsom, William Dilwyn, Robert Robeson, and William Hollick of the Kingdom of Great Britain,

And Le Abbe Raynal, Le Marquis de La Fayette, I. P. Brissot de Warville, Charton de La Terrierre and Francis Clery Du Pont of the Kingdom of France and such other person and persons as shall be hereafter elected and chosen in the manner hereinafter mentioned and their successors be and they are hereby declared to be one body politic and corporate in deed and in law by the name and style and title of "The Pennsylvania Society for promoting the abolition of slavery and for the relief of free negroes unlawfully held in bondage and for the improving the condition of the African race," and by the same name shall have perpetual succession and shall be able to sue and be sued, implead and be answered unto in all courts of law and equity, and to make, have and use one common seal to give authenticity to their acts, deeds, records and proceedings and the same at their pleasure to break, alter, change and make anew and to purchase, take and hold by gift, grant, demise, bargain and sale, will and demise, bequest, testament, legacy or by any other mode of conveyance any lands, tenements, goods, chattels, or estate, real, personal or mixed, or choses in action, not exceeding at any one time the yearly value of fifteen hundred pounds lawful money of Pennsylvania in the whole, and the same to give, grant, bargain, sell, demise, convey and assure to others for the whole or any lesser estate that they have in the same in such manner and form as the said society at their future meetings hereinafter described shall order and direct and to apply the rents, issues and profits, income and interest of such estate and the moneys arising from the sale of any parts thereof to the uses, ends, intents and purposes of their institution according to the rules, orders, regulations and constitutions of the said society now in force or which according to the provisions hereinafter made shall from time to time be declared and ordained touching and concerning the same as fully and effectually as any natural person or body politic and corporate within this state by the constitution and laws of this commonwealth can do and perform the like things.

[Section II.] (Section III, P. L.) And be it further enacted by the authority aforesaid, That the officers of the said society shall consist of one president, two vice-presidents, two secretaries, one treasurer who shall also be the keeper of the common seal and so many councillors as the said society shall from time to time think proper from time to time to appoint and elect all of whom shall be chosen annually by ballot of a majority of votes of the whole number of members who shall be present at the quarterly meeting hereinafter mentioned, which shall be held on the first second day of the week, called Monday in

the first month called January in every year after the passing
of this act, or at such other time and at such place as the said
society shall by their rules and orders direct and appoint and
of such committees for carrying into execution the designs of
the said institution as the said society heretofore have appointed and hereafter at any of their quarterly or special
meetings shall agree to and appoint in the manner and form
to be hereafter agreed on.

[Section III.] (Section IV, P. L.) And be it further enacted
by the authority aforesaid, That the said society shall
and may hold four quarterly meetings in every year at such
place and hour of the day as they shall agree unto on every
the first second day of the week called Monday in every the
first, fourth, seventh and tenth months, called January, April,
July and October in every year forever hereafter and may adjourn the said meeting from time to time, and shall and may
hold such other special meetings as the society by their rules
and orders shall direct and appoint and shall hold such other
meetings as the president of the said society shall think necessary to call or one of the vice-presidents of the said society at
the request of any six members thereof shall call, of which
special meetings notice shall be given in two of the public
newspapers printed in the city of Philadelphia at least two
days before the time of meeting, at any of which quarterly or
special meetings or adjournements thereof it shall and may
be lawful for the said society or so many of them as shall meet
by a majority of voices to agree to, ordain and establish such
by-laws, rules, orders and regulations as they shall judge necessary for the well ordering and governing the said society and
for the well managing the affairs thereof and to appoint such
and so many committees consisting of such number of their
members as they shall think necessary to superintend the different departments of duties already undertaken by the society
heretofore subsisting or hereafter to be undertaken by the
society hereby established and to receive the reports of such
committees and take such order thereon as to them shall seem
proper, and to fix and ascertain the terms and conditions upon

which new members shall be admitted into the said society upon which former members may be removed and to define and ascertain the duties of the several officers and committees of the said society and to enforce the same by such reasonable fines and forfeitures to be imposed on delinquents as they shall think proper and for want of obedience in any of the members, committees or officers of the said society to remove and displace them and others to appoint and generally to agree to, ordain and establish such by-laws, rules, orders and regulations for the well governing the said society, for perpetuating a succession of its officers and performing the duties they have undertaken or shall undertake as the said society at any of their said quarterly meetings, or special meetings or adjournments thereof shall by a majority of voices determine to be right and proper. Provided always nevertheless, That no real or personal estate above the value of sixty dollars shall be disposed of or the right and estate of the society therein shall be lessened and altered for the less nor any by-law, rule, order or regulation of the said society enacted, repealed or altered nor any sum of money appropriated to any new use not before agreed upon by any of the said meetings or committees to be appointed unless the president or one of the vice-presidents and at least twenty members shall be present at such meeting and a majority of those present shall agree to the same. And provided also, That all and every the by-laws, rules, orders and regulations already enacted and made or hereafter to be enacted and made by the said society be reasonable in themselves and not contradictory to the constitution and laws of this commonwealth.

[Section IV.] (Section V, P. L.) And be it further enacted by the authority aforesaid, That the constitution of the Pennsylvania Society for promoting the Abolition of Slavery and for the relief of Free Negroes unlawfully held in bondage as enlarged at a meeting of the said Society held at Philadelphia the twenty-third day of April in the year one thousand seven hundred and eighty-seven and all rules, orders, regulations and proceedings made and had by the said society in pursuance thereof be and they are hereby declared to be in full force and binding upon the said society by this act created and incorporated until the same shall be repealed, altered or annulled at a quarterly or special meeting or adjournment thereof to be held in pursuance of this act as fully and effectually as if the same were to be originally adopted by the said society hereby incorporated and created at one of their said meetings.

[Section V.] (Section VI, P. L.) And be it further enacted by the authority aforesaid, That until the next election which shall be held by the said society in pursuance of this act the said Benjamin Franklin shall be the president thereof, the said James Pemberton and Jonathan Penrose, shall be the vice-presidents thereof, the said Benjamin Rush and Caspar Wistar shall be secretar[ies] thereof, the said James Starr shall be the treasurer thereof, and William Lewis, Miers Fisher, William Rawle and John D. Coxe shall be the councillors thereof, and that all and every the committee and committees heretofore appointed by the said Society for the Abolition of Slavery and for the relief of Free Negroes unlawfully held in bondage shall be and continue to be the officers and committees of the society hereby created and incorporated and shall report to and account with the same in the same manner as they would have done to the former society in case this act had not been passed.

[Section VI.] (Section VII, P. L.) And be it further enacted by the authority aforesaid, That this act shall in all things be construed in the most favorable and liberal manner to and for the said society in order to effectuate the privileges hereby to them granted, and that no misnomer of the said corporation in any deed, will, testament, gift, grant, demise or other instrument of contract or conveyance shall vitiate or defeat the same if the said corporation shall be sufficiently described to ascertain the intent of the party or parties to give, devise, bequeath, convey or assure to or contract with the said corporation hereby created by the name aforesaid. Nor shall any non-user of the said privileges hereby granted create any forfeiture of the same but the same may be exercised by the said corporation and notwithstanding their failure to meet at any of the times herein specified to hold their annual elections, the officers elected at any of the said annual elections shall con-

tinue to hold and exercise their offices until others shall be duly
elected to succeed them at some future meeting of the said
corporation.

Passed December 8, 1789.   Recorded L. B. No. 4, p. 46.

CHAPTER MCDLXXVII.

AN ACT FOR INCORPORATING THE METHODIST EPISCOPAL CHURCH
(KNOWN BY THE NAME OF SAINT GEORGES CHURCH) IN THE CITY
OF PHILADELPHIA IN THE COMMONWEALTH OF PENNSYLVANIA.

(Section I, P. L.) Whereas the congregation of the Methodist
Episcopal church in the city of Philadelphia have prayed that
their said congregation may be incorporated and by law enabled as a body politic and corporate to receive, hold and enjoy such charitable donations and bequests as have heretofore been or which hereafter may be made to their society and
vested with such powers and privileges as are enjoyed by other
religious societies who are incorporated in this commonwealth:

And whereas this house is disposed to exercise the power
vested in the legislature of this commonwealth for the encouragement of pious and charitable purposes:

[Section II.] (Section II, P. L.) Be it therefore enacted and
it is hereby enacted by the Representatives of the Freemen of
the Commonwealth of Pennsylvania in General Assembly met
and by the authority of the same, That the Reverend John Dick-
ins, the present minister, Robert Fitzgerrald, Jacob Baker,
Thomas Armat, James Doughty, Josiah Lusby, John Hood,
Burton Wallace, John Bond and Henry Manly and their successors duly elected and appointed in such manner as is hereinafter directed be and they are hereby made, declared and
constituted to be a corporation and body politic and corporate
in law and in fact to have continuance forever by the name,
style and title of "The Methodist Episcopal Church in the city
of Philadelphia in the commonwealth of Pennsylvania."

[Section II.] (Section III, P. L.) And be it further enacted by the authority aforesaid, That the said corporation and their successors by the name, style and title aforesaid shall forever hereafter be persons able and capable in law as well to take, receive and hold all and all manner of lands, tenements, rents, annuities, franchises and other hereditaments which at any time or times heretofore have been given, granted, bargained, sold, enfeoffed, released, devised or otherwise conveyed to the said church and congregation or to any other person or persons to their use or in trust for them and the same lands, tenements, rents, annuities, liberties, franchises and other hereditaments are hereby vested and established in the said corporation and their successors forever according to the original use and intent for which such devises, gift and grants were respectively made and the said corporation and their successors are hereby declared to be seized and possessed of such estate and estates therein as in and by their respective grants, bargains, sales, enfeoffments, releases, devises or other conveyances thereof is or are declared and limited or expressed. As also that the said corporation and their successors at all times hereafter shall be capable and able to purchase, have, receive, take, hold and enjoy in fee simple or other lesser estate or estates any lands, tenements, rents, annuities, liberties, franchises, and other hereditaments by the gift, grant, bargain, sale, alienation, enfeoffment, release, confirmation or devise of any person or persons, bodies politic and corporate capable and able to make the same. And further, that the said corporation and their successors may take and receive any sum or sums of money and any portion or portion[s] of goods and chattels which have been or at any time hereafter may or shall be given or bequeathed to them or to the said church by any person or persons, bodies politic and corporate able and capable to make a bequest or gift thereof, such money, goods or chattles to be laid out and disposed of for the use and benefit of the said church and congregation agreeably to the true intent and meaning of the respective donors.

[Section III.] (Section IV, P. L.) Provided always and be it
28—XIII

enacted by the authority aforesaid, That the clear yearly value
interest, or income of the lands, tenements, rents, annuities
or other hereditaments and real estate of the said corporation
shall not exceed the sum of five hundred pounds, gold or silver
money at the present current value thereof in the commonwealth aforesaid exclusive of the voluntary contributions of
the members of the said church from time to time for the support of their minister or ministers for the time being.

[Section IV.] (Section V, P. L.) And be it further enacted
by the authority aforesaid, That the rents, issues, profits and
interests of the said real and personal estate of and belonging
to the said church and corporation and their successors shall
from time to time be applied and laid out for the maintenance and support of the minister for the time being who shall
and may from time to time be duly appointed to the pastoral
charge of the said church and congregation by the bishop or
bishops, elders, deacons and preachers who compose the assembly and conference of the Methodist Episcopal Church held in
the commonwealth of Pennsylvania or elsewhere within the
United States of America. As also for repairing and maintaining their said church or place of public worship, lot or lots
of land burial grounds, parsonage house or other houses and
buildings which now do or at any time hereafter may or shall
belong to the said church and corporation as shall
from time to time be thought proper or expedient by two thirds
of the trustees for the time being, nevertheless when two thirds
of the trustees are not agreed with respect to the application
of money as aforesaid then and in such case the minister for
the time being duly authorized and appointed as aforesaid shall
have a voice which with either the majority or minority of
the trustees present shall be final and decisive.

[Section V.] (Section VI, P. L.) And be it further enacted
by the authority aforesaid, That the said corporation and their
successors shall not by deed or any otherwise grant, alien, convey or otherwise dispose of any part or parcel of the estate
real or personal in the said corporation vested or to be vested
or charge or encumber the same to any person or persons
whatsoever except it be with the approbation and consent of

the minister or ministers for the time being duly authorized
and appointed as aforesaid and concurrence of two thirds of
the regular male members of the said church of at least twenty-
one years of age and of one year's standing.

[Section VI.] (Section VII, P. L.) Be it further enacted by
the authority aforesaid, That the said corporation and their
successors [by the name of the Methodist Episcopal Church in
the city of Philadelphia in the Commonwealth of Pennsylvania]
shall have full power and authority to make, have and use
one common seal with such device and inscription as they shall
think fit and proper and the same to break, alter and renew at
their pleasure.

[Section VII.] (Section VIII. P. L.) Be it further enacted by
the authority aforesaid, That the said corporation and their
successors by the name of "The Methodist Episcopal Church in
the city of Philadelphia in the Commonwealth of Pennsylvania," shall be able and capable in law to sue and be sued,
plead and be impleaded in any court or before any judge or justice in all and all manner of suit, complaints, pleas, matters and
demands of whatsoever kind, nature and form they may be
and all and every matter and thing therein to do in as full and
effectual a manner as any other person or persons bodies politic
or corporate within this commonwealth may or can do.

[Section VIII.] (Section IX, P. L.) Be it further enacted
by the authority aforesaid, That no misnomer of the said corporation and their successors shall defeat or annul any gift,
grant, devise or bequest to or from the said corporation provided the intent of the party or parties shall sufficiently appear
upon the face of the gift, grant, will or other writing whereby
any estate or interest was intended to pass to or from the said
corporation and their seccessors, nor shall any disuser or non-
user of the rights, liberties, privileges jurisdictions and authorities hereby granted to the said corporation and their successors or any of them create or cause a forfeiture thereof.

[Section IX.] (Section X. P. L.) Be it further enacted by
the authority aforesaid, That the said corporation shall at
all times hereafter consist of the ministers of the said con-

gregation (who shall from time to time be duly authorized and appointed to the pastoral charge of the same by the bishop or bishops, elders, deacons and preachers who compose the assembly and conference of the Methodist Episcopal Church held in the commonwealth aforesaid or elsewhere within the United States of America) and nine trustees duly qualified chosen and appointed as is hereinafter mentioned described and directed; who shall be and continue members of the said corporation until they be removed in manner and form following, that is to say, one third part in number of the trustees aforesaid being the third part herein first named shall cease and be discontinued and their appointment determine on the day commonly called Easter Monday which shall be in the year of our Lord one thousand seven hundred and ninety, upon which day a new election shall be had and held of so many others in their place and stead by a majority of the male members of the said congregation met and qualified to note and elect as is hereinafter mentioned, described and directed; and that such election shall and may be held in such manner and at such place as the said corporation shall from time to time appoint and direct. And on the day commonly called Easter Monday which shall be in the year of our Lord one thousand seven hundred and ninety-one the second third part in number of the trustees aforesaid shall in like manner cease and be discontinued and their appointment determine and a new election [shall] be had and held in like manner of an equal number in their place and stead. And on the day commonly called Easter Monday which shall be in the year of our Lord one thousand seven hundred and ninety-two, the last third part in number of the trustees aforesaid shall cease and be discontinued and their appointment determine and a new election [shall] be had and held in like manner and by the like mode of rotation one third part in number of the trustees shall cease and be discontinued and their appointment determine and a new election of the said third part to be had and held in manner and form aforesaid, on the day commonly called Easter Monday in every year forever, to the intent that no person

or persons shall continue to be a trustee or trustees for any
longer time than three years without being re-elected but that
the electors qualified to vote as is hereinafter mentioned described and directed shall and may be at liberty to re-elect the
same trustees or any one or more of them whose times shall
expire on the day of the said annual election whenever and so
often as they shall think expedient. Provided always nevertheless, That whenever any circumstance or concurrence of circumstances shall prevent the holding of an election for trustees
at the period aforementioned in the stead and place of those
whose appointments shall have ceased and determined then
and in such case an election shall be held as soon as conveniently may be done in manner and form aforesaid and that the
remaining members of the said corporation shall have power to
call a meeting of the electors of the said congregation for such
purpose.

[Section X.] (Section XI, P. L.) Be it further enacted by
the authority aforesaid, That whenever any vacancy shall
happen by death, refusal to serve or expulsion from member-
ship (according to the discipline and rules of the said church)
of any [one] or more of the said trustees, the said corporation
shall have full power at their discretion to appoint the time
and place for the purpose of electing a trustee or trustees (as
the case may be) in their stead and that the person or persons
so elected shall be and continue in office so long as the person or persons in whose place or stead he or they may have
been so elected would or might have continued in order to keep
up the number of nine trustees forever. But before any of the
aforesaid elections are held public notice shall be given to the
congregation on the preceding Sunday after divine service and
before the congregation is dismissed or in any other convenient
manner which the said corporation shall think expedient.

[Section XI.] (Section XII, P. L.) Be it enacted by the authority aforesaid, That no person or persons shall be entitled
to a vote at an election for trustees who is not a regular male
member or members (according to the rules and discipline of
the said church) of at least twenty-one years of age and of

one year's standing. And that no person or persons whatsoever may or shall be eligible as a member of the said corporation who is not at the time of his election a regular male
member (according to the rules and regulations mentioned in
the form of discipline of the said church as composed, agreed
to and now established by the bishops, elders, deacons and
preachers who compose the assembly and conference of the
Methodist Episcopal Church in America) of twenty-one years
of age and of at least two year's standing.

[Section XII.] (Section XIII, P. L.) Be it further enacted
by the authority aforesaid, That the members of the said corporation shall and may from time to time elect by vote or
ballot from among their own [number] a president who shall
continue in office for one year and then another may be elected
or the former re-elected. And in case of the absence of the
president then and in such case any other member of the said
corporation may be elected and shall act as president for the
time being. And the said corporation may and shall elect
by vote or ballot a treasurer and secretary from among themselves or from among the regular male members of their church
and congregation and may remove them at their pleasure.
And that the minister or ministers for the time being or any
other three members of the said corporation shall be and they
are hereby authorized and empowered to call a meeting of the
corporation when and so often as he or they or any three
members as aforesaid shall deem it necessary or shall be requested so to do by a majority of the regular male members
(as aforesaid) of the said church, that the said corporation or
two thirds of them met and convened shall be authorized and
empowered and they are hereby authorized and empowered to
make such by-laws, rules and ordinances as they shall judge
necessary. Provided always, That the said by-laws, rules and
ordinances or any of them be not repugnant to the laws of
this commonwealth and to the laws of the United States. And
also that all their laws and proceedings from time to time be
by their secretary fairly and regularly entered in the books or
records of the said church.

[Section XIII.] (Section XIV, P. L.) Provided nevertheless, and be it enacted by the authority aforesaid, That no powers and authorities by this act given or intended to be given to the said corporation shall be understood taken or construed in any wise to prohibit, prevent or to take from the minister of the said church for the time being duly authorized and appointed as aforesaid the religious use, benefit and enjoyment of the said church (known by the name of Saint George's Church or of any other church or churches which may at any time hereafter be purchased or built by the said corporation) in the city of Philadelphia or the liberties thereof but that the same shall be and forever hereafter continue to be had, used and enjoyed by them as heretofore and by no other person or persons whatsoever unless by particular license and consent of the minister for the time being and concurrence of two thirds of the trustees for the time being anything in this act contained to the contrary notwithstanding.

Passed December 8, 1789.   Recorded L. B. No. 4, p. 51.

CHAPTER MCDLXXVIII.

A SUPPLEMENT TO AN ACT ENTITLED "AN ACT TO IMPROVE THE BREED OF HORSES, AND REGULATE RANGERS." [1]

(Section I, P. L.) Whereas the seventh section of an act of the general assembly of Pennsylvania entitled "An act to improve the breed of horses and regulate rangers," requires that horses taken up by the rangers of the respective counties shall be advertised in every county of the state before they may be sold, and the said act having been made at a period in the late province of Pennsylvania when the counties were but few and the settlements not very extensive:

And whereas the present state of population in this state and the extent of the settlements renders it very difficult, ex-

[1] Passed May 9, 1724, Chapter 279.

pensive and unnecessary to advertise stray horses in the hands of rangers in the manner prescribed in the aforesaid act:
Therefore:

[Section I.] (Section II, P. L.) Be it enacted and it is hereby enacted by the Representatives of the Freemen of the Commonwealth of Pennsylvania in General Assembly met and by the authority of the same, That it shall be lawful for the rangers of the respective counties into whose hands any stray horses may have come and the same having been registered for the space of one year in their respective counties to sell such strays as aforesaid by public vendue at some convenient place in their respective counties, first-advertising the sale thereof for at least two weeks immediately before the day of the sale and in at least six of the most public places of the said counties, and the said rangers are hereby required respectively to make sale of all stray horses now in their keeping as soon as they shall have been registered for [the space of] one year as aforesaid and to pay the moneys arising therefrom into the hands of the county treasurer for the use of the county after deducting reasonable charges for their trouble and expenses.

Passed December 9, 1789. Recorded L. B. No. 4, p. 56.

CHAPTER MCDLXXIX.

SUPPLEMENT TO AN ACT ENTITLED "AN ACT TO INCORPORATE THE CITY OF PHILADELPHIA." [1]

(Section I, P. L.) Whereas by an act of the general assembly of this commonwealth [enacted] the eleventh day of March in the year of our Lord one thousand seven hundred and eighty-nine entitled "An act to incorporate the city of Philadelphia and for other purposes therein mentioned," it was enacted, "That a court shall be and is hereby established by the name, style and title of the Alderman's Court and shall consist of three aldermen of the said city for the time being to hear, try

---

[1] Chapter 1394.

and determine in a summary way all such causes, matters and
things within the said city as are by law cognizable before any
justice of the peace within this state where the debt or demand amounts to forty shillings and does not exceed ten
pounds:

And whereas a court of record has been accordingly established for the said purpose but no provision being made in
the said act of assembly for compensating the services of the
clerk of the said court and the safety of the suitors rendering
it necessary that a fair docket of the cases in the said court
should be kept:

Therefore:

[Section I.] (Section II, P. L.) Be it enacted by the Representatives of the [Freemen of the Commonwealth] of Pennsylvania in General Assembly met and by the authority of the
same, That the fees belonging to the clerk of the said court
shall be as follows, to wit: For entering each action upon the
docket, six pence and no more; for filing and recording each
action six pence and no more and for every final judgment,
six pence and no more.

Passed December 9, 1759. Recorded L. B. No. 4, p. 56.

FOURTEENTH ASSEMBLY—SECOND SITTING.

CHAPTER MCDLXXX.

A SUPPLEMENT TO THE ACT ENTITLED "AN ACT TO PROVIDE FOR
THE SALARIES OF THE OFFICERS OF THE LAND OFFICE" ENACTED
THE EIGHTH DAY OF DECEMBER ONE THOUSAND SEVEN HUNDRED
AND EIGHTY-NINE. [1]

(Section I, P. L.) Whereas the act to which this is a supplement fixed and ascertained the salaries of the officers of the

[1] Chapter 1475.

land office but made no provision for their accounting for the
fees paid into their respective offices:
　　Therefore:
　　[Section I.] (Section II, P. L.) Be it enacted and it is hereby
enacted by the representatives of the Freemen of the Commonwealth of Pennsylvania in General Assembly met and by the
authority of the same, That the secretary of the land-office, the
surveyor-general and receiver general, shall collect the fees
hereafter accruing by reason of their respective offices and
once in every three months from the date of this act shall account for the same upon oath or affirmation to be administered
by the treasurer of this state for the time being and pay them
to the said treasurer for the use of this commonwealth.
　　Passed February 19, 1790. Recorded L. B. No. 4, p. 68.

CHAPTER MCDLXXXI.

AN ACT FOR FOUNDING AND ENDOWING A PUBLIC SCHOOL IN THE TOWN AND COUNTY OF HUNTINGDON.

　　(Section I, P. L.) Whereas it has been represented to this
house by sundry inhabitants of the town and county of Huntingdon that considerable sums of money have been subscribed
and contributed and convenient lots of ground appropriated
for founding and carrying on a public grammar school for the
said town and county according to the following fundamental
articles, that is to say, First, The said school shall be governed
by seven trustees residing in the town and township of Huntingdon to be chosen by contributors towards the school, of
twenty shillings and upwards residing in the said town and
township and one trustee for each township in the county to
be chosen by contributors of twenty shillings and
upwards resident in that township and whose whole
contributions at the time of such election shall
amount to fifteen pounds or upwards. Secondly, When any

trustee shall die, resign or remove out of the township for
which he was elected or be otherwise disabled from acting
as a trustee or shall neglect to attend the visitation of the said
school for four succeeding quarterly meetings or visitations
without such plea or excuse of absence as shall be deemed
reasonable and satisfactory to the majority of a quorum or
legal board of seven or more trustees duly assembled at such
quarterly meetings, then and in every such case within three
months after such death, resignation, removal out of the township or other disability or disqualification as aforesaid such
board or quorum of seven or more surviving and remaining
trustees shall cause ten days notice to be given in the township
where the trustee or trustees resided whose seat hath been
vacated by any of the means aforesaid appointing a time and
place in such township for the election of a new trustee or trustees to supply such vacant seat or seats, at which election all
freeholders who have either contributed twenty shillings or
upwards towards founding the said school or who have paid
that sum in tuition money for the education of any child or
children shall be entitled to give their vote, provided that a
majority out of seven such votes at least shall be deemed necessary for an election, and provided further, that if there be no
such majority to vote or if the township shall neglect to make
any choice according to notice given as aforesaid, then a board
or quorum, not less than seven of the remaining trustees at
any quarterly meeting, if they shall think it necessary. may
nominate, elect and appoint a trustee or trustees to supply
such vacant seat or seats in all which cases the person so to
be chosen or appointed shall be resident in the town or township in which the person resideth whose seat he shall be chosen
to supply. Thirdly, A charter of incorporation agreeably to
the foregoing articles shall be applied for as soon as thirty
or more contributors meeting in the town of Huntingdon shall
choose the first seven trustees resident in the said town and
township, which seven trustees shall be a quorum to apply
to the legislature for a charter of incorporation and a grant
of a proportionate part of the lands reserved as a fund for
the endowment of public schools, agreeably to the forty-

fourth section of the constitution of this Commonwealth, and the said seven trustees shall also be a quorum to solicit and procure subscriptions and contributions in the other townships of this county and of strangers and also to agree with and employ a school-master and to carry on a proper building for a school-house and lastly to direct new elections or appointments to be held to fill up any vacancies that may happen in their own number, although fewer than seven be assembled at a quarterly meeting as must be the case should any vacancy happen among the first seven trustees for the town or township of Huntingdon before any election in the other townships.

And whereas it hath been further represented to this house that agreeably to the articles aforesaid thirty and more subscribers to the said school residing in the town and township of Huntingdon have duly elected Benjamin Elliot and Andrew Henderson, Esquires, the Honorable John Cannon, Esquire, and George Folkner, Alexander Dean, John Dean, and John Williams, Gentleman, as the first seven trustees, resident in the said township for beginning and carrying on the said school and the said seven trustees and other inhabitants of the said town and county of Huntingdon have humbly prayed, that a charter of incorporation may be granted to them:

And whereas this house are desirous to propagate the true principles of religion and liberty, virtue and knowledge with an equal and liberal hand through every part of this state agreeably to their duty and the great trust committed to them by the constitution and laws of the same.

[Section I.] (Section II, P. L.) Be it enacted and it is hereby enacted by the Representatives of the Freemen of the Commonwealth of Pennsylvania in General Assembly met and by the authority of the same, That the said Benjamin Elliot, Andrew Henderson, John Cannon, George Folkner, Alexander Dean, John Dean and John Williams and such other persons as shall be duly elected trustees according to the articles hereinbefore recited shall be and they are hereby declared to be one community, corporation and body politic to have continuance forever according to the said articles by the name and style of "The Trustees of the Public School of the County of Hunting-

don in the Commonwealth of Pennsylvania ," and by the same
name they and their successors shall be capable to purchase,
have, receive, take, hold and enjoy to them and their successors in fee or for any less estate or estates, any lands, tenements, rents, annuities or other hereditaments within this state
by the gift, grant, bargain, sale, alienation, enfeoffment, release, confirmation or devise of any person or persons, bodies
politic or corporate capable in law to make, give, grant and
transfer the same and such lands, tenements, rents, annuities
and other hereditaments or any less estates, rights and interest of in or to the same in anywise belonging and appurtenant
at their pleasure to grant, alien, sell and transfer in such
manner as they shall think meet and convenient for the further-
ence and continuance, (but in no way to the diminishing or injury) of the capital estate and foundation of the said school
or the value of the lands and estates herein and hereby granted
and given to the use of the said school or of any charitable
grants, gifts and bequests heretofore given and granted or
which may hereafter be given, granted, devised or bequeathed for the maintenance, furtherance and endowment
of the same, and the said trustees and their successors may take and receive any lands, tenements and hereditaments and any sum or sums of money and any kind, manner
or portion of goods and chattels, that shall be given, sold, devised or bequeathed to them by any person or persons, bodies
politic or corporate, capable to make a gift sale or bequest
thereof and employ the same towards erecting, setting up and
maintaining the said school in such manner as they shall judge
most convenient and useful for instruction, improvement and
education of the youth of the said county and others as well
for hire and reasonable tuition money as of poor children gratis
and without pay to be admitted and received by them on their
own knowledge or upon the recommendation of the justices
of quarter sessions and overseers of the poor within the county.

[Section II.] (Section III, P. L.) Be it further enacted by
the authority aforesaid, That the said trustees and their successors by the name and style aforesaid shall be able and

capable in law to sue and be sued, plead and be impleaded in
any court or courts and before any judge, judges or justices
within this commonwealth and elsewhere in all manner of
suits, complaints, pleas, causes, matters and demands of whatsoever kind, nature or form they be and to make, have and
use one common seal in their affairs, and the same to change
break, alter and renew at their pleasure, and to employ one
or more masters, tutors and instructors for the education of
the youth in the said school and to make, alter and continue
such laws, ordinances and regulations for the government of
the same not repugnant to the laws and constitution of this
Commonwealth as they and their successors from time to time
shall think most convenient and salutary and to do all and
every matter and thing for establishing, carrying on and perpetuating the said school in as full and effectual a manner
as any other person or persons, bodies politic and corporate
within this state in like case or cases may, can or ought to do.

[Section III.] Provided always, That the clear yearly value
of the messuages, rents, tenements, annuities or other hereditaments and real estate of the said school and corporation
shall not exceed two thousand bushels of wheat or the value
thereof in current money of this Commonwealth, and provided
further that the said trustees and their successors shall annually at the court of quarter sessions of the peace which shall
be held in and for the said county in the month of September
in every year or oftener if required lay an account of the state
and progress of the said school and of its fund and estate,
yearly expenditures and accounts before the justices and grand
jury of the said court or such commissioners and visitors as
the general assembly of this commonwealth may at any other
time specially appoint for the visitation of the said school
and an examination into the condition and conduct of the
affairs thereof.

Passed February 19, 1790.   Recorded L. B. No. 4, p. 71.

CHAPTER MCDLXXXII.

AN ACT TO REGULATE THE EXPORTATION OF POTASH AND PEARL-ASH

(Section I, P. L.) Whereas potash and pearlash are likely to become considerable articles of exportation from this state and inconveniences may arise from a want of their being inspected:

Therefore:

[Section I.] (Section II, P. L.) Be it enacted and it is hereby enacted by the Representatives of the Freemen of the Commonwealth of Pennsylvania in General Assembly met and by the authority of the same, That the president or vice-president and supreme executive council shall be and they are hereby authorized and empowered to appoint a skillful and discreet person to be inspector of pot and pearl ash for this state whose powers and duties shall be as they are hereinafter described who shall be empowered to appoint a suitable number of deputies under him. That such inspector and every of his deputies previously to entering on the execution of their respective offices shall take an oath or affirmation before a magistrate of the city or county in which they shall be appointed, faithfully and impartially to perform their trust and duty to the best of their skill and understanding according to the directions of this act. And in case of death, misbehavior in office or inability it shall be lawful for the president or vice-president and supreme executive council to appoint another inspector from time to time as the case shall require. That none of the said inspectors or his deputies during their continuance in office shall directly or indirectly vend, barter or trade in pot or pearl ash under the penalty of one hundred pounds to be recovered by action of debt by any person who will sue for the same, the one moiety thereof to the use of the person suing and the other moiety thereof to the use of this state, and every inspector or deputy inspector being so thereof convicted shall thenceforth be disabled from holding their respective offices.

[Section II.] (Section III, P. L.) And be it further enacted by the authority aforesaid, That from and after the enacting hereof no person or persons whatever shall ship or cause to be shipped any pot or pearl ash for exportation out of this state before he or they shall submit the same to the examination of the inspector of the port from whence the same shall be shipped or intended to be shipped, or his deputy. That the said inspector or his deputy, shall cause all pot and pearl ash submitted to his examination to be started out of the cask and shall carefully inspect and try the same and if fit for exportation shall sort it according to its quality into three sorts. That each sort shall be separately packed in tight casks, well hooped and coopered, the tare of which shall be previously marked by such inspector or his deputy on the head of each cask who shall also mark thereon with a branding iron the name of the port from whence shipped with the words potash or pearlash, the first, second, or third sort as the case may be.

[Section III.] (Section IV, P. L.) Be it further enacted by the authority aforesaid, That the said inspector or his deputy respectively shall be entitled to receive of the possessor of such pot or pearl ash as a full compensation for his services in examining, sorting and repacking the same, in coopering, weighing and marking the casks and delivering a note by him signed of the weight of each cask when empty the sum of six-pence for every hundredweight so inspected and for all pot or pearl ash adjudged to be unfit for exportation the sum of two-pence for every hundredweight. Provided, That the expense of additional cooperage or of new casks when necessary in the opinion of the inspector or his deputy, shall be paid by the possessor of the pot or pearl ash and that such possessor shall be at liberty to employ any other person for that purpose.

[Section IV.] (Section V, P. L.) Be it further enacted by the authority aforesaid, That if any dispute shall arise between

such inspector or his deputy and the possessor of any pot or
pearl ash concerning the quality, inspection or package thereof upon application to any magistrate of the city or county
where the case may happen, such magistrate shall issue his
warrant to three indifferent persons to view and examine the
same and make report thereof and the said magistrate is hereby empowered and required to give judgment agreeable to the
report of the said viewers or any two of them and the said inspector or his deputy shall thereupon proceed to repack the
same, if judged fit for exportation and mark the casks according to the direction of such viewers and for his services therein shall have the same fees as is hereinbefore directed and if
judgment shall be given upon such report in favor of the said
inspector or his deputy the said magistrate shall moreover
award the sum of three pence for each hundredweight of the
said pot or pearl ash, with costs to be paid by the possessor
thereof but if such judgment shall be given against such inspector or his deputy the costs and all reasonable charges shall be
awarded to be paid by such inspector or his deputy as the case
may be.

[Section V.] (Section VI, P. L.) Be it further enacted by
the authority aforesaid, That any person or persons whatever
who shall knowingly ship or cause to be shipped or who shall
receive on board any ship or vessel for exportation out of this
state any pot or pearl ash not inspected, marked and branded
in manner before directed or the marks and brands whereof
shall have been altered or counterfeited or which shall have
been condemned as unfit for exportation, shall forfeit and pay
the sum of twenty-five pounds for every such offence, and that
any person or persons who shall mark or brand any cask or
other vessel containing or intended to contain pot or pearl ash
or shall alter or efface any marks or brands made or impressed
by such inspector or his deputy with design to evade the intent
and meaning of this act shall forfeit and pay the sum of fifty
pounds for every such offense, and shall also suffer imprisonment without bail or mainprize for the term of three months
and until such fine and the costs of prosecution shall be paid.

[Section VI.] (Section VII, P. L.) Be it further enacted by the authority aforesaid, That such inspector or his deputy shall have full power and authority, by virtue of this act to enter on board any ship or vessel suspected to have received pot or pearl ash for exportation contrary to the provisions of this act in order to search for and examine the same and any person or persons whatever who shall obstruct and resist the said inspector or his deputy therein shall forfeit and pay the sum of twenty pounds for each such offense.

[Section VII.] (Section VIII, P. L.) Be it further enacted by the authority aforesaid, That all pot and pearl ash which shall be shipped for exportation out of this state or which shall be brought to any quay, wharf or other place in order to be shipped for such exportation contrary to the true intent and meaning of this act shall be forfeited and may be seized by the inspector or his deputy who after condemnation thereof in due course of law shall cause the same to be publicly sold and one moiety of the money arising therefrom after deducting the costs and charges shall be paid to the treasurer of the county in which such seizure and condemnation shall take place for the use of the commonwealth and the moiety thereof to the inspector or his deputy who shall seize and prosecute the same to judgment.

[Section VIII.] (Section IX, P. L.) Be it further enacted by the authority aforesaid, That the fees given and the fines inflicted by virtue of this act shall be recovered in the same manner as debts of like value are recovered by the laws of this state, and all the said fines except such as may be incurred by the inspector or his deputies shall be distributed in the manner hereinbefore directed with regard to the articles forfeited.

[Section IX.] (Section X, P. L.) Be it further enacted by the authority aforesaid, That this act shall continue and be in force for the term of two years and from thence to the end of the next session of the general assembly of this commonwealth.

Passed February 22, 1790. Recorded L. B. No. 4, p. 58.

CHAPTER MCDLXXXIII.

AN ACT TO REPEAL PART OF THE ADDITIONAL SUPPLEMENT TO THE ACTS FOR THE REGULATION OF THE MILITIA OF THIS COMMON-WEALTH.

(Section I, P. L.) Whereas it has been found on experience that the second section of the additional supplement to the acts for the regulation of the militia of this commonwealth passed the twenty-second day of March, one thousand seven hundred and eighty-eight authorizing the lieutenants of the city and county of Philadelphia and the several counties within this commonwealth to furnish the officers commanding battalions or corps with thirteen cartridges for every militia-man actually bearing arms in each battalion or corps on every battalion day hath not been productive of the advantages expected from it but on the contrary is found unnecessarily expensive: Therefore:

[Section I.] (Section II, P. L.) Be it enacted and it is hereby enacted by the Representatives of the Freemen of the Commonwealth of Pennsylvania in General Assembly met and by the authority of the same, That so much of the additional supplement to the acts for the regulation of the militia of this commonwealth as authorizes or directs the city and county lieutenants to furnish the militia with cartridges on battalion days shall be and is hereby repealed.

Passed March 3, 1790. Recorded L. B. No. 4, p. 63.

CHAPTER MCDLXXXIV.

AN ACT TO DIVIDE THE COUNTY OF FAYETTE INTO ELECTION DISTRICTS.

(Section I, P. L.) Whereas by the eighteenth section of the constitution it is provided that each county at its own choice may be divided into districts, hold elections therein and elect their representatives in the county and their other elective officers, and as a division of the county of Fayette would contribute to the ease and convenience of the good citizens thereof in holding their annual elections:

[Section I.] (Section II, P. L.) Be it enacted and it is hereby enacted by the Representatives of the Freemen of the Commonwealth of Pennsylvania in General Assembly met and by the authority of the same, That from and after the enacting hereof the elections of the county of Fayette which is hereby divided into four districts shall be held in four places, to wit, the freemen of the townships of Union, Franklin and Wharton, the first district, shall hold their elections at the court-house in Uniontown; the freemen of the townships of Springhill, German and George's, the second district, shall hold their elections at the house now occupied by Nicholas Riffle in German Township [aforesaid]; the freemen of the townships of Luzerne, Manallen and Washington, the third district, shall hold their elections at Fort Burd; and the freemen of the townships of Tyrone and Bulskin, the fourth district, shall hold their elections at the house now occupied by Samuel Hicks in Bulskin township aforesaid anything in the act entitled "An act to regulate the general elections of this commonwealth and to prevent frauds therein,"[1] contained to the contrary in anywise notwithstanding.

¹ Passed September 13, 1785, Chapter 1175.
Passed March 3, 1790. Recorded L. B. No. 4, p. 62.

CHAPTER MCDLXXXV.

AN ACT TO COMPENSATE WILLIAM LYON, ESQUIRE.

(Section I, P. L.) Whereas it appears to this house that the dwelling house and office of William Lyon, Esquire, prothonotary of the county court of common pleas for the county of Cumberland, having caught fire on the night of the first day of April one thousand seven hundred and eighty-nine were to-

gether with his household furniture and the wearing apparel
of himself and his family, entirely consumed, while the public
papers and records in his custody, by his spirited exertions
were preserved from destruction and the said William Lyon
hath requested this house, in consideration of the preceding
circumstances to exempt him from the payment of the tax imposed by an act of the general assembly passed [on] the
twentieth day of March one thousand seven hundred and
eighty-three upon certain writs issuing out of the said court:

And whereas it appears to this house to be reasonable that
a compensation should be made for losses occasioned by conduct so public spirited and disinterested:

[Section I.] (Section II, P. L.) Be it therefore enacted and
it is hereby enacted by the Representatives of the Freemen of
the Commonwealth of Pennsylvania in General Assembly met
and by authority of the same, That the said William Lyon,
Esquire, shall be and he is hereby exonerated from the payment
of the said tax upon all writs otherwise liable thereto which
have been issued out of the said office since the term of October
one thousand seven hundred and eighty-eight and also upon all
such writs which shall be issued out of the said office before
the term of April one thousand seven hundred and ninety-one.

Passed March 3, 1790. Recorded L. B. No. 4, p. 56.

CHAPTER MCDLXXXVI.

AN ACT TO REIMBURSE GABRIEL COX, GEORGE VALENDIGHAM AND
ANDREW SWERINGEN FOR MONEYS ADVANCED BY THEM IN THE
DEFENSE OF THE FRONTIERS OF WASHINGTON COUNTY.

(Section I, P. L.) Whereas Gabriel Cox, George Valendigham and Andrew Sweringen have by their petitions set forth
that in the year one thousand seven hundred and eighty they
engaged Captain Thomas Bay to raise a company of rangers
for the defense of the frontiers of Washington county and
gave their assumption for payment on which assumption the
said Captain Thomas Bay commenced a suit at law and recovered the sum of two hundred and fifty-five pounds damages and

five pounds costs and it being just and reasonable to reimburse
the said Gabriel Cox, George Valendigham and Andrew Swer·
ingen the moneys so recovered of them:

Therefore:

[Section I.] (Section II, P. L.) Be it enacted and it is here·
by enacted by the Representatives of the Freemen of the Commonwealth of Pennsylvania in General Assembly met and by
the authority of the same, That the comptroller general be
and he is hereby authorized and required to issue certificates
to Gabriel Cox, George Valendigham and Andrew Sweringen
for their respective shares of two hundred and sixty pounds
the certificates bearing interest from the first day of Septem·
ber in the year one thousand seven hundred and eighty-three.

Passed March 3, 1790. Recorded L. B. No. 4, p. 63.

CHAPTER MCDLXXXVII.

AN ACT DIRECTING THE PAYMENT OF THE ACCOUNTS OF SUNDRY DEPUTY SURVEYORS OF THE DEPRECIATION LANDS.

(Section I. P. L.) It appearing to this assembly that sundry de·
puty surveyors were employed in surveying the tract of land
appropriated by law for the redemption of [the] certificates for
the depreciation on the pay of the officers and soldiers of the late
line of this state in the service of the United States and that
by reason of the suspension of the sales of the said lands the
just demands of money of the [said] surveyors remain unsatis·
fied, there being no other fund on which orders can legally be
drawn for the amount of such demands.

[Section I.] (Section II, P. L.) Be it therefore enacted and
it is hereby enacted by the Representatives of the Freemen
of the Commonwealth of Pennsylvania in General Assembly
met and by the authority of the same, That the president or
vice president in council be and they are hereby authorized and
empowered on the accounts of those deputy surveyors who have
under the authority of this state surveyed the depreciation

lands or any part thereof and whose demands for such services
still remain unsatisfied being adjusted and settled as the law directs to draw orders for the amount of the balances due to
such deputy surveyors respectively on the treasurer of this
state, who shall pay the amount of such orders out of the fund
appropriated for claims and improvements by an act entitled,
"An act to appropriate divers funds accruing and growing due
to this commonwealth towards the expenses of government
and to provide a fund for other purposes:" [1] Provided the payment of such orders shall not interfere with the appropriation
of part of the said fund, made and directed by an act, entitled
"An act to appropriate the sum of five thousand pounds annually for the purposes therein mentioned"; [2] any act or part
of an act to the contrary hereof in anywise notwithstanding.

[Section II.] (Section III, P. L.) Be it further enacted by
the authority aforesaid, That whensoever a sum sufficient to
replace the sums which may or shall be paid by virtue of this act
shall be raised and paid into the treasury of this state by the
sales of the said depreciation lands or any part or parts thereof, so much of the moneys arising from such sales as shall be
equal to the amount of the sums which may or shall be paid
by virtue of this act shall be applied to the said fund set apart
for claims and improvements as aforesaid to replace the sums
for which orders shall be drawn in pursuance of directions
of this act.

Passed March 3, 1790.   Recorded L. B. No. 4. p. 64.
[1] Passed March 26, 1789, Chapter 1404.
[2] Passed September 28, 1789. Chapter 1446.

CHAPTER MCDLXXXVIII.

AN ACT RELATING TO THE SECURITIES TO BE GIVEN BY SHERIFFS AND CORONERS.

(Section I, P. L.) Whereas the security heretofore given by
sheriffs and coroners for the faithful execution of their respective offices being of a personal nature is inadequate to the importance of the trusts reposed in them

[Section I.] (Section II, P. L.) Be it enacted and it is hereby enacted by the Representatives of the Freemen of the Commonwealth of Pennsylvania in General Assembly met and by the authority of the same, That before any commission shall be granted to the sheriff or coroner of the city and county of Philadelphia or of any county in this state he shall enter into a recognizance before the president and supreme executive council or before commissioners by them for that purpose specially to be appointed in the several sums which by law the sheriffs and coroners of the city and county of Philadelphia and of each respective county are now required to give bond in, which recognizances shall be in the nature and effect of judgments obtained in the supreme court and shall bind the lands, tenements and hereditaments of the said sheriffs and coroners in the same manner as such judgment to the amount of the security by law required in each county respectively and to prevent injury to purchasers the said recognizances shall, as soon as may be after taking the same be delivered to and filed by the prothonotary of the supreme court who shall cause a docket to be made of the same for the information of persons applying and such sheriff or coroner shall also find two or more sufficient sureties to be approved by the president and supreme executive council who shall become bound to this commonwealth in the sum of money herein directed for the faithful performance of the respective trusts and duties of such sheriff or coroner which bonds, the execution thereof being first proved before the president of the court of common pleas of the respective county or in case of his death or absence before one of the judges of the said court shall be delivered to and filed by the prothonotary of the supreme court and copies of such bonds authenticated under the seal of the supreme court shall be admitted as legal evidence in any suit or suits that shall be brought thereon against the obligators, their heirs, executors or administrators.

(Section III, P. L.) That when the commonwealth or any individuals shall be aggrieved by the misconduct of any sheriff or coroner it shall be lawful as often as the case may require to institute actions of debt or of scire facias upon such recognizance against such sheriff or coroner, their heirs, executors

or administrators, or actions of debt upon such bonds against
such sureties, their heirs, executors or administrators and if
upon such suits it shall be proved what damage hath been sustained and a verdict and judgment be thereupon given execution shall issue for so much only as shall be found by the said
verdict and judgment with costs, which suits may be instituted
and the like proceedings be thereupon had as often as damage
is so aforesaid sustained. Provided that such suits against
such sureties shall be instituted within seven years after the
date of their several bonds.

[Section II.] (Section IV, P. L.) And be it further enacted
by the authority aforesaid, That until such securities shall be
given as aforesaid all commissions granted to and all acts and
things whatsover done by any such sheriff or coroner under
color of office shall be void and of none effect.

Passed March 5, 1790. Recorded L. B. No. 4, p. 66. See the note
to the Act of Assembly passed August 24, 1717, Chapter 222; and the
Act of Assembly passed March 12, 1791, Chapter 1532.

CHAPTER MCDLXXXIX.

AN ACT TO SUSPEND FOR A LIMITED TIME SO MUCH OF THE ACT OF
ASSEMBLY TO REGULATE THE FISHERY IN THE RIVERS CODORUS
AND CONEWAGO IN YORK COUNTY AS RELATES TO THE ERECTING
OF PLATFORMS TO THE DAMS THEREIN MENTIONED.

(Section I, P. L.) Whereas complaints have been made by
a number of the inhabitants of the borough and county of
York that they are deprived of the benefit of fish in the rivers
Codorus and Conewago by the obstructions on said rivers and
praying for an amendment to the act passed the ninth day of
March one thousand seven hundred and seventy-one entitled
"An act for regulating the fishery in the rivers Codorus and
Conewago in York County." [1]

And complaints also from the owners of said dams together
with a number of the inhabitants of said county that some of
the water works have lately been renewed at very great expense to the owners and are also of public utility to the community at large and that the platforms prayed for by the pe-

titioners in favor of the fisheries will be an additional expense
and tend to injure such dams and pray for a repeal of the said
law:

And whereas it appears that the said law to regulate the
fisheries in said rivers has not hitherto had the desired effect
either through inattention to it or by a defect in the platforms
described therein:

And as the erecting the platforms prayed for (wholly at the
expense of the owners of such water works) might be oppressive at this time:

Therefore:

[Section I.] (Section II, P. L.) Be it enacted and it is hereby
enacted by the Representatives of the Freemen of the Commonwealth of Pennsylvania in General Assembly met and by
the authority of the same, That so much of the act of assembly
passed the ninth day of March in the year of our Lord one thousand seven hundred and seventy-one entitled "An act for regulating the Fishery in the rivers Codorus and Conewago in York
county," [1] as relates to the erecting or opening platforms to the
mill dams and other obstructions across said rivers be suspended for the term of three years from and after the passing of
this act anything in the said recited act to the contrary in anywise notwithstanding.

Passed March 5, 1790. Recorded L. B. No. 4, p. 67.

CHAPTER MCDXC.

AN ACT FOR SETTLING THE ACCOUNTS OF JAMES ROWAN LATE COL-
LECTOR OF TAXES IN THE COUNTY OF PHILADELPHIA AND FOR
OTHER PURPOSES THEREIN MENTIONED.

(Section I, P. L.) Whereas it appears to this house that
James Rowan was appointed collector of taxes in the city and
county of Philadelphia and collector of certain rate or tax imposed upon the real and personal estates in the district of
Southwark in the county of Philadelphia by virtue of an act
entitled "An act to enable the commissioners therein named

[1] Chapter 623.

to purchase public landings in the district of Southwark in
the county of Philadelphia and for raising a fund to pay
the purchase money thereof," enacted the twentieth day of
September one thousand seven hundred and eighty-two, in
which capacities he has received and is accountable for large
sums of money which he is at present unable to discharge although no accident or casual misfortune has happened to prevent him from so doing, that his ostensible real and personal
property have been seized by due course of law and that he
has been committed to the gaol of the said city and county
where he now lies, that his accounts have not yet been settled
nor the proper steps taken to collect such arrearages of the said
taxes as he may not have received:

And whereas this commonwealth, disposed to temper justice with mercy, is willing by relieving the said James Rowan
from imprisonment to enable him to maintain his family and
at the same time to endeavor to compensate for his said breach
of trust:

[Section I.] (Section II, P. L.) Be it therefore enacted and
it is hereby enacted by the Representatives of the Freemen of
the Commonwealth of Pennsylvania in General Assembly met
and by the authority of the same, That upon the said James
Rowan's entering into bond with two sureties to be approved
by the commissioners of the county of Philadelphia for the
time being in the sum of two thousand pounds conditioned
that the said James Rowan shall within six months after the
date thereof render upon oath or affirmation a just and true
account of all the public money received by him or by persons
acting under his authority together with the names of the persons from whom received and the time when received and shall
also from time to time when thereunto required during the said
term answer upon oath or affirmation all such questions touching and concerning the premises as shall be proposed to him by
the said commissioners of the county aforesaid or the commissioners appointed by virtue of the act hereinbefore mentioned,
it shall be lawful for the sheriff or other officer in whose custody the same James Rowan may be to enlarge him

from imprisonment during the said term. And that it shall be lawful for the judges of the county court of common pleas for the county of Philadelphia upon the application of the said James Rowan and reasonable cause by him shown and due notice thereof given to the commissioners to enlarge the term hereinbefore allowed for such settlements of his accounts. Provided such enlarged term do not exceed six months and provided security be taken for such enlarged term in like manner as is hereinbefore required. And that the said James Rowan shall at all seasonable times during such term as shall be allowed for the purpose of settling his said accounts be at liberty to inspect his books and papers in the presence of the said commissioners or of some person to be appointed by them and to bring with him for his assistance such persons as he shall think fit and to make extracts and copies thereof for the purpose aforesaid.

[Section II.] (Section III, P. L.) Be it enacted by the authority aforesaid, That when the said James Rowan shall have in all things complied with the directions hereinbefore contained it shall be lawful for the judges of the court aforesaid upon his petition praying the benefit of this act and due notice thereof given as well to the said commissioners as to the private creditors of the said James Rowan to afford the like relief to him in like manner and upon the like terms and conditions as is provided by the several acts of assembly for the relief of insolvent debtors, save only that the said James Rowan shall assign to the commissioners of the said county for the time being all and singular his estate and effects for the use and benefit of the county of Philadelphia including the said district and for the said district respectively to be divided in ratable proportions according to the amount of the balances from him to them respectively due, and the surplus of his said estate and effects if any to the use and benefit of all his other creditors. Provided that such assignment shall not be deemed or taken to affect any seizure, attachment or execution of the estate and effects of the said James Rowan already made or levied. Provided, That nothing in this act contained shall extend to exonerate the said county of Philadelphia from any part of its quota or proportion of taxes or assessments due to this state by reason of the default of the said James Rowan as aforesaid nor to exonerate annul or lessen the force and effect of any security or engagement entered into by any other person for securing the payment of the moneys collected by him or for his good behavior in the duties of his office.

And whereas since enacting the act hereinbefore mentioned Robert Knox, Joseph Bleuer and Isaac Penrose, three of the commissioners therein named and authorized, have departed this life and it has been doubted whether the three surviving commissioners are authorized to proceed in the execution of the said act:

[Section III.] (Section IV, P. L.) Be it enacted by the authority aforesaid, That the three surviving commissioners, to wit, Joseph Turner, William Clifton and John Brown or any two of them in case of death or removal from this state the surviving or only remaining commissioners shall be and he or they are hereby authorized and empowered to execute and perform all the trusts and duties which are required in the said act to be performed by the commissioners herein appointed.

Passed March 6, 1790. Recorded L. B. No. 4, p. 67.

CHAPTER MCDLXCI.

AN ACT TO ALTER THE PLACE OF HOLDING ELECTIONS IN THE SECOND DISTRICT OF WASHINGTON COUNTY.

(Section I, P. L.) Whereas the people of the second district of Washington county have by their petition set forth that the line which divides the counties of Washington and Allegheny has passed through said district in such direction as to render the place of holding their public elections not central for the people of said district to meet at and it being necessary to fix the place of the election so as to suit the convenience of the people:

Therefore:

[Section I.] (Section II, P. L.) Be it enacted and it is hereby enacted by the Representatives of the Freemen of the Commonwealth of Pennsylvania in General Assembly met and by the authority of the same, That the freemen of the second district of Washington county (known by the name of "Bentley's district") shall from and after the passing of this act meet and hold their elections at the house of Thomas Hill on the road leading from the town of Washington to Brownsville, anything in the law which divides the county of Washington into election districts to the contrary notwithstanding.

Passed March 8, 1790.   Recorded L. B. No. 4, p. 69.

CHAPTER MCDLXCII.

AN ACT DECLARING THE ASSENT OF THIS STATE TO CERTAIN AMENDMENTS TO THE CONSTITUTION OF THE UNITED STATES.

(Section I, P. L.) Whereas in pursuance of the fifth article of the constitution of the United States certain articles of amendment to the said constitution have been proposed by the congress of the United States for the consideration of the legislatures of the several states:

And whereas this house, being the legislature of the state of Pennsylvania, having maturely deliberated thereupon have resolved to adopt and ratify the articles hereafter enumerated as part of the constitution of the United States,

[Section I.] (Section II. P. L.) Be it therefore enacted and it is hereby enacted by the Representatives of the Freemen of the Commonwealth of Pennsylvania in General Assembly met and by the authority of the same, That the following amendments to the constitution of the United States proposed by the congress thereof, viz:

Article 3. Congress shall make no law respecting an establishment of religion or prohibiting the free exercise thereof, or abridging the freedom of speech of the press or the right of the people peaceably to assemble and to petition the government for a redress of grievances.

Article 4. A well regulated militia being necessary to the security of a free state the right of the people to keep and bear arms shall not be infringed.

Article 5. No soldier shall in time of peace be quartered in any house without the consent of the owner nor in time of war but in a manner prescribed by law.

Article 6. The right of the people to be secure in their persons, houses, papers and effects against unreasonable searches and seizures shall not be violated and no warrants shall issue but upon probable cause supported by oath or affirmation and particularly describing the place to be searched and the persons or things to be seized.

Article 7. No person shall be held to answer for a capital or otherwise infamous crime unless on a presentment or indictment of a grand jury except in cases arising in the land or naval forces or in the militia when in actual service in time of war or public danger, nor shall any person be subject for the same offense to be twice put in jeopardy of life or limb, nor shall be compelled in any criminal case to be a witness against himself nor to be deprived of life, liberty or property without due process of law, nor shall private property be taken for public use without just compensation.

Article 8. In all criminal prosecutions the accused shall enjoy the right of a speedy and public trial by an impartial jury of the state and district wherein the crime shall have been committed, which district shall have been previously ascertained by law, and to be informed of the nature and cause of the accusation, to be confronted with the witnesses against him, to have compulsory process for obtaining witnesses in his favor and to have the assistance of counsel for his defense.

Article 9. In suits at common law where the value in controversy shall exceed twenty dollars the right of trial by jury shall be preserved and no fact tried by a jury shall be otherwise re-examined in any court of the United States than according to the rules of the common law.

Article 10. Excessive bail shall not be required nor excessive fines imposed nor cruel nor unusual punishments inflicted.

Article 11. The enumeration in the constitution of certain rights shall not be construed to deny or disparage others retained by the people.

Article 12. The powers not delegated to the United States by the constitution nor prohibited by it to the states are reserved to the states respectively or to the people.

Be and they are hereby ratified on behalf of this state to become, when ratified by the legislatures of three fourths of the several states, part of the constitution of the United States.

Passed March 10, 1790. Recorded L. B. No. 4, p. 70

CHAPTER MCDLXCIII.

AN ACT TO PROVIDE FOR THE MORE EFFECTUAL RELIEF OF THE WIDOWS AND CHILDREN OF THE OFFICERS AND PRIVATES OF THE MILITIA WHO HAVE LOST THEIR LIVES IN THE SERVICE OF THEIR COUNTRY.

(Section I, P. L.) The benevolent provisions heretofore made by the legislature of this state for the widows and children of the officers, non-commissioned officers and private men of the militia who have been killed or died of their wounds in the service of this state or of the United States having from several causes proved ineffectual:

[Section I.] (Section II, P. L.) Be it enacted and it is hereby enacted by the Representatives of the Freemen of the Commonwealth of Pennsylvania in General Assembly met and by the authority of the same, That the widows of such officers, non-commissioned officers and private men of the militia, who at the time of their being called into service resided within this state and who have been killed or have died of their wounds received in the service of this state or of the United States, shall, during their widowhood, be respectively entitled to receive pensions not exceeding the half-pay and value of the rations that such officer or private was entitled to at the time of his death, and in case any such widow has since departed this life or hath

married again or such officer or private left no widow, the child
or children of such officer or private shall be entitled to the
like pension or such proportionable part thereof as upon the
circumstances of the case and conformably to the true intent
and meaning of this act the justices of the court hereinafter
mentioned shall adjudge reasonable and just until such child
or children respectively shall attain the age of fourteen years,
and the said court shall appoint one or more suitable persons
to be guardians of such child or children for the purpose of
receiving and applying such pensions or proportionable parts
of pensions.

[Section II.] (Section III, P. L.) And be it further enacted
by the authority aforesaid, That every such person claiming the
benefit of this act shall make application to the orphans'
court of the county wherein he or she may reside, and it shall
be lawful for such court upon due proof to them made that
such applicant is the widow or lawfully begotten child of such
officer or private, if a widow, if she remains unmarried, if a
child, that he or she is under the age of fourteen years, that
such officer or private was at the time of being called into service resident within this state and was killed or died of his
wounds received in the actual service of this state or of the
United States, to grant a certificate, setting forth the name,
age, rank and regiment or other corps in which such officer or
private served at the time of his death, the time, place and
manner of his death and the pension to which they have adjudged such applicant entitled according to this act, which
certificate shall be transmitted to the comptroller general of
this state who shall examine the same and if need shall be return it to the said court to be revised and corrected in manner
hereinafter mentioned.

[Section III.] (Section IV, P. L.) And be it further enacted
by the authority aforesaid, That the comptroller general shall
cause all such certificates as shall be by him examined and approved to be registered in alphabetical order and having first
submitted the same to the examination of the register general

shall transmit such certificates to the supreme executive council who are hereby authorized to draw orders upon the state treasurer for payment thereof.

And as it is expedient from time to time to revise the orders, adjudications and decrees which have heretofore been made by virtue of the act of assembly entitled "An act for the more effectual supply and honorable reward of the Pennsylvania troops in the service of the United States of America"[1] passed the first day of March one thousand seven hundred and eighty, the act entitled "A supplement to the act entitled 'An act for the more effectual supply and honorable reward of the Pennsylvania troops in the service of the United States of America'" and the act entitled "An act to settle and adjust the accounts of the troops of this state in the service of the United States, and for other purposes thereinafter mentioned,"[2] passed the first day of October one thousand seven hundred and eighty-one or which may be made by virtue of this act.

[Section IV.] (Section V, P. L.) Be it enacted by the authority aforesaid, That the justices of the orphans' court in their respective counties shall have power as often as they respectively shall think proper and are hereby required at least once in every year to revise the respective orders, proceedings and adjudications, which by virtue of the before mentioned acts have been made or by virtue of this act shall be made in their respective counties, and to cause any such pensioner or pensioners or the guardians of any such pensioner or pensioners to appear before them with such evidence as may be necessary and may and shall thereupon make new orders, adjudications and certificates as the nature of the case and the true construction of the beforementioned act or of this act may require, and if any alteration or further order may be made it shall be certified in manner aforesaid for the purpose aforesaid.

---

1 Chapter 880.
2 See Chapter 955.
Passed March 27, 1790. Recorded L. B. No. 4, p. 73. See the Act of Assembly passed April 11, 1793, Chapter 1696; April 9, 1799, Chapter 2068.

[Section V.] (Section VI, P. L.) And be it further enacted by the authority aforesaid, That so much of the act of assembly entitled "An act for the regulation of the militia of the commonwealth of Pennsylvania" passed the twentieth day of March one thousand seven hundred and eighty as authorizes and directs the justices of the orphans' court in the several counties to draw orders on the county lieutenants in the cases 'herein mentioned shall be and is hereby repealed.

CHAPTER MCDLXCIV.

AN ADDITIONAL SUPPLEMENT TO THE SEVERAL ACTS OF ASSEMBLY RESPECTING PUBLIC AUCTIONS AND AUCTIONEERS.

(Section I, P. L.) Whereas the acts of assembly now in force in this commonwealth for regulating sales by public auction within the districts in the same acts specified have been found defective in some important particulars:

Therefore:

[Section I.] (Section II, P. L.) Be it enacted and it is hereby enacted by the Representatives of the Freemen of the Commonwealth of Pennsylvania in General Assembly met and by the authority of the same, That it shall and may be lawful for the president or vice president in council to appoint and license two additional auctioneers, one for the city of Philadelphia, and one for the Northern Liberties for the sale of estates, real and personal within the same respectively who shall continue in office for and during the will and pleasure of the said president and council and shall severally give bond to the president and his successors with two or more sufficient securities in the sum of two thousand pounds conditioned for the faithful discharge of their and every of their respective duties and for well and truly performing the terms and payments in and by this act and the several acts of general assembly to which this is a supplement directed and required, and the said auc-

tioneers who shall be appointed and licensed in pursuance of
this act shall severally and respectively have and possess
within the said city and Northern Liberties [township and district respectively] the like powers and exclusive authorities and
be under the like regulations, provisions and restrictions and
subject to the like pains and penalties which the auctioneers
within the said city, townships and district respectively had
possessed or were subject to before the passing of this act within their respective districts.

[Section II.] (Section III, P. L.) And be it further enacted by the authority aforesaid, That from and after the passing of this act the duties to be paid to the treasury of this commonwealth on the sale of all goods, wares and merchandise by
public auction shall be one per centum and no more.

Passed March 27, 1790. Recorded L. B. No. 4, p. 82. See the acts
of Assembly passed March 19, 1789, Chapter 1400; February 26, 1791,
Chapter 1529.

CHAPTER MCDLXCV.

AN ACT TO PROVIDE FOR THE SAFETY OF THE RECORDS OF THE
SEVERAL COUNTIES IN THIS COMMONWEALTH, AND FOR OTHER
PURPOSES THEREIN MENTIONED.

(Section I, P. L.) Whereas the safety of the papers and records belonging to or in the custody of the prothonotaries, reg-
isters and recorders of the several counties of this commonwealth is an object of great importance to the good citizens
thereof:

[Section I.] (Section II, P. L.) Be it therefore enacted and it
is hereby enacted by the Representatives of the Freemen of
the Commonwealth of Pennsylvania in General Assembly met
and by the authority of the same, That the commissioners of
each county of this commonwealth, with the approbation of
the justices of the county court of quarter sessions and grand
jury of their respective counties, shall be and they are hereby
authorized and empowered to cause to be erected a suitable
building or buildings of brick or stone on the most safe and

secure plan to avoid the ravages of fire at the place appointed
by law for holding the courts in their respective counties for
the reception and safe keeping of the records and other papers
belonging to and in the custody of the prothonotary of the
county court of common pleas, the clerk of the county court of
quarter sessions, the clerk of the orphans' court, the recorder
of deeds and the register for the probate of wills and the granting of letters of administration of their respective counties.

[Section II.] (Section II, P. L.) [Sic.] And be it further
enacted by the authority aforesaid, That the several officers
before mentioned upon due notice from the commissioners of
the respective counties as soon as such suitable buildings shall
have been constructed as aforesaid in their respective counties
shall be and they are hereby required to deposit and keep the
records and papers belonging to their respective offices in the
said buildings under the penalty of two hundred pounds to be
recovered by action of debt, bill or information, the one half to
be paid to the county treasurer of the county in which such
courts shall be respectively held and applied to the payment for
or repairing of the buildings herein directed to be erected, the
other half to the use of him or her who shall sue for the same.

And whereas suitors and others having business to transact at the different public offices in the several counties of this
commonwealth are frequently subjected to great delays, trouble and inconvenience by reason of the several public offices
being held at a distance from each other and it is just and reasonable that those persons who hold public offices of trust and
profit should accommodate their residence to the ease and con
venience of the public:

And whereas some time may elapse before the buildings
hereinbefore directed may be prepared for the reception and
safe keeping of the records and papers aforesaid:

[Section III.] (Section IV, P. L.) Be it therefore enacted
by the authority aforesaid, That from and after the first day
of January one thousand seven hundred and ninety-one as well
the officers herein mentioned as the sheriff of each respective
county shall keep their offices in such town or place as is or

shall be by law established for holding the courts for such
counties under the penalty of two hundred pounds to be recovered by action of debt, bill or information, the one half to
be paid to the county treasurer of the county in which such
courts shall respectively be held and applied to the payment
for or repairs of the buildings herein directed to be erected, the
other half therefor to the use of him or her who shall sue for
the same.

Passed March 27, 1790. Recorded L. B. No. 4, p. 77.

CHAPTER MCDLXCIV.

A FURTHER SUPPLEMENT TO THE ACT OF ASSEMBLY ENTITLED "AN
ACT FOR THE RELIEF OF INSOLVENT DEBTORS WITHIN THE PRO-
VINCE OF PENNSYLVANIA."

(Section I, P. L.) In order to remedy several defects and inconveniences in the laws now in force within this state for the
purpose of granting relief to insolvent debtors:

[Section I.] (Section II, P. L.) Be it enacted and it is hereby
enacted by the Representatives of the Freemen of the Commonwealth of Pennsylvania in General Assembly met and by
the authority of the same, That if upon hearing the petition of
any insolvent debtor praying relief from personal imprison
ment according to the several acts of assembly in such case
made and application on the part of any the creditors of such
debtor it shall appear to the court having cognizance thereof
to be reasonable and expedient to allow further time for such
cerditor or creditors to make inquiry relative to the estate and
effects of such debtor it shall be lawful for such court to re-
mand such debtor for such time as in their discretion shall be
thought sufficient for such inquiry.

[Section II.] (Section III, P. L.) Be it further enacted by
the authority aforesaid, That where any such debtor has been
or shall be remanded to gaol by reason of a strong presumption of fraud within the meaning of the several acts of assem-

bly in such case made and provided, it shall be lawful for the
court having cognizance thereof to discharge such person from
imprisonment upon the like terms and conditions and in the
like manner as in the said acts of assembly is made and provided in such reasonable time after having been so remanded
as the court having regard to the misconduct of the party shall
in their discretion think expedient: Provided that no such person be discharged from imprisonment until he or she shall
have been in actual confinement twelve calendar months from
the time of being so remanded.

[Section III.] (Section IV, P. L.) Be it further enacted by
the authority aforesaid, That where any person hath been or
shall be adjudged a bankrupt and may not have obtained a
certificate of conformity within the several acts of assembly
of this state for the regulation of bankruptcy and shall upon
his petition to the court having cognizance thereof pray relief
from personal imprisonment it shall be lawful for the court,
due notice having been given as well to the creditors of such
petitioner as to the commissioners named and authorized in
such commission of a bankruptcy, to discharge such petitioner
from imprisonment. Provided no such person shall be discharged from imprisonment until he shall have been in actual
confinement for the space of twelve calendar months.

[Section IV.] (Section V, P. L.) Be it further enacted by the
the authority aforesaid, That where any person hath been or
convicted and sentenced among other things to make restitution to the party aggrieved it shall be lawful for the court
in which such felony shall have been convicted upon his petition praying the benefit of this act and upon due notice to
the creditors of such petitioner to order and direct such additional labor to be performed by such felon in like manner and
for the like uses and purposes as were before awarded by the
court in which said felon was convicted as shall in their judgment be a sufficient commutation for such restitution and it
shall be lawful for such court upon due proof that such additional term of labor hath been fully complied with to order
such felon to be discharged from further imprisonment so far

as relates to the claims of any person or persons entitled to restitution as aforesaid.

[Section V.] (Section VI. P. L.) Be it further enacted by the authority aforesaid, That where any insolvent debtor being of the age of fifty years or upwards and married or having a charge of children shall by his petition pray the benefit of this act it shall be lawful for the court having cognizance thereof besides the like relief upon the like terms and conditions as by the several acts of assembly for the relief of insolvent debtors is made and provided to give such petitioner a certificate which shall operate with regard to all debts due previously to granting the same as a discharge both of the persons of such petitioner and of such property as he or she may afterwards acquire. Provided, such debtor shall not at the time of making such application for the benefit of this act be indebted to any one person in a greater sum than twenty pounds. Provided also, That any person who having received such certificate shall afterwards be imprisoned on account of any debts contracted after receiving the same shall not again be entitled to the like benefit.

[Section VI.] (Section VII. P. L.) Be it further enacted by the authority aforesaid, That it shall not be lawful to discharge any insolvent debtor from imprisonment unless at least fifteen days notice of the time appointed for hearing such debtor shall have been given to his or her creditors under the regulations and restrictions in the several acts of assembly in such cases provided.

[Section VII.] (Section VIII, P. L.) And be it further enacted by the authority aforesaid, That where at the time of any debtor's application to the court for the benefit of the said insolvent acts there shall be any action or actions depending in the said court or any other court within this state or judgments obtained against such debtors at the suit of any person or persons not inhabitants of this state it shall and may be lawful for the said court to order the discharge of the said debtor from imprisonment as to the debt or debts demanded in such action or judgments on due notice having been given

to the attorney at law for the plaintiffs in the said actions or to
the attorney in fact or known agent of the said plaintiff although the creditor or creditors may not have been personally
served with any such notices.

Passed March 27, 1790. Recorded L. B. No. 4, p. 83. See the Act
of Assembly passed February 14, 1729-30, Chapter 315.

CHAPTER MCDLXVII.

AN ACT TO AUTHORIZE AND DIRECT THE SUPREME EXECUTIVE
COUNCIL TO APPOINT COMMISSIONERS TO AUDIT AND SETTLE THE
ACCOUNTS BETWEEN BEDFORD AND HUNTINGDON COUNTIES AND
FOR OTHER PURPOSES THEREIN MENTIONED.

(Section I, P. L.) Whereas the commissioners and treasurer
of Huntingdon county have represented to this house that for
several years previous to the erection of the said county greater
sums in county taxes were laid in the county of Bedford than
the amount of the current appropriations to which the same
were subject and that considerable sums of money have arisen
from the sale of stray horses before that period and have
prayed the house to provide by law for a just settlement of the
accounts of the commissioners, treasurer and wood rangers
of the said county of Bedford so far as relates to the premises
and it appears to this house reasonable and proper to grant
the prayer of the said petition:

[Section 1.] (Section II, P. L.) Be it therefore enacted and
it is hereby enacted by the Representatives of the Freemen of
the Commonwealth of Pennsylvania in General Assembly met
and by the authority of the same, That the supreme executive
council are hereby authorized forthwith to appoint three commissioners who or any two of them shall audit and settle the
accounts of the commissioners, treasurer and wood rangers
of the county of Bedford relative to the county taxes and
moneys arising therefrom and from the sale of stray horses
prior to the twentieth day of September one thousand seven

hundred and eighty-seven on which day the said county of Huntingdon was erected; for which purpose they shall have power to send for persons and papers and administer the necessary oaths and affirmations and shall be respectively allowed a compensation of ten shillings for every day in which they or any two of them shall be employed upon such service to be paid out of the moneys remaining after the deductions hereafter mentioned if any there be otherwise to be paid by the commissioners of the county of Huntingdon.

[Section II.] (Section III, P. L.) Be it further enacted by the authority aforesaid, That after deducting all such county debts and legal charges and appropriations as may have been made or incurred previous to the twentieth day of September one thousand seven hundred and eighty-seven the residue of [the] said moneys in hand and also of such arrearages thereof as were due on the said twentieth of September one thousand seven hundred and eighty-seven so often as thirty pounds thereof shall from time to time hereafter be received shall be divided between the said counties of Bedford and Huntingdon in a ratio to be fixed by the said commissioners to be appointed by virtue of this act proportionably to the taxable property in the said counties respectively at the period of time before mentioned.

[Section III.] (Section IV, P. L.) Be it further enacted by the authority aforesaid, That all arrearages of taxes, excise duties or militia fines which before the twentieth of September one thousand seven hundred and eighty-seven became due within that part of the late county of Bedford which is now comprised in the county of Huntingdon shall be levied and collected with like powers and authorities and under the like penalties and restrictions as if the act entitled "An act for erecting part of Bedford county into a separate county"[1] had not been made.

CHAPTER MCDXCVIII.

A SUPPLEMENT TO THE ACT ENTITLED "AN ACT FOR ERECTING THE
SOUTHWEST PART OF THE COUNTY OF CUMBERLAND INTO A NEW
COUNTY.

(Section I, P. L.) Whereas doubts have arisen concerning
that part of the boundary line between the counties of Cumberland and Franklin near the town of Shippensburg:

For remedy whereof and to the end that the boundaries between the said counties of Cumberland and Franklin be cer-
tainly known:

[Section I.] (Section II, P. L.) Be it enacted and it is hereby
enacted by the Representatives of the Freemen of the Commonwealth of Pennsylvania in General Assembly met and by
the authority of the same, That a line beginning at York
county line in the South Mountain at the intersection of Lurgan and Hopewell townships, thence by a line composed of
part of the original line of Lurgan township and one to be
run so as to leave the tract of land now or late of Edward
Shippen, Esquire, wherein the town of Shippensburg is erected
within the county of Cumberland to the line of Fannet township thence by the lines of the last mentioned township (leaving
the same in Franklin county) to the line of Bedford county
shall be and the same is hereby declared to be the boundary
line between the counties of Cumberland and Franklin.

CHAPTER MCDXCIX.

AN ACT FOR THE RELIEF OF JOHN LYTLE, JOHN WEBB AND WILLIAM MURRAY.

(Section I, P. L.) Whereas John Lytle, John Webb and William Murray by their petitions have represented to this house that they in order to improve their farms borrowed money from the loan office in the year one thousand seven hundred and seventy four and that in the late Indian war they were driven from their habitation and lost all their personal property, by which means they are rendered at this time unable to discharge the several sums due by them to the state and have prayed this house to grant them a longer time to discharge the same:

And whereas it is just and reasonable that the prayer of their petition should be granted:

Therefore:

[Section I.] (Section II. P. L.) Be it enacted and it is hereby enacted by the Representatives of the Freemen of the Commonwealth of Pennsylvania in General Assembly met and by the authority of the same, That no further proceedings shall be had against John Lytle, John Webb and William Murray for five years from and after the enacting hereof.

Passed March 27, 1790. Recorded L. B. No. 4, p. 75.

CHAPTER MD.

AN ACT FOR COMPENSATING LAUGHLIN McCARTNEY AND OTHERS THEREIN MENTIONED FOR SUPPLIES BY THEM FURNISHED THE CIVIL OFFICERS OF NORTHUMBERLAND COUNTY IN THE YEAR ONE THOUSAND SEVEN HUNDRED AND SEVENTY-FIVE.

(Section I, P. L.) Whereas Laughlin McCartney, John Simpson, Thomas Gaskins, William Sayers, William McKim, Fred-

erick Stone, Aaron Levy, Robert Martin and William Mackey
by their petition to this house have represented that in consequence of the orders of John Penn, Esquire, late Governor
of Pennsylvania to enforce the execution of the laws in the
county of Northumberland dated the twenty fifth day of November one thousand seven hundred and seventy-five they furnished sundry supplies to the persons employed to execute the
said orders and as the said accounts cannot be settled and
adjusted under any of the existing laws of this commonwealth
and as it is just and reasonable that compensation should be
made to those who furnished supplies for the use of government:

Therefore:

[Section I.] (Section II. P. L.) Be it enacted and it is hereby
enacted by the Representatives of the Freemen of the Commonwealth of Pennsylvania in General Assembly met and by
the authority of the same, That the comptroller-general of this
state be and he is hereby authorized and required to examine
and settle the said accounts admitting them or such parts of
them as appear to be just and equitable and the same being
examined and approved by the register-general and afterwards
confirmed by the president and supreme executive council and
thereupon issue certificates in favor of the said Laughlin Mc-
Cartney, John Simpson, Thomas Gaskins, William Sayers, William McKim, Frederick Stone, Aaron Levy, Robert Martin and
William Mackey for such sums as they shall respectively be
entitled to which certificates shall bear interest from the first
day of January one thousand seven hundred and eighty-five.

Passed March 27, 1790.   Recorded L. B. No. 4, p. 85.

CHAPTER MDI.

AN ACT IN FAVOR OF READING HOWELL AND FOR OTHER PURPOSES THEREIN MENTIONED.

(Section I, P. L.) Whereas it appears to this house that Reading Howell of the city of Philadelphia hath at great expense

of labor and money procured materials for compiling an accurate map of Pennsylvania including the lands lately purchased of the United States and he hath nearly compiled the same, which map when completed will give more perfect knowledge of geography of the State and more especially of the uninhabited parts of it and will afford much assistance in the laying out of roads and the improvement of the inland navigation which will be of great advantage to the citizens of the commonwealth:

And whereas it is just and right for government to give encouragement to men who devote their time and money in pursuits which promote the public good:

And whereas it appears to this assembly that the lines of the state ought to be perpetuated and generally known to the citizens of this commonwealth which may be conveniently done by their being engraved and described in the said map:

[Section I.] (Section II, P. L.) Be it therefore enacted and it is hereby enacted by the Representatives of the Freemen of the Commonwealth of Pennsylvania in General Assembly met and by the authority of the same, That in order to enable the said Reading Howell to complete the said map, the president or vice-president in council be authorized to issue their warrants on the state treasurer requiring him to pay to the said Reading Howell the sum of three hundred pounds to be paid out of the moneys appropriated for claims and improvements when the same shall become sufficiently productive.

[Section II.] (Section III, P. L.) And be it enacted by the authority aforesaid, That the supreme executive council be and they are hereby authorized and requested to direct that all the lines of this state as established by law or otherwise fixed and ascertained be delineated and engraved on the said map to be published by the said Reading Howell together with [such] marginal notes relative thereto as shall be deemed necessary to explain the same, all expenses accruing in execution hereof be included in the sum hereby granted and so much of the law directing the northern boundary of this state to be engraved under the direction of the supreme executive council shall be and is hereby repealed. And the said Reading Howell shall be entitled to receive [only] the sum of two hundred pounds part of the sum herein granted until he shall have completed and published the said map. Provided nevertheless, That if the said Reading Howell his executors or administrators shall not complete the said map within the space of two years and six months from and after the enacting hereof then and In that case the said Reading Howell his executors or administrators shall repay into the state treasury all the moneys received by him in pursuance of this act.

[Section III.] (Section IV, P. L.) Be it further enacted by the authority aforesaid, That the said Reading Howell, his executors or administrators, shall deliver to the executive authority of this Commonwealth twenty-five of the said maps when completed for the use of the state.

Passed March 27, 1790. Recorded L. D. No. 4. p. 76.

CHAPTER MDII.

AN ACT FOR FURTHER ENLARGING THE TIME LIMITED BY THE ACT ENTITLED "AN ACT FOR FACILITATING THE REDEMPTION OF THE BILLS OF CREDIT EMITTED IN THE YEAR ONE THOUSAND SEVEN HUNDRED AND EIGHTY-ONE AND FOR REDEEMING PART OF THE FUNDED DEBT OF THIS STATE, FOR EXPENDING THE TIME FOR PATENTING LANDS WHICH WERE LOCATED BEFORE THE DECLARATION OF INDEPENDENCY AND FOR GIVING A RIGHT OF PRE-EMPTION TO ACTUAL SETTLERS FOR PROCURING WARRANTS FOR THE LANDS BY THEM OCCUPIED."[1]

(Section I, P. L.) Whereas in and by the act entitled "An act for facilitating the redemption of the bills of credit emitted in the year one thousand seven hundred and eighty-one and for redeeming part of the funded debt of this state, for extending the time for patenting lands which were located before the declaration of independency and for giving a right of preemp-

[1] Passed March 29, 1788, Chapter 1348.

tion to actual settlers for procuring warrants for lands by them
occupied, the time limited by the act enacted the twenty-eighth
day of March one thousand seven hundred and eighty-seven for
paying or securing to the state the payment for lands held
or claimed by any citizen of this commonwealth by location or
any other office right obtained before the tenth day of December one thousand seven hundred and seventy-six and yet remaining unpatented was extended under the terms and conditions therein mentioned to the tenth day of April one thousand seven hundred and eighty-nine:

And whereas in and by the same act the time limited by the
act enacted the thirtieth day of December one thousand seven
hundred and eighty-six entitled, "An act for giving during a
limited time a right of pre-emption to the actual settlers within
this state" [1] was further extended in every matter and thing
therein contained to the tenth day of April one thousand seven
hundred and eighty-nine:

And whereas by an act enacted the twenty-first day of
March in the year of our Lord one thousand seven hundred and
eighty-nine entitled, "An act for enlarging the time limited by
the act entitled, An act for facilitating the redemption of the
bills of credit emitted in the year one thousand seven hundred
and eighty-one and for redeeming part of the funded debt
of this state, for extending the time for patenting lands which
were located before the declaration of independency and for
giving a right of pre-emption to actual settlers for procuring
warrants for lands by them occupied within this state," [2] was
further extended in every matter and thing therein contained
to the said tenth day of April one thousand seven hundred and
ninety:

And whereas the said limitations so extended [us] aforesaid
will expire on the tenth day of April next and it is deemed just
and expedient that they should be extended:

[Section I.] (Section II, P. L.) Be it therefore enacted and it
is hereby enacted by the Representatives of the Freemen of

---

[1] Chapter 1259.
[2] Chapter 1402.

the Commonwealth of Pennsylvania in General Assembly met and by the authority of the same, That the times so as afore-said limited and extended be and they are hereby respectively further extended to the tenth day of April in the year of our Lord one thousand seven hundred and ninety-one and from thence to the end of the next sitting of the General As-sembly as fully and amply to all intents and purposes as they were by the aforesaid acts hereinbefore mentioned extended to the said tenth day of April one thousand seven hundred and ninety.

[Section II.] (Section III, P. L.) And be it further enacted by the authority aforesaid, That the receiver-general of the land-office shall receive any part of the purchase money for the lands mentioned in the act which this act is made to continue, one fourth being in lawful money of this State or in the bills of credit emitted by virtue of an act enacted the seventh day of April one thousand seven hundred and eighty-one and three-fourths thereof in depreciation certificates or other certificates of original state debts on which interest is payable annually at the treasury of this state. Provided each payment so made shall not be less than one-fourth part of the original purchase due on such lands.

Passed March 29, 1790. Recorded L. B. No. 4, p. 84.

CHAPTER MDIII.

AN ACT TO AUTHORIZE THE SALE OF THE BARRACKS IN THE BOR-OUGH OF LANCASTER AND THE LOT OR LOTS ON WHICH THEY ARE ERECTED AND FOR OTHER PURPOSES THEREIN MENTIONED.

[Section I.] Whereas the barracks in the borough of Lan-caster are become entirely useless to the state and an annual expense arising thereon for the ground rent and it is proper that the whole should be disposed of:

31—XIII

And whereas the roof of the public magazine or powder-house in said borough is in a state of decay, the ammunition or powder subject to damage, and as there are no moneys assigned for the repairs thereof it is proper that provision should be made for that purpose:

Therefore:

[Section I.] (Section II, P. L.) Be it enacted and it is hereby enacted by the Representatives of the Freemen of the Commonwealth of Pennsylvania in General Assembly met and by the authority of the same, That the president or vice-president in council be and they are hereby authorized and empowered to appoint two or more commissioners who shall expose to public sale and sell to the highest bidder or bidders the lot or lots of ground and the barracks thereon erected in the borough of Lancaster, one half of the purchase money shall be paid at the time of the sale and the remainder in six months after. And in case of neglect or refusal to pay such remaining part of the purchase money the premises shall revert to the state and be sold again by direction of council, and the first payment be forfeited for the use of the state.

[Section II.] (Section III, P. L.) And be it further enacted by the authority aforesaid. That the supreme executive council may (if they shall judge it necessary) direct the commissioners to apportion and lay off the said grounds into as many lots as the nature of the case may require with one or more streets as shall best accommodate the same and promote the interest of the commonwealth. And the said president or vice-president in council when the whole of such purchase moneys for such lot or lots respectively shall be paid to the said commissioners shall be and they are hereby authorized to make good and effectual conveyances for every such lot or lots to the purchasers thereof respectively.

[Section III.] (Section IV, P. L.) And be it further enacted by the authority aforesaid, That the president and supreme executive council are hereby authorized to employ a suitable person or persons by contract or otherwise to put a new roof upon the powder house in the borough of Lancaster of such materials as may be judged most proper and to direct the same to be paid for out of the moneys arising out of the sale of the barracks aforesaid.

[Section IV.] (Section V, P. L.) And be it further enacted by the authority aforesaid, That the remainder of the moneys arising from the sale of the said lots and barracks shall be paid into the state treasury for the support of government, first deducting such reasonable allowances to the commissioners for their trouble in the execution of this act as to the president and supreme executive council may appear just and right.

Passed March 30, 1790.	Recorded L. B. No. 4, p. 88.

CHAPTER MDIV.

AN ACT TO REDUCE THE TAX UPON WRITS ISSUED OUT OF THE COUNTY COURT OF COMMON PLEAS OF PHILADELPHIA COUNTY DURING THE TIME THEREIN LIMITED.

(Section I, P. L.) Whereas by an act of general assembly enacted on the twentieth day of March one thousand seven hundred and eighty-three a tax of five shillings and seven pence was imposed upon every writ whether original or judicial, mesne process or any writ which shall be issued in the course of any action (subpoenas for witnesses and writs in behalf of this commonwealth only excepted), to be paid by the prothonotary of the county of Philadelphia out of the fees of his office:

And whereas the division of the county of Philadelphia and the vesting original jurisdiction within the remaining part of that county in the supreme court with other causes have reduced the profits of the said office far below a competent provision for the difficult and professional duties required in the execution of it:

[Section I.] (Section II, P. L.) Be it therefore enacted and it is hereby enacted by the Representatives of the Freemen of the Commonwealth of Pennsylvania in general assembly met and by the authority of the same, That for each of the said writs which shall be issued from and after the enacting hereof

for and during the term of one year the said prothonotary
shall pay only the sum of two shillings and six-pence instead
of five shillings and seven-pence, any act of assembly of this
state to the contrary in anywise notwithstanding.

Passed March 30, 1790. Recorded L. B. No. 4, p. 69.

CHAPTER MDV.

AN ACT TO REPEAL AN ACT ENTITLED "AN ACT FOR ASCERTAINING
AND CONFIRMING TO CERTAIN PERSONS CALLED CONNECTICUT
CLAIMANTS THE LAND BY THEM WITHIN THE COUNTY OF LUZERNE
AND FOR OTHER PURPOSES THEREIN MENTIONED." [1]

(Section I, P. L.) Whereas an act of assembly enacted the
twenty-eighth day of March one thousand seven hundred and
eighty-seven entitled, "An act for ascertaining and confirming
to certain persons called Connecticut claimants the lands by
them claimed within the counties of Luzerne and for other purposes therein mentioned," [2] hath been found in its principles
and operations to be unjust and oppressive in as much as it
divested many citizens of this state of their lands without their
consent and without making them any just compensation:

And whereas depriving individuals of their property in such
a summary way is unconstitutional and of the most dangerous
consequence:

And whereas said act was enacted by the legislature hastily
without due consideration had and proper information of the
magnitude of the grant:

And whereas carrying said act into effect would impose a
grievous burden on the good citizens of this state to make compensation to those who would thereby be divested of their
property:

And whereas the reasons set forth in the preamble of said
act do not appear to warrant any legislative interference or
departure from the established rules of justice in respect to
private property nor hath had the effect proposed:

[1] Chapter 1265.
[2] Ante.

[Section I.] (Section II, P. L.) Be it therefore enacted by the Representatives of the Freemen of the Commonwealth of Pennsylvania in General Assembly met and by the authority of the same, That the act entitled, "An act for ascertaining and confirming to certain persons called Connecticut claimants the lands by them claimed within the county of Luzerne and for other purposes therein mentioned," [1] be and the same is hereby repealed and all proceedings had under said act are hereby rendered void and declared to be null and of no effect and all titles and claims which might be supposed to be affected by said act are hereby revested in the former owners in as full and ample a manner as if the said had never been enacted anything in the same to the contrary notwithstanding.

And whereas it has been represented to this house that judgment has been obtained in sundry actions of ejectment brought in the court of common pleas for the county of Northumberland for sundry tracts of land now lying within the county of Luzerne at the suit of persons claiming under titles derived from the late Proprietaries of Pennsylvania in which judgment by default has been recovered by persons holding such lands by virtues of rights or titles derived from or under the state of Connecticut and it is right and just that the defendants in such actions should not be dispossessed without a trial by jury.

[Section II.] (Section III, P. L.) Be it therefore enacted by the authority aforesaid, That no writ or writs of scire facias or habere facias possessionem shall issue from the said court to revive such judgments or to carry them into effect, but original [suits] in ejectment for recovery of any such tracts of land within the said county may be brought at the suit of such Pennsylvania claimants or any of them.

Passed April 1, 1790. Recorded L. B. No. 4, p. 96.

CHAPTER MDVI.

AN ACT TO ENFORCE THE DUE COLLECTION OF THE REVENUES OF THE STATE AND FOR OTHER PURPOSES THEREIN MENTIONED.

(Section I, P. L.) Whereas the interest of this commonwealth requires that the collection of the [public] revenues should be effected with greater regularity than has of late been practiced:

[Section 1.] (Section II, P. L.) Be it therefore enacted and it is hereby enacted by the Representatives of the Freemen of the Commonwealth of Pennsylvania in General Assembly met and by the authority of the same, That from and after the passing of this act all accounts of fees received by the secretary of the supreme executive council and the surveyor general, receiver general and secretary of the land-office, all accounts of moneys or certificates received by the receiver general in payment for lands which shall be purchased of this state or which have been purchased of the late proprietaries and are payable to this state, all accounts of moneys received or to be received for the use of the state by the prothonotary of the supreme court and the prothonotaries of the several county courts of common pleas or the clerk of the mayor's court of the city of Philadelphia, the clerks of the several courts of quarter sessions or other officers receiving or accountable for fines or forfeitures, moneys paid or to be paid for marriage [or] tavern licenses or taxes upon legal process and all accounts between this state, the several collectors of excise duties, the treasurers of the different counties and the several auctioneers of the city of Philadelphia, the district of Southwark and the townships of Northern Liberties and of Moyamensing shall once in every six months or oftener if thereto required by the treasurer of this state be rendered unto him, who shall without delay examine, liquidate and adjust the same, for which purpose the said treasurer of the state shall be and he is hereby authorized by subpoena and attachment to call before him any witness or witnesses and administer all necessary oaths and affirmations and every such account being so examined, liquidated and adjusted shall be transmitted by the said treasurer together with the evidence and vouchers thereto belonging to the register general for his examination and approbation, who if he approve thereof shall forthwith transmit the same with the vouchers and evidence accompanying it to the president and supreme executive council for their final approbation and the president and supreme executive council having approved thereof shall by their secretary return the said account with the vouchers and evidence to the register general who shall cause the same to be registered as the law directs in cases of accounts settled by the comptroller general, and to prevent error or fraud the register general shall make upon each of such vouchers a mark or note of reference to the account or accounts to which it referred when produced by the said treasurer and the said accounts being so approved and registered shall be returned with the said vouchers to the treasurer who shall be thereupon authorized and required either to give discharges or to take legal and effectual measures for recovering the moneys thereon due to the commonwealth as the nature of the case may require.

[Section II.] (Section III, P. L.) And be it further enacted by the authority aforesaid, That the said treasurer shall and he is hereby required and enjoined to furnish to the register general on the first day of every month (with a due exception of Sundays) an account of all moneys received and paid by virtue of his office during the preceding month and the register general is hereby required to transfer all such receipts and payments to the proper accounts in his books and the said treasurer shall settle annually with the register general in the manner hereinafter directed with regard to accounts hereafter arising between the commonwealth and individuals or bodies politic.

And whereas it is expedient to enable the comptroller general to state the account between this state and the United States and to settle and adjust to the twenty-eighth day of March one thousand seven hundred and eighty-nine all accounts depending between this state and individuals or bodies politic other than the United States and to report to the register general all such balances as were then due to or from any individuals or bodies politic in account with this state for the purposes directed in and by the act entitled "An act for the appointment of a register general for the purpose of registering the accounts of this state"[1] enacted the twenty-eighth day of March one thousand seven hundred and eighty-nine and the supplement thereto enacted the thirtieth day of September one thousand seven hundred and eighty-nine,[2] for which purpose it is necessary that the settlement of all accounts beween this state and individuals or bodies politic except the accounts hereinbefore mentioned should be vested in the first instance in the register general subject to the examination and control hereinafter mentioned:

[Section III.] (Section IV, P. L.) Be it therefore enacted by the authority aforesaid, That all demands hereafter made by individuals or bodies politic except what is hereinbefore excepted and all accounts hereafter to be opened between this state and such bodies politic or individuals shall in the first instance be submitted to, examined, liquidated and adjusted by the register general who shall for that purpose have the like powers and authorities as by any of the laws of this commonwealth are vested for such purposes in the comptroller general and the register general shall after liquidation and adjustment of every such account transmit the same with the vouchers and evidence in manner hereinbefore directed to the comptroller general for his examination and approbation, who having examined and approved be same and caused proper entries to be made thereof in his books of office shall in like manner transmit such accounts to the president and supreme executive council for their final approbation and the president and supreme executive council having approved thereof shall by their secretary return the same to the register general to be by him registered in manner hereinbefore directed, and all such accounts and vouchers shall be carefully filed and deposited in his office.

---

[1] Chapter 1422.
[2] Chapter 1463.

[Section IV.] (Section V, P. L.) Be it further enacted by the authority aforesaid, That all such settlements of accounts shall have the like force and effect and be subject to the like appeal at the instance of the party as settlements heretofore made by the comptroller general.

And whereas considerable sums in certificates [issued] by or under the authority of this state or the United States have from time to time been received by the comptroller-general for the use of this state and considerable sums in certificates have been issued by virtue of the act entitled "An act for the further relief of the public creditors who are citizens of this state by receiving on loan certain debts of the United States of America and for funding the same and for paying the annual interest of such loans and the interest of certain debts of this state every six months"[1] enacted the first day of March one thousand seven hundred and eighty-six and the supplement thereto enacted the twenty-eighth day of March one thousand seven hundred and eighty-seven, some of which last described certificates have by virtue of the said act been received in payment for lands by the receiver general and by him delivered to the comptroller general and others are from time to time returned by the possessors in exchange for the certificates of debts due by the United States received on loan by this state in pursuance of the said acts and it is expedient that proper measures should be taken to preserve such of the said certificates of debts due by the United States as were or shall be received for the use of this state and to cancel and render useless such as have been issued by or under the authority of this state:

[Section V.] (Section VI, P. L.) Be it therefore enacted by the authority aforesaid, That the comptroller general, the register general and the treasurer of this state shall in the presence of two members of the supreme executive council whom the president and supreme executive council are hereby requested to appoint from time to time for that purpose forthwith examine all certificates received by the said comptroller general and shall cause four exact lists to be made of the certificates of debts due by the United States including those certificates

---
[1] Chapter 1202.

denominated facilities or indents in his possession other than
those received on loan as aforesaid and which have not since
become the property of this state by receiving the new loan
certificates issued in lieu thereof in payment of lands as aforesaid specifying particularly in such lists the date, sum, number, time when interest commenced, amount of interest paid
and name of the payee of each certificate and each of the said
lists being signed in the margin of each page by such members
of the supreme executive council and by every of the said officers one of them shall be delivered to the president and supreme executive council, one to the register general to be by
him registered, one to the comptroller general which with the
credit given to him in the books of the [said] register general
on behalf of this state shall be in full acquittance and discharge
for all such of the said certificates as shall be delivered to the
treasurer and one of the said lists shall be delivered with the
said certificates to the treasurer, and the said treasurer shall
cause proper books to be opened containing an account of such
certificates as draw interest from the United States and shall
from time to time apply for and receive such interest and enter the same in such books to the debit of this state in account
with the United States and he shall take such proper measures
for the safety and security of all such certificates [and facilities or indents] as the president and supreme executive council
shall from time to time advise and direct. Provided, That before any of the pages in such lists shall be signed in manner
aforesaid the comptroller general shall in the presence of the
said two members of the supreme executive council deliver
into the hands of the said treasurer all such certificates and
facilities or indents as shall be enumerated and specified in
such page. And whereas it hath sometimes happened that certificates of debts due by the United States received by this
state in payment for lands or otherwise and not upon loan
have, to accommodate the parties, been delivered out by the
comptroller general in exchange for certificates granted by this
state in pursuance of the act aforesaid enacted the first day of
March one thousand seven hundred and eighty-six:

[Section VI.] (Section VII, P. L.) Be it therefore enacted

by the authority aforesaid, That in all such cases a certificate
or certificates of the like kind corresponding in amount and
value with those received on loan as aforesaid shall be delivered by the said comptroller general to the said treasurer in
manner aforesaid and proper entries shall be made thereof
in the said lists and where it shall be necessary in order to
effect the said exchange that any of the said certificates deposited with the treasurer in pursuance of the directions of
this act should be delivered out in lieu of a certificate received
on loan it shall be lawful for the president in council upon application from the comptroller-general approved and countersigned by the register-general to issue a warrant or warrants
for that purpose.

[Section VII.] (Section VIII, P. L.) Be it enacted by the
authority aforesaid, That all certificates issued by or under
the authority of this state which have been received by the said
comptroller-general in payment for lands or otherwise for the
use of this state or have been returned by the parties who received them in exchange for certificates of debts due by the
United States pursuant to the act aforesaid enacted on the
first day of March one thousand seven hundred and eighty-six
shall be examined in like manner and shall be cancelled by the
use of a proper instrument that shall cut each certificate in
the middle in the form of a cross without taking out any part
of the certificate or rendering it illegible and such certificates
shall thereupon be delivered to the register-general who shall
preserve the same by pasting them in numerical order in books
of coarse paper leaving so much of each certificate free as will
discover the indorsements of interest paid thereon. And
whereas it is expedient to effect with less circuity and expense
the receipt of the moneys remaining due to this state from its
citizens for moneys received on loan by virtue of an act entitled "An act for emitting the sum of one hundred and fifty
thousand pounds in bills of credit on loan and providing a fund
for payment of public debts," [1] passed by the assembly of the
late province of Pennsylvania on the twenty-sixth day of February one thousand seven hundred and seventy-three and by

---
[1] Chapter 672.

virtue of an act entitled "An act for erecting and opening a
loan office for the sum of fifty thousand pounds"[1] enacted the
fourth day of April one thousand seven hundred and eighty-
five.

[Section VIII.] (Section IX, P.L.) Be it therefore enacted
by the authority aforesaid, That all the powers and duties in
and by the acts hereinbefore mentioned or in or by any other
act or acts now vested in David Rittenhouse, George Schlosser
and Robert Smith, Esquires, or either of them jointly or severally as trustees of the said loan-offices respectively shall be and
they are hereby transferred to and vested in the treasurer of
the state and the said David Rittenhouse, George Schlosser and
Robert Smith, Esquires, shall and they are hereby required
to deliver in the space of thirty days after demand all the
books, records, deeds and papers in their custody and possession by reason of their said trusts.

[Section IX.] (Section X, P. L.) Be it further enacted by the
authority aforesaid, That in case any difference of opinion
should arise between the register-general, comptroller-general
or treasurer of the state or either of them relative to the duties
hereinbefore directed and required to be done by them or by
either of them they shall and are hereby required to apply
forthwith to the president and supreme executive council for
their orders and directions therein, which orders and directions
shall in such cases indemnify and save harmless all such
officers paying obedience thereto.

[Section X.] (Section XI, P. L.) Be it further enacted by
the authority aforesaid, That if the said comptroller-general,
the said trustees of the loan office or any other person or persons having in his or their possession any public records, books,
papers, accounts, vouchers, certificates of debts or other matters or things belonging to this commonwealth or wherein this
commonwealth is interested and concerned and which conformably to the true intent and meaning of this act ought to
be delivered to the said register-general or to the said treasurer of the state shall refuse or neglect within sixty days after
demand made by the said register-general or treasurer of the

[1] Chapter 1159.

state to deliver up to them or either of them all and every such records, books, papers, accounts, vouchers and certificates, every such person so offending against this act shall forfeit and pay a sum not exceeding five thousand pounds to be recovered by indictment or information to the use of this state.

[Section XI.] (Section XII, P. L.) Be it further enacted by the authority aforesaid, That the comptroller-general shall proceed in the exchange of the certificates issued in lieu of those received on loan as is hereinbefore mentioned under such orders and directions as have been heretofore given or may hereafter be given by the president and supreme executive council for that purpose and the comptroller-general and register-general shall once in each month in the presence of two members of the supreme executive council examine all certificates granted by this state and so received in exchange by the comptroller-general and after taking lists thereof in the manner hereinbefore directed such certificates shall be delivered to the register-general for the purpose of being cancelled and preserved in manner aforesaid and so much of the act of assembly entitled "A supplement to the act entitled 'An act for the appointment of a register-general for the purpose of registering the accounts of this state' " [1] as directs the comptroller general to submit the accounts of certificates and certificates by him to be given or received in exchange as aforesaid to the inspection of the register general shall be and the same is hereby repealed.

[Section XII.] (Section XIII, P. L.) Be it further enacted by the authority aforesaid, That the treasurer of the state shall be allowed the sum of two hundred pounds per annum for the expenses of providing an additional clerk and the necessary books and stationery by reason of the additional duties hereinbefore imposed upon him and in lieu of all charges or commission for receiving the certificates of the United States and drawing the interest thereon accruing as before directed.

---

[1] Passed September 30, 1789, Chapter 1463.
Passed April 1, 1790. Recorded L. B. No. 4, p. 90.
See the Acts of Assembly passed March 30, 1791, Chapter 1542;
April 4, 1792, Chapter 1627; April 11, 1793, Chapter 1693.

CHAPTER MDVII.

AN ACT TO MAKE PROVISION FOR REPAIRS AT MUD ISLAND.

(Section I, P. L.) Whereas the banks of Mud Island in the river Delaware have been and still are in a very dangerous and imperfect state notwithstanding that four hundred and ninety-six pounds eight shillings and three pence hath been expended thereon by direction of council very considerable repairs are still wanting to preserve the fort and other buildings from destruction:

And whereas no appropriation hath us yet been made by the legislature either for the sum already expended or for what may be farther necessary to complete said repairs:

And whereas the interest of the state requires that such provision should be made:

Therefore:

[Section I.] (Section II, P. L.) Be it enacted and it is hereby enacted by the Representatives of the Freemen of the Commonwealth of Pennsylvania in General Assembly met and by the authority of the same, That the sum of one thousand pounds moneys arising from the interest of the fifty thousand pounds loan be specially appropriated for the purpose of replacing the four hundred and ninety-six pounds eight shillings and three pence already expended on the banks of Mud Island by order of council as well as to provide a fund to complete the further repairs required on the banks of said Island.

[Section II.] (Section III, P. L.) And be it enacted by the authority aforesaid, That the president and supreme executive council be and they are hereby authorized to employ suitable persons by contract to put the banks of Mud Island into good and desirable repair and to pay for the same by a warrant or warrants drawn upon the state treasury for any sum or sums to be paid out of the fund hereinbefore provided which together with the four hundred and ninety-six pounds eight shillings and three pence already drawn for shall not exceed one thousand pounds.

Passed April 2, 1790. Recorded L. B. No. 4, p. 100. See the Act of Assembly passed April 13, 1791, Chapter 1563.

CHAPTER MDVIII.

AN ACT FOR APPOINTING TWO ADDITIONAL TRUSTEES FOR THE COUNTY OF HUNTINGDON.

(Section I, P. L.) Whereas by the act for erecting part of Bedford county into a separate county by the name of Huntingdon county three of the five trustees therein named were appointed as residents in the town of Huntingdon for the greater convenience of forming a necessary quorum in order to the execution of the trust committed to them:

And whereas by the death of one of the said trustees, the removal of another from said town and the intention of a third to remove soon from the county there remains but one of the said trustees who has his usual residence in the said town and it is become difficult to assemble any three of the said trustees for the necessary business of the [county]:

For remedy whereof:

[Section I.] (Section II, P. L.) Be it enacted and it is hereby enacted by the Representatives of the Freemen of the Commonwealth of Pennsylvania in General Assembly met and by the authority of the same, That Andrew Henderson and Richard Smith of the town of Huntingdon aforesaid be and they are hereby appointed trustees in conjunction with the surviving trustees named in the said act and now residing within the said county, and they or a majority of them, heretofore and now appointed and residing within the said county shall have and execute all the powers, trusts and duties committed to the five trustees in the act for erecting the said county in the same manner and as fully as if the said Andrew Henderson and Richard Smith had been originally appointed trustees in the said act.

Passed April 2, 1790. Recorded L. B. No. 4, p. 103.

CHAPTER MDIX.

A FURTHER SUPPLEMENT TO THE ACT ENTITLED "AN ACT TO IN-
CORPORATE THE CITY OF PHILADELPHIA."[1]

(Section I, P. L.) Whereas the power of appointing collectors of the taxes for paving, lighting and watching the streets of the city of Philadelphia was formerly vested in the city assessors and since those officers have been by law directed no longer to be chosen the authority of appointing such collectors has lapsed:

And whereas by the thirty-fifth section of the act to incorporate the city of Philadelphia the mayor recorder, aldermen and common councilmen are empowered to execute and perform all such matters and things as the wardens and street commissioners were at and immediately before the passing of the said act respectively authorized and enabled by law to do, and by the thirty-sixth section of the said act the mayor or recorder and four of the aldermen are empowered to do and perform all such matters and things as the said wardens and street commissioners were respectively at [and] immediately before the enacting the said act authorized and enabled by law to do and perform in conjunction with any justice or justices of the peace of and for the city and county of Philadelphia or either of them:

And whereas it will be more convenient and beneficial that instead of separating and dividing the above mentioned powers as the said act directs that the whole of the said powers should be vested in and exercised by such person or persons and in such manner as the said mayor or recorder, aldermen and common councilmen in common council assembled shall regulate, ordain, enact and appoint: And whereas some of the existing laws relative to the paving, lighting and watching the streets of the city of Philadelphia contain regulations which are [now]

_____

[1] Passed March 11, 1789, Chapter 1394.

and authority to make, ordain, constitute and establish such
and so many laws, ordinances, regulations and constitutions
as shall be convenient and necessary for the purposes of
estimating, assessing, raising and levying of taxes upon the
persons of single men and upon the estates real and personal
of the inhabitants of the city of Philadelphia for the purposes
of lighting, watching, watering, pitching, paving and cleaning
of the streets, lanes and alleys of the said city and directing,
appointing and regulating the time, order and manner of estimating assessing, raising, levying and collecting of the said
somewhat inconvenient and others which may be improved,
wherefore it will be most convenient and proper to invest the
said mayor, aldermen and citizens of Philadelphia with the
power of legislating, estimating and raising of taxes so far
as respects the lighting, watching, watering, pitching, paving
and cleaning the streets of the city unrestrained by any of
the said existing laws relative thereto.

[Section I.] (Section II, P. L.) Be it therefore enacted and
it is hereby enacted by the Representatives of the Freemen of
the Commonwealth of Pennsylvania in General Assembly met
and by the authority of the same, That from and after the
passing of this act the mayor, recorder, aldermen and common
councilmen in common council assembled shall have full power
taxes and of lighting, watching, watering, pitching, paving
and cleaning the said streets, lanes, and alleys any law of the
general assembly of Pennsylvania heretofore made to the contrary in anywise notwithstanding.

And whereas by acts of assembly existing at the time the
said act to incorporate the city of Philadelphia was enacted
the late wardens of the city with two justices of the peace
were empowered to regulate and fix the rates and prices to
be taken by wagoners, carters, draymen, porters and wood-
sawyers:

And whereas it is reasonable that the prices and rates to
be taken by chimney-sweepers should be regulated by mayor,
aldermen and citizens of Philadelphia and that all the various
powers and authorities which at the time of making the said

32—XIII

act to incorporate the city of Philadelphia were vested in the
said wardens and street commissioners jointly or severally or
which were vested in said wardens and street commissioners
respectively in conjunction with one or more justice or justices
of the peace for the city and county of Philadelphia should
be vested in the said mayor, aldermen and citizens of Philadelphia:

Therefore:

[Section II.] (Section III, P. L.) Be it further enacted by
the authority aforesaid, That from and after the enacting hereof the mayor, recorder, aldermen and common councilmen in
common council assembled shall have full power and authority to make, ordain, constitute and establish such and so many
laws, ordinances, regulations and constitutions as shall be
necessary and convenient for the purposes of fixing, ascertaining and regulating from time to time the rates and prices
which shall be demanded and received by wagoners, carters,
draymen, porters, wood-sawyers and chimney-sweepers for each
and every labor and service which they shall respectively do
and perform within the said city of Philadelphia and also for the
doing, performing and executing all and every [other] power,
authority, act, matter and thing whatsoever which the said
wardens and street commissioners separately of themselves
or they or either of them in conjunction with one or more justice or justices of the peace or with any other person or persons
whatsoever were authorized and empowered or might or could
lawfully do or perform by or under any laws in force at the
time the act to incorporate the city of Philadelphia was made.

[Section III.] And be it further enacted by the authority
aforesaid, That so much of the thirty-fifth and thirty-sixth sections of the act to incorporate the city of Philadelphia as is
by this act altered or supplied is hereby declared to be repealed. Provided nevertheless, That the consent and approbation of the mayor or recorder and of a majority of the aldermen and also of the common councilmen who shall from time
to time be present and in common council assembled shall be
necessary to the making, ordaining or establishing of all such
rules, regulations, appointments, laws, ordinances and con-

stitutions as the said mayor, recorder, aldermen and common
councilmen in common council assembled shall make, ordain
and establish.

Passed April 2, 1790.   Recorded L. B. No. 4, p. 100.   See the Act of
Assembly passed March 9, 1771, Chapter 6361.

CHAPTER MDX.

AN ACT FOR ALTERING A CERTAIN CLAUSE IN THE CHARTER OF THE
CORPORATION FOR THE RELIEF OF THE WIDOWS AND CHILDREN
OF CLERGYMEN OF THE PROTESTANT EPISCOPAL CHURCH IN THE
UNITED STATES OF AMERICA.

(Section I, P. L.) Whereas it hath been represented to this
general assembly by the "Corporation for the relief of the
widows and children of the clergymen of the Protestant Episcopal Church in the United States of America" that the good
and charitable purposes for which the said corporation was
instituted are in danger of being defeated by the disappoint-
ments the corporation experience in their endeavors to assemble the quorum required by their charter to make, repeal
or alter fundamental laws, which has been often in vain at-
tempted and a considerable majority of the said corporation
having requested by their petition that the clause in their
charter requiring a majority of all the members to make, repeal or alter any fundamental law may be so altered that a
less number than a majority of the whole may be vested with
the powers by the said charter given to such majority, and it
appearing to this assembly that such alteration is not only
agreeable to the members of the said corporation but is also
proper and necessary for the preservation of their funds and
to enable them to carry into effect the laudable purposes of
their institution:

Therefore:

[Section I.] (Section II, P. L.) Be it enacted and it is hereby
enacted by the Representatives of the Freemen of the Commonwealth of Pennsylvania in General Assembly met and by
the authority of the same, That it shall and may be lawful for
a majority of any twenty or more members of the said cor-

poration met at any annual or other meeting duly assembled
to propose any new law or regulation or the repeal, alteration
or amendment of any former one whether fundamental or not
in the form of a bill for the better ordering the affairs of the
said corporation and to cause the same to be published in one
or more of the public newspapers in each of the states of Pennsylvania, New Jersey and New York, and if at the next meeting of the said corporation to be held at any time not less
than six months after such publication thirty or more members
shall be duly assembled and three fifths of the members so
assembled shall approve and ratify such proposed new law or
regulation or such proposed repeal, alteration or amendment
of a former law whether fundamental or not the same shall
be and is hereby declared to be as valid and effectual to all
intents and purposes for carrying on the charitable designs
of the said corporation as if the majority of all the members
had been met anything in their said charter to the contrary
notwithstanding.

[Section II.] (Section III, P. L.) And be it further enacted
by the authority aforesaid, That any failure of the meeting
of a sufficient number of the said corporation heretofore at
any of the stated days or times of meeting for that purpose
directed by the said charter shall not be nor shall be considered,
taken, held or adjudged to be a forfeiture of the said charter or
a legal dissolution of the said corporation nor shall the rights
and powers of the said corporation be in anywise lessened or impeached thereby, but their said charter and every part thereof not altered by this act or by an act of the legislature of this
commonwealth passed on the nineteenth day of February one
thousand seven hundred and eighty-five, shall be good and
availing in all things in the law according to the true intent
and meaning thereof and shall [be] construed, reputed and
adjudged in all cases most favorably on the behalf and for the
best benefit and behoof of the said corporation and their successors so as most effectully to answer the good and valuable
purposes of their institution and incorporation.

Passed April 2, 1790. Recorded L. B. No. 4, p. 102. See the Act of
Assembly passed March 28, 1797, Chapter 1929.

CHAPTER MDXI.

————

(Section I, P. L.) Whereas it appears to this assembly that
in the year one thousand seven hundred and twenty-four a
number of the house carpenters of the city and county of Philadelphia formed themselves into a company for the purposes
of obtaining instruction in the science of architecture and assisting such of their members as should by accident be in need
of support or the widows and minor children of members and
for the furtherance of the said charitable and useful designs did for many years pay into the hands of the masters of
the said company considerable sums of money a great part
whereof was expended in the relief of their unfortunate members and the remainder was appropriated in the year one thousand seven hundred and sixty-nine to the obtaining a large lot
of ground on which were several buildings and other improvements and towards erecting of the house known by the name
of the Carpenter's Hall in the said city:

And whereas the members of the said carpenter's company
have prayed that they may be incorporated in such manner as
to secure the said estate to them and their successors, in order
to further the useful and charitable design of the institution:

And whereas this assembly is disposed to exercise the power
vested in the legislature of the commonwealth for the encouragement of useful and charitable purposes:

[Section I.] (Section II, P. L.) Be it therefore enacted and it
is hereby enacted by the Representatives of the Freemen of the
Commonwealth of Pennsylvania in General Assembly met and
by the authority of the same, That for the purpose of promoting
the useful and charitable objects before mentioned the present
members of the carpenter's company, that is to say, Isaac Zane,
John Mifflin, Joseph Thornhill, Benjamin Loxley, James Worrel, Gunning Beadford, Thomas Nevell, James Armtiage, Sam-

rel, Gunning Beadford, Thomas Nevell, James Armitage, Sam-
James Potter, George Wood, Joseph Rakestraw, Silas Englis,
William Lownes, Samuel Powel, William Robinson, James
Bringhurst, James Graysbury, Thomas Shoemaker, David
Evans, William Colliday, William Ashton, Samuel Jervis,
Samuel Wallis, Matthew M'Glathery, Thomas Proctor, Adam
Zantzinger, John Keen, John Lort, Joseph Govett, Joseph Ogil-
by, William Williams, Robert Allison, George Forepaugh,
John Smith, Matthias Sadler, James Gibson, George Ingels,
Frazer Kingsley, James Corkrin, Joseph Rakestraw, Junior,
Joseph Thornhill, Junior, John King, Andrew Boyd, Conrad
Bartling, William Garrigues, John Rugan, Mark Roodes,
Robert Evans, Joseph Wetherel, Hugh Roberts, Isaac Jones,
Samuel Pancoast, Matthias Val Keen, William Stevenson,
Robert Morrel, Richard Mosley, John Reinhard, Samuel Pas-
torius, Josiah Matlack, John Piles, Joseph Clark, William
Zane, Benjamin Mitchell, Thomas Savery, Nathan Allen Smith,
Samuel Jones, John Hall, Joseph Howell, Junior, Israel Hallowell, John Harrison, Ebenezer Ferguson, John Cooper, William Linnard, Jonathan Evans, Joseph Worrel, James Boyer,
be and the same persons are hereby created a body corporate
and politic in deed and in name by the name and style of "The
Carpenters' Company of the city and county of Philadelphia;"
and by the same name they and their successors are hereby
constituted and confirmed one body corporate and politic in
law to have perpetual succession and to be able and capable
to receive any sum or sums of money or to receive, purchase,
have, hold and enjoy any goods, chattels, lands, tenements,
rents, hereditaments, gifts, devises and bequests of what nature
soever either in fee simple or any less estate or estates or otherwise:

And also to grant, alien, assign or let the same lands, tenements, rents, hereditaments and premises according to the ten-
ures of the respective grants and bequests made to the said
corporation and of the estate of the corporation therein. Provided, That the clear yearly value of such real estate exceed
not the sum of one thousand pounds lawful money of this commonwealth.

[Section II.] (Section III. P. L.) And be it further enacted
by the authority aforesaid, That the said corporation by the
name style title aforesaid be and shall be forever hereafter
able and capable in law to sue and be sued, plead and be impleaded, answer and be answered unto, defend and be defended
in any court or courts or other places and before any judge or
judges, justice or justices or other persons whatsoever within
this commonwealth or elsewhere in all and all manner of suits,
actions, complaints, pleas, causes, matters and demands of
whatsoever kind or nature they may be in as full and effectual
a manner as any other person or persons, bodies politic and
corporate may or can do.

[Section III.] (Section IV, P. L.) And be it further enacted
by the authority aforesaid, That the said corporation
shall have full power and authority to make, have
and use one common seal with such device and inscription as they shall judge proper and the same to break,
alter or renew at their pleasure.

[Section IV.] (Section V, P. L.) And be it further enacted
by the authority aforesaid, That for the well ordering the
affairs of the said corporation there shall be a general meeting
held of the members on the third Monday or second day of
the week in January in every year hereafter at the Carpenters'
Hall or such other place as they may direct when a majority
of those convened shall choose by ballot a president, a treasurer and such and so many assistants and such other officers or
committees as they may judge necessary or useful, and shall
have full power and authority to order quarterly or special
meetings of said corporation and do and transact all business
and matters appertaining thereunto agreeably to such rules,
ordinances, regulations and by-laws as may hereafter be made
concerning the premises. And the corporation at any of their
said meetings shall have full power and authority to make
and ordain such rules, ordinances, regulations and by-laws as
a majority of the company met shall from time to time judge
necessary or convenient and the same to put in execution or
to revoke, disannul, alter or amend at their pleasure. Provided always, That the said rules, ordinances, regulations and

by-laws relate only to the useful and charitable purposes before mentioned and be not repugnant to the laws of this commonwealth.

[Section V.] (Section VI, P. L.) And be it enacted by the authority aforesaid, That the duties and authorities of the officers, the times of meeting of the corporation, the admission of members and the other concerns of the said corporation shall be regulated by the by-laws and ordinances thereof. Provided that no by-laws or ordinances of the said corporation shall be binding on the members or officers thereof unless the same shall be proposed at one regular meeting of the corporation and received and enacted at another after the intervention of at least thirty days, and that no sale, alienation or lease for more than two years of any part of the real estate of the said corporation shall be valid unless the terms and nature of such sale or lease be proposed at a previous meeting of the corporation as aforesaid.

[Section VI.] (Section VII. P. L.) And be it further enacted by the authority aforesaid, That no misnomer of the said corporation and their successors shall defeat or annul any gift, grant, devise or bequest to the said corporation if the intent of the donor shall sufficiently appear by the tenor of the gift, testament or other writing whereby any estate or interest was intended to pass to the said corporation nor shall any nonuser of the rights, liberties, privileges and authorities or any of them hereby granted to the said corporation create or cause a forfeiture thereof.

[Section VII.] (Section VIII. P. L.) And be it further enacted by the authority aforesaid, That the president, assistants, wardens and committee appointed by the company at their meeting on the eighteenth day of January one thousand seven hundred and ninety shall continue to act in their several stations and do and perform the duties assigned them for and during the remainder of the year or unto the third Monday (or second day of the week) in January one thousand seven hundred and ninety-one.

Passed April 2, 1790. Recorded L. B. No. 4, p. 96.

CHAPTER MDXII.

A SUPPLEMENT TO THE SEVERAL ACTS OF ASSEMBLY OF THIS STATE RELATIVE TO THE INSPECTION OF STAVES, HEADING AND LUMBER.

(Section I, P. L.) Whereas it frequently happens that staves and heading are suddenly taken from the lumber yards on board vessels without affording an opportunity to inspect and cull the same:

And whereas the penalty [for] mixing cullings and unmerchantable staves and heading with such as have been adjudged merchantable is confined to the exporter and thus the innocent may suffer while the guilty escape:

And whereas the acts of assembly of this state for regulating the exportation of lumber have been found in other repects inadequate to the purposes intended:

[section I.] (Section II, P. L.) Be it therefore enacted and it is hereby enacted by the Representatives of the Freemen of the Commonwealth of Pennsylvania in General Assembly met and by the authority of the same, That all staves and heading brought into the city of Philadelphia, the District of Southwark or Northern Liberties shall before they are delivered to the person or persons to whom the same may be consigned or sold and before the same are received into any lumber-yard or other place for sale or exportation, be inspected and culled by the officer or officers appointed by the laws now in force or by his or their deputy or deputies and if any person or persons shall offend in the premises he or they shall forfeit the staves or heading delivered or received as aforesaid one half to the use of the commonwealth the other half to the use of the informer.

[Section II.] (Section III, P. L.) And be it further enacted by the authority aforesaid, That if any person or persons shall mix any staves or headings which shall have been adjudged merchantable with any cullings or unmerchantable staves or headings or with any staves or heading which have not been inspected, he or they shall forfeit the whole so mixed, one half to the use of the commonwealth and the other half to the use of the informer.

[Section III.] (Section IV, P. L.) And be it further enacted by the authority aforesaid, That it shall and may be lawful to export staves commonly called and known by the name of Leogan staves and used for sugar hogsheads, provided they be four feet six inches long, three and an half inches broad, including sap, if it be sound and half an inch thick, any law, usage or custom to the contrary notwithstanding subject nevertheless to the same inspection as other staves.

[Section IV.] (Section V, P. L.) And be it further enacted by the authority aforesaid, That the officer appointed for inspecting and culling staves shall have four shillings and two pence for every thousand of pipe staves and hogshead headings and three shillings and four pence for every thousand of all other kind of staves and heading. Provided always, That nothing in this act contained shall debar any cooper from purchasing a sufficient quantity of staves or heading uninspected and unculled to make up into casks or to use in the way of his business within this state.

[Section V.] (Section VI, P. L.) And be it further enacted by the authority aforesaid, That so much of the act of assembly entitled "An act to prevent the exportation of bad or unmerchantable staves, heading, boards and timber"[1] and of the act entitled "An act to amend the act entitled 'An act to prevent the exportation of bad and unmerchantable staves, heading boards and timber'"[2] as is hereby altered and supplied shall be and is hereby declared to be repealed and made void and that the residue thereof shall be and is hereby declared to be in full force and virtue to all intents and purposes as if this act had not been made.

[Section VI.] (Section VII, P. L.) Be it further enacted by the authority aforesaid, That any person whatever who shall act as a deputy inspector of staves, heading or lumber not

[1] Passed April 21, 1759, Chapter 439.
[2] Passed May 20, 1767, Chapter 562.

being lawfully authorized and deputed so to do shall forfeit
and pay for every such offence the sum of five pounds to be
recovered as debts of like value may be recovered by the laws
of this commonwealth, one half to the use of the person suing
the other half to the use of the poor of the city and county of
Philadelphia.

Passed April 5, 1790. Recorded L. B. No. 4, p. 119.

CHAPTER MDXIII.

A SUPPLEMENT TO AN ACT ENTITLED "AN ACT TO ESTABLISH A
BOARD OF APPEAL WITHIN THE SEVERAL COUNTIES OF THIS STATE
AND TO GRANT EXONERATIONS IN CASES OF MILITIA FINES."[1]

(Section I, P. L.) Whereas it hath been represented to this
house that the commissioners authorized to receive appeals
for militia fines have in some counties exercised unlimited
powers by granting certificates of exoneration to all delinquent applicants without any distinction or exception whatever, which renders it necessary to define the powers which
shall be exercised by said board in future:

Therefore:

[Section I.] (Section II, P. L.) Be it enacted and it is hereby
enacted by the Representatives of the Freemen of the Commonwealth of Pennsylvania in General Assembly met and by
the authority of the same, That the said commissioners con-
stituting a board as by the said act is directed shall have
no power from and after the enacting hereof to grant exonerations to any person whatever liable to a fine or fines by reason
of non-attendance in the militia except such person be actually
insolvent or unless it shall appear to them that such person
was at the time or times when he was required to perform
such duties in the militia unable to attend by reason of in-
disposition of body or unavoidable absence from the city or
county in which such person shall reside.

---

[1] Passed March 27, 1789, Chapter 1416.

[Section II.] (Section III, P. L.) And be it further enacted by the authority aforesaid, That the fourth section of the said act shall be and it is hereby repealed.

Passed April 5, 1790. Recorded L. B. No. 4, p. 118.

CHAPTER MDXIV.

AN ACT TO SUSPEND FOR A LIMITED TIME THE OPERATION OF AN ACT ENTITLED "AN ACT FOR THE INSPECTION OF SHINGLES," AND FOR OTHER PURPOSES THEREIN MENTIONED.

(Section I, P. L.) Whereas by an act of general assembly enacted the twenty-ninth day of September in the year of our Lord one thousand seven hundred and eighty-nine entitled "An act for the inspection of shingles"[1] it is enacted, That no shingles shall be exported from this state unless the same shall be of one of the kinds therein mentioned and described:

And whereas it is represented that the immediate operation of the said act would be productive of great inconvenience and disadvantage to sundry inhabitants of the state of New Jersey who before and shortly after the enacting of the said act were and still are possessed of large quantities of shingles the dimensions whereof do not correspond with those prescribed in the said act of which said act the inhabitants of that state were not generally apprized till after the first day of March last:

And whereas the inhabitants of this commonwealth principally derive their supplies of shingles from the state of New Jersey and it is just and reasonable that the citizens of that state who had either before the enacting of the act aforesaid or since the said act was enacted without notice thereof prepared quantities of the said articles for the purpose of furnishing this state therewith should receive every indulgence consistent with the public welfare:

[Section I.] (Section II, P. L.) Be it therefore enacted and it is hereby enacted by the Representatives of the Freemen of the Commonwealth of Pennsylvania in General Assembly met

---

1 Chapter 1451.

and by the authority of the same, That the said act and all
and every the provisions and regulations therein contained
shall take effect and be in force from and immediately after
the first day of January next and not before that time anything in the said act contained to the contrary thereof in anywise notwithstanding.

[Section II.] (Section III, P. L.) And be it further enacted
by the authority aforesaid, That the shingles of the third kind,
mentioned in the said act when sold in bundles shall be packed
in a close and compact manner in the same bundles each of
which shall contain one hundred and twenty five shingles and
no more, and each row in every of the said bundles shall contain three shingles and no more and shall measure fifteen inches, and that no such shingle shall measure less than three
inches and half in breadth anything in the said act to the contrary hereof in anywise notwithstanding.

Passed April 5, 1790. Recorded L. B. No. 4, p. 118.

CHAPTER MDXV.

AN ACT FOR APPOINTING AN ADDITIONAL TRUSTEE FOR THE COUNTY
OF MIFFLIN.

(Section I, P. L.) Whereas by the ninth section of an act of
this commonwealth entitled "An act for erecting certain parts
of Cumberland and Northumberland counties into a separate
county"[1] John Oliver, William Brown, Daniel Beal, John
Stewart, David Bowel and Andrew Gregg of said county were
appointed trustees for the county aforesaid with full authority
for them or a majority of them to purchase or take and receive
by grant, bargain or otherwise any quantity or quantities of
land not exceeding one hundred and fifty acres of land on the
north side of Juniata river and within one mile from the mouth
of the Kishacoquillis creek for the use, trust and benefit of

---

[1] Passed September 19, 1789, Chapter 1436.

said county and to lay out the same into regular town lots and
to dispose of so many of them as they or and four of them
may think best for the advantage of said county and
they or any four of them, are thereby authorized
to sell and convey so many of them as they may
think proper and with the moneys so arising from the sale
of said lots and with other moneys to be duly assessed,
levied and collected within the said county of Mifflin for that
purpose which is hereby declared it shall and may be lawful
for the commissioners thereof to do or cause to be done to
build and erect a court-house and prison suitable and convenient for the public on the public and such other square as
shall be reserved for that purpose, and the said trustees shall
from time to time render true and faithful accounts of the
expenditures of the same not only to the commissioners but
to the grand jury for inspection, adjustment and settlement of
the accounts of said county:

And whereas David Bowel one of the said trustees does not
reside within the limits of the said county of Mifflin and as the
act erecting Mifflin county requires four trustees to concur in
every transaction done under and in virtue of their appoint
ment:

[Section I.] (Section II, P. L.) Be it therefore enacted and
it is hereby enacted by the Representatives of the Freemen of
the Commonwealth of Pennsylvania in General Assembly met
and by the authority of the same, That Dr. James Armstrong
is hereby appointed a trustee in and for the county of Mifflin
and is hereby vested with like powers and authorities in every
matter and thing whatsoever that of right belongs to any trustee appointed for the county of Mifflin by the act hereinbefore
recited.

Passed April 5, 1790. Recorded L. B. No. 4, p. 117.
See Act of April 5, 1797, Chapter 1958, appointing William Harris
as trustee in lieu of. See the Act of Assembly passed April 5,
1797, Chapter 1598.

CHAPTER MDXVI.

. ———

AN ACT TO REFORM THE PENAL LAWS OF THE STATE.

(Section I, P. L.) Whereas by the thirty-eighth section of the second chapter of the constitution of this state it is declared, "That the penal laws as heretofore used should be reformed by the legislature as soon as may be and punishments made in some cases less sanguinary and in general more proportionate to the crimes;" and by the thirty-ninth section "That to deter more effectually from the commission of crimes by continued visible punishment of long duration and to make sanguinary punishments less necessary houses ought to be provided for punishing by hard labor those who shall be convicted of crimes not capital wherein the criminal shall be employed for the benefit of the public or for reparation of injuries done to private persons." And whereas the laws heretofore made for the purpose of carrying the said provisions of the constitution into effect have in some degree failed of success from the exposure of the offenders employed at hard labor to public view and from the communication with each other not being sufficiently restrained within the places of confinement, and it is hoped that the addition of unremitted solitude to laborious employ ment as far as it can be effected will contribute as much to reform as to deter:

[Section I.] (Section II, P. L.) Be it therefore enacted and it is hereby enacted by the Representatives of the Freemen of the Commonwealth of Pennsylvania in General Assembly met and by the authority of the same, That the pains and penalties hereinafter mentioned shall be inflicted upon the several offenders who shall from and after the passing of this act commit and be legally convicted of any of the offences hereinafter enumerated and specified, in lieu of the pains and penalties which by law have been heretofore inflicted; that is to say, every person convicted of robbery, burglary, sodomy or buggery or as accessory thereto before the fact shall forfeit to the commonwealth all and singular the lands and tenements, goods and chattels whereof he or she was seized or possessed at the time the crime was committed and at any time afterwards until conviction and be sentenced to undergo a servitude of any term or time at the discretion of the court passing the sentence not exceeding ten years in the public gaol or house of correction of the county or city in which the offence shall have been committed and be kept at such labor and fed and clothed in such manner as is herein after directed.

[Section II.] Provided always and be it further enacted by the authority aforesaid, That no person accused of [any of] the aforesaid crimes shall be admitted to bail but by the judges of the supreme court or some or one of them nor shall he or she be tried but in the supreme court or in a court of oyer and terminer or general jail delivery held in and for the county wherein the offence shall have been committed and that peremptory challenges shall be allowed in all such cases wherein they have been heretofore allowed by law but no attainder hereafter shall work corruption of blood in any case nor extend to the disinherison or prejudice of any person or persons other than the offender.

[Section III.] (Section IV, P. L.) And be it further enacted by the authority aforesaid, That every person convicted of horse-stealing or as accessory thereto before the fact shall restore the horse, mare or gelding stolen to the owner or owners thereof or shall pay to him, her or them the full value thereof and also pay the like value to the commonwealth, and moreover undergo a servitude for any term not exceeding seven years in the discretion of the court before which the conviction shall be, and shall be confined, kept to hard labor, fed and clothed in manner hereinafter mentioned. Every person convicted of simple larceny to the value of twenty shillings and upwards or as accessory thereto before the fact shall restore the goods or chattels so stolen to the right owner or owners thereof or shall pay to him, her or them the full value thereof or of so much thereof as shall not be restored, and moreover shall forfeit and pay to the commonwealth the like value of the goods and chattels

stolen and also undergo a servitude for any term of years not
exceeding three at the discretion of the court before which
the conviction shall be, and shall be confined, kept to hard
labor, fed and clothed in manner hereinafter directed.

And whereas by the ninth section of the first chapter of
the constitution it is declared, "That in all prosecutions for
criminal offences a man has a right to be heard by himself and
his counsel to demand the cause and nature of his accusation,
to be confronted with the witnesses, to call for evidence in his
favor and a speedy public trial by an impartial jury of the
county, without the unanimous consent of which jury he cannot be found guilty." Since which declaration it is not proper that persons accused of small or petty larcenies should be
tried and convicted before two magistrates or justices of the
peace without the intervention of a jury.

[Section IV.] (Section V, P. L.) Be it therefore enacted by
the authority aforesaid, That the act of assembly entitled "An
act for the trial and punishment of larceny under five shillings"¹ be and the same is hereby repealed and [that] if any person or persons shall hereafter feloniously steal, take and carry
away any goods or chattels under the value of twenty shillings,
the same order and course of trial shall be had and observed
as for other simple larcenies and he, she or they being thereof legally convicted shall be deemed guilty of petty larceny and
shall restore the goods and chattels so stolen or pay the full
value thereof to the owner or owners thereof and also forfeit
and pay the like value to the commonwealth and be further
sentenced to undergo a servitude for a term not exceeding one
year in the discretion of the court before which such conviction
shall be, and be confined, kept to hard labor, clothed and fed
in manner as herein after directed. And every person convicted of bigamy or of being an accessory after the fact in any
felony or of receiving stolen goods knowing them to have been
stolen or of any other offence not capital for which by the
laws in force before the act entitled "An act to amend the penal

---

¹ Passed February 24, 1720, Chapter 243.

laws of this state"[1] burning in the hand, cutting off the ears,
nailing the ear or ears to the pillory, placing in and upon the
pillory, whipping or imprisonment for life is or may be inflicted, shall instead of such parts of the punishment be fined
and sentenced to undergo in the like manner and be confined,
kept to hard labor fed and clothed as is hereinafter directed
for any term not exceeding two years which the court before
whom such conviction shall be may and shall in their discretion
think adapted to the nature and heinousness of the offence.

[Section V.] (Section V, P. L.) And be it further enacted by
the authority aforesaid, That robbery or larceny of obligations
or bonds, bills obligatory, bills of exchange, promissory notes
for the payment of money, lottery tickets, paper bills of credit,
certificates granted by or under the authority of this commonwealth or of all or any of the United States of America shall
be punished in the same manner as robbery or larceny of any
goods or chattels. And whereas by the eighth section of the
act of assembly entitled "An act for the advancement of justice and more certain administration thereof"[2] it is enacted that
if any woman shall endeavor privately to conceal the death of
her child which by being born alive should by the law be
deemed a bastard so that it may not come to light whether it
was born alive or not and be convicted thereof shall suffer
death as in case of murder "except such mother can make
proof by one witness at the least that the child whose death was
by her so intended to be concealed was born dead" whereby the
bare concealment of the death is almost conclusive evidence of
the child's being murdered by the mother or by her procure-
ment.

[Section VI.] (Section VI, P. L.) Be it therefore declared and
enacted by the authority aforesaid, That from and after the
publication of this act the constrained presumption that the
child whose death is concealed was therefore murdered by the
mother shall not be sufficient evidence to convict the party
indicted without probable presumptive proof is given that the
child was born alive.

1 Passed September 15, 1786, Chapter 1241.
2 Passed May 31, 1718, Chapter 236.

[Section VII.] (Section VII, P. L.) And be it further enacted by the authority aforesaid, That every other felony or
misdemeanor, or offence whatsoever not specially provided for
by this act may and shall be punished as heretofore.

[Section VII.] (Section VIII, P. L.) Be it enacted by the authority aforesaid, That the commissioners for the county of
Philadelphia with the approbation of the mayor and two of
the aldermen of the city of Philadelphia and two of the justices
of the court of the quarter sessions for the county of Philadelphia shall as soon as conveniently may be cause a suitable number of cells to be constructed in the yard of the gaol of the said
county each of which cells shall be six feet in width, eight feet
in length and nine feet in height and shall be constructed
with brick or stone upon such plan as will best prevent danger
from fire and the said cells shall be separated from the common yard by walls of such height as without unnecessary ex-
clusion of air and light will prevent all external communication for the purpose of confining therein the more hardened and
atrocious offenders who by virtue of the act entitled "An act
for amending the penal laws of this state" have been sentenced to hard labor for a term of years, or who shall be sentenced thereto by virtue of this act.

[Section IX.] (Section IX, P. L.) Be it enacted by the authority aforesaid, That for the purpose of defraying a proportionable part of the expense of erecting such cells and walls
the president and supreme executive council shall be and they
are hereby authorized to draw orders on the state treasurer
for the sum of five hundred pounds to be paid out of the funds
especially appropriated for claims and improvements when
the same shall be sufficiently productive and for defraying the
residue of the expense it shall be lawful for the commissioners
of the said county or a majority of them to assess, levy and
collect within the said county so much money as they with the
concurrence and approbation of the said mayor, aldermen and
justices shall judge necessary, Provided, The same does not
exceed the sum of one thousand pounds.

[Section X.] (Section X, P. L.) Be it enacted by the authority aforesaid, That the said cells shall be and are hereby de-

clared to be part of the gaol of the city and county of Philadelphia and the residue of the said gaol shall be appropriated to the purposes of confining as well such male convicts sentenced to hard labor as cannot be accommodated in the said cells as female convicts sentenced in like manner, persons convicted of capital crimes, vagrants and disorderly persons committed as such and persons charged with misdemeanors only, all which persons are hereby required to be kept separate and apart from each other, as much as the convenience of the building will admit and to be subject to the visitation and superintendence of the inspectors hereinafter appointed.

[Section XI.] (Section XI, P. L.) Be it further enacted by the authority aforesaid, That it shall be lawful for the mayor or any alderman of the city of Philadelphia and any justice of the peace of the said county to commit any vagrant or idle and disorderly person (being thereof legally convicted before him as by law is directed) to the said gaol to be kept at hard labor for any term not exceeding one month any law of this state to the contrary notwithstanding.

[Section XII.] (Section XII, P. L). Be it enacted by the authority aforesaid, That in order to prevent the introduction of contagious disorders every person who shall be ordered to hard labor in said gaol shall be separately lodged, washed and cleaned and shall continue in such separate lodging until it shall be certified by some physician that he or she is fit to be received among the other prisoners and if such person be a convict the clothes in which he or she shall then be clothed shall either be burnt or at the discretion of two of the said inspectors be baked, fumigated and carefully laid by until the expiration of the term for which such offender shall be sentenced to hard labor to be then returned to him or her.

[Section XIII.] (Section XIII, P. L.) Be it enacted by the authority aforesaid, That all such convicts shall at the public expense of such county during the term of their confinement be clothed in habits of coarse materials uniform in color and make and distinguishing them from the good citizens of this commonwealth, and the males shall have their heads and beards close shaven at least once a week and all such offenders shall during the said term be sustained upon bread, Indian meal or other inferior food, at the discretion of said inspectors and shall be allowed one meal of coarse meat in each week and shall be kept as far as may be consistent with their sex, age, health and ability to labor of the hardest and most servile kind in which the work is least liable to be spoiled by ignorance, neglect or obstinacy and where the materials are not easily embezzled or destroyed, and if the work to be performed is of such a nature as may require previous instruction, proper persons for that purpose to whom a suitable allowance shall be made shall be provided by order of any two of the inspectors hereafter named, during which labor the said offenders shall be kept separate and apart from each other if the nature of their several employments will admit thereof and where the nature of such employment requires two or more to work together the keeper of the said gaol or one of his deputies shall if possible be constantly present.

[Section XIV.] (Section XIV, P. L.) Be it enacted by the authority aforesaid, That such offenders unless prevented by ill health shall be employed in work every day in the year except Sundays and the hours of work each day shall be as many as the season of the year with an interval of half an hour for breakfast and an hour for dinner will permit, but not exceeding eight hours in the months of November, December and January, nine hours, in the months of February and October and ten hours in the rest of the year and when such hours of work are passed the working tools, implements and materials or such of them as will admit of daily removal shall be removed to places proper for their safe custody until the hour of labor shall return.

[Section XV.] (Section XV, P. L.) Be it enacted by the authority aforesaid, That the keeper of the said gaol shall from time to time with the approbation of any two of the inspectors hereafter mentioned provide a sufficient quantity of stock and materials, working tools and implements for such offenders for the expense of which the said inspectors or any two of them shall be and they are hereby authorized to draw orders to be countersigned by the commissioners of the county on the treasurer of the county if need shall be specifying in such orders the quantity and nature of the materials, tools or implements wanted, which orders the said treasurer is hereby required to discharge out of the county stock, for which materials, tools and implements when received the said keeper shall be accountable, and the said keeper shall with the approbation of any two of the said inspectors have power to make contracts with any person whatever for the clothing, diet and all other necessaries for the maintenance and support of such convicts and for the implements and materials of any kind of manufacture, trade or labor in which such convicts shall be employed for the sale of such goods, wares and merchandise as shall be there wrought and manufactured and the said keeper shall cause all accounts concerning the maintenance of such convicts and other prisoners to be entered regularly in a book or books to be kept for that purpose and shall also keep separate accounts of the stock and materials so wrought, manufactured, sold and disposed of and the moneys for which the same shall be sold and when sold and to whom in books to be provided for those purposes, all which books and accounts shall be at all times open for the examination of the said inspectors and shall be regularly laid before them at their quarterly or other meetings as hereinafter is directed for their approbation and allowance.

[Section XVI.] (Section XVI, P. L.) Be it enacted by the authority aforesaid, That if the said inspectors at their quarterly or other meetings shall suspect any fraudulent or improper charges or any omissions in any such accounts they may examine upon oath or affirmation the said keeper or any of his deputies, servants or assistants or any person of whom any necessaries, stock, materials or other things have been purchased for the use of the said gaol or any persons to whom any stock or materials wrought or manufactured therein have been sold or any of the offenders confined in such gaol or any other person or persons concerning any of the articles contained in such accounts or any omission thereout and in case any fraud shall appear in such accounts the particulars thereof shall be

reported by the said inspectors in writing to the mayor of the
said city for the purposes hereinafter mentioned.

[Section XVII.] (Section XVIII, P. L.) Be it enacted by
the authority aforesaid, That in order to encourage industry
as an evidence of reformation separate accounts shall be opened
in the said books for all convicts sentenced to hard labor for
six months and upward in which such convicts shall be
charged with the expenses of clothing and subsistence and such
proportionable part of the expenses of the raw materials upon
which they shall be employed as the inspectors at their quarterly or other meetings shall think just and shall be credited
with the sum or sums from time to time received by reason of
their labor and if the same shall be found to exceed the said
expenses one half of said excess shall be laid out in decent rai-
ment for such convicts at their discharge or otherwise applied
to their use and benefit as the said inspectors shall upon such
occasions direct and if such offender at the end or other determination of his term of confinement shall labor under any acute
or dangerous distemper he shall not be discharged unless at
his own request until he can be safely discharged.

[Section XVIII.] (Section XVIII, P. L.) Be it enacted by
the authority aforesaid, That no person whatever except the
keeper, his deputies, servants or assistants, the said inspectors,
officers and ministers of justice, counsellors or attorneys at law
employed by a prisoner, ministers of the gospel or persons producing a written license signed by two of the said inspectors
shall be permitted to enter within the walls where such offenders shall be confined and that the doors of all the lodging
rooms and cells in the said gaol shall be locked and all lights
therein extinguished at the hour of nine and one or more
watchmen shall patrol the said gaol at least twice in every
hour from that time until the return of the time of labor in the
morning of the next day.

[Section XIX.] (Section XIX, P. L.) Be it enacted by the
authority aforesaid, That the walls of the cells and apartments
in the said gaol shall be whitewashed with lime and water at
least twice in every year and the floors of the said cells and
apartments shall be washed once every week or oftener if the

said inspectors shall so direct by one or more of the said prisoners in rotation who at the discretion of the said keeper shall have an extra allowance of diet for so doing and the said prisoners shall be allowed to walk and air themselves for such stated time as their health may require and the said keeper shall permit and if proper employment can be found such prisoners may also be permitted with the approbation of two of the said inspectors to work in the yard provided such airing and working in the yard be in the presence or within the view of the said keeper or his deputies or assistants.

[Section XX.] (Section XX, P. L.) Be it enacted by the authority aforesaid, That one or more of the apartments in the second story of the said gaol and at the extreme end of the west wing shall be fitted up as an infirmary and in case any such offender being sick shall upon examination of a physician be found to require it he or she shall be removed to the infirmary and his or her name shall be entered in a book to be kept for that purpose and when such physician shall report to the said keeper that such offender is in a proper condition to quit the infirmary and return to his or her employment such report shall be entered by the said keeper in a book to be kept for that purpose and the said keeper shall order him or her back to his or her former labor so far as the same shall be consistent with his or her state of health and the said mayor, aldermen and justices shall from time to time appoint a physician to attend at said gaol.

[Section XXI.] (Section XXI. P. L.) Be it enacted by the authority aforesaid, That the keeper of the said gaol shall have power to punish all such prisoners guilty of assaults within the said gaol when no dangerous wound or bruise is given, profane cursing and swearing, indecent behavior, idleness or negligence in work or wilful mismanagement of it or of disobedience to the orders and regulations hereinafter directed to be made by confining such offenders in the dark cells or dungeons of the said gaol and by keeping them upon bread and water only for any term not exceeding two days and if any such prisoner shall be guilty of any offense within the said gaol which the said keeper is not hereby authorized to punish or for which

he shall think the said punishment is not sufficient by reason
of the enormity of the offense he shall report the same to two
of the said inspectors who if upon proper inquiry they shall
think fit shall certify the nature and circumstances of such
offense with the name of the offender to the mayor of the said
city and the mayor shall thereupon order such offenses to be
punished by moderate whipping or repeated whippings not exceeding thirteen lashes each or by close confinement in the said
dark cells or dungeons with bread and water only for sustenance for any time not exceeding six days or by all the said
punishments.

[Section XXII.] (Section XXII, P. L.) Be it enacted by the
authority aforesaid, That it shall be lawful for the mayor and
two aldermen of the said city and two of the justices of the
peace of the said county on the first day of May annually to
appoint a suitable person to be keeper of the said gaol who
shall however be liable to be removed by the mayor, aldermen
and justices aforesaid when occasion may require in which
case another shall from time to time be appointed in like manner who shall receive as full compensation for his services
and in lieu of all fees and gratuities by reason or under color
of the said office so much per annum as the said mayor, aldermen and justices at the time of such appointment shall direct
to be paid in quarterly payments by orders drawn on the treasurer of the said county by said mayor and also five per centum
on the sales of all articles manufactured by the said criminals
and such keeper shall have power with the approbation of the
mayor, aldermen and justices aforesaid, to appoint a suitable
number of deputies and assistants at such reasonable allowances as the mayor, aldermen and justices aforesaid shall think
just which allowances shall be paid quarterly in like manner
and before any such gaoler shall exercise any part of the said
office he shall give bond to the treasurer of the county with
two sufficient sureties to be approved by the said mayor in the
sum of five hundred pounds upon condition that he, his deputies and assistants shall well and faithfully perform the trusts
and duties in them reposed, which bond the due execution
thereof being proved before and certified by any of the alder-

men of the said city shall be recorded in the office of the recorder of deeds for the county of Philadelphia and copies thereof exemplified by the said recorder of deeds shall be legal evidence in all courts of law in any suit against such gaoler or his sureties.

[Section XXIII.] (Section XXIII, P. L.) Be it enacted by the authority aforesaid, That it shall be lawful for the said mayor, aldermen and justices aforesaid on the first Monday in May next to appoint twelve inspectors, six of whom shall be in office until the first Monday in November next and six until the first Monday in May following, and so from time to time six inspectors shall be appointed in manner aforesaid on the first Mondays in May and November annually, and if any person so appointed not having a reasonable excuse to be approved of by the said mayor, aldermen and justices shall refuse to serve in the said office he shall forfeit and pay the sum of ten pounds to be recovered by action of debt as debts of like value are recoverable by the laws of this commonwealth, the one half thereof to the use of the person suing, the other half to be paid to the treasurer of the said county to be applied to the purposes hereinbefore mentioned.

[Section XXIV.] (Section XXIV, P. L.) Be it enacted by the authority aforesaid, That the said inspectors, seven of whom shall be a quorum, shall meet once in three months, in an apartment to be provided for that purpose in the said gaol and may be especially convened by the two acting inspectors when occasion may require, and they shall at their first meeting appoint two of their members to be acting inspectors who shall continue such for such time as shall be directed by the said inspectors or a majority of them when met together. And the acting inspectors shall attend at the said gaol at least once in each week and shall examine into and inspect the management of the said gaol and the conduct of the said keeper and his deputies so far as respects the said offenders employed at hard labor and the directions of this act and shall do and perform the several matters and things hereinbefore directed by them to be performed.

[Section XXV.] (Section XXV, P. L.) Be it further enacted

by the authority aforesaid, That the board of inspectors at
their quarterly or other meeting shall make such further orders and regulations for the purpose of carrying this act into
execution as shall be approved of by the mayor and recorder
of the said city and such orders and regulations shall be hung
up in at least six of the most conspicuous places in the said
gaol and if the said keeper or any of his deputies or assistants shall obstruct or resist the said inspectors or any of them
in the exercise of the powers and duties vested in them by this
act such person shall forfeit and pay the sum of twenty pounds
to be recovered as aforesaid and shall moreover be liable to be
removed in manner aforesaid from his respective office or employment in the said gaol.

[Section XXVI.] (Section XXVI, P. L.) Be it further enacted by the authority aforesaid, That the present house of
correction in the city of Philadelphia shall be reserved for the
exclusive reception and confinement of debtors and persons
committed to secure their appearance as witnesses in criminal
prosecutions and not charged with any misdemeanor or higher
offense, which witnesses if bound in recognizances for their
appearance in favor of the prosecution shall be allowed the
sum of six pence per diem to be paid out of the county stock,
and the commissioners of the said county are hereby authorized
to make such alterations in the same not exceeding the sum
of sixty pounds as shall be necessary to accommodate all such
prisoners and to distinguish the said house of correction by a
proper title henceforward it shall be called and known by the
name of "The Debtors' Apartment."

[Section XXVII.] (Section XXVII, P. L.) Be it further enacted by the authority aforesaid, That the keepers of the said
gaol and of the said house of correction respectively shall
forthwith exchange the several prisoners in their respective
custody conformable to the true intent and meaning of this
act and shall be and are hereby indemnified for all such prisoners as shall be safely delivered into proper custody pursuant
to the directions of this act:

And whereas it may not at present be practicable to introduce all the above mentioned regulations into each of the

counties of this state although it is necessary that an uniformity of punishment should as much as possible prevail in all:

[Section XXVIII.] (Section XXVIII, P. L.) Be it enacted by the authority aforesaid, That the malefactors sentenced to hard labor as aforesaid in the several counties of this state other than the county of Philadelphia shall be employed in the several gaols and work houses in the respective counties in such hard and servile labor and fed and clothed in such manner as is hereinbefore directed. And the sheriff of the proper county to whom the said malefactors shall be committed in execution of their sentence shall from time to time with the approbation of the justices of the court of quarter sessions of the proper county in open court appoint so many keepers of the said malefactors as shall be necessary, whose wages shall be ascertained and allowed by the said court and paid by the treasurer of the county out of the moneys in his hands raised for the use of the said county by a warrant drawn by the said sheriff and at least one of the commissioners of the proper county and that the duty of the said keepers shall be to superintend and direct their labors, manage and attend to their clothing, diet and lodging and take care that they be safely kept and the better to effect this purpose they shall have authority to confine in close durance apart from all society all those who shall refuse to labor, be idle or guilty of any trespass and during such confinement to withhold from them all sustenance except bread and water, and also to put iron yokes around their necks, chains upon their leg or legs or otherwise restrain in irons such as shall be incorrigible or irreclaimable without such severity.

[Section XXIX.] (Section XXIX, P. L.) Be it enacted by the authority aforesaid, That the court of quarter sessions of any such county shall have power either ex officio or upon information against any such keeper for partiality or cruelty to call before them such keeper together with the material witnesses and inquire into his conduct and if it shall appear that he hath been guilty of gross partiality or cruelty it shall and may be lawful for the said court to suspend or remove him, and any of the judges of the supreme court when upon the cir-

cuit in such county either on their own motion or on complaint
made by any other may take original cognizance of the misbehavior of any keeper and remove him from office if they see
cause and in case of suspension or removal of all or any of the
said keepers either by the justices of the quarter sessions or
the judges of the supreme court the sheriff of the proper county
with the approbation of the justices of the quarter sessions of
the same county shall and he is hereby authorized and directed
to appoint another keeper or keepers in the room of such as
shall have been so suspended or removed.

[Section XXX.] (Section XXX, P. L.) Be it further enacted
by the authority aforesaid, That the keepers of the gaols and
workhouses or houses of correction in such counties shall once
every three months or oftener if required furnish the commissioners of their respective counties with a complete calendar or
list of all persons committed to their respective custody under
sentence of such servitude, together with the names of their
crimes, the term of their servitude, in what court condemned,
the ages and the description of the persons of such as shall appear to be too old and infirm or otherwise incapable to undergo
hard labor out of the gaols or work houses, and the said commissioners shall at the charge of the proper county provide the
clothing and the food hereinbefore directed for them as also
such articles and materials of labor and manufacture as shall be
most suitable for the employment of all those who are capable
of labor or manufacture and deliver the same to the said gaoler
or workhouse keeper, taking a receipt therefor; and that the
gaoler or workhouse keeper shall render an account quarterly
or oftener if required to the commissioners of the work done by
the said malefactors and dispose of the same in such manner
as the commissioners shall direct and the said commissioners
are hereby authorized from time to time to draw orders or
give their warrants on the treasurer of the proper county for
the advance of such sums as they shall think reasonable and
necessary for carrying this act into execution and all expenses
and charges incurred or to be incurred by virtue of this act
shall be levied and raised as other county charges are and be
accounted for in like manner excepting the said sum of five

hundred pounds directed by this act to be paid out of the treasury of the state towards erecting the said cells in the yard of the gaol of the county of Philadelphia.

[Section XXXI.] (Section XXXI, P. L.) Be it enacted by the authority aforesaid, That the said keepers of any of the gaols, and houses of correction within this commonwealth, their deputies and assistants in case any of the said offenders shall escape from confinement without the knowledge or consent of the said keepers, deputies or assistants shall forfeit and pay the sum of ten pounds to be recovered and applied in manner aforesaid. Provided, That nothing in this act contained shall be deemed or taken to extend to escapes voluntarily suffered by any such keepers of the said gaols or workhouses.

[Section XXXII.] (Section XXXII, P. L.) Be it enacted by the authority aforesaid, That if any such offender sentenced to hard labor shall escape, he or she shall on conviction thereof suffer such additional confinement at hard labor agreeably to the directions of this act and shall also suffer such additional corporal punishment not extending to life or limb as the court in which such offender shall have been convicted shall adjudge and direct. And if any such offender shall after his or her escape be guilty of any offense for which he or she would have been sentenced to death by the laws in force before the passing of the act entitled "An act for amending the penal laws of this state" [1] he or she shall suffer death as if the said act or this act had not been made.

[Section XXXIII.] (Section XXXIII, P. L.) Be it enacted by the authority aforesaid, That any such offenders who have been or shall be pardoned for the offenses or crimes of which he or she hath been or shall be convicted in pursuance of the said act or of this act, provided such offense was by any law in force before the passing of the said act made capital and who shall be convicted of a second offense of the like nature shall suffer death on such conviction without the benefit of clergy and any constable who shall take up and convey to gaol any convict who shall escape from his confinement shall be allowed mileage at the same rate as constables are commonly allowed to be paid by the treasurer of the proper county.

[Section XXXIV.] (Section XXXIV, P. L.) Be it enacted by the authority aforesaid, That any felon convicted in any county in this state other than the county of Philadelphia of any felony or felonies for which he or she shall be sentenced to hard labor for the space of twelve months or upwards may at the discretion of the court in which such felon shall be convicted within three months after such conviction be removed at the expense of the said county under safe and secure conduct to the gaol in the said county of Philadelphia and therein be confined, fed, clothed and employed at hard labor as is hereinbefore directed for the remaining part of the time for which by such sentence he or she shall be liable to imprisonment, and the commissioners of the said county of Philadelphia upon the application of the said inspectors shall have authority from time to time to draw orders upon the treasurer of the county from which such felon shall have been so removed for the expenses of feeding and clothing such felon, if the labor of such felon shall not be sufficient to pay the same, which orders the treasurer of such county shall accept and pay.

[Section XXXV.] (Section XXXV, P. L.) Be it enacted by the authority aforesaid, That if any gaoler or other person whatever shall introduce into or give away, barter or sell within any gaol or house of correction in the said city or any of the counties of this state any spirituous or fermented liquors excepting only such as the gaoler or keeper of such gaol or house of correction shall make use of in his own family or such as may be required for any prisoner in a state of ill health and for such purpose prescribed by an attending physician and delivered into the hands of such physician or other person appointed to receive them, such person shall forfeit and pay the sum of five pounds to be recovered as debts of like value may be recovered by the laws of this state, one moiety thereof to the use of the person suing, the other moiety to be paid to the said inspectors for the purposes in this act contained.

[Section XXXVI.] (Section XXXVI, P. L.) Be it enacted by the authority aforesaid, That the act entitled "An act for amending the penal laws of this state" [1] and the act entitled

---

[1] See Ante.

"An act to amend an act entitled 'An act for amending the penal laws of this state'" [1] shall be and they are hereby repealed.

[Section XXXVII.] (Section XXXVII, P. L.) Be it enacted by the authority aforesaid, That this act shall be in force for the term of five years and from thence to the end of the next session of the general assembly and no longer.

[Section XXXVIII.] (Section XXXVIII, P. L.) And be it further enacted by the authority aforesaid, That the force and operation of the act hereinbefore mentioned entitled "An act for amending the penal laws of this state" [2] shall notwithstanding the said act is herein repealed remain valid and effectual as to all persons convicted and sentenced to confinement, servitude and hard labor conformably to the true intent and meaning of the said act and of this act.

Passed April 5, 1790. Recorded L. B. No. 4, p. 105. See the Acts of Assembly passed September 23, 1791, Chapter 1513; April 4, 1792, Chapter 1636; April 22, 1794, Chapter 1777; April 18, 1795, Chapter 1861; March 20, 1797, Chapter 1929; April 4, 1799, Chapter 2051.

Sections 1, 2, 3, 4, 5, 6, 7, 32 and 33 repealed by the Act of Assembly passed March 31, 1860. Chapter 376. P. L. of 1860, p. 452.

CHAPTER MDXVII.

AN ACT FOR THE PAYMENT OF THE CLAIM OF TURNBULL, MARMIE AND COMPANY.

(Section I, P. L.) Whereas it appears to this house that Messrs. Turnbull, Marmie and Company late contractors for a part of the continental army had on the first day of June one thousand seven hundred and eighty-seven a warrant drawn by the board of treasury of the United States on Thomas Smith, Esquire, continental loan officer, for the sum of three thousand

---

[1] Passed March 27, 1769, Chapter 1409.
[2] Ante.

dollars and by him accepted and placed to the credit of this state in account with the United States. In order to satisfy which warrant an order was afterwards drawn on the treasurer of this state for the like sum which was accepted but the money has not been paid:

[Section 1.] (Section II, P. L.) Be it therefore enacted and it is hereby enacted by the Representatives of the Freemen of the Commonwealth of Pennsylvania in General Assembly met and by the authority of the same, That the president and supreme executive council be authorized and they are hereby authorized to draw an order on the treasurer of this state for the sum of eleven hundred and twenty-five pounds together with lawful interest from the first day of June one thousand seven hundred and eighty-seven and until the said principal sum with interest shall be paid, to be paid out of the fund of five thousand pounds annually set apart and particularly appropriated by law for the payment of claims.

Passed April 5, 1790. Recorded L. B. No. 4, p. 104.

CHAPTER MDXVIII.

AN ACT IN FAVOR OF ROBERT THORN

(Section 1, P. L.) Whereas Robert Thorn of the county of Bucks by his petition hath represented to this assembly that encouraged by a number of inhabitants of this state and New Jersey who entered into subscriptions for raising a sum of money to remove some obstructions in the river Delaware that greatly impeded the navigation thereof at the places called Wells's Falls and Howell's Falls and also encouraged by a very favorable season he was induced to hire a number of hands for the purpose aforesaid and hath expended therein over and above what he hath been able to obtain from the aforesaid subscriptions the sum of forty pounds, twelve shil-

34—XIII

lings and eight pence for which he hath received no compensation and prays for assistance from this house therein:

And whereas it appears to this assembly that the said representation is just and true and that the said money hath been expended in such manner and places as considerably to improve the navigation aforesaid:

Therefore:

[Section I.] (Section II, P. L.) Be it enacted and it is hereby enacted by the Representatives of the Freemen of the Commonwealth of Pennsylvania in General Assembly met and by the authority of the same, That the president or vice president in council be and they are hereby authorized and empowered to draw an order on the treasurer of this state in favor of Robert Thorn for the sum of forty pounds, twelve shillings and eight pence to be paid out of the fund especially appropriated by law for the payment of claims and improvements as soon as that fund shall become sufficiently productive.

Passed April 5, 1790.   Recorded L. B. No. 4, p. 105.

CHAPTER MDXIX.

AN ACT RELATING TO THE SALE OF LANDS THEREIN MENTIONED.

(Section I, P. L.) Whereas an act of assembly of this commonwealth entitled ".An act further to continue an act entitled '.An act to suspend the sale of lands for non-payment of taxes and for other purposes therein mentioned' "[1] has expired by its own limitation. And whereas many inconveniences may arise to the owners of unsettled lands in this commonwealth if the said lands shall be set up and sold for the taxes due thereon without further notice to the said owners:

To prevent the said inconveniences, and that all such owners may have reasonable time and notice of the taxes in arrear upon their said lands:

[1] Passed September 26, 1789, Chapter 1442.

[Section I.] (Section II, P. L.) Be it enacted and it is hereby enacted by the Representatives of the Freemen of the Commonwealth of Pennsylvania in General Assembly met and by the authority of the same, That previous to any sale to be held by the commissioners of the several counties of this commonwealth of any of the lands within the meaning and intention of the said recited act for any taxes or arrears of taxes due to this commonwealth the commissioners of the respective counties in which such lands lie shall cause the said lands and the taxes due thereon and the owners' names thereof to be publicly advertised in their respective counties and in one or more of the public papers of the city of Philadelphia for at least twenty-six weeks successively and in default of the owners thereof or some persons for them discharging the said taxes the said commissioners shall cause the said lands the taxes on which shall not be so discharged to be set up to public sale agreeably to the laws now in force in this commonwealth but the present commissioners of the several counties wherein the lands of non-resident holders are situate shall and may on the application of any such holder or his or her agent or attorney rectify any mistakes or remedy any injustice which shall be made appear to such commissioners respectively in the assessments either of the present or any former year of the lands of such non-resident holder from whom taxes are now due provided no such application shall on any pretence whatsoever cause delay in the payment of such arrears as are justly due in the opinion of the said commissioners respectively within the time hereinbefore limited and appointed.

[Section II.] (Section III, P. L.) Be it enacted by the authority aforesaid, That if at such sale no person shall bid the sum due on each tract then and in that case the said commissioners shall cause the same to be bid in for the use of this commonwealth and make return thereof to the treasurer of the commonwealth due and legal notice being first given of the time and place of such sale.

Passed April 6, 1790.   Recorded L. B. No. 4, p. 124.

CHAPTER MDXX.

AN ACT FOR RAISING BY WAY OF LOTTERY THE SUM OF EIGHT HUN-
DRED POUNDS FOR REDEEMING THE HOUSE OF PUBLIC WORSHIP
BELONGING TO THE HEBREW CONGREGATION, OF THE CITY OF
PHILADELPHIA FROM THE MORTGAGE AND ENCUMBRANCE
THEREON.

(Section 1, P. L.) Whereas it hath been represented to this
assembly that the house of public worship belonging to the
members of the Hebrew congregation of the city of Philadelphia is now under execution upon several judgments for the
payment of the sum of eight hundred pounds and which they
are unable to discharge without the permission of the legislature to raise the aforesaid sum by lottery:

And whereas it is just and proper that all religious societies
should be protected so far as is consistent with the principles
of the constitution of this commonwealth:

Therefore:

[Section I.] (Section II, P. L.) Be it enacted and it is hereby
enacted by the Representatives of the Freemen of the Commonwealth of Pennsylvania in General Assembly met and by
the authority of the same, That Manuel Josephson, Solomon
Lyon, William Wistar, John Duffield, Samuel Hayes and Solomon Etting be and they are hereby appointed managers and
directors of the lottery hereby instituted and directed to be
drawn for the preparing and disposing of tickets to oversee
the drawing of the lots and to order and perform all such
other matters and things as are hereinafter directed and appointed to be done and performed and that the said managers
or any four of them shall meet together at some convenient
place to be by them appointed for the execution of the powers
and trusts reposed in them by this act and shall cause proper
books to be prepared in which each leaf shall be divided into
three columns upon the innermost of which shall be printed
two thousand one hundred and sixty tickets, numbered one,
two, three, and so onwards in arithmetical progression where

the common excess is but one until they rise to the number
two thousand one hundred and sixty, upon the outside column
there shall be printed the like number of tickets of the same
breadth and form and numbered in like manner and in the
middle column shall be printed a third set of tickets of the
same number with those of the two other columns, which tickets shall be joined with oblique lines or devices in such manner
as the said managers shall direct and [after] (sic.) of the last
mentioned tickets shall have written or printed thereupon
(besides the number of such tickets and the year of our Lord)
the following words, viz., "Hebrew Congregation Lottery
This ticket entitles the bearer to such prize as may be drawn
against its number if demanded within nine months after the
drawing is finished subject to a deduction of twenty-five per
cent."

[Section II.] (Section III, P. L.) And be it further enacted
by the authority aforesaid, That the said managers shall have
full power and authority to sell and dispose of to such person
or persons as shall choose to adventure in the said lottery the
tickets of the middle column aforesaid at the rate of four dollars each for ready money and not otherwise and upon the
receipt of such sum of four dollars shall deliver to the said adventurer one of the said tickets signed by one of the said managers and cut out of the said books through the said oblique
lines and devices indentwise to be kept [and used] for the better ascertaining his, her or their interest in the said tickets.

· [Section III.] (Section IV, P. L.) And be it further enacted
by the authority aforesaid, That for the greater security of the
adventurers and punctual payment of the prizes that shall be
drawn in the said lottery the said managers shall pay weekly
into the bank of North America all the moneys received by
them for tickets sold for which they shall receive from the said
for the purpose in this act mentioned as are usually given by
there shall be printed the like number of tickets of the same
said bank for other moneys deposited therein.

[Section IV.] (Section V, P. L.) And be it further enacted
by the authority aforesaid, That for enabling the said mana-

gers to pay off the prizes as they are severally drawn and for
discharging the incidental expenses attending the management
and drawing of said lottery orders shall be drawn on the said
bank by one or more of the said managers in checks provided
for that purpose expressing that such drafts are on account of
such lottery.

[Section V.] (Section VI, P. L.) And be it further enacted
by the authority aforesaid, That as soon as the tickets of the
middle column shall be sold the said managers or any four or
more of them shall cause all the tickets of the extreme column
in the said books, the same being cut out indentwise through
the said oblique lines or devices, to be carefully rolled up and
made fast with silk or thread and shall cause them to be put
into a box to be prepared for that purpose marked with the
letter A and to be immediately after sealed with the several
seals of the said managers until the said tickets are to be drawn
as is hereinafter mentioned, but the tickets of the innermost
column shall remain in the said book for the discovering any
mistake or fraud if such should happen to be committed contrary to the meaning of this act.

[Section VI.] (Section VII, P. L.) And be it further enacted
by the authority aforesaid, That the said managers or any
four or more of them shall also prepare or cause to be prepared
two thousand one hundred and sixty prize tickets on which
shall be written or expressed, as well in figures as in words at
length as follows, that is to say: Upon one of them one thousand dollars, upon one other of them five hundred dollars, upon
one other of them three hundred dollars, upon one other of
them two hundred dollars, upon one other of them one hundred
dollars, upon ten others of them severally fifty dollars, upon
four others of them severally forty dollars, upon eight others
of them severally thirty dollars, upon sixteen others of them
severally twenty dollars, upon thirty others of them severally
ten dollars, upon seventy-two others of them severally five dollars, and upon two thousand and thirteen others of them severally two dollars, and put the same prizes into a box marked
B, which principal sums so to be expressed upon the said tick-

ets will amount in the whole to the sum of eight thousand and
twenty-six dollars out of which the said managers are hereby
authorized and required to deduct twenty-five per centum and
no more amounting in the whole to eight hundred pounds, the
sum intended to be raised by this act for the purposes therein
mentioned and specified.

[Section VII.] (Section VIII, P. L.) And be it further enacted by the authority aforesaid, That the said managers or
any four or more of them shall cause the said boxes with all
the ticketes therein to be carried to some public and convenient room in the city of Philadelphia by ten o'clock in the forenoon on some certain day to be by them appointed and placed
on a stage or table, and shall then and there severally attend
this service and cause the two boxes to be unsealed and opened
and the tickets or lots being in presence of the managers and
such of the adventurers as shall think proper to attend well
shaken and mixed together in each box, some one fit and indifferent person to be appointed by the said managers shall
draw one ticket from the box A in which the said numbered
tickets shall have been put as aforesaid and one other indiffer-
erent and fit person appointed and directed in like manner shall
at the same time draw one ticket or lot from the box B in which
the said two thousand one hundred and sixty prize tickets
shall have been promiscously put as aforesaid and the tickets
so drawn shall be immediately opened and the number of the
ticket drawn from the box A and the value of the prize drawn
out of the box B shall be called aloud and the number and prize
shall be filed together and entered in books by clerks whom
the managers are hereby authorized and empowered to employ
and oversee for this purpose and so the drawing to continue
by taking one ticket at a time out of each box and opening,
calling aloud, filing and entering the same as before mentioned
until the whole number of tickets and prizes aforesaid shall
be drawn and if the drawing aforesaid cannot be performed
in one day the said managers shall cause the said boxes to be
sealed up in manner aforesaid and adjourn until the next day
and so from day to day (Saturdays and Sundays excepted) until the drawing shall be finished and completed as aforesaid,

and the tickets so drawn shall remain in the custody of the managers.

[Section VIII.] (Section IX, P. L.) And be it further enacted by the authority aforesaid, That as soon as the drawing is finished the books of the several clerks compared and lists made out therefrom the managers shall cause a list of the numbers and prizes to be published in two English and one German newspaper, printed in the city of Philadelphia and immediately thereafter proceed to the payment of the prize money and if any dispute shall arise in adjusting the property of any of the said prizes the managers shall determine to whom it doth or ought to belong.

[Section IX.] (Section X, P. L.) And be it further enacted by the authority aforesaid, That if any of the adventurers shall neglect to apply to the said managers for the sum due on his, her or their tickets respectively within the space of nine months after the publication of the prize list, such sum or sums of money so due to him, her or them shall be applied to the uses, intents and purposes to which the sum hereby intended to be raised is ordered to be appropriated and applied.

[Section X.] Provided always and be it enacted by the authority aforesaid, That before any of the [said] managers shall take upon himself the duties and offices hereby enjoined or any clerk employed by the said managers shall act in such employment they and each of them shall respectively before the mayor, or one of the aldermen of the city of Philadelphia take the following oath or affirmation, viz: I, A. B., do swear (or affirm) that I will faithfully execute the trust reposed in me and that I will not use or permit or direct any person to use any indirect act or means to obtain a greater or more fortunate prize either for myself or any other person whatsoever and that I will to the best of my judgment declare to whom any prize, lot or ticket of right does belong according to the true intent and meaning of the act of assembly entitled "An act for raising by way of lottery the sum of eight hundred pounds for redeeming the House of Public Worship belonging to the Hebrew congregation of the city of Philadelphia from the mortgage and encumbrance thereon."

[Section XI.] (Section XII, P. L.) And be it further enacted
by the authority aforesaid, That the moneys arising from the
lottery hereby instituted shall be and hereby are appropriated
to the discharge of the judgments now in force and operation
against the said Hebrew congregation and to and for no other
use and purpose whatsoever.

Passed April 6, 1790. Recorded L. B. No. 4, p. 121.

INDEX.

544 *Index.*

HAGUE, JOHN.

Supreme Executive Council authorised and directed to draw on State
Treasurer for £100 in favor of, as a
reward for introducing into this
State a cotton carding machine, ... 13b

HAWKERS. See Markets.

HEADINGS. See Staves and Headings.

HEBREW CHURCHES. See Churches.

HEWSON, JOHN. See Acts of Assembly (Private.)

HIGH TREASON. See Treason.

HIGHWAYS.

Supreme Executive Council directed
to apply moneys previously raised
by lottery, to repairing certain pub-
lic roads, ... 21
Certain roads in Northampton and
Luzerne counties opened and estab-
lished, ... 46
Direction of the same, ... 48
Width of the same, ... 49
Supreme Executive Council to appoint
commissioners, ... 49
Commissioner to lay out and open
said roads, ... 49
And to report proceedings and ex-
penditures to the President or Vice-
President in Council, ... 49
Who are empowered to establish said
roads as reported, ... 49
When established, said roads to be
public state highways, ... 49
Courses and distances to be entered in
council book, ... 49
Such entry to be deemed a record
thereof, ... 50
£1,000 appropriated for these purposes, ... 50
President or Vice-President authorised to draw on State Treasurer for
such sum in favor of commission-
ers, ... 50
Commissioners to enter security for
faithful discharge of trust, ... 50
Appropriation for reviewing state
road west of Bedford, ... 278

HIGHWAYS—Continued.

Fund out of which appropriation is
to be paid, ... 275
Further appropriation for opening a
road between the river Susquehanna
and the Lehigh, ... 275
Appropriation for completing the road
through Black's Gap, between
Chambersburg and Yorktown, ... 276
Orders to be drawn on State Treasurer for sums mentioned, ... 276
Commissioners to be appointed to view
the roads and highways of the
State, ... 356
The general road law continued for
seven years, ... 413

HOLY TRINITY CHURCH. See Churches.

HORSES.

Stray horses to be sold at public sale
after having been registered for one
year, ... 440
Such sales to be advertised, ... 440
Disposition of proceeds of such sales, 440

HORSE-STEALING.

Penalty for, and as accessory before
the fact, ... 312

HOUSE OF CORRECTION.

To be converted into "The Debtors'
Apartments," 523
Prisoners to be exchanged by the
keepers of the jail and the, ... 523

HOUSE OF EMPLOYMENT. See Criminal Law.

HOUSE OF REPRESENTATIVES.

Joseph Fry, doorkeeper of, released
from all claims for rent, etc., growing out of his occupancy of apartments in the State House, ... 51

HOUSTON, JOHN.

Supreme Executive Council authorised
to draw an order on the Treasurer,
in favor of, ... 356

HOWELL, READING. See Acts of Assembly (Private.)

574 *Index.*

Index.